for women
First
SMART
SOLUTIONS

for women First

SMART
SOLUTIONS

Compiled by Kayla Smull and Rachel Schnalzer

RODALE ®

First for Women is a registered trademark of Bauer Publishing Co., L.P.

Printed in the United States of America

Rodale Inc. makes every effort to use acid-free ♾, recycled paper ♻.

Illustrations by Mona Daly

Compiled by Kayla Smull and Rachel Schnalzer

Book design by Christina Gaugler

Library of Congress Cataloging-in-Publication Data is on file with the publisher.

ISBN 978-1-62336-504-2 hardcover

2 4 6 8 10 9 7 5 3   hardcover

We inspire and enable people to improve their lives and the world around them.
For more of our products visit rodalestore.com or call 800-848-4735.

Contents

We Put You FIRST

Want a great deal on jeans? Looking for shortcuts in the kitchen? Wondering which hairstyle is right for your face shape? Look no further! *First for Women* magazine has featured inspiring tips and creative information for more than 25 years, and each issue brings new shortcuts, ideas, and terrific advice so you can live well, feel great, look beautiful, and love every day of your life. And now we've collected our favorite tips from the past few years and compiled them into *First for Women Smart Solutions*—a jam-packed, helpful guide to beautifying your home, balancing family and work, preparing great meals, and being smart about money.

We know you're busy and on the go, so we keep things short and simple. Open to any page, and you'll find amazing ideas for cleaning, cooking, decorating, and shopping, as well as pampering yourself (and your favorite pooch or kitty, too). And when life's little mishaps come your way, we're there to help you save time, money, and effort!

What's more, we tapped leading experts and scientific research in a variety of fields for up-to-date information you can use to navigate the complexities of our fast-paced world. From ways to lower your electric bill (in 2 minutes or less!), to negotiating your way out of a cell phone contract, getting a salon-style blowout at home, haggling on auto repair, or looking 10 years younger, we've asked the brightest minds for what really works. Their ideas will inspire you, motivate you to try new things, and ensure that you're on the road to happiness.

You can count on *First for Women Smart Solutions* to help you sidestep expensive repairs, get the most out of every dollar you spend, cash in on your clutter, and make cooking a breeze. No matter how creative, clever, and careful you are, you may have to contend with a rust ring on your counter, a missing sock that never finds its way out of the dryer, and a soggy quiche crust. But, don't worry—we have you covered with more than 1,800 ideas and tips to ease your stress and get your day back on track. Need an idea for cleaning carpets? Check. Looking for advice for reviving a shrunken wool sweater? No problem. Want to prevent taco fillings from spilling? Yes, we have ideas for that, too.

With hundreds and hundreds of tips to choose from, we certainly have a few favorites we're eager to share with you. Let us show you how to:

- Fight fleas on Fido (pages 38 and 288)
- Save 50 cents per gallon of gas (page 170)
- Extend the life of a wireless mouse (page 327)
- Double your garage sale profits (page 175)
- Salvage an overcooked turkey (page 79)
- Use Bubble Wrap 11 new ways (pages 64, 135, and 196)
- Seed chile peppers without the burn (page 84)
- Get whiter teeth in under 1 minute (page 256)

Throwing a party or hosting a crowd? We offer hundreds of ideas, activities, décor, and beauty tips you need to pull off an unforgettable bash on any budget. And you'll find so many clever ideas for table settings, centerpieces, and themed celebrations that you'll want to make every day a holiday.

More than 1.3 million women read our magazine every month for great tips and amazing ideas, and now we've collected our best ideas into a book to inspire you even more. Grab a cup of tea, cozy into a soft chair, and enjoy *First for Women Smart Solutions*.

Chapter 1

SMART HOME SOLUTIONS

Kitchen Confidential

Where does the time go? Between planning meals, making a healthy dinner, and doing dishes, it can be hard to find time to get everything done in the kitchen. But don't worry, *First for Women* is here to help. In this chapter, you'll find countless tips and tricks to help make cooking fun again.

CLEANING CLUES

De-gunk an old cookie sheet

To get a rusty cookie sheet into like-new shape for your afternoon of baking, sprinkle a layer of baking soda onto stains, then pour on enough hydrogen peroxide to cover. Let sit for 15 minutes before washing as usual. The alkaline baking soda and oxidating hydrogen peroxide will loosen baked-on grease so it can be wiped away. Money saved: $9 for a new baking sheet

Easily clean a crusty casserole dish

Your lasagna is always a hit with your loved ones, but no one looks forward to scouring the pan after dinner. To make cleanup easier, sprinkle Epsom salts over any crusted-on food and let sit for 10 minutes. The absorbent salts will dry out the residual moisture that bonds the food to the pan, causing the pieces to flake off. And a quick scrub with the rough salts is all it will take to remove any extrastubborn bits that remain.

15 seconds to a clean blender

You've been feeling more energized than ever, thanks to your morning smoothies, but you could do without the hassle of cleaning the seeds and pulp out of your blender. Forget the elbow grease! Simply fill the blender three-quarters of the way with warm water and a bit of liquid dish soap. Cover and blend on high for 15 seconds, then rinse thoroughly. Food bits will be washed away, even from tricky crevices the dishwasher doesn't reach.

Ensure knives are clean and sharp

Although scrubbing pads do a good job of removing stuck-on residue from kitchen knives, the rough texture can damage the blade's finish. To keep your knives looking and cutting their best, enlist the help of a wine cork. Simply angle the blade away from your body as you slowly run the cork over the knife. Next, wash the utensil in hot, soapy water with a soft sponge. The cork is strong enough to scour away the most stubborn residue but gentle enough to do the job without damaging the knife's blade.

Safely pick up glass shards

While you were unloading the dishwasher, a glass got away from you and shattered on the floor. And although you were able to quickly take care of the big pieces, what about all the little shards? The save: Moisten one side of a slice of bread with a few drops of water, then slowly wipe the floor with the bread, wet side down. The damp, sticky slice will attract and lift every last bit of glass, safely clearing the floor.

In-a-pinch dish detergent

When your dishwasher is full but you're out of detergent: Pour 1 tablespoon each of borax and baking soda (or 2 tablespoons of baking soda and 2 drops of dish soap) into the wash compartment, then add 1 tablespoon of vinegar to the rinse compartment and run as usual. The mild abrasives in borax and baking soda will scrub away food particles and the vinegar will dissolve soap scum, leaving dishes spotless.

 ## Get "sticky" oven racks to glide smoothly

"I cleaned my oven last month, and the racks have been sticking ever since. I'm hosting Thanksgiving, so I worried I'd spill dishes when I tried to pull them out. Then I had the idea to spritz a cotton ball with cooking spray and run it over the sides of the racks. Now they slide without a hitch!"

—*Donna Heller, Baltimore, MD*

Quick fix for a grease-blocked drain

Oops! While cleaning up after breakfast, you accidentally spilled some bacon grease down the drain—and now the sink is clogged. If you don't have a plunger handy, squirt a generous amount of liquid dish soap (about ½ cup) into the drain, then follow immediately with a kettle full of boiling water. The soap will act as a lubricant to soften and break up the blockage, while the hot water will dissolve and flush any leftover residue. Within minutes, the pipes will be clear. Money saved: $10 for a plunger

Clean burners while you sleep

Trying to scrub the grime off gas-stove burners can be a workout. The no-sweat solution: Pour ¼ cup of household ammonia into a large zipper-lock bag, place the burner inside, and seal. Let sit overnight. The ammonia's fumes are so effective at dissolving the mess, you'll be able to wipe it away with a damp sponge the next morning.

Then simply rinse and dry the burners before placing on the stove.

Outsmart stubborn stove-top splatters

Mmm . . . homemade tomato sauce. The only downside? The sauce bubbles energetically as you stir, splashing all over your stove top and leaving you with hardened, crusty spots that won't budge without lots of elbow grease. Save yourself the aggravation by giving the range a light coating of cooking spray before you begin cooking. The oils in the spray will prevent any spills from hardening on the stove's surface. With one swipe of a damp dishcloth or paper towel, your appliance will look as good as new.

Quickly remove melted-on plastic

You absentmindedly set down a bag of bread too close to a warm stove burner, and the plastic melted immediately. To remedy, saturate a cloth with rubbing alcohol and rub it into the mess, then scrape with a spatula. The alcohol's solvents will dissolve the polymers in the plastic, making it easy to remove. If any residue remains, sprinkle it with baking soda and buff with a damp cloth.

Make old copper look like new

You finally found the perfect hanging pot rack for your kitchen, but one look at the tarnish on your copper pots makes you reluctant to install it. For a natural copper polish, mix together equal parts salt and all-purpose flour, then add enough white vinegar to form a paste. Use a soft cloth to rub the mixture into tarnished areas. The vinegar's acetic acid will break down the oxide coating that's causing the tarnish, and the abrasive salt particles will scour it away. And the flour thickens the paste, ensuring it stays put long enough to work.

Restore shine to silverware

There's no need to buy polish if your silver looks dull. Instead, line a glass pan with foil, then fill with hot water and 2 tablespoons of baking soda; soak the silver for 5 minutes. The mix of baking soda, aluminum, and silver sulfide (in the tarnish) will create a chemical reaction that fades discolored spots. Then simply buff the silver dry. Money saved: $5 for a bottle of silver polish

Keep silver from tarnishing

To prevent the disappointment of pulling out your best silverware only to find it tarnished, wrap a few pieces of chalk in cheesecloth and tuck them in with your utensils. The chalk will absorb tarnish-causing moisture, keeping your silver perfectly polished. No chalk? Try one of the silicone mini sacks that come with shoes—they work the same way!

Stainproof plastic storage containers

The leftovers from a batch of tomato sauce or chili cut down on kitchen duty—until you have to scrub the tomato stains from the plastic storage containers. Prevent stains from forming in the first place by soaking the containers in cold water for 5 minutes before filling with warm sauce or soup. Chilling the plastic will make it less porous, so it won't be as likely to absorb food's pigments—or leach the chemical bisphenol A—as room-temperature plastic. The result: clear containers every time.

Make old "etching" disappear

"The other day I noticed black and gray lines that looked like spiderwebs on my white dishes. I mentioned it to a friend who runs a café, and she said the scratches are actually scuff marks caused by utensils. Luckily, she had an easy fix: Combine 2 tablespoons of cream of tartar and enough water to make a paste, then massage the mixture into the marks with your fingers. After about a minute of rubbing, the scratches vanish!"

—*Gail Turco, Bath, ME*

Pull the fridge out with ease

You need to scoot your fridge away from the wall so you can vacuum the coils, but it's so heavy! The fix: Spray window cleaner on the floor in front of the appliance's feet. The liquid will cut down on traction, while the cleaner's alcohol will make the floor slick so you can gently move the fridge. (Just take care not to scratch your floor.)

NIX STINKY SMELLS

Outsmart lingering food odors on skin

To erase the smell of garlic from your hands, squirt a dollop of nongel toothpaste onto your palms, then wash as you would with soap. The paste's abrasive texture will scrub away the offending molecules.

Easy way to deodorize jars

You're all set to can your homemade berry jam, but your jars still smell faintly of last year's pickles. The remedy: Combine 1 teaspoon of mustard powder (available in the spice aisle) and 1 quart of water. Pour the solution into the jars and swish for 15 seconds before rinsing with water. Canning experts swear by mustard as a top-notch deodorizer, so you'll be canning that jam in no time.

No more stinky sponges!

If you're as frustrated as we are by sponges that get smelly after just a few dish-washing sessions, try this clever trick: After each use, wring out the sponge, then attach a binder clip to one side so you can stand the sponge upright on the clip's "wings," rather than laying it flat on the counter or sink. This will allow the kitchen staple to thoroughly air-dry, preventing odor-causing mildew from forming. Problem solved!

Freshen up a smelly garbage disposal

Your kitchen sink is causing quite a stink! Curb the odor with frozen citrus peels: Freeze a few orange, lemon, or lime peels. Then, whenever your disposal needs cleaning, drop in a few of the peels and run the machine for 10 seconds. The hardened skins will leave behind a citrusy scent, as well as dislodge any buildup on the blades to keep the disposal running smoothly.

No more garbage odor

"With all the cooking I do, my kitchen trash is always full of food scraps. Inevitably, some get lodged between the bag and garbage can, causing a stink—and forcing me to clean the dirty can. Then my mom suggested placing newspaper under the bag to absorb smells and keep the can clean. Such an easy fix!"

—*Linda Fortine, Waco, TX*

BE A GROCERY GENIUS

Genius way to keep coupons handy

You dread the thought of holding up the checkout line for 5 minutes while you search for that two-for-one coupon floating around in your purse. To keep all your coupons organized, enlist the help of an old checkbook wallet. Simply insert one coupon into each slot while you clip. The enclosed compartments will allow you to keep the vouchers sorted by category, brand, savings amount, or store—so you can easily grab just the one you need, when you need it.

Tote groceries with ease

"I always leave the market with an overloaded cart, which means multiple trips from my car to the house—a major pain on hot summer days. So I tossed an old laundry basket in my trunk. Now I just load the bags into the basket and carry it into the house. It even prevents my purchases from toppling over on my drive. I wish I'd thought of this sooner!"

—*Liv Schreyer, Provo, UT*

Never buy duplicate spices again

Now that you've started mixing your own spice rubs for grilled chicken and steak, you're always looking for new flavors to add to the rotation. Trouble is, you can never remember which seasonings you've already purchased. The genius way to avoid picking up duplicates: Line up your spices and take a picture with a camera or your cell phone. Next time you're thinking of buying a new spice, take a quick look at the picture to remind yourself of what you already have. Spice rack clutter—cured!

Never forget the milk again!

"I used to keep my grocery list on the kitchen counter, but it always got stained or lost in a stack of papers. I wanted a paperless list, so I came up with this idea: I add the items I need to a dry-erase board and take a picture of it with my cell phone. Now I always have my list on hand. Plus, if someone else in my family is able to stop at the store, I can text them the photo. So easy!"

—*Lena Dalton, Indianapolis, IN*

EASY KITCHEN ENTERTAINING

Prevent an ice-pop mess

You love surprising the little ones in your life with frozen ice pops on hot days—but the fast-melting treats end up turning your sweeties into sticky messes. To prevent this, make a "drip catcher." Simply poke a small hole in the bottom of a muffin liner (foil liners work especially well because they won't get soggy) and slip the stick of the ice pop in. Problem solved!

Save yourself a serving trip

You love hosting your annual Fourth of July barbecue, but trekking in and out of the house to grab various condiments and seasonings can make it hard to enjoy the company of your guests. The easy solution: Place your favorite fixings in cupcake liners and carry them in a muffin tin. The 12 wells will keep each condiment separate and steady so you can easily carry out more at once.

Short a trivet? Try this!

The family's all here, the turkey's done, and you're ready to enjoy your Thanksgiving feast. But as you bring all the dishes to the table, you realize you need another trivet. The save: Grab a computer mouse pad (just make sure it doesn't have a plastic coating). The heatproof pad is the perfect size to fit under plates and baking dishes, plus the rubberized bottom will prevent slipping and sliding. *Bon appétit!*

Cool down drinks—fast!

Oops! Your barbecue guests are due to arrive in just 30 minutes and you forgot to chill the drinks. The save: Wrap a wet paper towel around each bottle and can and stash in the freezer for 15 minutes. As water from the paper towels evaporates (after removal from the freezer), it draws heat away from the drinks so they cool off quickly.

Transport salad dressing sans mess

Toting a salad to work can be a hassle when the lid pops off your dressing container, spilling oily vinaigrette everywhere. Next time, pour the dressing into an empty spice jar. Its airtight seal will prevent spills en route. Then, at lunchtime, just shake and sprinkle onto your salad—the jar's holes make for easy pouring.

HELPFUL KITCHEN HINTS

See recipe cards at a glance

A clever way to make a favorite recipe easier to follow as you cook: Tape the card behind the clear plastic cover of an old CD jewel case. You'll be able to adjust the angle of this makeshift stand for optimal viewing—no more bending over the counter as you try to read the next step. Plus, you'll safeguard your cards from food splatters.

Retrieve trinkets from a drain

If you accidentally drop an earring down the sink, just grab your vacuum, put on the hose attachment, and slip the foot of a pair of panty hose tightly over the end. Then hold the hose over the drain and turn on the vacuum. Sink drains often use U-bend pipes, so it's likely that the trinket is sitting in the bend below the basin. The vacuum will suck the earring out of the drain, while the panty hose will keep it from being inhaled into the vacuum. Money saved: $120 for a plumber's visit

No more lost or crushed cupcake liners!

"Baking is my favorite pastime—I especially love making cupcakes. My signature touch is to use colorful liners that coordinate with special events, so I always keep a bunch on hand. But the boxes the liners come in create clutter in my pantry and often end up getting crushed. Luckily, I came across this storage idea on Torie Jayne's Web site

The simple way to keep ice from turning to slush? Enlist a colander!

to use glass jars. Now I can see what I have at a glance, plus the liner-filled Mason jar looks so pretty on my counter!"

—Diane Merryman, Columbus, OH

Never struggle with plastic wrap again

A simple task like putting away the leftovers from dinner can become a pain when you can't easily locate the loose end of your roll of plastic wrap. Avoid the hassle by placing the roll in the freezer for 5 minutes. The cold air will tamp down static electricity so the plastic won't stick to the roll—or your hands—when you pull off a piece. (The wrap will regain its clinging properties as it warms back up.)

Reader Tip — Quick fix for a missing cork

"While cleaning up after my girls'-night-in gathering, I noticed a half-empty bottle of wine with no cork in sight. Luckily, I remembered my pal's trick of 'sealing' the bottle with a candle. I microwaved an old unscented taper for 3 seconds to soften the wax, cut an inch off the bottom, and stuck the piece in the neck of the bottle. The makeshift stopper fit perfectly, and when I wanted a glass of wine the next day, it pulled out just as easily as a regular cork."

—Allison McAdams, Baltimore, MD

Nifty trick for a lost pot-lid knob

The knob from your favorite pot came unscrewed, and now it's nowhere to be found. The throwaway that makes a perfect replacement: a wine cork. Simply push a sharp, pointed screw up through the hole of the pot lid and carefully twist the cork onto it from the top until it's secure. The heat-resistant cork will allow you to continue to use the cookware safely until you find the knob (or can purchase a new one).

Tool-free way to test oven calibration

If you suspect your oven is improperly calibrated, perform this quick test: Pour a spoonful of sugar into an oven-safe bowl or onto some foil on a baking sheet and place it in a 350°F oven. After an hour, the sugar should still be granulated (though it might turn slightly brown). If it has started to melt, your oven is running too hot.

Erase heat marks from a wooden table

When a piping-hot bowl of soup or cup of coffee leaves a white heat ring on your table, try this: Mix a dab of nongel toothpaste with a pinch of baking soda to make a paste. Rub gently over the stain until the paste feels warm, then wipe clean with a damp cloth. (Repeat as necessary.) The slightly abrasive toothpaste–baking soda combo will lift the discoloration from the wood's surface. When finished, buff with furniture polish to restore the table's luster.

No more freezer burn!

To avoid the disappointment of opening your favorite sorbet only to discover it's covered with ice particles, try this: Place a sheet of aluminum foil over the open carton, then put the lid on top before freezing. Since the thin metal sheet will insulate your frosty treat from the moisture that sneaks in and causes freezer burn, you'll be able to savor every sweet scoop.

(continued on page 10)

10 Brilliant Uses for HYDROGEN PEROXIDE

1 Safely disinfect meal-prep areas

To keep cutting boards and counters free from bacteria without resorting to chemical-laden cleansers, just give the surface a wipe with a paper towel or clean dishcloth soaked in 3 percent hydrogen peroxide. The solution will kill salmonella and other harmful organisms, preventing the spread of germs to nearby surfaces.

2 Green up a yellowed plant

The leaves of your indoor plants are starting to turn yellow—a sign of root rot. To help them bounce back, first repot the plants, then water the soil with a solution of 1 cup of water and 1 ounce of 3 percent hydrogen peroxide. (Continue doing this even after the plant is healthy.) The antimicrobial hydrogen peroxide acts as an oxygen supplement, which will aerate the soil and nourish the plants.

3 Lift bloodstains from a white shirt

If a shaving nick or bloody nose leaves a white shirt stained, pour a mixture of equal parts 3 percent hydrogen peroxide and water directly onto the affected area. Let it sit for 30 minutes, then launder as usual. The hydrogen peroxide will react with the blood to break down the stain, gently erasing the unsightly mark without damaging the fabric (unlike bleach, which can turn whites gray).

4 Save a scorched tablecloth

Oops! You accidentally burned the tablecloth while ironing. The fix: Grab a rag big enough to cover the stain and soak it in 3 percent hydrogen peroxide. Lay the rag over the scorch mark, then iron on a medium setting until the mark disappears. The hydrogen peroxide's gentle bleaching agents (along with the iron's heat) will loosen and lift the stain, while the saturated cloth will protect the linen from scorching further.

5 Eliminate between-teeth stains

Nix stubborn stains between your teeth with this trick: Dip regular dental floss in a bowl of 3 percent hydrogen peroxide, then floss as usual. Hydrogen peroxide (the main active ingredient in most tooth-whitening products) releases oxygen to break down the stain and whiten discoloration without damaging tooth enamel. You'll see an improvement within 2 to 3 weeks.

6 Extend the life of fresh flowers

To make a beautiful bouquet last 4 or 5 days longer, try this trick: Fill your vase a little less than halfway with lukewarm water and add 1 teaspoon of 3 percent hydrogen peroxide. The antimicrobial solution will kill any harmful bacteria in the water so your blooms can thrive.

7 Stop a blister from becoming infected

Your new shoes look fabulous, but now you have blisters—ouch! To ward off infection, fill a large bowl with equal parts water and 3 percent hydrogen peroxide, then soak your feet for about 30 minutes before bedtime. The antibacterial solution will kill germs, plus increase oxygen to the injured skin to promote cell renewal and speed healing.

8 Soak away nail discoloration

When a dark polish causes your nails to take on a yellowish tinge, simply fill a bowl with enough 3 percent hydrogen peroxide to cover your fingertips, then place your nails in the liquid and soak for 1 to 2 minutes. (Use a cotton swab dipped in the solution to wipe under nail tips.) The hydrogen peroxide will oxidize the pigment molecules from the polish, restoring your nails to their natural color.

9 Remove pesticides from produce

Hydrogen peroxide can rid fruit and vegetables of harmful pesticides. Simply combine one part 3 percent hydrogen peroxide and nine parts water in a spray bottle and spritz generously on each piece of produce. Scrub with a vegetable scrubber, then rinse thoroughly with water. Hydrogen peroxide is study proven to eradicate *E. coli* and other bacteria, guaranteeing your produce is safe to eat.

10 Whiten dirty, dingy tile grout

The grout-cleaning combination that works even better than bleach: hydrogen peroxide and baking soda. Combine one part 3 percent hydrogen peroxide and three parts baking soda to make a paste. Scrub it on the grout with an old toothbrush and let it sit for 30 minutes, then rinse with warm water. The peroxide will release oxygen to break down the stain, while the abrasive baking soda will help scrub the marks from the grout's surface.

Add these to ease a freezer's workload

Hot temperatures can cause your freezer compressor to go into overdrive to keep the interior cold—and that can drive up your electric bill. The fix: freezer blocking. Just take a few empty cardboard boxes (like the ones that hold ice cream bars) and fill with leftover foam packing peanuts. Then tape shut and place in any empty areas in your freezer. (Aim to keep the freezer about two-thirds full for maximum efficiency.) The peanuts will act as insulation, helping to keep the space cold so the compressor doesn't have to run as often. Money saved: $90 per year on your electric bill

In-a-pinch blender jar

Oops! Your glass blender jar slipped out of your hands and shattered—but there's no need to rush out to get a new one. Most blender-blade attachments screw securely onto a standard-mouthed ($2^5/8$-inch) Mason jar or 15-ounce mayonnaise jar. Simply toss the ingredients into the jar, remove the blade cap from the blender, and twist it onto the jar. Then screw the cap back into the appliance and blend as usual. Money saved: $15 for a new glass blender jar

Fridge won't shut? Try this

Ugh! Every time you walk into the kitchen, you find the fridge open a crack because the door isn't "sticking" like it's supposed to. The fix: Wedge two $1/4$-inch-thick blocks of scrap wood under the front corners of the appliance. This creates a slight upward tilt that allows gravity to pull the door shut, locking in the cold air.

Keep chips fresh with a wine cork

Even with a good stash of chip clips, you can always use one more! Make your own clip by cutting a lengthwise slit in a wine cork to turn the bottle topper into a fast-and-easy way to keep your snacks crisp.

DIY select-a-size paper towels

We love the idea of those paper towels that allow you to choose full or half sheets, but they can cost up to twice as much as regular rolls. The simple solution? Cut a regular roll in half. Just place the roll on a cutting board and use a sharp serrated or electric knife to carefully slice through the center, then store the two halves on your paper towel holder. Genius!

Fast Bathroom Fixes

Wouldn't it be terrific if the bathroom cleaned itself? Well, look no further for tips that help you clean in a jiffy and make your beauty routine a snap.

CLEAN SHOWER SHORTCUTS

Naturally disinfect a showerhead

Yuck! Showerheads aren't just a landing strip for mineral deposits—they're also a breeding ground for bacteria. To get rid of germs in no time, remove the showerhead and place it in a shallow bowl with enough mouthwash to completely cover it. Let it sit for 10 minutes, then rinse with water and screw the head back into place. Mouthwash contains sodium benzoate, a disinfectant that will make the surface 100 percent germ-free without leaving a harsh chemical odor.

Mildewproof a shower curtain

Try as you might to keep the bathroom spotless, you seem to be losing the battle against the heat and humidity. The proof: a new layer of mildew clinging to the bottom of the shower liner every week. But you can outsmart the mold for good with the help of baby oil. Next time you clean, just rub a thin layer of the oil over the bottom 3 inches of the dry shower curtain. The slick stuff will form a waterproof seal that will lock out mildew-promoting moisture.

Eliminate shower curtain mold

Prevent mold and mildew from forming on your plastic liner by trimming off the bottom inch or two with pinking shears. These sewing scissors will create a ridged hem that gives water more places to drip off, speeding drying time so mold doesn't have a chance to grow. For extra spot-fighting power, spritz the liner with a solution of ¼ cup of table salt and 1 pint of water once a week. The sodium crystals will help prevent mold from forming, plus break down soap scum stains. Money saved: $12 for a new liner

No more shower curtain mildew

The fuss-free way to prevent mold and mildew from growing on your shower liner: Soak the curtain in salt water. Fill your tub with a solution of 2 tablespoons of salt per gallon of water and submerge the liner for 20 minutes. Then, without rinsing, hang the curtain as usual. The invisible coat of sodium crystals left on the liner will seal gaps in the fibers, preventing mildew from latching on. Money saved: $10 for a new liner

Make your shower self-cleaning

With hard-water deposits, soap scum, and tough-to-clean tile grout, scrubbing the shower can be a nightmare. Nix the hassle with this daily cleaner: Combine ⅓ cup of rubbing alcohol and 1 cup of water in a spray bottle. After every shower, spritz the walls and tub with this mixture—no rinsing or scrubbing necessary. The rubbing alcohol's solvents will dissolve shower grime as the solution slides down the walls. Plus, the mixture evaporates quickly, so it won't leave behind streaks.

Cut your bathroom cleaning time in half

Scrubbing the bathroom is nobody's favorite chore—especially in the hot, sticky summer, when stubborn water spots and soap scum seem to crop up in the shower every day. Keep the stall clean for twice as long by spraying furniture polish onto the tile walls and buffing away with a clean cloth. (Skip the floor and holding bar, which can get slippery.) The polish will create an invisible barrier that repels water and soap, preventing unsightly buildup and stains.

Clean the bathroom with half the effort

This trick (a favorite of hotel housekeepers) will help you spend less time scouring—so you can spend more time relaxing: Before you start cleaning the bathroom, fill the tub with a few inches of the hottest water you can draw from the tap. Once the room is steamy, spritz surfaces with cleaners and let sit for 5 minutes before scrubbing as usual. The hot, moist air will loosen dirt and grime so the cleaning agents can do a better job of getting surfaces spotless.

Silence an annoying drippy faucet

The repairman can't come to fix your leaky faucet until tomorrow, and the sound is driving you crazy! For a temporary fix, tie a length of dental floss around the spout, letting the other end rest in the basin. Water will flow silently down the string, keeping you sane until help arrives.

Clear a clogged drain naturally

The chemical-free fix for a slow-draining sink: Pour 3 tablespoons of baking soda down the drain and follow with 1 cup of vinegar. Wait 20 minutes, then run the hot water for 10 seconds. The fizzy baking soda–vinegar combo will dissolve grease and loosen buildup, while the scalding water will wash away any remaining grime. Money saved: $7 for a bottle of drain cleaner

Unclog a pipe for pennies

Need another low-cost, chemical-free fix for a slow-draining sink? First, put a kettleful of water on to boil. Next, mix 2 tablespoons of table salt and 2 cups of club soda, then pour the solution down the drain. Wait 1 minute, then pour the boiling water into the sink. The abrasive salt-and-seltzer combination will break down grease and grime, while the scalding water will dissolve the mess within seconds. Money saved: $7 for a bottle of drain cleaner

De-grime grout for pennies

To get dingy grout looking like new, mix 3 cups of water, ½ cup of baking soda, ⅓ cup of lemon juice, and ¼ cup of vinegar in a spray bottle. Spritz on the grout and let sit for 3 minutes, then wipe dry. The baking soda and vinegar will cut through soap scum, while the citric acid in lemon juice will erase stains. Money saved: $8 for grout cleaner

Whiter, brighter grout sans scrubbing

To eliminate mold and hard-water deposits, spread foam shaving cream on the grout lines after your next shower. Let sit for 10 minutes, then wash away with water. The steam from the shower will loosen the grime, making it easier for the foam's alcohols to soak into crevices and break down stains so you can wipe clean with a damp cloth. Bonus: Since shaving cream is bleach-free, it works on both light and dark grout. Money saved: $10 for grout cleaner

Reader Tip: Clean dingy grout in minutes

"It seems like whenever I notice that my bathroom tile grout looks dingy, I'm too busy to scrub it. Then one day I was using my bleach-to-go pen on a stained shirt and had an idea—I drew lines of the bleach gel on my grout, then tidied up the rest of the room. After 15 minutes I wiped the gel away with a damp cloth and voilà—the pen's bleach left the grout white and gleaming! Plus, the thick gel formula kept it from bleeding onto my tile."

—Kay O'Neill, Beaverton, OR

Get shower door tracks gleaming

When you stepped out of the shower this morning, you noticed the door tracks were in desperate need of a good cleaning. But the space between them is so narrow that you aren't sure how to get to the grime. To effectively clean even the tiniest areas, spray the tracks with your favorite all-purpose cleaner and let sit for a few minutes. Then grab a screwdriver from your toolbox, wrap a soft cloth around the pointed end, and quickly rub it back and forth along the inside of the tracks. The cleaner will loosen the built-up dirt, dust, and soap residue, making it a snap to scrub away. And the screwdriver's narrow tip will easily fit into the tight spaces your fingers can't reach. The result: sparkling shower tracks in no time!

CLEVER ADVICE FOR A CLEAN VANITY

Liquid hand soap for pennies

Your crew goes through hand soap like crazy, and the cost of replacements is eating up your household budget. For a cheaper (and healthier) alternative, buy a large bottle of inexpensive shampoo, fill an empty hand-soap dispenser with equal parts water and shampoo, and give it a shake. The surfactants in the diluted solution are just as effective as regular soap at removing dirt and grime from hands. Money saved: $3 per bottle of hand soap

Display extra guest towels perfectly

You're hosting a few out-of-town guests this weekend and need a convenient place to store a few extra washcloths and bath towels—but there aren't enough spare hooks in your bathroom. If you have an old wine rack lying around, put it to use as a towel holder. Just roll up the cloths and place one in each slot. The neatly spaced partitions will keep the towels organized and readily available without taking up a lot of extra space.

Squeeze out every last bit of toothpaste

Uh-oh—you just about finished the toothpaste, and your husband still has to brush his teeth. Instead of dashing to the drugstore, submerge the tube in a glass of hot water for 1 minute. The warmth will expand the tube and loosen any trapped toothpaste so your husband can get in one final round before buying a replacement tomorrow.

Double the life of bar soap

Ugh! You just set out that soap last week, and it's already becoming a gunky mess. To avoid this: Each time you place new soap in the shower, unwrap a second bar and stash it in the linen closet. Exposure to air will evaporate moisture within the bar, causing it to compress so it will last longer. Plus, the soap will keep your linens and towels smelling fresh.

Mess-free way to refill a soap bottle

File under *totally frustrating*: It's hard to keep your hand steady when refilling your liquid-soap dispenser—and even the slightest move can leave you with a stream of soap running down the outside of the bottle, forming a puddle on your countertop. The save: Place a chopstick in the empty bottle, then pour as usual. The chopstick will help direct the soap so it flows easily into the dispenser. No waste, no mess!

Ward off rust rings on counters

To prevent a can of hair spray or shaving cream from leaving a pesky rust ring on your bathroom vanity or in your shower, coat the bottom of the can with two layers of clear nail polish and let dry completely. The polish will create a seal that keeps water from mixing with metal and creating rust. Already have a rust-ring mark in your bathroom? Try this: Combine 1 tablespoon of lemon juice and enough salt to form a paste, then apply the mixture to the stain and let sit for 24 hours before blotting with a clean cloth and rinsing with cool water. No more rust!

Reader Tip — Freshen up a bathroom

"My teen boys share a bathroom, and as you can imagine, it's tough to keep it smelling nice. I used to set out candles, but they objected to the 'girly' look. So now I place a few drops of essential oil on the inside of the toilet-paper tube. When the roll is spun, the subtle scent is released. Problem solved!"

—Nicole Tan, Avalon, CA

All Around the House

Welcome home to your sanctuary! Learn how to start a cozy fire, plump your bedding, and keep your day running smoothly.

Get a cozy fire roaring in no time!

There's simply nothing more relaxing than spending a night by the fire. The fast way to get the flames going: Fill empty toilet-paper rolls with dryer lint, then stick two or three under the wood and carefully light with a long match. The makeshift fire starters will easily catch and burn long enough to ignite the wood.

Make fireplace sweeping a cinch

Get your fireplace clean—minus the mess of flying ash—with this trick: Save the grounds from a pot of coffee (or the leaves from a few used tea bags) and sprinkle them over the sooty remains before you sweep. The damp bits will settle the flaky ash particles and keep them from rising while you sweep up.

 Safeguard delicate curtains from snags

"Every spring, I switch out my heavy winter drapes in favor of lighter curtains. But when I tried to hang them this year, the delicate material kept catching on the curtain rod's jagged metal ends. Then I had the idea to grab a couple plastic sandwich bags from the pantry and slip one over each end of the rod before sliding on the curtains—and it worked! The plastic kept the fabric from snagging and was easy to remove when I was finished."

—*Martha Levin, Lewis, KY*

Slip-proof an indoor welcome mat

If your doormat just won't stay put, try this to prevent accidental slips and falls: Cut an old mouse pad into four squares and use a hot-glue gun to attach the pieces to the corners of the mat's underside. The mouse pad's rubber backing will grip the floor to keep the mat from sliding. Money saved: $10 for a rug grip

Quick fix for flat, lumpy pillows

The simple way to perk up a pillow that's no longer pleasant to sleep on: Toss it into the dryer with two tennis balls for 30 minutes on low heat. The pounding of the tennis balls will fluff up the flattened fabric and stuffing, restoring the pillow to its cushy best. Bonus: The heat and movement of the dryer will shake any dust particles loose. (This trick works equally well for synthetic and down pillows.)

Stop a mattress from slipping

If every little toss and turn causes your mattress to slide around, place a large nonskid pad (like the kind used under area rugs) on top of the box spring, trimming any edges that hang over. The added traction from the rubber padding will secure the mattress so you can enjoy a deep, refreshing sleep.

Easy way to fill a duvet cover

Your new duvet cover is gorgeous, but getting a comforter inside is trickier than you anticipated. To the rescue: large binder clips. Simply slip the duvet in the cover and secure the top corners with clips, then shake to evenly distribute the comforter. Place on your bed and smooth out any lumps, then remove the fasteners. Money saved: $7 for a set of duvet clips

Wallpaper removal trick

"I recently decided to repaper my bedroom but couldn't get the old paper off. Then a friend said to use Pine-Sol—pine oil acts as a solvent to dissolve adhesives. I mixed one part cleaner with four parts water in a spray bottle and soaked the walls. After 20 minutes, I was able to easily peel off the old paper."

—*Cherise Wood, Chicago, IL*

No more hot-glue strings!

That picture-frame craft you saw online turned out great, except for the weblike strings left by your glue gun. To prevent this next time, place your glue sticks in the freezer for 20 minutes before using. This helps ensure that the sticks aren't exposed to moisture in the air, which is the main cause of strings. Your project will be perfect!

Add extra "grip" to worn winter boots

If your tried-and-true snow boots aren't giving you the traction they used to, the nonslip tread may be starting to wear down. The easy fix that can help you get through the rest of the icy season without having to invest in a new pair: After taking off the boots, use a razor blade to carefully cut ¼-inch-deep V shapes into the soles about 1 inch apart. The cut rubber creates new "treads" that will grip the ground and provide you with firmer footing in wintry conditions. Money saved: $50 for a new pair of snow boots

Revive a dead ballpoint pen

"It's so frustrating when a ballpoint pen stops writing—and I know there's plenty of ink left inside. That's why I was thrilled when a friend of mine shared this easy trick: Just dip the tip of the 'dead' pen in boiling water for 10 to 15 seconds. This will melt away any clogged-up ink on the ball so it can flow freely again."

—*Gina Zigler, St. Louis, MO*

No-sew for torn lace

There's no need to pull out your sewing kit when you spot a tear in your lace tablecloth. Simply place a piece of waxed paper behind the rip and brush a layer of clear nail polish over the area. Let dry completely, then remove the paper. The nail polish will leave behind a thin coating of polymers that will invisibly seal the hole.

Revive potpourri instantly

When your favorite potpourri starts to lose its scent, pour ¼ cup rubbing alcohol or vodka into a spray bottle and generously spritz over the top, then stir to ensure every piece is saturated. The colorless, odorless liquid will gently break down the potpourri's hardened, dried-out surface, exposing the still-scented layers underneath.

Unseal an envelope without ripping it

Oops! You forgot to include a photo in one of the thank-you notes you just sealed. The solution: Stick the sealed envelope in the freezer for 2 hours, then gently slide a letter opener or butter knife under the envelope's flap to open. The cold temperature will cause the glue to become brittle and crack, so you can open the envelope without a problem. To reseal, simply tape shut, then send the card on its way.

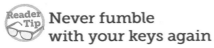
"My husband often forgets to turn on the porch light, so it's hard to find the door lock or pick the right key after a night out. Then one day I saw a bottle of my daughter's glow-in-the-dark nail polish, and a lightbulb went off. I put a dab of the liquid above the lock and on the top of the house key. The polish gives off just enough glow to make getting in the door a cinch."

—*Kathy Cornell, Utica, NY*

Fast Storage Suggestions

Dealing with piles, stacks, and clutter takes up your precious time every day. Discover ideas and tricks for organizing, storing, and tackling the storage issues in your home.

STOW IT

Store more on the door

Store more . . . right on your door! These clever hanging strategies will keep essentials at your fingertips.

Use DVD baskets for bath supplies: When bathroom storage space runs low, extra supplies end up crowding the linen closet. The fix: hanging a trio of woven DVD baskets on the door. They act as convenient catchall bins for items like toilet paper, bath toys, and curlers. To affix baskets, drive short wood screws through the backs of the bins into the door. Also handy: Place removable self-adhesive hooks on the door to hang odds and ends.

Use clotheslines for pantry overflow: When the kids get the munchies, your pantry goes from orderly to out of control in a flash. To avoid this, make their favorites easily accessible by tacking up a clothesline. You'll be able to hang snack bags with clothespins, which will keep bags folded shut so snacks will stay fresh longer. Also handy: Tack a tissue box to the door to hold grocery bags.

Use shoe pockets for fitness gear: Finally! No more digging through piles of hand weights and running shoes on the closet floor—a repurposed shoe organizer (hung on the door with screws) features pockets that are perfect for tucking in weights, jump ropes, and more. Also handy: Attach two cable ties to the door with screws so you can stash hard-to-stow items like a yoga mat.

Use bag caddies for crushable items: Family-size snack bags can easily get crushed in cramped pantries. But hanging wire baskets (originally intended for holding trash bags in the kitchen cabinet) on the inside of your door provides a simple, fast fix. Bonus: The baskets are also wonderful for storing delicate loaves of bread or keeping bags of pasta upright.

Perfectly styled shelves guaranteed!

Display knickknacks, ceramics, and candles on horizontal stacks of books to add interest to your bookshelf. To add dimension to the shelf, be sure to include varying heights of horizontal stacks.

Make "bookends"

By placing books on either side of the shelf, you instantly frame any objects placed on the inside of the shelf, calling attention to picture frames and keepsakes positioned in the middle. Place books both ways (horizontally and vertically) to add depth to an otherwise drab shelf.

Add frames

Placing picture frames behind stacks of books is a great way to add an interesting, personal touch to a bookshelf. Plus, family photos make a great background for your books!

Rotate accessories

Don't just place knickknacks and decorative items face forward on your bookshelf. Instead, angle them about 25 degrees to the side for a casual, not-too-fussy look.

KITCHEN KEEPERS

No more kitchen cabinet clutter!

If your cabinets are crammed full of pots, pans, lids, and other cookware, try this trick to keep the lids organized and free up space: Remove the backing from two adhesive hooks (like 3M Command brand hooks), then latch the hooks around the bottom of the lid at the 4 and 8 o'clock positions. Next, stick the adhesive to the inside of the cabinet door. The lids will be out of the way yet easy to access.

Out of counter space? Try this!

You're hosting a buffet dinner for friends, and counter space is shrinking fast! The in-a-pinch fix: Open a kitchen drawer and place a cutting board across it, then shut the drawer until the board fits snugly. (If it doesn't feel secure, place a dish towel under the board for added traction.) Voilà—an instant counter extension!

Easily access appliances

You prefer to have your coffeemaker tucked back by the wall when it's not in use, but every morning when you pull it out, the screeching makes you cringe. Keep it quiet with this quick trick: Apply felt protectors (like the ones used to prevent chairs from scratching the floor) under the appliance. The soft fabric will allow it to glide smoothly across the countertop.

Never run out of baking staples again

"I do a lot of baking at this time of year, and it's frustrating when I go to retrieve a cup of flour or sugar from my opaque storage canisters only to discover there isn't enough left for my recipe. To help keep track of my supplies, I started placing a rubber band around each container, lining it up with the level of the contents inside. Then I move the band down as I use more. This makes it easy to see at a glance how much I have left."

—*Megan Peterson, Nashville, TN*

Unstick a stubborn Mason jar

Your neighbor just gave you some of her delicious homemade preserves. But when you try to open the jar, the ring won't budge. Mason jar rings sometimes form a vacuum seal with the jar and flat lid, making them tough to remove. The fix: Fill a bowl a third of the way with warm water, invert the jar so it's standing on its lid in the water, and let sit for 20 minutes. Keeping the jar upside down will help break the vacuum seal, and the warm water will soften any sticky jam that may have leaked out of the jar, so the ring will come off with ease.

CLUES FOR CLOTHING

Smooth rough wooden hangers

Several of the wooden hangers in your closet have jagged areas, and you worry they'll snag your delicate tops. The quick fix: Buff the worn areas with a sheet of waxed paper, waxed side down. The paper's rough surface will smooth away loose splinters, while the wax will lubricate the area and leave behind a clear, slick coating that will keep lightweight garments safe from snags.

 ## Genius idea for organizing delicates

"Every so often I organize my underwear drawer and promise myself it will stay that way. But a few weeks later, it's back to its haphazard state. Then I had this helpful idea: I cut a few shoe boxes in half horizontally and cut another vertically. Then I fitted them inside my drawer and placed my folded items in the compartments. Now it's easy to keep everything neat!"

—*Kelly Flannery, Pocatello, ID*

SOS for stored clothing snafus

When the weather is finally warm enough to trade in those heavy layers for flirty skirts and airy sweaters, your spring duds may need a little TLC after months of storage before you can slip them on. That's why we asked the experts how to fix the most common problems—fast!

Wrapping rubber bands on hangers stops wide-neck tops from slipping.

Yellowed armpits

Pesky sweat stains in clothing don't go away when stored over the long winter. The problem: During months in storage, the acids in sweat react with the aluminum compounds in most deodorants, slowly causing the fabric to yellow. To fix this, dampen the area, then sprinkle on unseasoned meat tenderizer (containing papain or bromelain) or a powdered detergent and work into a paste. Let sit for 1 hour and rinse with cool water.

Insect holes

It figures: Bugs such as moths and silverfish are especially attracted to high-end fabrics like cashmere. To mend the damage these pests cause: Turn the garment inside out and gently stretch the hole over a darning mushroom or tennis ball. Using matching thread, weave a circle around the perimeter of the hole to reinforce gnawed-on edges. Next, make vertical stitches to sew the top to the bottom, picking up the open loops from the stitch of the fabric. To finish, tie off the thread and gently press with a steam iron.

Off odor

Any smell—from mildew to mothballs to cedar blocks—will intensify in storage and be tough to eradicate. That's especially true if the source of the odor is oily in nature (as is the case with mothballs), since oil-based chemicals are poorly soluble in water and won't rinse out in the wash. The save: Toss five pieces of activated charcoal, which is a superior odor absorber, into a paper bag and tape shut. Place this sachet and the clothing in a plastic bin (to avoid staining, don't let the bag touch the clothes), then cover the container and leave overnight. Your clothes should be odor-free in the a.m.

Stretched-out cuffs

If you're like us and have a habit of pushing up your sleeves as the day gets warmer, the cuffs of last year's spring sweaters and cardigans were probably already losing their shape before they were packed away in the fall. The problem gets worse in storage, though: When the strained fabric dries out, it loses whatever shape it had left. To remedy this, dip cuffs into very hot water for about 5 seconds, then use a hair dryer set on hot to blow them dry. The combination of hot water and air will shrink cotton or cashmere fibers so the cuffs return to their original shape.

Set-in wrinkles

No matter how carefully you fold and pack your spring wardrobe, creases are a given—especially with lightweight fabrics like linen, rayon, and cotton. To easily smooth away even the deepest wrinkles, try this trick that will double the power of your iron: Place a large sheet of aluminum foil beneath your ironing board's cover, then lightly spritz each garment with water and press as usual. The conductive foil will retain heat and warm up the backs of the garments as you press the fronts, so it will be like you're ironing the clothes on both sides simultaneously. The result: You get neatly pressed clothes in half the time.

10 Brilliant Uses for BEER

1 Restore volume to limp locks
To add oomph to strands, combine 3 tablespoons of beer and ½ cup of water. After washing your hair as usual, rub the mixture into locks and let sit for 5 minutes, then rinse. The beer's B vitamins and proteins will heal damaged hair and add body. And don't worry—rinsing will remove the beer smell. Bonus: Beer adds shine and helps ward off dandruff!

2 Quickly clean and season cast iron
An easy way to get your cast iron in tip-top shape: Pour enough fresh beer to cover the bottom of your still-warm pan and let sit for 5 to 10 minutes. The carbonation will keep food particles from sticking to the pan's surface, plus the beer will leave behind a subtle nuttiness that will enhance the flavor of your future dishes.

3 Attract butterflies to your garden
These beauties actually love the smell of beer! To welcome them into your yard, mix a small amount of flat beer with some mashed, overripe banana (ripe fruit is another butterfly favorite) and spread it on a tree trunk or rock near your garden. Then sit back, relax, and watch pretty insects flutter about.

4 Restore shine to gold jewelry
If your gold necklace looks dull but you don't have polish on hand, pour a bit of beer (a light or medium brew—avoid dark ale) onto a soft cloth and rub it into the bangle, then buff with a clean cloth. Beer's carbonic acid will dissolve oil and dirt so your jewelry sparkles.

5 Green up your lawn in no time
Brown spots creeping up on your lawn? Professional gardeners suggest pouring beer (just enough to wet the grass) on discolored areas. The brew's acids kill fungus, while its fermented sugars feed the grass to stimulate healthy growth.

6 Quickly get rid of skunk stink
Fido crossed paths with a skunk and smells so foul, we can barely get near him! But that curious dog has gotten into this bind before, so we know the fix: Rub a can or two's worth of beer into his coat, then rinse with water and bathe him with doggy shampoo to remove any beer scent. Beer's yeast cultures will penetrate the skunk spray's water-resistant oils so the brew's carbonic acid can dissolve them. Plus, the alcohol will kill odor-causing bacteria, resulting in a fresh-smelling cuddle buddy!

7 Spruce up wood furniture

Guests are arriving soon for your dinner party, and a quick inspection of your wooden coffee table has you wishing you had furniture polish on hand. The in-a-pinch fix: Wipe down the furniture with a soft cloth saturated in beer, then buff dry with a clean, dry cloth. The drink's slight foaminess loosens dust, while the color of the malt brings out the wood's hue and the alcohol boosts shine.

8 Keep wasps from spoiling outdoor fun

Your gang is out in the yard enjoying the beautiful weather when wasps come buzzing about, ruining the fun. To keep the pests at bay, make a wasp trap. To do: Fill a jar halfway with beer, then spread a thin coating of petroleum jelly along the upper inside area of the jar. Next, poke a hole in the lid that's about the diameter of your pinkie, then screw it on top. Wasps are attracted to the sugar and protein in beer, so they'll fly into the trap but won't be able to climb out. Just be sure to place the trap away from where people gather or play.

9 Remove rust marks with ease

You scored a set of metal lawn chairs for a song at a yard sale. The only hitch: There are a few rusty spots. Beer to the rescue! Simply cover the problem areas with a beer-soaked rag and let sit for about an hour. The brew's carbonic acid will dissolve the rust so your yard sale find will look as good as new.

10 Tenderize tough cuts of meat

It figures! We've got all the fixings for a tasty rump roast dinner . . . except tenderizer. Luckily, a foodie friend clued us in to the perfect save: Put the roast in a large, zipper-lock bag and pour in one can of beer, then let it soak in the fridge for at least 1 hour before cooking. Beer's carbonic acid softens the muscle fibers that make meat tough. But beer isn't as acidic as vinegar-based marinades, so it doesn't render the roast mushy or impart a strong flavor.

Faded colors

If your duds look duller than they did in the fall, the culprit may be exposure to light: Even if you keep the garments in a windowless closet, light from a fluorescent bulb can be enough to break down color pigments. Leftover chemicals (including body oil or even chlorine from your water) can also gradually degrade the garment's dye. The solution: Wash the items in a like-color load. Sometimes color on one fabric can bleed into another fabric, which can restore color to faded clothing. If that fails, buy fabric dye like Rit and use as instructed.

Do this for fluffier cashmere

As you're laying out an outfit for tomorrow, you notice that the cashmere sweater you wanted to wear looks a little limp because it's been in the back of your closet for months. The quick fix: Put the sweater in a large zipper-lock bag, then stash it in the freezer overnight. The cold air will make the cashmere fibers plump up, so by morning the sweater will look extra plush and luxurious. (Don't forget to take it out of the freezer a half hour before getting dressed so it can warm up.)

NICE-AND-NEAT LINENS

Clever storage solution for extra sheet sets

If the shelves of your linen closet are crammed full of sheets and pillowcases, try this: Designate an extra set of sheets for each bed in the house, then fold the linens and store them flat between the box spring and mattress. When it's time to change the sheets, instead of digging through the linen closet, you can just grab the fresh set from under the mattress.

Rank sheet sets from king to twin

Make it easy to find sheets for every bedroom. Just fold the sheets and place them inside their pillowcases, then use towel-rod clips to hang them on curtain rods installed on the door. Each rod can be designated for one room: your set on top, guests' in the middle, and kids' on the bottom.

Prevent blanket fallout

It always seems like a good idea to store extra throws, blankets, and pillows on the top shelf . . . until you pull out an item and the whole pile falls down. To avoid this mess, store throws in individual bags or bins so that when you grab one bin, you get a single throw blanket, not an avalanche.

Corral bath-time supplies

Not enough room in your bathroom for everyone's toiletries? Relocate some items to the linen closet and store them in portable plastic buckets. Just designate one for each person, and your shampoo will never get lost among your kids' Mr. Bubble again.

Outsmart "towel towers"

Piles of towels can become a storage nightmare in even the neatest linen closet. The fix: Place a repurposed shoe-storage bin on your closet shelf to create cubbies for folded towels and rolled washcloths.

NIX INDOOR PESTS NOW

Chemical-free way to keep ants at bay

To avoid a repeat of last summer's ant infestation without resorting to poisonous traps, try this child- and pet-safe solution: In a bowl, combine ½ cup of molasses, ¼ cup of sugar, and ¼ cup of active dry yeast (found in the baking aisle). Pour ⅛ inch of the mixture into shallow jars or bowls and leave them on counters, in cabinets, under the fridge— anywhere you've spotted ants before. The molasses and sugar will attract the pests, but since they can't digest the yeast, they'll die after eating the mixture.

Say good-bye to pesky fruit flies

To keep produce on the counter without having to deal with hordes of fruit flies, leave 1 to 2 inches of cola in a plastic screw-top bottle and use a nail to poke a small hole in the cap before setting the bottle out on your counter. The sugary-smelling cola will attract the pests, but once they fly into the bottle, they won't be able to get back out and will eventually drown. Replace every week. Money saved: $5 to $15 for fruit-fly traps

A natural way to repel pests

Keep bugs and little critters away by pouring a few drops of peppermint oil (available at most health-food or grocery stores) on cotton balls and placing them wherever the pests tend to gather. Ants, silverfish, caterpillars, and mice register the mint's strong menthol scent as an olfactory alarm, which will make them get out and stay out.

Keep clothes safe from pests

Reader Tip "My bedroom closet is tiny, so I always swap out clothing when the seasons change and store off-season garments in boxes under my bed. Since I hate the smell of mothballs, I use my mom's trick to keep my stored clothes safe: Saturate a few cotton balls in lavender essential oil, wrap them in cheesecloth, tie closed, and place a bundle or two in each box. The herbal scent repels pests just as effectively as mothballs. Plus, it leaves my clothes smelling lovely!"

—Alexa Hammon, Harrisburg, PA

Ward off pantry pests

Springtime is mealworm mating season—the time of year when these bugs are most likely to be in your kitchen. But you can keep them out of your flour, pasta, and other staples by tucking a bay leaf inside each container (or tape it to the inside of a cabinet door). Since mealworms hate the herb's smell and taste, they'll stay away.

Keep mice out of your house

To stop critters from invading your space, pinpoint where the pests can gain entrance, then stuff the openings with dryer sheets. The intense aroma is so unappealing to mice that they won't want to chew through the sheets to get inside. (Replace the sheets when you notice their scent fading.)

Genius trick for keeping ants at bay

If you notice ants marching toward your home's entryway, grab a stick of chalk and draw thick lines around the perimeter. Chalk's calcium carbonate is a nontoxic ant repellent, so the insects won't cross the border. You can also draw lines around outdoor pet bowls to keep pests away from Fido's food.

Happy Houseplants and Flowers

It's so special to have floral bouquets and houseplants decorating your living space, and you'll want to keep your plants and flowers looking their best. Try these tips to keep your vases sparkling, keep your blooms everlasting, and find shortcuts to watering.

VASE CLEANING

Corral blooms in a wide vase

You can't wait to display the flowers your neighbor brought over from her garden. The only problem? The arrangement is a tad too small for your vase, so some of the weaker stems are flopping over to the side. To the rescue: dental floss! You can use the invisible string to tie the stems together so they stand beautifully upright.

Fast fix for a foggy glass vase

The blooms you snipped from the garden are going to look beautiful in your living room, but first you have to get that foggy film off your glass vase. To do: Fill the container with hot water and drop in two Alka-Seltzer tablets. The citric acid and sodium bicarbonate in the heartburn remedy will form bubbles that break down caked-on plant residue, so your glass will be crystal clear and bouquet ready in minutes.

LONG-LASTING BLOOMS

Double the life of fresh flowers

Keep a bouquet looking beautiful by dropping two aspirin tablets into the water-filled vase. The acidic aspirin will decrease the pH level of the water, making it inhospitable to the harmful bacteria that cause flowers to wilt before their time.

Simple fix for droopy flowers

Displaying freshly cut hydrangeas, roses, and daisies from your garden really livens up your house, but you hate watching the blooms droop after just a few days. Make bouquets last longer by adding a few drops of vodka (about 1 teaspoon) to the vase water. Vodka inhibits the production of ethylene, a molecule that accelerates aging in plants, so the fading flowers will perk up and look fresh longer.

Quick help for wimpy leaves

To perk up indoor plants that look like they've seen better days, try this trick: The next time you boil eggs, save the cooled cooking water and use it instead of tap water to nourish your plants. This supercharged H_2O will have absorbed growth-stimulating nutrients like lecithin and protein from the eggs, so just a few "sips" will help your droopy houseplants stand tall again.

Reader Tip: Droop-proof a tulip bouquet

"I love decorating my home with tulips from my garden. But within days, the stems start flopping over because the blooms are so heavy. When I told a florist friend about the problem, she suggested I lightly spray the top of each stem with aerosol hair spray before arranging the flowers. The stiff, invisible coating helps strengthen the stems. Now my tulips look beautiful for over a week!"

—Candace Shumerk, Avon, CT

Quick fix for brown leaf tips

If the leaf tips of your indoor houseplants are tinged brown, the culprit may be your water. Chlorine, present in most tap water, can harm a sensitive plant's growth, but letting water sit out overnight before using it will allow the chlorine to dissipate. This works especially well for plants with thin leaves, like spider plants, which are particularly sensitive to chlorine.

Use charcoal for better bouquets

To keep a bouquet looking gorgeous for more than a week, drop a piece of charcoal (without lighter fluid) into an opaque, water-filled vase, then add the flowers. The briquette will act as a water filter, trapping chlorine and other contaminants that speed wilting.

Make fresh-cut flowers last longer

To extend the life of your arrangement, try this recipe recommended by florists: For every liter of lukewarm water, combine 2 tablespoons of fresh lime juice, 1 tablespoon of sugar, and ½ teaspoon of bleach. The lime juice will help optimize the pH level of the water, the sugar will provide nutrients that help the buds open, and the bleach will ward off bacterial growth. Your bouquet will last for an extra week or more!

Fix a broken flower stem

"I was arranging a bouquet of beautiful blooms that had been sent to me when I discovered a broken stem. Instead of tossing that flower out, I placed its stem in a drinking straw, secured it with masking tape, and trimmed the plastic so the flower was the same length as the others. Then I placed it in the middle of the bouquet to mask the alteration. The stem 'extension' worked perfectly—no one noticed the difference!"

—*Samantha Lepo, Oakland, MD*

END WATERING WOES

Water hanging plants with ease

The potted flowers in your living room look stunning, but they're slightly out of reach, which makes them hard to water—if you don't drag out a chair to stand on, you end up soaking yourself as you try to angle the watering can. An easier way: Simply drop three or four ice cubes into each pot. You'll save yourself the trouble of lugging around a watering can, and, because the ice melts slowly, your plants will absorb more water.

Mess-free way to refresh a bouquet

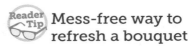

"After I spend time carefully arranging flowers, I don't want to ruin the bouquet by yanking out all the blooms when it comes time to change the water. So I was happy when a friend shared this easy trick: Use an old turkey baster to suction out the old water, then fill the baster with fresh water and squeeze it into the vase. Genius!"

—*Kimberly Thorr, Salisbury, MD*

Ensure houseplants thrive with a cloche

Tropical and Mediterranean plants favor more humid environments than most homes afford. The easy fix? Make a homemade cloche to help keep the plant safe from heating- and cooling-vent drafts and contain its own humidity. To do: Using a knife or box cutter, carefully remove the bottom few inches from a clean 1- or 2-liter soda bottle and place it on top of your planter. Water as usual and enjoy!

Electronics with Ease

All of our favorite gadgets simplify our lives and keep us connected. But every once in a while, we have an "oops" moment and can use some pointers to smooth the situation.

SOS for a soaked phone

Oops—your husband forgot he had his cell phone in his pocket until after he dove into the pool! To sidestep water damage, turn off the phone immediately and remove the battery, then fill a container or bag with dry rice, put the parts inside, and seal. Let sit overnight. The rice will absorb the moisture that's shorting out the phone. Once you reassemble it, it'll be as good as new! Money saved: $50 to $100 for a new cell phone

Amplify a cell phone alarm

If your deep-sleeping teen has trouble hearing his cell phone alarm in the mornings (even with the volume maxed out), try placing the device inside a tall, clean drinking glass. When the alarm goes off, the sound will reverberate inside the glass and become amplified, so he can't help but hear it.

Use tape to mark cords

If you've ever unplugged cords from your computer or television to clean or move furniture and then felt lost when it came time to replace the cords again, try this: After you unplug each item, place a small piece of masking tape over the plug so you can remember where to plug it in later. If you need to unplug several cords, write numbers on the masking tape for both cord and device.

Clean a keyboard with ease

You go to your home office to finish a last-minute work project and find the computer keyboard coated with sticky fingerprints. To get rid of the grime in a flash, just wet a cotton swab with your facial astringent and lightly squeeze out any excess. Then swipe it over and between the keys, using new swabs as necessary. The solution's alcohol will break down oil and dirt while disinfecting the keys.

Remove keyboard gunk in seconds

A sure sign that school is back in session: the food bits stuck in the computer keyboard, compliments of the kids' snacking while doing homework. To lift the grime, dip a clean eyeshadow applicator into rubbing alcohol and sweep between the keys. The tool's spongy head fits into the crevices, where it will whisk away dust and crumbs. You can also use the alcohol-soaked sponge to disinfect the keys—a top spot for household germs.

Easily reach computer ports

"I like my desktop computer, but whenever I want to plug a cord into the back of the monitor, I end up having to stand up and bend awkwardly over the screen to find the ports. Then one day I caught sight of my old lazy Susan and had an idea. I stuck the rotating platform under my computer monitor, gave it a couple spins to make sure the cords had enough room to move, and voilà—easy access to the plug ports in an instant!"

—Rachel Hausman, Lakeville, CT

Keep a computer screen crystal clear

Your computer monitor is a magnet for dust and fingerprints, but household cleaners contain solvents like ammonia and alcohol that can damage the screen or antiglare coating. Rather than purchase a specialized screen cleaner, cut a rag-size square from an old pair of panty hose, lightly spritz it with water, and use it to dust the screen. The mesh nylon will act like microfiber, gathering dust without redistributing it, while the water will safely remove grease and fingerprints. (This trick works for TV screens, too.) Money saved: $4 to $8 for computer cleaner or cleaning wipes

Double the life of printer ink

"The black ink in my printer always seems to run out faster than the colors. So I was thrilled when my friend suggested this easy trick: Change the font color to gray before printing to-do lists, driving directions, and other casual documents. The lighter hue uses up less black ink, so my cartridge will last twice as long."

—Emma Kim, Boise, ID

Printer out of ink? Try this!

We all know how frustrating it is to be in a hurry to print something, only to discover that the printer cartridge is so low on ink that the document is illegible—and you don't have another cartridge handy. The save: Remove the cartridge from the printer and blast it with warm air from a blow-dryer for 60 seconds. The heat will thin out the remaining ink so you'll be able to print a few more pages. (For best results, put the cartridge back in while it's still warm.)

More power from your laptop

While dashing off an urgent e-mail, you notice that your laptop battery is running dangerously low—and there's no charger on hand. The fix: After quitting all unnecessary programs and dimming the energy-sapping backlight as much as possible, press Control+Option+Command+8 for Macs or LeftAlt+LeftShift+PrintScreen for PCs. This will invert the colors of your screen, making it mostly black. (To return your screen colors to normal, simply press those keys again.) The less color on your screen, the more energy you ultimately save. You can also activate gray scale (under "display settings" on most computers), which turns off all power-exhausting colors.

Save power on your cell

The next time your low-battery alarm goes off when you're expecting a call, take your phone out of your pocket or purse and keep it away from direct sunlight. The reason: When a cell phone is warm, its electrons move faster, which depletes the battery faster as well. Other sneaky energy sappers to switch off: vibrate mode, keypad tones, and any open applications such as e-mail, Wi-Fi, and Bluetooth.

ELECTRONICS + SUMMER = UH-OH

Heat, outdoor activities, and sticky warm-weather treats can wreak havoc on electronics. Here are six fix-it tricks that will help you beat any gadget disaster this season.

Sand vs. handheld games

Sand in the keypad of a handheld toy or cell phone can jam buttons and cause internal damage. The save: Hold the game upside down and use a clean, soft-bristled toothbrush to brush around and between the keys. The thin, flexible bristles will safely dislodge the sand grains. To prevent the problem next time, seal games and cell phones in zipper-lock bags before a beach trip—you can still use buttons and even touch screens, but this will keep the devices sand-free.

Airborne debris vs. laptops

You left your laptop on your patio table while you did some weeding, then you closed it up and brought it inside. But when you open it back up, the screen stays mostly dark. The culprit: airborne pollen, dust, or even just humidity jamming the laptop's lid switch. The easy fix: Locate the lid switch—usually near the laptop's hinges—and jiggle it back and forth to clear debris.

Lightning storms vs. computers

If your computer won't reboot after a thunderstorm, even after you've unplugged it and tried new outlets, try unplugging your keyboard, too. Keyboards and other external devices may have been affected by the surge as well, which could be why your computer won't turn back on. Let the computer sit for 20 to 30 minutes after unplugging it to drain any electricity that's interfering with the start-up cycle, then power it back up.

Hot cars vs. cell phones

You accidentally left your cell phone in your sizzling-hot car while grocery shopping, and now it won't turn on. To rescue the device, crank up your car's AC and direct it at the phone. Once home, place the device in front of a fan until it no longer feels hot to the touch, then seal it in an airtight bag and stow it in your fridge (not the freezer) for 5 to 10 minutes before removing and trying to power it up again.

Cool drinks vs. keyboards

To save a soda-soaked keyboard, first unplug it, hold it upside down to drain the liquid, and pat it dry with a towel. Then dampen a clean cloth with rubbing alcohol and use it to clean the keyboard. To clean under the keys, cover one end of a toothpick with cotton (from a cotton ball), wet it with rubbing alcohol, and gently slide it into the cracks between the keys, changing the cotton when it gets dirty. Leave the keyboard upside down on a towel to dry overnight.

Pools vs. digital cameras

You wanted to take a cute shot of your niece playing in the pool, but an ill-timed splash soaked your digital camera. Remove the battery immediately to protect it from damage. Then pat the battery and camera dry and seal both pieces in an airtight zipper-lock bag with several silica gel packets (the ones that come inside shoes and electronics packaging) or dry rice, which will absorb the moisture. Wait until the camera is completely dry before turning it on.

Battery basics for digital cameras

Oh, no! Your camera's battery light starts blinking just as your baby niece goes into supercute mode. To maximize the rest of your battery life, be sure to turn off the LCD screen and resist using flash and zoom, which all use up more energy. Also, in cold weather, outdoor shooters should keep cameras or batteries close to their bodies when not in use. Cold weather can deplete a battery quickly, so keeping it warm with body heat will extend its life.

Don't stop the music

You still have 20 minutes to go on the treadmill, but your MP3 player's battery looks perilously low. To squeeze out another few songs, select a playlist or album. Switching back and forth between songs causes the device to use power looking for each file, and browsing through songs activates the energy-draining backlight. But MP3 players can "cache" albums or playlists, storing the data in a way that lets the hard drive retrieve it faster and with less battery power. Another tip: Keep the volume as low as possible.

Warm up your remote batteries

You finally have a chance to catch up on the backlog on your DVR, but your remote control's batteries are dying—and what's the point of recording if you can't fast-forward through the commercials? The save: Remove the batteries and tuck them behind your knee for a few minutes to warm them up before popping them back into the remote.

Handy Holiday Tips

Use this to water a Christmas tree

There's no need to crawl under the tree and wrestle with the lower branches every time you need to refresh the water—an empty wine bottle can make the task much easier! The bottle's long neck will allow you to keep a little distance as you refill the basin, and the thin opening helps ensure that the water goes right where you want it to instead of splashing all over the floor.

Reader Tip — Ensure holiday cards arrive

"After I sent out my cards last year, I was disappointed to hear some people never received theirs. It turned out that some of the local cards got caught in a rainstorm, so the addresses were smudged and the envelopes couldn't be delivered. I mentioned it to a letter-carrier friend, who suggested brushing a coat of clear nail polish over the addresses—it's the perfect sealant."

—Pat Jones, Brookings, OR

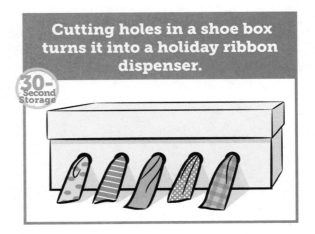

Cutting holes in a shoe box turns it into a holiday ribbon dispenser.

30-Second Storage

SOS for squashed bows and ribbons

You're putting the final touches on your wrapped gifts when you realize the bows and ribbons you saved from last year have been crushed and wrinkled. To restore their beauty, toss them in the dryer (set on low heat) with a clean, damp cloth for 2 minutes. The low heat combined with the cloth's moisture will expand the plastic bows to their original shape, plus take wrinkles out of fabric ribbons. Money saved: $6 per bag of gift bows

 ## Smooth ribbon wrinkles in minutes

"After the Christmas presents under my tree are unwrapped, I gather all the fancy fabric ribbons that have been tossed around the room so I can reuse them to pretty up gifts throughout the year. But before I pack them away, I grab my flatiron and run it over each ribbon once or twice to smooth out any creases. They end up looking brand-new!"

—Katherine Tracey, Bloomfield, IN

Prevent gift wrap from unraveling

No matter how tightly you roll up your wrapping paper, the loose end always unravels—and securing it with rubber bands or tape won't do because that creates creases and tears. Instead, grab an empty cardboard wrapping-paper tube and cut it open lengthwise. Then slip the tube around a full wrapping-paper roll so the free end of the paper hangs slightly through the slit. The tube will keep the paper neatly bound, plus act as a handy dispenser the next time you need to wrap a gift.

Nix wrapping-paper chaos

For an easy way to keep your gift-wrapping supplies from unraveling and cluttering your floor or closets, place each roll in the leg of an old, clean pair of panty hose, then straddle the legs over a closet rod or on a hanger. The nylons will keep the rolls neatly contained, plus allow you to see them all at a glance.

Genius way to display photo cards

You love looking at all the holiday photo cards you've been receiving in the mail, but since they don't stand up like regular cards, they're hard to display around your home. The save: Grab a handful of small binder clips. Simply slip the photo between the two "arms" of a clip, then stand it up on a flat surface. Bonus: Your cards won't be damaged by tape or pushpin holes.

Beautiful Backyards and Gardens

Now that you have your home looking beautiful, it's time to focus on the yard. How do you keep weeds at bay? Or raccoonproof your garbage cans? Read on for tons of helpful hints that will keep your garden, your driveway, and even your car looking picture-perfect.

DAILY GARDENING ADVICE

Keep garden tools looking like new

When it's finally warm enough to work in your garden, it seems the damp weather wreaks havoc on your metal tools. To stave off rust, toss a few silica gel packets (the ones that come in shoe boxes, electronics packaging, and food containers) into your toolbox. The packets will pull moisture and sulfide vapors from the air, preventing rust-causing oxidation. Bonus: Put some in your jewelry box to keep silver free of tarnish, too!

Keep garden shears from sticking

Warmer weather inspires you to do some trimming around your yard, but your trusty garden shears keep sticking and jamming. What can help: Rub a bit of car wax onto the hinge of the shears. The wax will lubricate the metal so you can make cleaner cuts and use less elbow grease in the process—your arms will thank you!

Quick help for rusty gardening tools

After pulling out your trusty snipper and trowel, you see that they've fallen victim to rust. The fix: Fill a bowl with white or apple cider vinegar and let the tools soak overnight. The vinegar's acetic acid will break down the rust, leaving the tools looking brand-new by morning.

Outsmart pot pileups with a ladder

It's easy to get carried away at the garden center, and the horticultural haul can eat up backyard space. The solution: going tall. A tiered A-frame display shows off the maximum number of plants in the minimum number of square feet. Simply rest wood planks on the ladder's rungs.

Brighten up any corner with a to-go window box

A wooden tote filled with pots of flowers lets you change out blooms—something that isn't easy to do in a traditional window box. Plus, the handle turns the contained arrangement into a go-anywhere centerpiece.

Complement a garden bed with a border of blue

Take a stone border beyond basic by painting it blue, a hue that coolly contrasts garden greens. Hint: Spray paint ensures pigment gets into the small grooves of masonry.

Optimize an outdoor wall with pot holders

An exterior wall can add at least 15 square feet to your garden when fitted with potted-plant hangers. Plus, the suspended pots allow gravity to take care of drainage, and excess water travels down to hydrate the plants below. To install hanging rings, drill holes into the wall and screw in place.

Stop hanging plants from dripping

If you accidentally pour a little too much water into one of your hanging plants, grab a shower cap and slide it over the bottom of the pot. The cap's elastic band will fit snugly around most midsize planters, allowing the cap to collect any excess liquid as it drains. (If your planter is on the smaller side, be sure to secure the shower cap with tape or a rubber band to keep it from slipping.)

Reader Tip — Never lug another mulch bag

"As much as I love gardening, when the weather heats up, the last thing I want to do is make a dozen trips back and forth from the shed to grab bags of mulch, potting soil, my toolbox, and other heavy supplies. But I had an aha moment the other day when I spotted my son's plastic snow sled lying in the corner of the garage. I placed everything I needed for an afternoon of gardening on the sled and was able to easily pull it across the yard in one trip. I didn't even break a sweat!"

—Alexandra Grimes, Dalton, NH

Water your garden half as often

Thanks to the recent streak of dry, blazing-hot weather, you've been watering your garden every day—but your roses and geraniums still look a little lackluster. The grilling staple that can help them stay hydrated: charcoal. Simply break several briquettes into 1-inch pieces and sprinkle them on flower beds or beneath bushes and hedges. The porous, absorbent charcoal will retain rain and hose water and slowly release it into the ground, so the soil will stay moist for twice as long. The carbon in the charcoal will also provide vital nutrients to the plants. Plus, the dense briquettes will block sunlight to the soil around the plants to discourage weeds from growing.

Genius way to grow herbs

You love to cook with fresh herbs, so you make a point of growing your own. But last year some (like mint and chives) spread so fast that they threatened to overtake the whole garden. To the rescue: a canvas over-the-door shoe organizer. Just poke a few small drainage holes in the bottom of each pocket and hang it over a shed door or tall railing. Fill the pouches with potting soil, leaving 1 inch of headspace, then plant an herb variety in each one. The pockets will organize and contain even the most aggressive herbs.

Easily patch a torn garden hose

While watering your tomato plants, you notice that your hose has sprung a small leak. To seal it temporarily, jam a toothpick or wooden matchstick (with the flammable end removed) into the leaky spot, then break off the excess. Use the hose as you normally would. The wood will swell when it gets wet, sealing off the hole until you can get to the hardware store to buy a new garden hose.

Prevent tracked-in messes

To avoid bringing postgardening grime indoors with you, make an outdoor cleanup station: Cut the foot off an old pair of nylons and throw in all your leftover soap slivers, then tie the stocking around the neck of your outdoor spigot. When you're done gardening, turn on the tap and use the soap to wash away any muck before going inside. (Kids can also use the cleanup station after playing outdoors.)

Storing seeds safely

Your garden has produced such delicious tomatoes that you'd like to hold on to the leftover seeds for next season. A trick to ensure you won't lose them: Staple their packets shut and slip each into a plastic photo sleeve, then clip the sheet into a three-ring binder. (Hint: If you're missing the packet, fold the seeds into a piece of paper and label it with a picture of the plant.) The page protectors will hold everything in place while letting you see what each plant is.

TRICKS FOR A GREAT YARD

Banish weeds—for pennies!

Your yard looks fabulous . . . except for the crabgrass sprouting up in the cracks of your walkway. To eliminate it, pour a 1/8-inch-thick layer of salt on the weeds, then sprinkle with water. The sodium will dissolve into the soil and block weeds' access to water, causing them to die. (Note: Salt shouldn't be used near plants that you don't want killed.) Money saved: $10 for a 32-ounce bottle of weed killer

Nontoxic weed killer

For a kid- and pet-friendly way to eliminate the weeds sprouting through the cracks in your walkway, mix 1 cup of salt and 1 gallon of white vinegar, pour into a spray bottle, and spritz on the cracks. The sodium will dehydrate existing weeds, while the vinegar will make the soil inhospitable to growth. (Note: This works so well, you should spray only where you never want plants to grow.)

Quick fix for splintered lawn tools

Ouch! The task of raking leaves is tough enough—the last thing you need to deal with is shards of wood from the rake's handle poking into your hands. The good news: You can smooth out a worn handle by applying a coat of lemon-oil furniture polish to the wood with a soft cloth. The moisture-rich oil will soften and seal the splintering cracks, then work to cure the wood to a hard, polished finish. Enjoy a little breather while the wood dries—after about an hour, you'll be able to speed through your yard work pain-free!

10 Brilliant Uses
for BUTTER

1 Restore sheen to weather-worn hair

If the combination of chilly winter winds and drying indoor heat has your hair feeling brittle, try this: Rub 2 to 3 teaspoons of butter into your hair, focusing on the ends. Then cover with a shower cap or towel and let sit for 30 minutes before shampooing. The butter's fat will seep into hair cuticles, soothing and nourishing the keratin, a protein that makes up healthy hair. This will cause the cuticles to lie flat, leaving your tresses shiny.

2 Eradicate a fishy smell from hands

Tonight's homemade fish-and-chips dinner was delicious, but preparing the fillets left an unpleasant fishy odor on your hands. To nix the smell fast, rub ½ teaspoon of butter into your hands and wait 1 minute, then wash with soap and warm water. When the butter's fats seep into your pores, they will dissolve the trapped fish oils responsible for the persistent smell. (This trick works for any odor.) Bonus: The emollients in the spread will leave your hands feeling soft and smooth.

3 Remove white residue from colored candles

You want to surprise your husband with a candlelit meal for Valentine's Day. But when you grab your festive pillar candles from storage, they're covered with a filmy white residue. The quick fix: Rub ½ teaspoon of butter on a soft cloth and use it to buff the wax. The friction created by the rubbing will dislodge dirt and dust on the surface of the candles, while the butter's milk fats will infuse the wax with moisture, leaving the pillars refreshed and glossy in no time.

4 Strip stubborn bathtub decals

Sure, your son loved the rubber duck decals in the tub . . . when he was 3. Now that he's approaching his tween years? Not so much. To remove them with ease, cover each sticker with 1 teaspoon of butter. Let sit for 10 to 15 minutes, then use a butter knife to gently loosen the decals. Repeat if sticky residue remains. The butter's oils will dissolve the adhesive, so the decals and glue will peel away sans struggle.

5 Revive old, damaged leather goods

Oops! Your husband just discovered his "lost" glove on the front steps—but not before the freezing temperatures left the leather stiff and brittle. Give the glove new life with butter: Use your fingers to gently knead the leather, then rub in 1 teaspoon of the spread. Seal the glove in a plastic bag and let sit overnight. In the morning use a soft cloth to buff away all remaining greasy residue. The porous leather will absorb the butter's fatty acids to restore lost moisture, while the milk fats will renew the leather's original luster.

6 Lift water rings from wood furniture

When a misplaced glass of water leaves a white ring on your wooden coffee table, reach for a pat of butter. Apply 1 tablespoon of the spread to the mark and rub it in with a soft cloth. Let it sit overnight, then wash away any excess grease with soapy water. The oils in the butter will seep into the wood's pores, displacing the trapped moisture that's causing the pesky ring. Plus, the milk fats will reseal the wood's grain, so it will look as good as new.

7 Prevent jar lids from getting stuck

There are times when you'd rather skip adding honey to your tea than wrestle with a stuck-shut jar lid. To stop sticky drips from cementing the lid closed, simply rub ¼ teaspoon of butter on a soft cloth and swipe it around the lip of the jar and the inside of the lid. The film of oily butter will repel any drips and keep the lid lubricated, allowing it to open easily every time.

8 Make large pills easier to swallow

Your kids are finally getting over their strep throat—just in time for you to catch it. But the antibiotic pills your doctor prescribed are so large, you're having trouble swallowing them. The remedy: Roll each pill in butter before washing it down with a glass of water. The greasy butter will coat the capsule and act as a lubricant, so the pill will slide right down your throat.

9 Quickly soothe a fussy cat

Thanks to a last-minute mix-up with the kennel, you had to bring your cat with you to visit your sister's family—and the new environment has Muffy stressed out. Soothe her nerves by rubbing 1 to 2 teaspoons of butter on her front paws. The urge to lick off the creamy spread will distract her from the commotion and unfamiliar surroundings just long enough to make her comfortable again. Plus, the butter will pick up the scents of the new house, so your cat will get more accustomed to it with every sniff and lick.

10 Keep leftover onions fresh longer

Your favorite marinara sauce recipe calls for half an onion. But more often than not, the other half spoils before you can use it. Next time, coat the onion's cut surface with butter, wrap it in foil or plastic wrap, and store it in the fridge. The butter's milk fats will create an airtight seal on the surface of the onion that will prevent bacteria from growing, so it stays fresh longer—without leaving a taste behind.

Fill in balding lawn spots with gelatin

Bare areas can make even the most manicured yard look bedraggled. To the rescue: gelatin, which is rich in plant-nourishing nitrogen, a key ingredient in fertilizers. To do: Pour unflavored gelatin powder into a bowl (you'll need about 6 ounces per square foot), then stir in enough cool water to achieve a ketchuplike texture and mix in 2 tablespoons of grass seed per 6 ounces of gelatin. After loosening the top ½ inch of bare soil with a hoe, pour the mixture into a zipper-lock plastic bag, snip off one corner, and squeeze out rows about an inch apart, letting them bleed into the surrounding grass. Bonus: Gelatin's thick texture will prevent the seed from being blown away by wind, so you won't have to repeat the job.

Easier hedge pruning

Due to months in storage, your garden shears are sticking—so it's taking twice as long as usual to prune the bushes. The save: After removing any rust, use a lint-free cloth to buff car wax into the clipper's hinges. The slick coating will decrease friction and improve the mobility of the tool's axis, preventing sticking and future rust buildup. Plus, car wax is designed to be long lasting, so just one treatment will do the trick for months.

Recycle spring grass clippings

For the first mowing in spring, be sure to save those grass clippings, because they contain more nutrients than grass at any other time of the year. And they come with the lowest number of weed seeds, too. Put the clippings on your compost pile or leave them on the lawn, where they'll return those nutrients directly to the soil.

Make postpruning cleanup a breeze

You don't mind pruning the hedges—it's raking up all the little leaves and twigs afterward that drives you crazy. The stress-saving fix: Before you start working, lay an old sheet under the bushes to collect all the clippings. Then the only thing you'll need to do is toss the debris when you're finished.

Easy way to paint a fence

Trying to stain or paint the bottom of a fence can be tricky—you end up either dripping paint all over the lawn or sweeping bits of dirt and grass onto the wet wood. To eliminate these hassles, place a dustpan under the fence as you paint, sliding it along the ground as you finish each section. The pan will keep the grass out of your way and catch drips, enabling you to breeze through the task.

PATIO POINTERS

Store an outdoor umbrella this way

It's depressing enough when we have to take down our patio umbrella—can't summer last a little longer? But then we have to figure out how to cover the thing. To cope, we grab a pair of panty hose and stretch one leg over the umbrella's tip until it covers the base. Then we knot the second leg around the covered handle to secure and store upright. The tight weave of the hose keeps dirt out, so next spring we'll get 15 more minutes to just relax in the sun.

Fast fix for a grimy patio umbrella

Your patio umbrella must have been damp when you packed it away last year—when you dig it out of storage, it's mildewed and grimy. To freshen it up, mix 2 cups of white vinegar with 2 tablespoons of liquid dish soap in a large bucket, fill with warm water, and use a sponge or soft-bristled brush to scrub the canvas with the solution. Rinse with cool water and let dry in the sun. Vinegar's acetic acid will kill mildew, while the soap will cut through dust, pollen, and grime, so your umbrella will look and smell like new.

Spruce up wicker without the fuss

After surviving the harsh winter elements, your wicker patio furniture looks a little dingy. But the tight weave makes removing dust and grime difficult. The fix: Mix ¼ cup of ammonia and 1 gallon of water and use the solution to liberally spritz the furniture. After 10 minutes, rinse off with a garden hose and let air-dry. The gaseous quality of ammonia lets it slip between the weave, where its ionizing agents will dissolve hard-to-reach dirt and mildew. Then the water will rinse the mess away—no wiping required!

Clean a patio with this

A simple way to tackle dirt, mildew, and moss buildup on your patio: Combine equal parts hydrogen peroxide and hot water in a bucket, then dunk a stiff broom (without wire bristles) into the mixture and firmly sweep the area. The hydrogen peroxide will kill mold and mildew, while the hot water will loosen stuck-on dirt so you can easily sweep away the mess. Then just sit back and enjoy your outdoor space!

Remove mildew from a deck with white vinegar

After months of being soaked with snow and rain, your favorite outdoor gathering spot may be marred by mildew. To remedy this, spray the wood with undiluted white vinegar and let sit for about an hour before hosing it off. (You can use white vinegar on mildewed patio cushions, too—just test on an inconspicuous corner first.) The vinegar's acetic acid will quickly kill mildew and mold spores. If any stains remain, spritz the discolored areas with a mild bleaching agent, like 3 percent hydrogen peroxide. Let sit for a half hour, then rinse with water.

Restore weather-worn furniture with beer

Wood tables and chairs often look dingy after a season of sitting out in the elements (or are dusty from sitting in storage). To revive your patio furniture, pour flat beer onto a soft cloth and use it to buff the wood. Beer's alcohol will cut through dust, debris, and buildup, plus proteins in the beverage's hops will seal in moisture to leave behind a subtle shine. And malt (which is responsible for beer's hue) will bring out the natural color of the wood. After wiping down the furniture, rub it dry with a clean cloth to banish any beer odor, which could attract pests.

Keep patio furniture spotless all season

Apply a light coat of car wax to your clean plastic or metal patio and lawn chairs before setting them out for the season. The slick substance will keep dirt, pollen, and tree sap from sticking to the furniture, making it a cinch to wipe clean as needed. Plus, the wax will protect the chairs from sun-induced fading. (And since you're applying such a light coating, there's no need to worry about wax rubbing off on your clothing.)

SUMMER HEADACHES?

Try These Swaps!

PAIN TRIGGER: Liquid lawn fertilizer
SMART SWAP: Epsom salts

Many weed-and-feed treatments contain heavy-duty chemicals (including phenoxy herbicides like 2,4-D, which is an ingredient in Agent Orange) that can trigger headaches, rashes, and other illnesses. Even worse, these chemicals can release harmful vapors for months after being applied.

A nontoxic option: Spray your lawn with a mix of 2 tablespoons of Epsom salts per gallon of water, then water as usual. The salts' magnesium promotes seed germination and chlorophyll production (to thicken grass), while the sulfur lowers the soil's pH to help grass absorb nutrients like iron (for hardier growth and brighter color). Note: A mixture with too much Epsom salts can burn grass, so test on a small spot first. If grass looks fine after 48 hours, it's safe to apply.

PAIN TRIGGER: Area bug repellent
SMART SWAP: Essential oil

Most brands of bug repellent rely on N,N-diethyl-meta-toluamide, aka DEET, to drive away pests. But DEET easily gets absorbed by skin, which is very harmful not only to your skin but also internal organs.

Luckily, many essential oils can effectively deter scent-sensitive pests. Try putting a drop of lavender, eucalyptus, citronella, pennyroyal, catnip, or cedarwood oil on a cool lightbulb near the area you want to protect. When you turn on the light, it will heat and diffuse the scent throughout the air. No bulbs nearby? Soak fabric scraps in essential oil and hang them around the area.

After winter, it feels great to enjoy the fresh air. But sometimes our outdoor adventures expose us to chemical-laden products that can trigger health problems like skin irritation, light-headedness, tiredness, and nausea. That just won't do! To the rescue: We rounded up some just-as-effective natural alternatives to common store-bought products so you can have your warm-weather fun—without the dizzying side effects.

PAIN TRIGGER: Flea collar
SMART SWAP: Salt water

Chemical-packed flea and tick repellents can expose you and your furry friend to levels of pesticides that are 1,000 times over the Environmental Protection Agency's "acceptable" threshold. Two biggies: tetrachlorvinphos, which can cause stomach upset and eye irritation, and propoxur, which can trigger nausea and increase heart rate.

A safer bet: Wash your pet (and his bed or doghouse) with a gallon of warm water mixed with $1/2$ cup of table salt, taking care to avoid his eyes, then rinse well with water. Salt will dehydrate and kill fleas and their larvae, stopping the infestation. For extra protection, consider adding $1/4$ to 1 teaspoon (depending on his size) of apple cider vinegar to your pet's water or wet food daily. This will give his sweat a faint acidic odor that fleas can't tolerate. Bonus: The vinegar's potassium will add a healthy shine to his coat.

DRIVEWAY DISASTERS— AVERTED!

Dissolve driveway oil stains fast!

While changing the oil in your lawn mower, your husband accidentally knocked over the oil can. To sop up the spill, cover it with powdered dish-washing detergent. After 10 minutes, scrub the spot with a stiff broom, then sweep the whole mess away. The grease-fighting ingredients that help detergent work on dirty dishes will break down the grease, then the absorbent powder will soak it all up, leaving the ground spotless.

Shovel snow 50 percent faster

A white Christmas is a beautiful sight, and you want to minimize shoveling time so you can enjoy it. The time-saving trick: Coat the shovel with cooking spray. The oil will form a water-resistant seal that keeps wet snow from sticking to the metal, so you'll clear twice as much snow with each scoop.

End rock-salt clumping

When you opened your new bag of rock salt at the start of the snowy season, it was filled with small granules that were easy to sprinkle on your walkways. But now the bag is loaded with big balls of stuck-together salt. The fix: Toss a few lumps of charcoal into the bag to absorb clump-causing moisture. Next time a storm hits, you'll be able to salt with ease.

SWIMMING POOL SPLASH!

Locate a leak in an inflatable pool toy

It figures—you finally get a chance to relax in the pool sans kids, and the inflatable raft is deflating.

Save adult swim with this easy way to find the leak: In a bucket, combine dish soap and water, then pour over the floatie, pressing down lightly. The air escaping from the tear in the raft will make the soapy water bubble, allowing you to pinpoint the exact spot that you need to patch.

Deflate pool toys in half the time

Bringing your own inflatable balls and rafts to the community pool is a great way to keep little ones occupied, but having to deflate everything at the end of the day is time-consuming. To speed up the task, pack a binder clip in your beach bag. You can use the clip to apply pressure to the valve so air will escape more easily. Then you'll have both hands free to press air out of the inflatables. You'll be done in a jiffy!

NIX OUTDOOR PEST PROBLEMS

Keep rabbits from nibbling your garden

Your small vegetable garden was thriving before a family of rabbits started snacking on your plot. Take a hot tip from gardening gurus and combine 1 tablespoon of Tabasco sauce and 1 gallon of water. Then transfer the solution to a spray bottle and spritz on your plants (reapplying after heavy rain). The diluted solution won't harm blooms, but the strong, spicy smell of the hot sauce will have rabbits, mice, squirrels, and chipmunks looking elsewhere for a free buffet.

Repel garden pests—without chemicals

You thought the bunny you spotted in the backyard was cute . . . until he started using your garden as a snack bar. To keep the furry nuisance away, place two cotton balls soaked in white vinegar inside empty film canisters or pill bottles, poke a few holes in the caps, and bury halfway in the soil near the nibbled-on plants. The vinegar's strong odor will ward off curious rabbits, cats, dogs, deer, and raccoons, and the plastic canisters will retain the scent for weeks. Replace as needed. Money saved: $10 to $20 for animal repellent

Raccoonproof garbage cans

To prevent those pesky critters from getting into your outdoor trash cans and making a mess, sprinkle about 5 tablespoons of Epsom salts around and on top of the rubbish. (Reapply after it rains or snows.) Raccoons dislike the taste of the mineral, so after one lick, they'll take off and stay away from the trash for good.

Do away with garden slugs

To ensure your vegetables and flower beds stay free of harmful slugs, bury a clean yogurt container (any size) in an area where you've spotted the slimy creatures, making sure the rim is even with the ground. Fill the container with beer, then bait the rim with small bits of raw potato. The slugs will be lured into the cup but won't be able to crawl out. Problem solved!

Bright idea for repelling mosquitoes

You love enjoying your after-dinner cup of coffee on the front porch. The only hitch: the bugs that swarm around your entrance light. To deter the pesky insects, screw a yellow lightbulb (a "warm" white bulb will work, too) into the offending light and a white lightbulb (like a "cool" white) into a farther-away lawn lamp. Since mosquitoes have a hard time seeing yellow light, they'll be attracted to the brighter white light—away from you.

Antproof your BBQ

Your outdoor dinners often lure a few uninvited guests: ants and other creepy-crawlies. For a chemical-free way to banish the bugs, coat the bottom 2 inches of each picnic-table leg with a thick layer of petroleum jelly. The gooey barrier is impossible for insects to cross, so you won't have to worry about them nibbling on your food.

Keep gnats from crashing your next party

Guarantee a bug-free barbecue with this trick: Fill a few small bowls with a solution of three parts vinegar and one part dish soap, then set the bowls around the party area (at least 3 feet away from food). The pests are attracted to the smell of vinegar, so they'll dive into the bowls—and the slippery soap will keep them from climbing back out. Money saved: $5 per citronella candle

Soothe a bee sting in seconds

Ouch! You were in the garden picking tomatoes for tonight's salad and a bee stung your forearm. For quick relief, grab a slice of raw onion and apply it directly to the sting. The sulfur in the bulb is a natural detoxifier that neutralizes venom, reducing inflammation on contact.

REPEL BUGS NATURALLY

To rub on arms and legs:

Slathering skin with an aromatic lotion can ensure that bugs find you positively unappealing—even though other people will think you smell terrific. Two standout oils: lemongrass (repels ticks and mosquitoes) and clove (study-proven to keep mosquitoes off skin for 2 full hours). Just rub an oil-infused lotion onto skin every hour or two to get the benefits.

Lemongrass lotion:

1 cup of body lotion + 5 drops of lemongrass oil + 5 drops of clove essential oil = Combine in a bowl, then transfer to a 12-ounce pump bottle and shake well.

To add to the tablescape:

Eucalyptus and lavender are especially effective at deterring winged pests—perfect for when you're unwinding with friends and want to keep invaders from flying into your space. Plus, lavender's aroma will make guests feel at ease. You can disperse the scent with reeds, which will draw the oils up and release them into the air. Refresh the repellent every 2 hours by flipping the reeds over.

Lavender-eucalyptus diffuser:

6 ounces of water + 5 drops of eucalyptus oil + 5 drops of lavender oil = Combine water and oils in a pretty container and drop in 10 reed sticks.

> No more bug-repellent headaches! These chemical-free homemade blends keep mosquitoes, bees, and more at bay.

To spray around the area:

When you know friends and family will be out and about in the yard, spray a blend of rubbing alcohol, lemon juice, and peppermint oil around the gathering area's perimeter. The intense aromas of lemon juice and peppermint oil are overwhelming to pests, so they act as a bug shield. And rubbing alcohol adds an extra measure of security, since it's toxic to insects if sprayed directly on them. Respray the perimeter every hour to renew the "border."

Citrus-mint patio spray:

$1/2$ cup of rubbing alcohol + $1/4$ cup of fresh lemon juice + 10 drops of peppermint oil = Combine in a 24-ounce spray bottle, fill with water, and shake well.

Prevent flies from crashing your picnic

Who doesn't love dining al fresco in the summertime? But when flies come to share the feast, it's hard not to take your lunch inside. To keep the pests away, cut a lemon into quarters and poke a dozen whole cloves into the fleshy part of each wedge. Then transfer the slices onto paper plates and place them where needed. Flies can't stand citrus and spicy scents, so the combination of lemon and cloves will ensure they'll take their hunger elsewhere.

Repel mosquitoes naturally

Rather than dousing yourself in chemical sprays or lighting pricey citronella candles when mosquitoes attack your deck, mix 2 tablespoons of garlic powder and 2 cups of water in a spray bottle and use it to spritz your outdoor light before turning it on. As the bulb heats up, it will disperse a faint garlicky scent across your entire deck. Mosquitoes' sensitive odor receptors hate the smell of garlic, so they'll stay away. Money saved: $5 to $15 for citronella candles

Instant itch relief—for less

If an evening spent out on the patio left the family covered in mosquito bites, try this: Mix 1 teaspoon of ammonia with 1 cup of water, then dip a cotton ball in the solution and dab the affected areas. Ammonia is the active ingredient in some after-bite remedies because its alkalinity neutralizes acidic insect venom, easing the itch in minutes. Money saved: $5 for a tube of anti-itch cream

Cruising with Cars

Whether your car is the Love Bug or the family van, you'll want to keep it in tip-top shape both inside and out. Follow this helpful advice to keep your vehicle looking almost brand-new.

MANAGING THE LITTLE THINGS

Get more life out of wiper blades

This winter's especially snowy, icy weather wreaked havoc on your car's wiper blades—they're smearing rain and muck across your windshield. If you don't have the time to get them changed right now, just grab an emery board from your purse and rub it gently over both sides of the blade. The roughness will dislodge smudge-causing residue from your wipers, giving them a few more weeks of life.

Freezeproof locks

When a sheet of ice covers your car's keyhole, making it impossible to insert the key, it can be tough to chip it away. To sidestep the annoyance, place a flat, wide refrigerator magnet over your car door and trunk locks whenever snow or sleet is in the forecast. The magnets will create a seal to prevent water from seeping into the lock and freezing. In the morning, you can simply slide the magnets off and hit the road.

Defog your windshield—fast

On busy mornings, who has time to wait for the defroster to kick in? Instead, try keeping a clean blackboard eraser in your glove compartment. The extra-absorbent felt will quickly remove the vision-impairing condensation. Simply wipe the windshield and any fogged-up windows, then safely pull out of your driveway.

Fend off a flat tire

One of your car tires is looking low on air, and you suspect a hole. To locate the puncture, fill a spray bottle with soapy water and spritz the tire all over. Keep an eye out for a cluster of air bubbles, which will form on the surface where the hole is. Once you spot it, you've found the problem area and can patch it up accordingly.

Fast fix for hazy headlights

If your car's headlights seem to be a bit dull, use a cloth to rub a dollop of nongel toothpaste onto each one for about a minute, then wipe with a clean rag. The paste is abrasive enough to remove grime, but it won't scratch the lenses. (Avoid using glass cleaner—experts say its ammonia and solvents may harm lenses.) Money saved: $12 for a headlight restoration kit

Clean the windshield with a mesh onion bag

If summer's insect population seems to have gone "splat" on your windshield, grab a mesh onion bag and a little dish-washing liquid. Squirt a small amount of the liquid onto your windshield, and then scrub with the mesh bag. The mesh won't harm the glass, and the dead bugs will come off easily. Finish by wiping the window with a clean cloth.

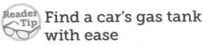

Find a car's gas tank with ease

"My family and I rented a car when we visited Florida last month, and when I went to get gas, I realized I had no idea which side of the car the tank was on. Of course I ended up choosing the wrong side! Then the gas station attendant shared this tip: Look for a small arrow near the car's gas gauge—the arrow is pointing to the side of the car the tank is on."

—*Amy Pasternak, Atlanta, GA*

DO AWAY WITH DENTS AND SCRATCHES

Frostproof a windshield

Why is it that your car always needs scraping on days when you're already running late for work? The save: The night before, slit open the sides of a plastic garbage bag, leaving it connected at the bottom. Then lay the bag flat across the windshield and secure under the wipers. Ice will form on the bag, not your windshield, so in the morning you can just pull it off, taking the icy layer with it—no scraping required!

Keep doors ding-free

To protect your car's finish (and your garage wall) from the dents and scratches that can occur when you open your door, create your own wall guard. To do: Cut an old pool noodle in half lengthwise, then screw or super-glue one half of the noodle to the wall where the front and rear doors would hit. (Or, if you always park in the exact same spot, you could mount an old mouse pad to the wall instead.) Money saved: $15 for a garage wall guard

"Erase" a scratch on your car's finish

Ugh—you were washing your car when you noticed a hairline scratch on the hood. The good news: There's no need to buy pricey touch-up paint or make a trip to the body shop. Instead, grab a crayon. Simply wash and dry the affected area, then slightly melt the tip of the crayon with a lighter or blow-dryer and "draw" over the scratch several times. The soft wax will dry into a hard, weatherproof filler. And since crayons are available in a wider array of colors than touch-up paint, you'll easily find the perfect match for your car.

Fix a dent for free

Oops! Instead of hitting his glove during a game of catch, your son's baseball hit your car. Before you make a trip to the body shop, try this: Coat the rim of a toilet plunger with petroleum jelly, place the tool over the dent, and pump as you would to unclog a toilet. The plunger will create a vacuum seal that pops the dent back into shape. Money saved: $250 per auto-body fix

Chapter 2

QUICK CLEANING AND FIX-ITS

Simple Laundry Smarts

Sometimes, between washing, drying, and folding, it seems laundry can take up an entire day. Then you have to worry about ironing out wrinkles and removing stains—who needs it? Here you'll find expert hints and tips for making laundry day as easy and effortless as can be.

END WASHING WOES

Safe way to wash delicates

Oh, no! You carefully hand washed your delicates, then noticed a few bleached spots on your best bras—even though the detergent you used didn't contain bleach. The possible culprit: chemical residue in your sink, like the peroxide in many toothpastes. To prevent this next time, place a colander in the sink, then put your garments inside and hand wash as usual. Problem solved!

No more mangled bras!

We admit it: We're often tempted to toss underwire bras into the washer instead of spending precious time hand washing . . . but that can twist the wire and ruin the bra. Luckily, we learned this trick: Place bras in a salad spinner with 3 tablespoons of baby shampoo and warm water, then spin for about a minute. The gentle cyclic motion gets delicates as clean as the washing machine does. Just be sure to thoroughly wash the spinner when done, or designate one for laundering.

In-a-pinch fabric softener

You planned to tackle a few loads of laundry this morning . . . until you saw that the fabric softener bottle was empty. For a quick substitute, mix 8 cups of white vinegar and 1¼ cups of warm water in a bucket, then add 1 cup of baking soda while stirring continuously. (The mixture will fizz.) Pour into a clean, gallon-size plastic jug; add 1 teaspoon of essential oil (like lavender); and seal. To use, shake the jug, then add ½ to 1 cup to your washing machine at the start of the rinse cycle. The vinegar and baking soda will soften the fibers in your clothes, while the essential oil will add a nice scent.

Coddle delicate clothing with castile soap

Gently cleanse away dirt with natural castile soap, which is free of additives like phosphates and phthalates that can wear down fabric fibers over time. Authentic castile soap is made with olive oil, which is very mild and suitable for sensitive skin, so it's ideal for delicate clothes, too.

You'll want to do laundry!

Laundry rooms are often neglected when it comes to decorating. But if you have to spend time working in the laundry room, wouldn't it be nice if it was beautiful? Here's how to turn a ho-hum room into a soothing, streamlined workspace.

Soothe stress with a spa-inspired shade: Cool colors instantly soothe the eye, so opt for blues when painting the walls. Who doesn't like to feel relaxed, especially when doing chores?

Elevate essentials with floating shelves: Laundry room clutter can certainly add up. To create more space, install floating shelves to store detergent and other laundry products. You can even take it one step further and store detergent in pretty glass containers from home-goods stores. Success secret: For adequate clearance and easy access, hang the lower pair of shelves 18 inches above the top of the washer and dryer, and the top shelves 15 inches higher.

Divvy up the work with a sorting station: Why should you be stuck with all the folding? Instead, install a large shelf and place a small laundry basket for each family member on the shelf. After drying, just place each piece of clothing into the appropriate basket for each person to fold.

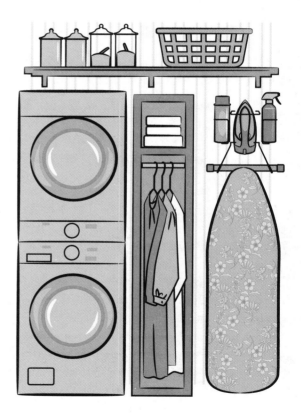

DOABLE DRYING

Soften up stiff towels

Ahhh . . . After a refreshing dip in the pool, it feels wonderful to wrap yourself up in a big, cozy beach towel as you dry off in the sun. To ensure that your towels feel soft and are superabsorbent, add ½ cup of vinegar to your laundry's rinse cycle (or to the detergent compartment of front-loading machines) every few washes. The vinegar will dissolve the buildup of detergent, fabric softener, and body oils that cause towel fibers to become stiff.

Dry clothes in a flash

You want to wear your favorite sweatshirt tonight, but it's still in the dryer and you have to leave soon. To speed things up, toss a dry towel in with the rest of your wet laundry. The towel will absorb some of the water, decreasing the moisture so clothes dry faster. Your sweatshirt will be ready to wear in no time!

Up your dryer's effectiveness

If your clothes dryer is taking longer and longer to dry a load, there may be an invisible film over the lint trap. To check, remove the lint trap and run it under the faucet—if water collects on top, use a toothbrush and warm, soapy water to scrub away the microscopic debris. Thoroughly cleaning the filter will prevent fire hazards and reduce your electric bill. It's a win-win!

Lifting out lint

Lately your clothes dryer has been taking forever to get the job done, even though you clean the lint-trap screen after each load. The probable culprit: lint caught inside the machine. But you can get things up to speed again with a pair of chopsticks.

Just pull out the lint screen and use the utensils to pluck any wayward fluff out of the slot, then replace the screen. You're all set!

Boost your dryer's efficiency

If drying loads of jeans, sweaters, and sweatshirts seems to be taking longer than it should, fabric softener–residue buildup in the lint trap could be to blame. To fix, remove the trap and scrub with a sponge dipped in a solution of 1 cup of water and 2 tablespoons of liquid dish detergent. Rinse well with warm water and slide the trap back in. The alkaline soap will dissolve the gunk to restore airflow and water drainage in your machine, so clothing can dry at top speed. Bonus: You can save up to $50 per year on your electric bills!

Restore a shrunken wool sweater

It's hard to complain when your guy does the laundry, but sometimes he flubs and throws your wool sweaters in the dryer. Before donating the too-small knitwear, fill a sink with warm water, add 1 tablespoon of hair conditioner, and soak the sweater for 30 minutes. The conditioner's oils will soften the wool fibers, making the fabric more pliable so you can stretch it back to its original shape. Lay flat to dry, then wash and dry as usual. Money saved: $30 for a new sweater

Air-dry sans collapses with a wooden rack

A freestanding plastic drying rack can be a bargain, but adjusting its rungs to get it upright feels like a game of Twister. An easier solution: a wall-mounted wooden rack. Its pegs and dowels are more securely anchored than plastic designs, reducing collapses. In addition, its simple style adds a peaceful touch to your routine.

SOS FOR SUMMER'S TOUGHEST STAINS

THE STAIN: Salad dressing, sunscreen

In the moment: Artificial sweetener

A blotch that spreads slowly, darkens fabric, and feels greasy is likely oil based. Since oil and water don't mix, H_2O is not the answer. Instead, cover the spot with a sweetener like Splenda or Equal and let sit for 10 minutes. The powdery granules will absorb the oil to minimize spreading and lighten the stain.

Back at home: Dish soap

Dish soap removes oil from dishes, so it's perfect for fixing an oil stain on clothing, as well. Softly massage a tiny drop of clear, unscented dish soap into the stain with your fingers. Flush with cold water, then repeat if needed.

THE STAIN: Grass, mustard, berries

In the moment: Hand-sanitizer gel

The pigments in dye-based stains bond to cloth fibers so well that they're actually used to color fabric. And while these stains may be stubborn, you can fade them with hand sanitizer. Simply work a bit into the mark and let sit for 5 minutes, then blot with a cool, damp cloth and pat dry. The sanitizer's alcohol will help dissolve the pigments, so the stain will be far less noticeable—and easier to remove later.

Back at home: Hydrogen peroxide

Soak the stained area in a bowl filled with equal parts 3 percent hydrogen peroxide and water for 30 minutes, then rinse with cool water. Repeat if needed. Why it works: Hydrogen peroxide is a mild bleach that releases oxygen, which agitates the stain to loosen the bond between the pigments and clothing fibers. Once loosened, the pigments will easily wash away. (Test on an inconspicuous area first.)

It figures! Just minutes after arriving at a barbecue bash for an afternoon of fun, mustard splatters on your white top. To the rescue: We've rounded up in-a-pinch fixes to minimize the appearance of a spot while you're out . . . plus the surefire ways to nix the stain for good when you get home.

THE STAIN: Wine, coffee, tea

In the moment: Salt

Wine and coffee stains are caused by tannins—acidic compounds that leave behind a yellowish-brown tinge. To minimize the mark, moisten it with water, then cover it with salt and let sit for 10 minutes. Absorbent salt granules will draw out excess liquid, while the sodium breaks down stain-setting pigments.

Back at home: White toothpaste

Wet the stain and squeeze on a pea-size dab of white (not gel) toothpaste. Rub it in with your fingertips and rinse with warm water, then repeat if needed. The mild bleaching agents in white pastes will help fade the brownish color, while the gentle abrasives work to dislodge stubborn residue. (Test on an inconspicuous area first.)

THE STAIN: Ice cream, blood, sweat

In the moment: Cold water

Compounds that originate in an animal's body (like milk) tend to be protein based. And since proteins bond to cloth fibers when they dry, it's easier to treat this type of stain while it's still wet. Simply flush the area with cold water or club soda and rub the fabric. Take care to avoid heat—it can solidify proteins, making them superstubborn.

Back at home: Alka-Seltzer tablets

Drop a tablet of Alka-Seltzer into a water-filled bowl and let the stained area soak for 30 minutes before rinsing with water. Alka-Seltzer's mildly abrasive sodium bicarbonate combined with the effervescence of the dissolving tablets works to force protein residue out of cloth fibers.

STAIN SOLUTIONS

Erase stubborn sweat stains

The summer heat has taken its toll on your family's shirts: You're preparing to wash a load of whites, but one after another has ugly perspiration stains. Rather than soaking the garments, grab some regular-strength aspirin. Add one pill prior to washing the shirts, then another right before the rinse cycle. Aspirin's salicylic acid will bleach the fabric and lift away stains, leaving your whites brighter and more resistant to future discoloration.

Help for dried-on mud stains

After working in the garden, your pants are covered in dried mud. To deliver the pants from destruction, take an uncooked potato and cut it in half crosswise. Rub the discolored areas with the cut end of the spud, soak the garment in a basin of cool water for 1 hour, and wash as usual. The potato's chlorogenic acid will seep into the material and break up the stain, so the pants will look just as good as they did pregardening.

Pretreat stubborn stains for pennies

There's always more laundry to do after the holidays—party clothes, tablecloths, guest sheets . . . So when your stain pretreater runs out, you need a substitute—stat! Just fill a jar halfway with leftover soap slivers and top off with hot water. Wait 3 minutes, then stir until the soap dissolves. Work this "soap jelly" into stains before laundering as usual. The mixture will lift and suspend stain molecules so they come out easily in the wash. Money saved: $5 for a commercial pretreater

Quick fix for mildewy towels

While cleaning out the trunk of your car, you notice a musty scent. The culprit: a mildewy towel from last week's trip to the beach. To eliminate the odor, just rub a mixture of 1/4 cup of white vinegar and 1 teaspoon of salt into any visible spots, then wash and dry the towel as usual. Vinegar's acetic acid will break down mildew (and soften fabric), while the abrasive salt will scour away residue, revealing a like-new towel. Money saved: $15 to $20 for a new beach towel

Pretreat stubborn stains for pennies

Instead of shelling out for store-bought stain remover, whip up this powerful, low-cost solution: In a clean spray bottle, combine two parts water and one part ammonia, then spritz on spots and wait 15 minutes before laundering as usual. This alkaline cleaner will neutralize and emulsify oil-based stains, including mayonnaise, gravy, salad dressing, butter, lipstick, and body lotion. (Test in a small area for colorfastness first.) Money saved: $5 per bottle of stain remover

Reader Tip: Lift an ink stain from suede

"When I finished my Sunday morning crossword puzzle last week, I noticed I'd left a small pen mark on my suede sofa cushion. Luckily, I remembered this easy trick: Rub the stain with an unused pencil eraser in the direction of the suede's grain. The eraser forms crumblike particles that get under the surface of the suede to lift the mark. Within seconds, the spot was gone and my sofa looked as good as new!"

—Alicia Clark, Boston, MA

SEWING CHAOS CURED!

Sew-simple solutions for bolts, bobbins, bits, and more!

Sort and stow "notions" with hanging jars

A clever rack of glass jars keeps buttons, bobbins, and other small sewing supplies in sight, plus makes the most of under-shelf space. Simply attach three to five jar lids to the bottom of a wall shelf with screws. Then place materials inside the empty glass jars and twist into their lids.

Prioritize projects with a numbered rack

Dedicated totes keep all the materials you need for a particular job right at hand, and hanging them from numbered knobs keeps crafts in order. To make, screw round cabinet knobs into a 6-inch by 42-inch wooden board, then mount onto your wall. Next, affix a numbered sticker (at office-supply and craft stores) onto the face of each knob.

Keep an emergency sewing kit ready in your space

A small, basic sewing kit can be a timesaver, since you can stick it on a shelf and grab it fast when you need to make a sewing repair, rather than sorting through your stash for supplies. Keep your kit in a plastic food-storage container—just add a small pair of scissors, needles, extra buttons, and spools of neutral thread.

Maximize creativity with color and space

Purple provides the perfect balance between calming blue and energizing red, plus it increases levels of the creativity-boosting hormone oxytocin, so adding this hue to your workplace will spark inspiration every day. To expand your artistic side even more, double your workspace with a sewing table made by stacking a plain door atop a pair of standard sawhorses for an impressive 24-by-80-inch work surface.

Create a to-go sewing kit with a shadow box

Placing sewing necessities in a hinged, sectioned box creates a portable kit ready for on-the-spot repairs. Simply tuck buttons, spools of thread, ribbons, fabric remnants, and trims into the compartments and label the box as desired.

Tape a paper lunch bag onto your ironing board

Keep a lunch bag taped to the edge of your ironing board so you can snip wayward threads and remove fuzz from clothes as you're pressing them.

10 Brilliant Uses
for APPLE CIDER VINEGAR

1 Green up yellowed plant leaves
No matter what potting soil you try, yellow spots keep popping up on your plants. The likely culprit: high pH levels in the soil caused by hard water. To remedy this, water your plants with a mixture of 2 tablespoons of apple cider vinegar and 1 quart of water. Repeat once weekly for 3 weeks. Apple cider vinegar's acidity will restore the soil's pH to optimal levels, plus nourish the plants with trace minerals. The result: vibrant green foliage.

2 Prevent a bang from bruising
If you bang your shin, soak a bit of gauze in apple cider vinegar and place it on the sore spot. Secure with a bandage or medical tape and leave in place for 1 hour. When applied topically, vinegar increases circulation to the skin's surface. This will prevent blood from pooling so a black-and-blue mark doesn't form.

3 Get pans sparkling sans scrubbing
Lasagna night was a hit, but now there's a cheese-crusted pan sitting in the sink. Rather than spending precious time scrubbing, fill the pan with warm, sudsy water and add 2 tablespoons of apple cider vinegar, then let soak for 30 minutes. The acids in the vinegar will work to dissolve stuck-on food, making cleanup a breeze.

4 Ward off pesky dandruff flakes
To combat flakes, pour equal amounts of apple cider vinegar and water in a spray bottle. Spritz on hair and scalp; wait 15 minutes, then shampoo. The vinegar's antimicrobial properties will kill the bacteria that cause dandruff.

5 Effortlessly trim stubborn fat
Sipping a blend of 2 tablespoons of apple cider vinegar and 8 ounces of water before meals can help you shed pounds with no struggle. Studies show that the vinegar's acetic acid boosts fat burning by 10 percent, plus it curbs hunger.

6 Remove rust spots with ease
After digging your trusty Christmas tree stand out of the garage, you notice a few spots of rust. Apple cider vinegar to the rescue! Simply soak the metal stand in enough of the kitchen

staple to cover the tarnished areas. The vinegar's acid will break down rust's iron oxide to leave your stand looking like new.

7 Tenderize a tough cut of meat

Everyone at your dinner table will be raving about how tender and juicy your roast is when you marinate it in apple cider vinegar, which will break down the meat's tough muscle fibers. A delicious marinade to try: Blend 2 cups of apple cider vinegar, ½ cup of vegetable oil, 2 tablespoons of soy sauce, 1 teaspoon of sea salt, and 1 to 2 tablespoons of fresh chopped garlic. Marinate the meat in the liquid for 3 hours before cooking.

8 Soothe a sore throat—stat!

The fast-acting remedy for a scratchy, irritated throat: Mix ¼ cup of apple cider vinegar and ¼ cup of water and gargle with the liquid for 15 seconds. Repeat every hour or so as needed. The acetic acid in apple cider vinegar destroys illness-causing bacteria, so you'll be feeling your best in no time.

9 Add shine to Fido's coat

While brushing your fluffy pal, you notice his fur looks a bit lackluster. What can help: Add ¼ teaspoon of apple cider vinegar to his water bowl daily and gradually build up to 1 teaspoon of vinegar for every 15 pounds of your pet's body weight. (The gradual increase helps him adjust to the taste.) The potassium and B vitamins in the vinegar will nourish and strengthen hair follicles to impart a healthy shine.

10 Clear a stubborn clog naturally

The nontoxic fix for a slow-draining sink: Pour ½ cup of baking soda down the drain, then 1 cup of apple cider vinegar. Wait 20 minutes, then run the hot water for 10 seconds. The vinegar's acid will react with the baking soda to create fizzy bubbles that will dissolve grease and loosen buildup. Bonus: The mixture neutralizes odors, too.

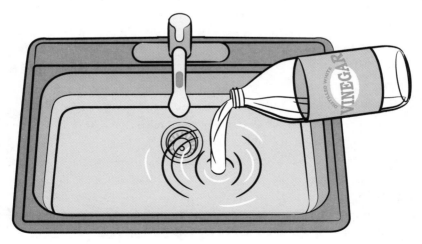

Quickly lift a food stain

The next time a blob of mustard, dribble of coffee, or dollop of raspberry jam ends up on your shirt, wet the spot with cool water, cover with foam shaving cream, and let sit for 5 minutes before laundering as usual. The shaving cream's alcohols will dilute the dyes in the stain to ensure it comes out easily in the wash.

Remove lipstick from cloth napkins

If a smudge of red lipstick ends up on your linens, simply rub the spot with a bar of wet white soap and let sit for 30 minutes, then rinse with cold water and wash as usual. The alkaline soap will thin the lipstick's oily base so it will come off easily.

Banish set-in stains in seconds

Someone must have spilled jam on the carpet this morning, and the stain is already dry. To eliminate the splotch, spritz with a solution of three parts water and one part white vinegar (test on an inconspicuous area first), then cover with a damp terry-cloth towel and iron it using the steam setting. The vinegar's acetic acid will break down the stain particles, while the steam will travel deep inside the carpet fibers, liquefying the loosened dye so the towel can absorb the stain.

Quick save for a yellow shirt collar

When stress at work leaves our husbands' collars yellow, we turn to baby powder: Just rub a bit into the stain, then hold a hot iron an inch away and press the steam button for 5 seconds before tossing the shirt into the washer. The powder will absorb oils that bind the stain to the fabric, and the steam will expand the shirt's fibers so the powder can go deeper. Money saved: $30 for a new shirt

EASY-PEASY IRONING

No-sweat wrinkle removal

You've sworn off ironing in this 100°F heat—until your husband announces that he's got a big meeting with corporate tomorrow and his shirt needs pressing. Before you spend time shvitzing over a hot ironing board, try this: Toss the wrinkled garment into the dryer with a damp towel, then run the machine for a few minutes. As the moisture from the towel heats up, it will create steam that will relax the shirt's wrinkles. Then simply take out the garment and hang it as usual—no sweating required.

Reader Tip: Get rid of wrinkles in a blink!

"It seemed like every time I was running late in the morning, the shirt that I wanted to wear needed ironing. Luckily, my friend told me I could simply tuck an ice cube into a clean sock and toss it into the dryer with the wrinkled shirt, then run the machine on the low or fluff setting for 2 to 5 minutes while I do my makeup. The heat melts the ice to generate steam, which releases the wrinkles. This only works for machine-washable garments, though."

—*Jessica Him, Tenafly, NJ*

Easily erase a scorch mark

Holidays can mean ironing table linens, and ironing when you're superbusy can mean—gulp—scorches. But there's an easy dodge: Simply rub the burn with the cut side of a halved raw white onion, then leave the onion on the spot for a few hours before laundering as usual. Compounds in the onion will break down carbon particles in the burned fabric to prevent the stain from becoming permanent.

The fuss-free way to iron delicates

You're about to dress for a party when you see that your silk top is wrinkled. Since the iron's steam setting might be too hot for the delicate fabric, try this: Wrap an ice cube in a soft cloth and run it all over the garment, then use your iron on warm. The slight dampness and warmth will create steam, so creases will smooth out in seconds.

Keep clothes fresh with linen ironing water

Lavender provides an instant mood boost—always a plus during laundry day. In addition, a Japanese study found that the linalool in the scent prompts the body to produce calming compounds. To make lavender linen water, steep two handfuls of dried lavender in 2 cups of boiling water and strain into a bottle. Apply before ironing.

Chase away moths naturally with cedar

Cedar is well known for nixing any pests that might destroy clothing. But cedar accessories can lose their potency within weeks. Instead of replacing them, mist with cedar spray—its essential oils instantly refresh the wood for a good-as-new result right now.

LEATHER CARE MADE EASY

Polish dull patent leather fast

You love your patent leather flats—and it shows. To restore their shine, just squirt glass cleaner onto a soft cloth and use it to buff the shoes. The cleaner's ammonia and isopropyl alcohol will dissolve the scuff marks and grime clinging to the leather's high-gloss finish and won't harm it. Your shoes will be as shiny as the day you bought them.

Restore shine to dingy leather

One upside to chilly weather: You get to bring your favorite leather boots and purses out of storage. If your accessories need a bit of TLC after last winter's wear and tear, dip a cloth into two beaten egg whites and lightly scrub the leather for a minute before wiping away any excess with a damp rag. Proteins in the egg will help remove dirt, dust, and grime to renew leather's luster.

Get scuffed patent leather gleaming

After pulling out your go-to patent leather pumps for date night, you see that they're sporting unsightly scuffs. The remedy: Dip a cotton swab in rubbing alcohol and dab on the marked areas, then wipe with a clean, absorbent cloth. Isopropyl alcohol is a powerful solvent that will break down the scuffs in seconds, leaving your footwear looking flawless.

SEWING SMARTS

Sew through any fabric with ease

Stitching jeans, window drapes, and other thick materials can be a tough task. To save yourself from tired, achy hands and pricked fingers, trade your pincushion for a bar of bath soap. Fatty acids in the soap will lubricate the tip of each pin and needle so you can effortlessly glide them through the thickest of fabrics. Bonus: The soap will lightly scent the needles so each stitch will give off a subtle hint of fresh fragrance.

Clever Cleaning Tricks

Let's face it: Cleaning makes you feel good, but it isn't always fun! But with these tips, cleaning is quick and painless, so you can spend less time scrubbing and more time with your family.

NIX GARBAGE-CAN SLIPUPS

Easily secure trash bags

Your garbage bags keep sliding down into the kitchen trash can once they start to get full, and you have to reach into the mess to fish them out. To the rescue: binder clips! Simply use two to four of the fasteners (depending on the size of your trash can) to attach the plastic bag to the can's top edges. Now the bag won't budge, even when you toss in something heavy.

Outsmart pesky trash-can leaks

A leaky garbage bag is a nuisance—besides the stench, it means you have to go through the process of washing the trash can. But you can outsmart leaks by sprinkling a shallow layer of kitty litter in the bottom of the can, under the bag. The absorbent material will sop up any wayward liquid (and the accompanying odors). Just replace the kitty litter each time you take out the trash.

SPOTLESS FLOORS

Spruce up hardwood floors naturally

While doing a quick inspection of your home before your in-laws arrive, you notice your living room floor is looking dingy. To the rescue: tea! Simply boil a kettle of water, transfer to a bucket, and add three bags of black tea. Give your floor a quick sweep while the tea steeps for 3 to 5 minutes, then dip your mop (or mop cover) into the bucket and clean as usual. The tea's tannins will bring out the wood's natural color and shine—without the sticky coating or strong artificial scent that chemical-based formulas leave behind. Money saved: $19 for hardwood-floor reviver

SOS for salt-stained floors

After a long winter, we all have some salt footprints to contend with. The easy fix: a 50:50 solution of white vinegar and water. Vinegar's acetic acid will neutralize the salt particles without damaging the wood's finish.

Sweep dusty floors in half the time

Taking a broom to your floors usually results in a cloud of lightweight dust flying all over the room instead of going into the pan. The solution: Stretch the leg of an old pair of panty hose over the bristles of your broom before you sweep. The tight-knit mesh will attract and trap dust, letting you gather the dirt in record time.

Spotless rugs for pennies

To lift carpet stains without harsh, pricey chemicals, try this: Sprinkle baking soda on the mark and let sit for 10 minutes. The alkaline cleanser will break down the stain and neutralize odor. Vacuum, then blot a mixture of ½ tablespoon of dish soap, ½ tablespoon of vinegar, and 1 cup of warm water onto the carpet until the stain is gone. Money saved: $8 for carpet cleaner spray

Touch up wood floors for pennies

Ugh! You just noticed a few tiny scratches on your new hardwood floor. To restore its pristine surface, rub a shelled walnut over the unwanted blemishes. The friction will cause the floor to absorb the nut's natural oils, darkening the marks in seconds. Money saved: $11 for a hardwood touch-up kit

Erase tea stains for pennies

Of course—the day you splash a few drops of tea onto your beige carpet, you find you're out of stain remover. No problem: Just combine equal parts water, milk, and household bleach in a small bowl, then use a sponge to wet the spot with the mixture. Once the area is saturated, blot with a towel and rinse with water. The milk's lactic acid will loosen the bond between the tea's tannins and the carpet fibers, while the bleach neutralizes the brownish color, making the spot vanish. Money saved: $5 to $10 for stain remover

Never miss another dirt particle

Use this trick to say so long to the frustrating dirt trails that remain after you've swept: Stick double-sided tape to the edge of your dustpan and sweep as usual. The adhesive will catch every last speck of dirt. When done, toss the tape.

OUST ODORS!

Neutralize paint fumes

You want to spruce up the guest room with a fresh coat of paint before the holidays, but the thought of lingering fumes gives you pause. A trick pro painters use to minimize the smell and ward off headaches: Stir 1 tablespoon of vanilla extract into each gallon of paint. Vanilla's potent scent will mask paint odor without altering the color or texture.

Easy way to scent your home

Friends are coming over in an hour or so, and you want the place to smell wonderful. The problem: Your favorite scented candle has burned down to the wick. For an easy save, put a drop or two of your favorite essential oil on a few lightbulbs throughout the house (checking that the bulbs are cool first), then turn on the lights. As the bulbs heat up, the aroma will spread from room to room—making your home smell positively inviting!

SOS for a musty basement

If spring rain showers have left your basement smelling a bit off, here's an easy way to eliminate the odor: Toss a few unused charcoal briquettes (without starter fluid) into empty coffee cans and seal. Punch holes in the lids, then place the cans throughout your basement where kids and pets can't get to them. The porous charcoal will absorb odor-causing moisture in no time.

10 Brilliant Uses
for CORKS

1 Get a campfire blazing
The easy way to get a roaring blaze going: Place a few corks in a jar and add enough rubbing alcohol to cover, then let soak for about an hour before you plan on lighting the fire. Next, place the corks under your logs and use a long match to ignite the stoppers. The corks will absorb the flammable alcohol, so they'll fire up quickly and keep the flames going strong.

2 Safely store sewing needles and pins
If searching through your sewing box often leads to a painful run-in with an errant needle (we've been there), try sticking your needles, pins, and tacks into a wine cork. If all won't fit in one, use different corks for each type of pin. The corks will firmly encase the needles, keeping fingers safe and instantly organizing your box.

3 Safely store knives in a drawer
To ensure no one gets jabbed by the tip of a sharp knife when reaching into the kitchen drawer, cut a slit along the side of a wine cork, then slide the tip of the blade inside. (Use more than one cork to cover the length of the blade, if needed.)

4 Easily sand small spaces
The ornate dresser you got at a yard sale will look amazing when you're done refinishing it, but sanding the curves is a challenge. Try wrapping the sandpaper around a cork. The rounded shape will make it easier to control the paper around the curves, so you'll get a cleaner look with less effort.

5 Protect wood floors from scrapes
An easy fix to ensure that your chairs won't scratch your beautiful floors: Using a sharp knife, carefully cut 1/4-inch-thick rounds from a cork. Apply a dab of wood glue to each disc, then attach to the bottoms of your chair legs. The cushiony material will work just as well as the felt pads found at hardware stores—but won't cost you a cent!

6 Stop cabinet doors from slamming
You love it when your kitchen is the center of activity, but the sound of cabinets banging shut as loved ones bustle about makes you feel a bit on edge. To quiet the noise, slice a cork into thin circles and use wood glue to affix two disks inside each cabinet door (one on each outer top and bottom corner). *Ahhh*—that's better.

7 Guarantee happy rocking

If the little one in your life has a rocking horse that sways so far back that it makes you nervous—or you have a rocking chair that tilts too far for comfort—try this: Carefully slice a cork in half lengthwise, then use wood glue to attach the halves to the underside of each back rocker, near the ends. These "stoppers" will prevent the rocker from tipping over.

8 Put an end to boot-tray puddles

Thank goodness for your boot tray—it keeps all the wet footwear off your floor so you spend less time cleaning. The only hitch: Puddles collect in the tray, preventing your boots from fully drying. For an easy fix, line the bottom of the tray with a layer of corks. The absorbent material will soak up water as it drips off your boots.

9 Brighten stainless steel in a blink

The chemical-free way to get your kitchen appliances looking like new: Dab any fingerprint smudges or water splatters with a cork dipped in olive oil, then wipe clean with a soft, dry cloth. The cork's textured surface will buff away any buildup without harming the stainless steel, and the olive oil will impart shine. Gorgeous!

10 Fix a wide-pour spout

The spouts on many olive oil bottles allow the liquid to spill out too quickly. To ward off the waste, cut a 1/4-inch-deep wedge down the length of one side of a cork, then slip the cork into the bottle. The slim opening will make it easy to pour the perfect amount of oil.

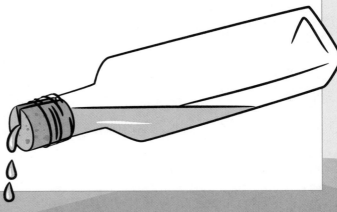

Odors—eliminated!

You can give your home that fresh scent you love without spending on store-bought odor-eliminating sprays, thanks to this easy recipe: In an empty spray bottle, add ⅛ cup of liquid fabric softener, 2 tablespoons of baking soda, and 20 ounces of hot tap water. Shake well, then spritz into the air or on any less-than-fresh surfaces. (Spot test in an inconspicuous area first.) Money saved: $6 for a bottle of odor eliminator

Nix nasty vacuum odor

Reader Tip

"Lately my vacuum has been releasing a musty smell every time I use it—not what I want when I have guests coming. So I had the idea to pour ½ cup of my favorite potpourri into the vacuum bag. Now when I turn on the appliance, it releases the potpourri's fresh scent into the air—so my house looks and smells great!"

—*Katie Larson, Wayne, PA*

Make a musty book smell like new

When you discovered your favorite childhood storybook in a box in your basement, you couldn't wait to read it to your daughter. But years spent in storage have left the tome smelling dank and mildewy. Eliminate the musty odor by placing a used dryer sheet in the center of the book for a day or two. The sheet's porous fibers will absorb the moisture in the paper and leave behind a laundry-fresh scent, so you and your little one can get lost in the tale instead of distracted by the odor.

DUST BE GONE!

The secret to a perfect polish

Ugh! You dusted a few days ago, but when sunlight streams through your window, you realize your table looks like it hasn't been cleaned in weeks. The culprit: Furniture polish can leave behind an oily residue that attracts dust and makes fingerprints more noticeable. But there's no need to dust daily. Instead, polish as usual, then sprinkle cornstarch on the fixtures and buff with a soft cloth. The granules will soak up the oil for results that last.

Genius way to dust radiators

To clean a dusty radiator without making a mess, hang a damp bath towel, sheet, or cloth behind it, then blast from the front with a blow-dryer on its highest cool setting. Dust and debris will be transferred onto the damp towel, which you can shake off outside and toss into your washer for no-fuss cleanup.

Ceiling-fan dust begone!

Reader Tip

"I always dread dusting the ceiling fan. Every time I do it, dust lands on the floor—and on my head. Then it occurred to me to make use of an old pillowcase. I simply slip each fan blade in the pillowcase and wipe so the dust lands inside the case. It's so easy—I wish I'd thought of it sooner!"

—*Jeanette Watters, Cleveland, OH*

Genius use for orphan socks

There's no need to delay your spring cleaning when you run out of individual sheets for your wet/dry mop. Just dampen an inside-out ankle sock with your favorite cleaner, stretch it around the mop head, and use as you normally would. The textured cotton sock will effectively pick up dust and dirt, leaving your floors spotless. Bonus: Instead of tossing the sock when you're done, you can wash and reuse as often as you like. Money saved: $11 for a box of dry-mop refills

SAFE-AND-SOUND CLEANERS

Three simple, homemade, natural solutions are all it takes to make every room in your home sparkle—and keep you headache free!

For dishes and more

A mixture of soap flakes, castile soap, essential oil, and water works wonders for hand washing dishes. The soap duo cuts through grease and leaves plates gleaming. And a few drops of an essential oil (like lavender, lemon, or rosemary) add a pleasing scent—plus boost the solution's antibacterial strength! Here, we used lavender castile soap and lavender oil for a lovely floral-themed liquid.

Lavender dish soap:

$1/4$ cup of soap flakes + $1/4$ cup of castile soap + 10 drops of lavender oil = Combine in a 24-ounce squeeze bottle, fill with warm water, and shake well.

For windows and more

For crystal-clear windows, a mixture of rubbing alcohol, white vinegar, cornstarch, and water will work just as well, if not better than, store-bought glass cleaners. Plus, all these ingredients can be found around the house. The rubbing alcohol teams up with vinegar to remove smudges and impurities from the surface of the glass. And cornstarch makes the solution thicker than traditional glass cleaners, which keeps it from dripping before you wipe.

Sparkling glass cleaner:

$1/4$ cup of rubbing alcohol + $1/4$ cup of white vinegar + 1 tablespoon of cornstarch = Combine in a 24-ounce spray bottle, fill with warm water, and shake well.

For counters and more

A combination of castile soap, fresh lemon juice, lemon essential oil, and water creates an effective cleaner that can be used anywhere—from kitchen counters to bathroom tile! The castile soap produces a nice, mild lather for deep cleaning without scratching. And the citric acid in the lemon juice and essential oil cuts through bacterial buildup while adding a crisp, clean scent.

Lemon all-purpose spray:

$1/4$ cup of castile soap + $1/4$ cup of lemon juice + 10 drops lemon oil = Combine in a 24-ounce spray bottle, fill with warm water, and shake well.

Revive an old dust mop in seconds

Even though you've had it for only a few months, your dust mop seems to be pushing around the dirt on your floors rather than picking it up. Don't lose faith in it just yet—simply trim ½ inch off the tool's cotton strands. Frayed ends lose their ability to attract dust bunnies, but a quick clip will refresh the fibers so they lift dirt with ease. Money saved: $14 for a new dust mop

Make a hand vac more powerful

If your hand vac isn't up to the task of suctioning the grime that gets tracked into your hallway, static buildup in the canister may be preventing dirt particles from flowing freely. To fix: Cut a strip off a dryer sheet and suck it up with the vacuum. Let it swirl around for a few minutes, then turn the vac off and empty it. The dryer sheet will neutralize static so your vacuum works like new.

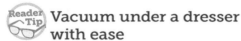 ### Vacuum under a dresser with ease

"I've always hated cleaning under my bedroom dresser—even the vacuum's extension hose never reached all the way underneath, so I'd end up on all fours, stretching as far as I could. But then my neighbor told me her simple trick: Just remove the dresser's lowest drawer and stick the vacuum hose into the extra space. Now I can finally get all the dust out from under the dresser without breaking a sweat!"

—Alicia Jackson, Rochester, NY

WIPES DONE WELL

Never buy household wipes again

You love the convenience of disposable cleaning wipes, but buying box after box can really add up. Save time and money by layering coffee filters in a resealable container and pouring in just enough multisurface cleaner to dampen each one. These homemade wipes will have all the power of your favorite cleaner. And since coffee filters are made with longer fibers than paper towels, they're durable enough to stand up to your toughest scrubbing. Money saved: $5 for store-bought wipes

SOS for dried-out baby wipes

You keep a canister of baby wipes handy so you can easily swipe anything that needs a quick cleaning, but the canister lid was left open and now the wipes have all dried out. To the rescue: baby oil. Just add a few drops to the bottom of the plastic container, then close the lid and turn the container upside down. Let sit overnight. By morning, the oil will have seeped into the cloth fibers and infused each wipe with moisture. Money saved: $7 for a new container of baby wipes

EFFORTLESS MARK REMOVAL

Wipe away water rings

You made sure to set out plenty of coasters, but some of your party guests forgot to use them—and your coffee table has the marks to prove it! To the rescue: rubbing alcohol. Simply soak a rag in the liquid, wring it out, and use it to lightly dab the stains until they disappear. (Don't vigorously scrub.) Why it works: Rubbing alcohol will penetrate the damaged varnish of the table and quickly evaporate, "dissolving" the water stains in minutes.

Lift heat marks from furniture

Wanting to make postcookout cleanup easier, you threw a plastic cloth over your outdoor table. But the hot sun warmed the plastic too much, leaving white heat marks all over the wood. To remove them, add enough olive oil to 1/4 cup of baking soda to form a paste, then gently buff the mixture into the marks. Wipe away the paste and rub in a little more olive oil. The absorbent baking soda will draw out the mark-causing moisture from beneath the wood's finish, and the oil will restore the table's luster.

Ward off mold on windowsills

The fresh air that drifts through your open windows on a summer day is delightful . . . but the breeze can also let in mold and mildew spores that gather and grow on the windowsills. To keep the fungus (and the allergy symptoms they trigger) at bay, rub your sills with a white candle. The wax will seal the trim to help prevent spores and moisture from seeping into cracks, so you can breathe easy.

FEEL-GOOD CLEANERS

Household headaches solved!

New research at the University of Washington reveals that many common cleaning products contain chemicals not listed on their labels—some of which can lead to headaches, dizziness, itchy skin, and more. Here are five chemical-free alternatives to everyday cleaners.

Alternative to air fresheners: Air fresheners can numb our nasal passages, which fools us into thinking that odors have dissipated. But in reality, it's our noses that are damaged. In addition, the air fresheners can cause headaches. For an all-natural household deodorizer, layer 1/2 inch of orange peels and 1/4 inch of salt in a glass jar, continuing until it is 2/3 full. Leave the uncovered jar in any musty room. The salt will draw moisture from the peels' thin outer membranes, releasing the fragrant oils within. (Rose petals and lavender blossoms work well, too.)

Alternative to oven cleaners: Oven cleaners are notorious for containing chemicals that can seriously corrode the skin, mouth, throat, and eyes. To get a squeaky-clean oven naturally, mix 1 cup of baking soda with 1/4 cup of salt, then add enough water to form a paste. Apply it to the inside walls of the oven, avoiding openings, bare metal, and racks, which could corrode. Leave overnight, then wipe away the paste using a damp sponge. The baking soda will absorb built-up grease, while the abrasive salt crystals will scour away food and grime to reveal a pristine oven.

Alternative to disinfectant wipes: Sure, it's convenient to clean surfaces with premoistened wipes and disinfectant sprays, but many contain chemicals like phenol and ammonia that can cause eye, skin, and lung irritation. The natural alternative: In a resealable container or a spray bottle, combine 2 cups of water, 3 tablespoons of liquid dish soap, and 10 to 20 drops of tea tree oil. The oil's terpenoids have powerful antiseptic and antifungal properties. Keep the solution on hand to disinfect surfaces anytime.

Alternative to wood polish: Petroleum distillates and other harsh chemicals in furniture polishes can irritate skin, aggravate asthma, and cause headaches and dizziness. Use lemon juice and olive oil instead. Just apply a solution of two parts oil and one part juice to furniture, let sit for 2 minutes, and wipe clean with a soft cloth. (Test on an inconspicuous spot first, since lemon juice could bleach darker wood finishes.) The lemon's citric acid will cut through grime and dust buildup,

SURPRISING GERM HOT SPOTS FIXED

Even spotless homes can harbor an unsettling number of pathogens—and cleaning can cause these health sappers to spread, researchers caution. Learn where bacteria hide so you can banish them for good!

HOT SPOT: Washing machine walls

When researchers at the University of Arizona in Tucson swabbed inside more than 100 washers, 60 percent tested positive for fecal bacteria and 20 percent for staph. The cause: "Bacteria from dirty clothing and dishcloths can settle into washing machine drums and breed," says lead scientist Charles Gerba, PhD.

Simple save: White vinegar

Vinegar has been shown to be such a powerful sanitizer that it even kills *E. coli.* To get the benefits, pour $\frac{1}{2}$ cup into the fabric-softener dispenser or add directly into the machine during the rinse cycle of every load. Also, make sure your water heater is set to a temperature high enough to kill potential pathogens (140°F). Another easy tip: Bleach instantly kills harmful organisms, so when you're doing a few loads of laundry, save a bleach load for last.

HOT SPOT: Crisper drawer

Refrigerator salad drawers contain an average of 7,850 colony-forming units (a measure of bacteria) per square centimeter, according to UK researchers. That's 750 times the level considered safe.

Simple save: Bubble wrap

Remove the crisper drawers and scrub them inside and out with soap and water, then rinse. Next, line each drawer with bubble wrap before returning it to the fridge. (Plastic wrap works in a pinch.) When the drawers get gunky (about once a month), throw out the bubble wrap and reline the drawers. Bonus: The packing material helps cushion produce so it will last longer.

HOT SPOT: Kitchen sink

The sink's top germ trap: The metal aeration screen in the faucet. Since the screens are oxygenated and constantly moist, they are a perfect breeding ground for bacteria. Over time, the bacteria can build up and form a biofilm, which can then come off onto your food, dishes, or hands. Another kitchen sink culprit is the drain, where an average of 500,000 bacteria (mainly from food prep) reside per square inch.

Simple save: Borax

Fill your sink with 1 gallon of water and add ½ cup of borax (a natural disinfectant). Dip a clean toothbrush in the water and use it to scrub the metal aeration screen. Let sit for at least 30 minutes (or overnight), then empty the sink and give the drain a vigorous scrub with the toothbrush.

HOT SPOT: Vacuum cleaner brushes

Half the vacuum cleaner brushes tested in a University of Arizona study were found to contain fecal bacteria, and 13 percent were contaminated with harmful *E. coli* bacteria. "Food particles often get trapped in the brushes, allowing bacteria to multiply," explains Dr. Gerba. "Then when you vacuum, the brushes spread the bacteria from room to room."

Simple save: Essential oil

Clean vacuum brushes with disinfectant after each use. A chemical-free option: Mix equal parts water and white vinegar in a spray bottle, then add 1 teaspoon of tea tree or thyme essential oil, both of which are effective against *E. coli* and other bacteria. After vacuuming, unplug the machine and spritz the brushes and attachments (including the insides), then wipe with a clean cloth. Bonus: Next time you vacuum, the oil's aroma will be carried throughout your house.

HOT SPOT: Spice rack

Wiping down cutting boards and countertops after meal prep is second nature, but spice jars and salt and pepper shakers are less likely to get cleaned. The problem: These containers are often touched after handling raw meat. Plus, they are "common touch" surfaces, so they are subject to the germs of multiple people. In fact, 100 percent of household salt and pepper shakers in one study tested positive for cold-causing rhinovirus bacteria.

Simple save: Wet wipes

A quick swipe with regular disinfectant wipes is enough to sanitize spice shakers, so keep a pack on hand for regular wipe-downs, especially if a cold is making the rounds. Also smart: Measure and pour spices into small dishes before beginning meal preparation. That way, you'll avoid touching jars after handling raw meat.

remove leftover polish, and leave behind a fresh scent. Plus, the oil will seep into the wood's pores to restore moisture and impart a natural shine.

Alternative to toilet bowl cleaners: Cleaning the toilet is no one's favorite job, but add in burning, itchy skin, eyes, and lungs—courtesy of the corrosive hydrochloric acid and hypochlorite bleach in most cleaners—and it's a real pain. Skip the chemical cocktail and pour ½ cup of baking soda and ¼ cup of vinegar into the bowl. Then add 10 drops of your favorite essential oil, if desired. The acidic vinegar and alkaline baking soda will react to create fizz, which will polish the porcelain. When the fizzing stops, give the bowl a quick scrub and flush for a spotless, deodorized toilet.

Touch-Ups and Repairs

As your home ages, it's likely you'll want to do a few touch-ups here and there. But what should you do when you just can't find your trusty screwdriver? Or when your paintbrushes are dried out? Read on for the answers to these questions and other helpful household repair advice.

PRO PAINTING HINTS

Rescue a hardened paintbrush

Oops! You forgot to wash your paintbrushes the last time you used them, and now the paint has hardened on the bristles. The fix: Pour some distilled white vinegar into an old saucepan and bring it to a boil over medium heat. Hold a paintbrush by the handle and dip the bristles into the boiling liquid, swiftly moving the brush back and forth and scrubbing the bristles against the bottom of the pan. Pull out the brush every 15 seconds to check if it's clean. Repeat the process if needed. The combination of the vinegar's high temperature and acetic acid will break up and dissolve the old paint, leaving you with like-new brushes without having to spend a dime.

The little trick to an easier paint job

The last time you painted your bedroom, it seemed like you spent more time rearranging the drip-catching newspaper under the can than actually painting. Prevent annoying drips by hot gluing a paper plate (or several) to the bottom of the can. The plate will capture the stray drops and go wherever you go, so you can complete the job without skipping a beat. When you're finished, simply remove the plate and store the can for next time.

Keep paintbrushes soft and pliable

Ugh! You pull out your brushes for a project, only to realize they're stiff from a previous paint job. The save: Add a drop of fabric softener to a cup of water and soak the brushes in the solution for a few minutes. Silicones in the laundry staple will condition the bristles so you can paint with ease. When it's cleanup time, rinse the brushes, then give them another softening soak before storing.

NO MORE SCREWDRIVER DILEMMAS

Quick fix for a jiggly doorknob

Uh-oh! Your bathroom doorknob seems to be getting looser each time you twist it. To repair it before guests arrive, remove the loose screws, dip them into clear nail polish, and let dry for about a minute before screwing them back into the knob. (They should still feel tacky.) The polish acts as an adhesive that will help the screws (and your doorknob) stay firmly in place.

Can't find the screwdriver?

A dime is the perfect thickness to fit into the groove of many flat-head screws, so it's a great in-a-pinch substitute when your screwdriver is missing in action but you need to complete a small task (like replacing the batteries in a remote control or toy). Another nagging "must remember to" you can cross off the list!

Help for a stripped screw hole

You're in the middle of tightening a chronically loose hinge on your bedroom door when you realize the screw hole is stripped. The speedy save: Break the flammable tip off a match, stick the remaining wood into the hole, and tighten the screw as usual. The metal will shred the matchstick, filling the hole and giving the screw something to catch hold of again.

The trick that keeps drilling mess-free

Your husband decided to get organized and mount Peg-Board to the garage wall. But using his electric drill on the drywall is sure to get dust into crevices—and boy, is that tough to get out! To contain the mess, put a sticky note directly under where he's going to drill, then fold the bottom up to the top edge to form a long V. The paper will form a ledge that'll capture drilling-induced dust and debris, eliminating cleanup.

10 Brilliant Uses
for BAKING SODA

1 Remove tarnish from silver effortlessly

To make quick work of polishing filigree silverware, line a pot with aluminum foil, add 2 tablespoons of baking soda, and drop in the tarnished pieces. Then fill the pot with boiling water. Once cool, remove the silver and rinse, scrubbing away any residual discoloration with a toothbrush. The alkaline baking soda will separate the acidic, tarnish-causing sulfur from the silver and transfer it to the foil, unveiling gleaming tableware.

2 Enjoy better-tasting coffee in the morning

If your a.m. coffee tastes bitter, the culprit may be a dirty coffeemaker. To clean the machine, fill it with a solution of 1/4 cup of baking soda and 1 cup of water and run a full cycle without adding coffee. Then discard the dirty water, rinse, and run again using only water to flush away any remaining baking soda. The powder's abrasive particles will get into every crevice of the machine, knocking loose the coffee residue responsible for the bad-tasting brew. The result: a squeaky-clean machine and the perfect cup of joe.

3 Soften fabric—the natural way

You've always relied on fabric softener to prevent static cling, but lately the flowery smell has been irritating your sinuses and skin. The natural alternative: Fill a plastic container with baking soda, adding two drops of your favorite essential oil per cup of powder. Then stir, seal, and set aside for 1 week. On laundry day, add 1/2 cup of this mixture to the wash cycle instead of softener. The baking soda will nix detergent residue, plus soften and deodorize fabric, while the essential oil will leave behind a light scent that won't irritate skin.

4 Wash away pesticides from produce

Though you try to buy organic fruit and vegetables, pickings are slim in the winter months. To ensure pesticide-free produce, lightly dust fruit and veggies with baking soda, brushing it in with your fingers before rinsing as usual. The tiny, abrasive particles will get into every nook and cranny in the peel to gently scrub away dirt and pesticides, leaving behind perfectly clean—and safe—produce.

5 Deice a walkway without harming it

Salt and commercial deicers sometimes work their way into cracks in walkways and driveways, staining or even eating away at concrete. The safer option: Sprinkle icy spots with 1 cup of baking soda mixed with 2 to 3 tablespoons of sand (to improve traction). Baking soda has a lower freezing point than water, so when it comes into contact with ice, it speeds melting time and prevents refreezing. But because baking soda particles are much finer than salt crystals, they are less abrasive and won't damage your driveway.

6 Cook fluffier omelets every time

You're long overdue for grocery shopping but feeling tired, so it's cheese omelets for dinner tonight. (We've been there!) However, the last time you cooked eggs, they came out bone-dry and flavorless. For better-tasting omelets, add $1/2$ teaspoon of baking soda for every three eggs used. As you cook, the kitchen staple's sodium bicarbonate will release carbon dioxide, leavening the eggs for a superfluffy main course.

7 Smooth away rough, itchy skin

If drying indoor heat tends to leave your skin flaky and irritated, try adding 1 cup of baking soda to your next bath. The slightly abrasive particles will gently slough off dead skin cells as you relax, so when you get out of the tub, you'll feel extra smooth and refreshed. Then apply moisturizer to prevent further drying. (This treatment soothes windburned skin, too.)

8 Whiten teeth for pennies

Next time your teeth need a pick-me-up, try this: Dip a wet toothbrush in baking soda, top with a dollop of toothpaste, and brush as usual. Repeat two to four times a month, depending on gum sensitivity. The tiny, abrasive baking soda particles will gently scour away plaque and stains that make teeth look dingy, revealing pearly whites after just one use. Plus, baking soda neutralizes bad breath–causing germs.

9 Freshen up your pooch in a pinch

With guests on the way, there's no time to give your dog a full-blown bath. The save: Stand Fido on top of a towel or newspaper and rub handfuls of baking soda into his coat for a minute or two, then brush him thoroughly. The absorbent particles will soak up offensive odors and excess body oils, leaving your pup's coat shiny, clean, and smelling fresh. And he'll be grateful to skip a cold outdoor bath!

10 Lift tomato sauce stains from plastic

To save time and money, you make large batches of tomato sauce to store in the freezer. The problem? The sauce leaves stubborn orange stains on your plastic containers. To remove them, add enough water to $1/4$ cup of baking soda to make a paste and apply to the stains. After 20 minutes, wipe the containers clean with a damp sponge. The alkaline baking soda will neutralize the acidic tomato stains, making it easy for the abrasive particles to scrub the color away. Bonus: The baking soda will also absorb any lingering odors.

Prevent annoying screwdriver slips

While you're assembling a bookcase, one frustrating screw keeps slipping as you try to drive it in. Just put a dab of nail polish on the screw's head, then screw in as usual. The tackiness of the nail polish will give the screwdriver a little more friction, keeping it in place for easy turning. But the polish won't cement the tool to the screw, so when you're done, you can simply wipe away the excess.

In-a-pinch screwdriver

If you need to remove a screw but don't want to schlep down to the basement and hunt for your trusty Phillips head, simply grab a metal potato or vegetable peeler from your kitchen drawer instead. The tool's curved top edge will fit perfectly into the star-shaped grooves on the screw head, so loosening it will be a breeze.

SHARPENING SMARTS

Sharpen a dull paper shredder

If your shredder has been working overtime this tax season and the blades are having a hard time slicing through paper, try running a few sheets of foil through the device. Dull blades are often the result of built-up dust from shredded paper, and the foil will remove the particles. (There's no need to sharpen with foil if you have a self-sharpening model, but the blades may need to be oiled—check the manual for details.)

Sharpen shears in seconds

Ugh! Your scissors are so dull, they can barely cut through paper, let alone the fabric for your craft project. To sharpen them stat, grab a piece of sandpaper from your husband's workbench and snip through it a few times with the scissors. The sandpaper's rough texture will instantly hone the tool without damaging or scratching the blades. Shear genius!

Little secret to perfect furniture touch-ups

When you're applying a fresh coat of paint or varnish to your patio chair, bench, or table, press a thumbtack or small nail into the bottom of each item's legs before starting the job. This will elevate them off the ground so you can easily reach the bottoms and undersides with your paintbrush. Plus, it will ensure the freshly painted pieces won't stick to the ground (or the newspaper you've laid underneath). After the paint is dry, simply remove the nails and voilà—beautifully spruced-up furniture, without the stress!

HANDY HOUSEHOLD HINTS

SOS for dried-out masking tape

You're just about to hang a few festive holiday decorations when you realize your old roll of masking tape has dried out, leaving it unsticky and totally unusable. The fast fix: Microwave the roll for 10 seconds. The heat will slightly melt the adhesive, restoring its tacky texture. Money saved: $3 for a new roll of masking tape

Re-adhere a loose vinyl tile

An easy fix for a tile that's loose and sticking up from the floor: Place a sheet of foil over the curled end, then press a hot iron onto the foil and hold for a few seconds. The iron's heat will reactivate the glue on the self-adhesive vinyl so it will lie flat again.

Never get poked by a nail again

Ouch! It seems like every time you reach into a container of nails while doing simple home repairs, you end up getting jabbed. The solution: Hot glue a small magnet to the bottom of your hammer's handle. When you need a nail, simply point the handle into the container. The magnet will attract the nails, eliminating the risk of a finger prick.

SOS for wooden furniture nicks

To remove small dents from wooden furniture, place a damp rag on the spot and run an iron set on steam over it five times. The heat and moisture will cause the wood fibers to swell and fill in the dent, restoring your table's flawless finish.

Fix a "sticky" sliding door

When weather finally starts to warm up, the sliding glass door in your kitchen gets a lot more use. The problem: It keeps catching and getting stuck, forcing you to jiggle it shut. To remedy this, simply rub an old candle stub against the door's tracks. The wax will lubricate the door, letting it glide smoothly.

Add tape to kitchen cabinet magnets

If you have to give a forceful yank to open your cupboard, the magnetic strip inside the door is probably more powerful than it needs to be. To fix: Stick a piece of clear tape over the magnet. This will slightly weaken the magnetic pull so the door will open with ease.

Can't find your ruler? Use this

When you need to take a measurement but don't have a ruler handy, reach for some spare change. A quarter's diameter is just a smidgen under 1 inch and a penny's is exactly 3/4 inch, so the coins can help you complete the task at hand without having to waste time searching for that measuring stick.

Chapter 3

FABULOUS FOOD AND HEALTHY MEALS

Meat on a Mission

A juicy, marinated steak or beautifully grilled salmon makes the perfect centerpiece for a family meal. Luckily, *First for Women* is here with expert tips guaranteed to make meat preparation quick, easy, and "wow" worthy.

GRILLING

Find your ideal grilling temperature

Yikes! Your salmon turned out blackened instead of beautiful. Next time, prevent the burn with this simple test: Hold your hand 6 inches above the heated grill grate. If you can stand it for 2 seconds, the grill is good for searing steaks; 4 seconds, it's ready for grilling chicken; 5 seconds, it's right for cooking more heat-sensitive foods like fish.

Tender grilled meat every time

If the high heat of the grill often leaves your steaks, pork chops, and chicken breasts tough and dry, try adding black or green tea to your marinade. Simply brew a cup, let it cool, and pour it over the meat along with your favorite seasonings. Let sit for 30 minutes before cooking. The tea's tannins will help break down the meat's tough proteins, leaving it tender and juicy (without adding a strong flavor).

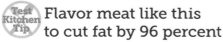

Flavor meat like this to cut fat by 96 percent

If you're all about the grill in the summer and use a lot of marinades on your meats, you may be surprised to learn that marinades tend to be high in fat and calories. Switch to making them with buttermilk instead of oil. The combination of acidity and fat in buttermilk is perfect for tenderizing. And as a fabulous bonus, it delivers energizing protein, plus healthy bacteria that help the liver burn up to 38 percent more stored fat. Since buttermilk is a little thicker than oil, though, bump up the herbs and seasonings in your marinade recipes, adjusting to taste, before adding to meat and vegetable dishes.

Easiest way to grill hot dogs

Cooking more than a few franks at a time can be a pain: It's easy to forget which ones you've already flipped, and the dogs often slip right out of your tongs. Instead, try threading an entire package of eight hot dogs onto two metal or water-soaked wooden skewers, one at each end of the franks. This will allow you to flip all the hot dogs at once, making grilling a cinch.

Get perfect grill marks on your meat

Want to impress your guests with beautifully seared steaks? Just lay a sheet of foil over the grill grate 10 minutes prior to cooking. This will trap the heat, making the grate extra hot—the key to getting dark, distinct grill marks. Remove the foil and grill as usual.

Grill sausages this way

High heat can cause sausage casings to shrink and curl, making it tough to fit the meat into sandwich buns. To keep the links straight, stick a metal or soaked bamboo skewer lengthwise through each one before grilling as usual. Allow the cooked sausages to rest for a few minutes, then remove the skewers and enjoy!

The secret shortcut to fall-off-the-bone ribs

For delicious, tender barbecued ribs in a half hour, place 2 pounds of meat (cut into four-rib sections) in a bowl and top with 1 cup of barbecue sauce. Cover and microwave for 10 minutes. Turn the ribs over and microwave for 8 minutes more, then grill as usual over high heat for 5 minutes on each side. The ribs will be supertender with a crisp glaze.

Make a grimy grill sparkle with an onion

If you lift up your grill lid and discover there's still grease, ash, and food residue left over from the last barbecue, don't sweat it. Cleanup will be a breeze with this trick: Fire up the grill for 10 minutes to soften the buildup, then turn it off and let it cool slightly. Next, spritz a halved onion with cooking oil spray, pierce it with a cooking fork, and use the flat side of the veggie to scrub the grates. Enzymes in the onion will break down grime so the vegetable's rough, layered surface can easily scour away dirt. And to make future cleanup easier, spray the cleaned grates with cooking oil. The slippery coating will repel food and grease, which means you'll have more time to focus on backyard fun.

BACON

An easier, healthier way to cook bacon

If visions of spattering grease make you hesitant to fry bacon, place the strips on a metal cooling rack set in a rimmed baking sheet, then cook in a 350°F oven for about 15 minutes. All the grease will be contained to the oven, plus it will drip away from the bacon, making strips supercrispy.

No-fuss bacon chopping

Bacon bits make a tasty base for soups and stews, but chopping the raw meat can be tough because the slices tend to stick together and slide around your cutting board. The fix: Wrap the bacon in plastic and freeze for 30 minutes before slicing. The fat will harden, making the slices easier to chop.

BEEF AND STEAKS

Tastier carved meat

You know to let steak sit for 5 minutes before slicing. But placing a hot steak on a cold cutting board can leave your dinner lukewarm. The fix: Run the board under hot water and towel dry it before setting down the meat. You'll get extra-juicy steak that tastes like it came straight off the grill.

Marinate steak in a jiffy

Grilled steak would be a perfect weeknight meal—but the recipe your family favors takes so long to marinate. The shortcut that saves time and improves flavor: Grill your steak without marinating, then let the meat sit in the marinade for 5 to 10 minutes. Cooked steak absorbs flavor faster, so it will take only a few minutes to get great flavor. And since dry steak sears easier, this method will also give you more of the charred taste that everyone loves.

Reheat rare steak without overcooking it

Your perfectly medium-rare steak sat out for too long and is now too cold to serve. To reheat it without cooking it further, place it in a metal pan, cover with lettuce, and broil for 2 minutes. The moist lettuce will keep the steak from overcooking and drying out.

Tenderize a cheap cut of meat

The secret to turning a tough steak into a juicy treat: Generously salt the meat and let it sit for about an hour before cooking. The salt will draw out water from the steak and dissolve. Then the salt water will be reabsorbed into the meat, where it will break down tough proteins. Wipe away any excess salt water from the steak and cook as usual.

Finish cooking roast beef in a hurry

If your roast is taking forever to cook through, this tip can help: Slice the top of the meat at 1-inch intervals (accordion style), making sure to cut only halfway down. Tie the roast with string and put it back in the oven until done. This will allow heat to penetrate the roast so it will finish cooking fast.

Sidestep smoky grease splatters

Roasting beef at a high temperature can result in a smoky kitchen—just what you don't want when you have guests in the house. Head this off by covering the bottom of the pan with water. The liquid will keep the fat in the meat drippings from splattering and burning, reducing the amount of smoke while the roast cooks.

Tender corned beef—guaranteed!

To ensure your St. Patrick's Day feast turns out tender, try this doneness-testing trick: Stick a carving fork into the meat and pull upward. If the fork slides out easily without lifting the entire roast, the meat is juicy, tender, and perfectly cooked.

Fastest way to defrost meat

Oops! It's 5 p.m. when you realize you forgot to take tonight's steaks out of the freezer. Instead of microwaving them, which can make the meat tough, try this USDA-studied quick-thaw method: Seal the steaks in zipper-lock bags and submerge in a bowl of hot tap water (about 125°F). The meat will defrost and be ready to cook in 15 minutes. (This works for chicken breasts and pork chops, too.)

Broil meat sans mess

When the weather calls for cooking steaks indoors, you turn to the broiler for its speed and ease. The only downside: The drippings that collect in the pan below often smoke, splatter, or flare up. To avoid this, line the bottom of the pan (under the rack) with slices of stale bread before placing in the broiler. The bread will soak up any fatty juices that fall, preventing them from smoking or catching fire.

Evenly sized meatballs—each and every time

If your homemade meatballs always start out one size and end up getting bigger and bigger as you work, leaving you with unevenly sized (and unevenly cooked) portions, try this: Roll the meat mixture into logs and cut each log into equal slices. Then roll each slice into a ball and cook as usual.

BURGERS

The secret to juicy burgers

Cold weather hasn't dampened your burger cravings, but cooking on the stove top often leads to dry patties. For tastier burgers, sprinkle the hot pan with a thin layer of kosher salt before adding the meat. The salt will draw out juices, then quickly set them, forming a tasty crust that will seal in moisture. (Brush off excess salt before serving.)

Extra-juicy lean burgers

In an effort to cook healthier, you've been making burgers with ground turkey or lean beef, but the patties turn out dry. The simple save: Try adding finely shredded zucchini or carrots to the meat before cooking. The vegetables will add moisture—plus a hint of natural sweetness—to the burgers.

Cook burgers with ice!

To prevent lean beef patties from becoming dried-out hockey pucks on the grill, try molding the ground meat around small ice cubes. As the burgers cook, the ice will slowly melt and baste the meat from the inside, leaving the patties moist and tender.

Always cook burgers evenly

Whenever you toss a batch of burgers into a frying pan, they end up burned on the edges and rare in the middle. The solution: Use your finger to poke a hole through the center of each patty before cooking. Heat will penetrate the middle of the meat to promote even cooking. (The hole will close up as the burger cooks.)

CHICKEN

A space-saving way to freeze chicken stock

Storing stock in plastic containers in the freezer can take up so much space. Instead, pour the stock into heavy-duty freezer bags, then lay the bags on the floor of the freezer so they'll harden into flat sheets. Once frozen, you can stack the bags or place them on their sides as needed.

Quick substitute for a roasting rack

You'd like to roast a chicken for dinner but can't find your roasting rack. The fix: Peel and slice two large onions in half and place them cut side down underneath the bird. This will allow air to circulate around the chicken for even browning, plus add savory flavor to the meat.

Slice stir-fry meat superthin with this trick

Thinly slicing a steak or chicken breast for a stir-fry can take twice as long as actually cooking the dish. Make quick work of the task by freezing the meat for 30 to 60 minutes before slicing. The partially frozen meat will stay firm under the pressure of a knife, allowing you to make thin, even cuts.

Juiciest roast chicken ever

Your roast bird always scores major raves, but you wish the breast would come out as moist and tender as the legs and thighs. What can help: Roast your chicken breast side down for the first 30 minutes of cooking, then flip the chicken over and finish cooking it on its back to let the skin crisp up. This will allow the juices to flow to the white meat, making every bite extra juicy.

Mess-free chicken carving

Cutting into a roast chicken can cause the juices to run all over your countertop. To make the job neater, place your cutting board inside a large rimmed cookie sheet, then carve as usual. The pan will contain all the runaway juices, so you can save them for gravy or pour them over the sliced meat.

Crispy roast chicken—guaranteed!

The secret to a crisp-skinned bird: Mix 1 teaspoon of baking powder, 1 tablespoon of water, and a pinch of salt until it forms a paste, then rub all over the chicken. Let sit for 15 minutes before rinsing with cold water. Roast as usual. The baking powder will dehydrate the skin and tenderize the meat, resulting in a moist-inside, crunchy-outside chicken.

The secret to better breaded chicken

Brush the egg onto the meat instead of dipping the meat into the egg. Dipping causes excess egg to attach to the cutlet, creating extra moisture under the breading. Then, as the egg cooks, steam separates the coating from the cutlet. But brushing on the egg keeps the crispy coating from falling off.

Ensure bread crumbs stick to meat

You carefully breaded your chicken cutlets, only to watch half the crumbs fall off in the skillet. Next time, swap your regular egg wash for a blend of flour and egg whites (1 tablespoon of flour for each white). Dip the cutlets in the egg mixture before coating in crumbs. This gluelike substance will help the breading adhere firmly to the meat.

LAMB

Your most flavorful Easter lamb ever

For the special family dinner you're hosting, you want to ensure your roast leg of lamb tastes fantastic. To boost the meat's flavor, use a paring knife to cut 1-inch slits all over the roast, then fill the holes with slivers of garlic. As the meat cooks, the garlic will infuse it with a nutty, savory taste. (Try this trick on beef and pork roasts, too.)

The better way to French lamb

To easily remove any traces of meat, try this butcher's secret: Wrap a piece of kitchen twine around the base of each bone, then tie one end of the string to a secure object (like a sink faucet). Grip the other end and slide it away from the meat. This will lift off any scraps, leaving the rack perfectly clean.

MEAT LOAF

Trick for tastier meat loaf

For a more robust and savory meat loaf, try baking the bread crumbs on a baking sheet at 350°F for 5 to 8 minutes, or until golden brown. Let the bread cool, then mix with the meat and other ingredients as usual. Toasting the crumbs yields new flavor compounds, giving the meat loaf a deeper, more complex taste.

Your best meat loaf ever!

The bread crumbs you use in your meat loaf do a great job of holding the mixture together, but you've noticed that the additional starch diminishes the beefy taste. Boost the flavor by stirring into your mixture 1 cup of sautéed mushrooms and 1/2 tablespoon of soy sauce (instead of salt) for every pound of raw meat. These ingredients will lend a robust savoriness to the dish.

The secret to ready-in-minutes meat loaf

To speed the cook time of this dish, trade your loaf pan for a muffin tin. Since the meat muffins are smaller, they'll cook up in about 20 minutes at 375°F. (Use a thermometer to check that they're at least 160°F.) Bonus: effortless portion control!

SEAFOOD

No-stick way to grill fish

You love the smoky flavor of grilled fish, but the delicate fillets often stick and fall apart on the grill no matter how much oil you use. For a healthier and tastier dish, cover the hot grates with thin lemon slices, then lay the fish on top to cook. The lemon layer will prevent the fillets from sticking while still allowing them to cook through. Plus, the citrus flavor will complement the fish.

Bone a salmon fillet in seconds

Ack! Even though the seafood-counter guy promised that the salmon fillet was boneless, we discovered a few sharp bones in our dinner. Next time, we'll use this quick double-checking trick: Drape each fillet over an overturned bowl. Any remaining bones will stand up for easy removal with tweezers.

Get all the sand out of clams

To prevent your crew from "gritting" their teeth, place the shellfish in a large bowl, fill it with cool tap water, and add 1 tablespoon of cornmeal for every pound of clams. Let sit for 20 to 60 minutes. Cornmeal irritates clams' digestive tracts, encouraging them to spit out more sand.

Grilled shrimp made easy!

When you grill skewered shrimp, do the pieces always spin around on the stick as you try to flip them, making it hard to grill both sides? For an easy fix, thread one skewer through one end of each shrimp and another through the opposite end of each shrimp. This will keep the pieces stable and allow you to flip with ease.

Upgrade for frozen shrimp

To ensure your frozen seafood cooks up firm and meaty (not limp and mushy), try this: Place the peeled raw shrimp in a bowl, generously sprinkle with salt (about 2 tablespoons per pound), and cover with cold water. Chill for 30 minutes, then rinse and cook as usual. The salt will change the structure of the shrimp's proteins, trapping moisture inside so the meat stays firm and juicy.

Prevent scallops from sticking to the grill

To ensure perfect results, combine 3 tablespoons of oil, 4 teaspoons of flour, and 1 teaspoon of cornstarch in a bowl and use a pastry brush to lightly coat the scallops with the mixture before grilling. The oil and starch will create a barrier to stop the seafood from sticking.

TURKEY

Meatier-tasting turkey burgers

Prevent lean poultry patties from tasting bland by mixing in 5 ounces of chopped mushrooms and 4 teaspoons of soy sauce (instead of salt) for every pound of raw ground turkey or chicken. Both ingredients are rich in glutamate, an amino acid that will add a savory, beefy flavor to burgers.

Quick solution for dried-out turkey

You cooked your turkey to the right temperature, but it still came out dry as a bone. Simply slice up the meat, place it in a baking dish, and pour chicken stock halfway up the sides. Cover with foil and put the turkey back in the oven for 10 minutes. This quick braise will add moisture back to the meat, leaving it plump and juicy.

Tastier ground turkey

You'd love to swap in ground turkey for beef, but the leaner meat makes the dish a tad bland. To "beef up" the flavor, dissolve 1 cube of low-sodium beef bouillon in 1/4 cup of hot water and stir it into the turkey as it cooks. The bouillon's aromatics will enhance the meat's taste without adding calories.

10 Brilliant Uses for EGGSHELLS

1 Pestproof garden in a jiffy

Between the deer, slugs, and snails, you're worried that come May, you won't have any plants left in your garden! To deter the hungry nuisances, scatter crushed eggshells on the leaves of the nibbled-on plants and around the perimeter of your garden. Snails and slugs can't safely go over the jagged corners of the crushed shells, and deer hate the smell of egg—so your garden will stay pest-free.

2 Quickly soothe sore, aching joints

Your weekend-warrior husband can't seem to go a day without developing a new ache or pain. Eggshells to the rescue! Break one up in a glass jar, then cover with apple cider vinegar and screw the jar shut. Let sit until the pieces dissolve (about 2 days). Eggshells contain nutrients that promote healthy joints, like collagen, chondroitin, glucosamine, and hyaluronic acid. These nutrients are infused into the vinegar as the eggshell membrane dissolves, providing quick relief when you rub the solution into sore spots. (The mixture will keep for months in the pantry.)

3 Relieve dry, peeling cuticles

After your burst of spring cleaning, the skin around your fingernails is dry and peeling. The remedy: Break off a couple pieces of eggshell with the membrane attached. Then tape the shells, membrane side down, to problem areas until the shells begin to feel dry. Eggshell membranes contain healing nutrients like hyaluronan, so your rough, peeling cuticles will be healthy and soft by the next day.

4 Uncover baby-soft skin in seconds

Spring is here, but your complexion still looks winter-dull. Freshen up your skin with this inexpensive mask: Finely crush one or two eggshells, whisk together with one egg white, and apply all over your face. Let dry, then rinse with warm water. The gently abrasive shells will buff away the dry, dead skin that's hiding your natural glow. Plus, the eggshells' calcium will promote cell regeneration and help even out your complexion. The result: soft, radiant skin after a single use!

5 Gently scour any surface— naturally!

Finding household cleaners that don't irritate your sensitive skin and sinuses can be a struggle. If your store-bought scouring powder inflames your eyes, skin, or lungs, try using eggshells as a chemical-free alternative. Just pulverize several dried eggshells and store them in a covered plastic container. When needed, dust the to-be-cleaned surface with the powder and use a sudsy sponge or dish towel to scrub away the mess. The abrasive particles will safely buff away stains and grease but won't irritate sensitive skin.

6 Keep drains running smoothly

If your kitchen sink is draining sluggishly, the culprit may be built-up grease or food in the pipes. Simply place a few well-crushed eggshells in the sink trap. When you run the water, the abrasive shell fragments will travel down the drain and help scrape away clog-inducing gunk, keeping the pipes clear and water flowing smoothly.

7 Brew a better cup of coffee

Lately your morning joe tastes bitter and acidic. The save: Add 1 teaspoon of crushed eggshells to the grounds before brewing. The shells' alkaline calcium carbonate will neutralize the acid content of the coffee, making it smoother tasting and easier on the stomach. Plus, if you use a percolator (when camping, for example), the shells will weigh down the grounds so they sink to the bottom of the pot.

8 Provide birds with a nutrient boost

When you set up your bird feeder this year, try this trick: Bake five eggshells in a 250°F oven until dry but not brown (about 20 minutes). Let cool, then crumble them into small pieces and sprinkle them in the feeder. The calcium-rich shells will act as a natural supplement to help female birds lay strong eggs (which are about 95 percent calcium) and maintain bone health. Birds can also use the shells to build nests.

9 Clean narrow-necked vases effortlessly

Cleaning all the residue from inside irregularly shaped vases (like the one your Easter bouquet came in) can be a pain. To easily scrub away even hard-to-reach grime, drop one or two crushed eggshells into the container, add warm water and a drop of dish-washing liquid, and give it a couple swirls. The soap will loosen the gunk so the abrasive shells can scrape it away, leaving every last nook gleaming. This trick works well on thermoses, too.

10 Grow healthier tomato plants

To give your tomatoes a head start this season, add one or two crushed eggshells to the soil before planting. As the eggshells decompose, they will release calcium into the dirt. This helps prevent blossom-end rot, a common problem with tomato plants. Calcium also helps almost any plant grow faster, so try sprinkling eggshells all around your garden. Bonus: Eggshells that are mostly whole can be used as healthy starter pots for seedlings.

Eat Your Veggies

Vegetables are an important part of any balanced diet, but it can be challenging to come up with new ways to cook and serve them. Here, you'll find clever tips for making your vegetable courses yummy, convenient, and irresistible.

COOKING HINTS

Little trick for yummier roasted veggies

For extra-delicious roasted carrots, parsnips, potatoes, and butternut squash, try slicing the vegetables on a diagonal instead of chopping into cubes. The angular cut will maximize the amount of surface area that gets caramelized in the oven's heat, delivering the most flavor and crunch.

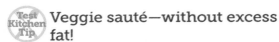 Veggie sauté—without excess fat!

Veggie sautés are the perfect side—they're quick, tasty, and healthy, but they're often cooked in butter, which adds unnecessary fat and calories. Sure, cooking spray would be a calorie-saving choice, but it just doesn't cut it in terms of taste. Instead, trying sautéing vegetables in low-sodium chicken broth. Simply use ¼ cup of chicken broth instead of 1 tablespoon of butter. The broth is much lower in calories, plus it makes the side even more savory and delicious. You might end up eating more nutrient-packed veggies!

ARTICHOKES, BROCCOLI, AND CAULIFLOWER

Key to tender artichokes

The foolproof way to ensure that your artichoke has been boiled to perfection: Pull on the top of an interior leaf. If it separates easily, then the veggie is ready. But if you need to tug a little before the leaf loosens, a bit more cooking time is required.

Remove mold spots on cauliflower

You just purchased a fresh head of cauliflower, but tiny black mold spots are already on its surface. The quick fix: Rub the blemishes with a fine Microplane zester until the discoloration is gone. The kitchen tool will remove just the top layer of cauliflower, ensuring the vegetable keeps its shape and less goes to waste.

SOS for "bendy" broccoli

When broccoli starts to lose its freshness, it makes like Gumby and bends easily. To bring a faded bunch back to life, trim ½ inch from the bottom of the stem, then stand the stalk in a liquid measuring cup filled halfway with cold water. Place in the fridge overnight. The water will replenish the broccoli so it returns to being crunchy and delicious.

Take the bite out of broccoli rabe

Although you blanched the broccoli rabe before sautéing, it's still bitter. The quick fix: Stir in a squeeze of lemon and sprinkle of salt. Acid and salt neutralize bitterness, resulting in a milder, sweeter veggie. (This works with any bitter greens, including kale, collards, and mustard greens.)

BEANS

Quick-soak dried beans

The cold weather has you craving chili for dinner, but your recipe calls for soaking the dried beans overnight. To speed up the process, place rinsed dried beans in a bowl and cover with water. Microwave until the water boils (5 to 10 minutes, depending on the amount of beans and microwave wattage). Let sit for 1 hour before draining and using the beans in your recipe.

The secret to tender bean dishes

If your bean recipes never turn out as soft as you'd like, hold off on adding acidic ingredients (like tomatoes, vinegar, or wine) until after the beans have fully cooked. The acid reacts with the beans' starch and prevents them from swelling and becoming tender.

Colander-free bean rinsing

Your signature baked-bean dish calls for rinsed and drained canned beans—but when you're in the middle of prepping for a holiday party, the last thing you need is another dish (the colander) to wash. Skip the extra cleanup by punching a few holes in the top and bottom of the can with a church key. Then hold the can under the faucet, allowing the water to drain from the bottom holes, until the liquid runs clear. Open the can and use the beans as usual.

BRUSSELS SPROUTS

Outsmart stubborn Brussels sprout odor

Boiling the tiny cabbages causes the release of stinky sulfur compounds that can permeate your kitchen. To prevent the odor from scaring away your dinner guests, add a stalk or two of celery to the cooking water with the sprouts. This highly absorbent vegetable will help neutralize the unwelcoming smell.

Take the bite out of Brussels sprouts

For a side dish everyone will love, blanch Brussels sprouts in boiling water for 5 minutes before sautéing or roasting. Parboiling will break down the veggie's bitter compounds, letting its natural sweet flavor shine through.

CHILES

Painlessly seed a chile
Test Kitchen Tip

If you love adding fresh hot peppers to homemade chili, you know that chopping them can be a pain—the seeds get under fingernails and may burn for hours. Try this chopping trick: Slice the chile lengthwise along one side, keeping the stem and seedpod intact. Then turn the pepper so it's cut side down and slice off another side. Repeat twice, leaving the seeds and stems behind. This way you get four big slices without having to handle the stinging seeds.

Simple way to seed a chile

Your enchilada recipe calls for serranos, but using your knife to remove seeds from a long, slim pepper is tough. The easier way: Trim the ends off the pepper, then firmly roll it against a cutting board. Next, hold the pepper upright and roll it between your palms. The pressure will loosen the seeds so they just fall out!

CORN

The trick for juicy corn

You love the smoky flavor of grilled corn on the cob, but sometimes the high heat of grilling makes the kernels shrivel up and get tough. The fix: Before placing your corn on the grill, soak the husked ears in salted water (about 1 tablespoon of salt for 8 ears) for 10 minutes. The salt water will act like a brine, so you'll have perfectly charred corn that's also plump and juicy. And as a bonus, the salt will intensify the natural sweetness of the corn.

Sweeten out-of-season corn
Test Kitchen Tip

Maximize corn's flavor even if it isn't quite in season: Just add a little sugar to the cooking water (about 4 teaspoons of sugar per gallon of water). Corn contains proteins called prolamins, which can taste bitter when out of season. But cooking the ears in a light sugar solution will restore the kernels' sweetness, masking any starchy bitterness. Just be sure not to add salt to the water when cooking, since it will toughen the kernels.

Perfect grilled corn every time

The secret to preventing corn on the cob from drying out or scorching on the grill: Soak the unshucked ears in cold water for 15 minutes, then grill with the silk and husks intact for 20 minutes or until tender, turning occasionally. The husks hold in moisture, allowing the kernels to gently steam on the grill so they come out juicy and succulent. Plus, the husks will peel back easily, removing the silk in the process and creating a handle for easy eating.

Quick trick for storing corn holders

Those quirky corncob holders look great on your table, but searching for the sharp tools in a crowded drawer often leads to pricked fingers. To keep hands safe, store each pair of holders in a wine cork—simply stick one in each end of the cork. They'll be easy to spot in a drawer, and you'll never end up with a mismatched set.

EGGPLANT

Foolproof trick for choosing eggplant

Who knew? Female eggplants have more seeds, so they taste harsher than their male counterparts. To determine the sex, look at the indentation on the bottom of the veggie—if it's deep and shaped like a dash, it's female; if it's shallow and round, it's male.

No more oily eggplant

Prevent pan-fried eggplant from soaking up grease by submerging the slices in ice water for 15 minutes. Blot dry with paper towels, then bread if desired and fry as usual. Saturating the veggie with water will stop oil from getting absorbed into the flesh.

Grease-free eggplant—guaranteed

An easy way to keep sautéed eggplant from soaking up too much oil: Simply brush a beaten egg white onto the surface of the slices before cooking. The egg will create a protective barrier to prevent the porous vegetable from absorbing excess grease as it cooks.

GARLIC

 Easy way to tame too-harsh garlic

Does your pesto recipe taste overly garlicky? Give the garlic a quick blanch before adding it to the food processor. Simply thread peeled cloves onto a skewer and submerge in boiling water for 1 minute. Your pesto will have just the right amount of bite!

Mince garlic effortlessly

Finely chopping garlic can be a hassle: The pieces tend to stick to the knife, forcing you to constantly stop and wipe the blade clean. Next time, after giving the cloves a rough chop, sprinkle on a couple of pinches of salt, then mince as usual. The salt will absorb some of the sticky juices, plus help break down the garlic, making the job easier.

Keep minced garlic from burning

To prevent sautéed garlic from burning the second you turn your back, try this: Instead of starting with oil, pour 4 tablespoons of water into the pan of minced garlic. Let cook for 2 minutes or until the water evaporates, stirring occasionally. Then add oil along with your other ingredients and continue to sauté until done. This will ensure that your garlic tastes sweet, not bitter and burned.

Speediest way to peel garlic

When your dish calls for lots of garlic, there's no need to peel the cloves individually. Instead, separate and lightly smash the cloves, then put them in a bowl with the peels still on. Cover with another bowl (ideally the same size) and shake for 10 seconds. The friction will cause the peels to slip right off!

LEAFY GREENS

Get the grit out of greens

No matter how thoroughly you wash leafy greens such as spinach and Swiss chard, traces of grit are always left behind. Next time, roll the leaves into a cigar shape, slice into 1-inch-long ribbons, and submerge the pieces in a bowl of water to wash. Cutting the greens into smaller pieces will ensure more surface area comes into contact with the water—so all the dirt will be washed away.

Core lettuce easily and without waste

Crisp, cool, and low cost, iceberg is your lettuce of choice for burgers when serving a crowd. To get the most leaves from each head, try this: Hold the lettuce so the core is parallel to a hard surface, then briskly bang it against the surface. The core will break free, leaving you with a head of just leaves.

Perk up wilted greens quickly

If the leafy greens you were planning on using in today's salad are already looking a little past their prime, try this: Fill a bowl with ice water and soak the veggies for 15 minutes, then spin dry. The icy water will replace the lost moisture that's causing the wilting, so the greens will crisp right up.

 ## No more soggy salad greens

Even after several whirls in the salad spinner, freshly washed lettuce can still leave a pool of water in the serving bowl. Place a saucer upside down in the bowl before filling with the greens. Any excess water will run off the leaves and collect underneath the saucer, leaving the salad dry and crisp.

OLIVES

Easier way to pit olives

Kalamata, niçoise, and Sevillano olives sold with the pits still in add a burst of salty tang to sandwiches and salads, but getting the pits out is a bit of work. The trick that makes it a cinch: Place olives on a cutting board, then gently press each one with the flat side of a chef's knife. The olive will split and the pit will slide right out.

ONIONS

Take the bite out of raw onions

You love the color and crunch that red onions add to salads, but their pungent flavor tends to overpower the rest of the dish. Next time, soak a sliced onion in cold water for 15 minutes. The water will draw out the acrid bite, leaving you with sweet, salad-ready onion slices.

Trick to chopping every last bit of onion

Whenever you're dicing an onion and reach the narrow area near the root end, it becomes difficult to chop without the onion slipping. The simple fix: Cut the onion in half with the skin on, then peel back the skin toward the root to form a handle. Use this as a grip and chop all of the onion with ease.

Choose the sweetest onions every time

The next time you need to use a raw onion (say, for salads, salsa, or guacamole), select the flattest, squattest one you can find. Sugar causes the fibers inside the onion to break down and collapse, resulting in a flatter shape—so these onions will have a higher sugar content and a sweeter taste.

Get onion flavor without the work

You think your homemade chicken soup could use a little onion flavor, but everyone's hungry and you don't have time to peel, chop, and sauté one. Instead, cut an onion in half and push it into a citrus reamer, just as you would a halved lemon or lime. Then pour a little of the fresh onion juice into your soup to instantly perk up its flavor.

PEAS

The best way to cook snow peas

It's easy to overcook fresh snow peas when you blanch them on the stove top. Instead, place the snow peas in a colander in the sink and pour boiling water over them until they turn bright green. Then rinse the veggies under cold water to stop the cooking process. Voilà—perfectly tender-crisp snow peas in seconds.

No-fuss way to cook frozen peas

Green peas are a vegetable your whole family can agree on—if only so many didn't end up in the sink during the straining process. Here's a hassle-free, one-step way to cook and strain: Pour the frozen vegetables into a mesh sieve, then place in the pot of boiling water, balancing the sieve atop the pot. When the veggies are tender, lift out the sieve.

PEPPERS

Keep a cut bell pepper from going soft

If you avoid recipes that call for half a bell pepper because the other half goes soft in 2 days, try this tip: Slice off the bottom half of the vegetable, leaving the top intact. Since the "lid" houses the seeds (which hold in moisture), the leftover pepper will stay fresh for a few extra days.

The genius way to keep stuffed peppers upright

Your stuffed peppers earn rave reviews from your crew. The only problem? The peppers often tip over when baking. To avoid this, arrange filled peppers in a muffin pan, then bake. The pan's wells are the perfect size to keep peppers upright.

POTATOES

Easiest way to bake potatoes for a crowd

Whenever you bake more than a few potatoes at a time, the spuds tend to roll all over the baking sheet (and often right onto the floor). Save yourself stress by standing the potatoes on end in a 12-cup muffin tin. This will make it easier to move them in and out of the oven, plus provide ample air space around each spud to ensure even cooking.

Boil potatoes sans the spills

Oops! You turned away from the pot of potatoes you were preparing for your St. Patrick's Day feast for just a second and the water boiled over, creating a huge mess. Next time, try rubbing oil or butter on the inside of the pot near the top before cooking potatoes (or any other starchy foods, like pasta). This will prevent the water from climbing up the sides and keep it contained in the pot.

Peel potatoes in a flash

To make the tedious task of peeling potatoes easier to bear, try this: Use a paring knife to score the spuds' skins around the middle (like a belt), then cook in boiling water for 15 minutes, or until done. Place the potatoes in an ice bath for 30 seconds to cool, and the skins will come right off.

Bake potatoes without turning on the oven

Too hot to even think about baking potatoes? Enlist your slow cooker for the job. Prick the spuds with a fork, stand them up on end (leaning them against the inner wall of the pot), and set to low. The potatoes will be perfectly cooked in 5 to 6 hours.

Keep boiled sweet potatoes bright

Mashed sweet potatoes are a family favorite, but sometimes the boiled spuds come out pale brown instead of bright orange. To keep your veggies vibrant, add a few slices of lemon to the cooking water. The fruit's citric acid will keep the potatoes from darkening while complementing their sweet flavor.

Key to prepping potatoes ahead

It's great to get a jump on holiday cooking by peeling and chopping the day before. But if you try it with potatoes, they turn brown and mushy. To prevent this: After prepping, submerge them in a bowl with 1 tablespoon of vinegar per 2 cups of water. When you're ready to use them, drain, rinse, and cook as usual. Vinegar's acidity will stop the potatoes from oxidizing, so they look freshly sliced even a day later.

ROOT VEGETABLES

Keep root veggies from drying out

Carrots, beets, and radishes add delicious crunch to salads. Unfortunately, even when you keep them wrapped in the fridge, they dry out and shrivel in just a few days. Ensure your veggies stay moist and crisp all week by removing their leaves before storing. The reason: Leaves leach moisture from the veggies.

Grate ginger with ease

The key to releasing the most flavor from fresh ginger: Store the fibrous root in a plastic bag in the freezer. (Thaw before using.) Freezing causes the water in the root to expand, breaking down its tough fibers. Once defrosted, you'll be able to extract the maximum amount of flavorful juice.

Outsmart ginger "strings"

Mincing ginger can be a pain—the fibrous root is difficult to cut up, and the pieces tend to fly everywhere. Next time, cut the ginger into cubes and press through a garlic press. The tool will catch the skin and fibers, leaving you with only the finely crushed flesh.

Mince ginger with ease

Fresh gingerroot is so fibrous that it can be tough to mince evenly. To make the job easier, place the peeled root on your cutting board and carefully strike it a few times with a meat mallet until it's flattened. This will help break down the root's fibers so you can easily run your knife through the knob, ensuring finely minced pieces in seconds.

SQUASH

Peel winter squash with ease

To make peeling and slicing butternut or acorn squash a cinch, poke a few holes in the squash with a fork, then wrap in a dish towel and microwave for 3 minutes. Let cool slightly, then peel, cut, and cook as usual. Par-cooking the squash will cause the peel to soften so it's easy to remove.

Seed a squash with ease

You love the flavor of butternut squash, but the tedious task of seeding the veggie is another story. Next time, reach for an ice cream scoop instead of a regular spoon. The scoop's sharp, rigid edge will readily cut through the squash's fibrous strings, and its deep bowl will remove plenty of seeds in a single swipe, enabling you to get the job done in half the time.

TOMATOES

Never waste tomato paste again!

Your barbecue sauce recipe calls for only 2 tablespoons of tomato paste, leaving most of the can unused. To keep it from going bad, drop it by tablespoonfuls onto a lined baking sheet and freeze until solid. Then place the paste in a zipper-lock bag and store in the freezer for up to 3 months. In the fall you can add the frozen paste to soups, stews, and chili.

No-cook tomato puree

You stocked up on summer's last blast of tomatoes, which are perfect for a puree. But it's too hot to turn on the stove, and the last time you used a food processor, the puree was watery with bits of skin mixed in. A better way: Halve your tomatoes and remove the seeds, then grate each tomato against the largest holes on a grater. When you're left holding only skin, throw it away; the grated pulp that remains is your puree.

Easy tomato paste removal

You love the extra punch that tomato paste gives soups and stews, but scraping out the last bit from the bottom of the tiny tin can is often a challenge. An easier way: Open the container on both ends with a can opener, then remove and discard the top lid. Use the bottom lid as a plunger to push all the paste up and out of the can.

Flavorful, Fresh Fruit

Fruit is the perfect treat—sweet and nutritious. Learn lots of tips and tricks, from keeping strawberries fresh to seeding a pomegranate. Read on to find out how to expertly store and prepare your produce!

The secret to perfectly poached fruit

Just a few minutes of overcooking pears can lead to a mushy mess. To ensure firm-tender results every time, bring the poaching liquid to a boil with the fruit and let simmer for 5 minutes, then turn off the heat. The residual heat will cook the fruit perfectly, so when the liquid cools, the fruit is done.

Help for a lackluster fruit salad

Your fruit salad *looks* beautiful, but the sweet-tart flavor you crave just isn't there. To give the fruit a boost, try making a quick dressing: Mix equal parts sugar and water in a saucepan and mash in a few spoonfuls of the prepared fruit. Add a squeeze of lemon juice and cook until the sugar dissolves. Let cool, then drizzle over the fruit salad.

Take the hassle out of chopping dried fruit

You love adding dried apricots and plums to baked treats, but cutting them into pieces can be a pain—the soft fruit always sticks to the side of your knife. To prevent this, freeze the fruit for 1 hour before chopping. The moisture in the fruit will temporarily firm up, making it less sticky.

Sweeten out-of-season fruit

Your little ones begged you to make your scrumptious strawberry pie, but you know the out-of-season berries will taste bland. For a pie that comes out sweet and delicious, toss the strawberries with 2 tablespoons of lemonade mix. The citric acid will brighten the berries' flavor, while the sugar will help balance tartness. Just be sure to cut 1 tablespoon of sugar from your recipe so the dessert is not too sweet.

Tastiest way to prevent fruit slices from browning

When hosting a party, you try to do as much in advance as possible—like cutting up apples and pears for the cheese plate. Usually, you sprinkle the slices with lemon juice to keep them from browning, but the fruit ends up tasting a bit too tart. You may be surprised to learn that seltzer, which has a lower pH level than regular water, wards off browning without leaving behind a sour taste. Simply place the slices in a bowl and add just enough seltzer to cover.

Make lemons last three times longer

Lemons were on sale this week, so you stocked up. To ensure they don't dry out too quickly, place them in a bowl of cold water and store in the fridge. (Change the water every week or so.) The water will keep the lemons hydrated, so they'll stay fresh for up to 3 months.

How to choose the juiciest lemons

Those lemons looked great at the market, but when you got home, you realized they were as hard as a rock. For juicy results every time, choose lemons by texture: Air tends to seep through the rinds of larger-pored lemons and dry out the pulp, so look for ones that are smooth and pore-free.

Better way to squeeze just a little bit of lemon juice

Sometimes a recipe calls for just a teaspoon of citrus juice, but when you cut off a small wedge to use, the rest of the lemon dries up in the fridge. Next time, use a skewer to poke a hole in the uncut lemon, then squeeze out the amount you need. Thanks to this trick, the inside of the lemon won't be exposed to air, so it will stay fresh in the fridge longer.

How to choose the sweetest oranges

At the market, look for citrus fruit with a slight greenish cast. Evenly colored oranges are often underripe ones that have been dyed. A faint touch of green indicates that the fruit was harvested from a warmer climate, which helps convert its starches into sugar.

Zest citrus with ease

Orange, lemon, and lime rinds make tasty additions to cakes, muffins, and puddings, but zesting can be tough if your fruit is too soft or your grater has become dull. The solution: Place the fruit in the freezer for 20 minutes before using. The firmed-up surface will be easier to zest, plus the peels will retain more of their flavorful oils.

Keep strawberries fresh for 2 weeks

Berries often spoil after just a few days, but you can extend their shelf life by washing them in a solution of 1 part vinegar and 10 parts water before storing. Vinegar will kill the mold spores and bacteria that cause the fruit to go bad.

Juicy watermelon without the mess

Slicing into a watermelon usually results in a countertop covered with sticky juice. Next time you have a hankering for the fruit, place your cutting board in a rimmed baking sheet first. When you're finished cutting, the sweet juice will be contained in the baking sheet, so you can easily save it to use in smoothies.

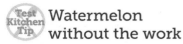

Watermelon without the work

Watermelon is such a healthy snack, but slicing through the hard rind is often tedious. Try this clever trick: Simply slice a fresh watermelon in half, then use an ice cream scoop to dish out the fruit like sorbet. The melon forms perfect easy-to-eat rounds—and saves a lot of slicing!

Seed a pomegranate without a mess

Pomegranate seeds add sweet-tart flavor to dishes, but removing the edible seeds is a messy task—the juice can splatter on counters, and the pink seeds can stain hands. To avoid this, cut the fruit in half and submerge the halves in a bowl of water. Keeping the fruit underwater, pull the seeds from the membrane. The seeds will fall to the bottom of the bowl as the membrane floats to the top, so you can just pick it out. Then strain over a mesh sieve to gather the seeds.

Keep cut avocado green

To prevent leftover avocado from browning, place red onion slices on the bottom of a dish and set the avocado, skin side down, on top; cover and refrigerate. Onion's sulfuric acid will stop the avocado from oxidizing, and since the onion won't touch the fruit's flesh, the flavor won't change.

Best way to stop avocado slices from browning

If you need only half an avocado, keep the rest fresh by coating the cut side with vegetable oil spray, then wrapping it tightly in plastic. This will prevent the fruit-browning oxidation that occurs when the flesh is exposed to air. The leftover avocado can be stored in the fridge for up to 3 days.

Pit cherries sans mess

Next time you have a bag of cherries to pit, try this: Place each cherry on top of an empty wine, beer, or vinegar bottle, then firmly push a chopstick through the center. The pit (along with any sticky red juice) will pop out into the bottle, ensuring your hands and counter stay clean.

Ensure pretty apple slices

You need uniform apple slices for the tart you're taking to a friend's party, but cutting out the seeds often causes the fruit to break. The save: Quarter the apples, then core them starting at the narrow blossom end instead of the stem end. Since the stem gives structure to the apple wedges, putting too much pressure on it can cause the fruit to snap in half.

Keep bananas fresh longer

To ensure that the bananas you just bought stay firm and yellow until you can finish the whole bunch, tightly wrap a piece of plastic wrap around the crown, where the pieces connect. Just be sure to reseal the plastic each time you break off a banana. The result: The fruit will keep fresh for up to 4 days longer.

Sweet pineapple guaranteed!

The pineapple you picked up looked like a gem, but some of the pieces taste totally bland. That's because pineapple ripens from the bottom (where it was connected to the plant), so the top section isn't as juicy and flavorful. To ensure every bite is equally delicious, cut off the leafy top, then set the pineapple upside down and let it sit for at least an hour before slicing. This will cause the natural sugars and juices to flow to the top of the fruit, infusing it with sweet, mouthwatering flavor.

Be "Side" Savvy

So much time is spent preparing main courses that sometimes soups and salads fall by the wayside. Read on and you'll learn how to make delicious, effortless sides that perfectly complement your main dishes.

CHICKEN SALAD

No more watery chicken salad

You love adding celery to your chicken or tuna salad, but it makes the dish watery after an hour. Next time, before mixing in the celery, sprinkle on ½ tablespoon of salt for every stalk of celery, let the pieces sit in a colander for 15 minutes, then rinse and add to the salad. The salt will extract water from the celery so your dish will be free of extra moisture.

COLESLAW

Keep coleslaw supercrisp

It never fails: An hour after you whip up a batch of coleslaw, the cabbage becomes soggy and limp. Prevent this by soaking the whole head of cabbage in ice-cold salt water (1 tablespoon of salt per 2 quarts of water) for 10 minutes. Rinse and dry, then chop as usual. The salt will help the cabbage retain water so it stays crunchy when mixed with the other ingredients.

FRIES

Perfectly crisp oven fries every time

Baked potato wedges tend to have a thick, chewy crust instead of a light, crispy one. The fix: Soak the raw, cut-up spuds in hot water for 10 minutes, then pat dry before seasoning and baking. The water will remove surface starch and sugars that hinder the development of a thin, crispy crust.

Soaking fries makes them crispy

For fluffy-inside, crispy-outside fries, soak the cut potatoes in a bowl of room-temperature water for 30 minutes, then pat dry and cook as usual. The water will remove some of the sugar from the surface of the spuds, making the exterior thin and crispy, and also permeate the starch molecules to make the interior fluffy.

POTATO DISHES

SOS for a mushy gratin

Cool weather put us in the mood for potatoes au gratin. But when we pulled the dish out of the oven, the top looked pale and tender instead of crisp. To remedy, we poured on a thin layer of cream and baked for another 20 minutes. The sugars in the cream caramelized and browned without becoming greasy.

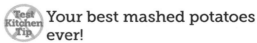 Your best mashed potatoes ever!

Here's the secret for the creamiest mashed potatoes: Melt the butter in a pan and stir it into the potatoes before adding milk or cream. When the milk is mixed in first, it binds to the potatoes' starch molecules and makes them gummy. But the fat in butter coats the starch and prevents the spuds from getting pasty. The result: a smooth, fluffy mash.

Keep baked-potato skins crisp with oil

For perfectly baked spuds, skip wrapping them in foil, which can make the skins soggy. Instead, coat them in vegetable oil, place directly on the middle oven rack, and bake at 350°F for about 1 hour. (Set a sheet pan on the rack below to catch drippings.) The oil will lock in moisture and make the skin golden and crisp.

Keep mashed potatoes hot— not soggy

Uh-oh—your roast chicken is taking more time than anticipated to cook, and your mashed potatoes are already done. To ensure that the spuds stay hot and fluffy, lay a kitchen towel over the pot, then cover with the lid. The closed top will keep warm air in and the towel will absorb any condensation that forms inside, preventing the potatoes from getting soggy.

Test Kitchen Tip Creamy mashed potatoes— without the fat!

Whenever you make mashed potatoes, skip the cream and cut way back on the butter. Instead, reserve the starchy cooking water that you boiled the potatoes in and mix ¾ to 1 cup of it into the mashed potatoes, along with a small pat of butter— about 2 tablespoons. The result: a comfort food favorite that's supercreamy and healthy!

Potato salad without the guilt

Grandmother's potato salad may be amazing, but the cup of mayonnaise in the recipe might make you think twice before indulging. Try lightening up the dish by using full-fat Greek yogurt instead of mayo. The slimmed-down salad tastes just as creamy, tangy, and delicious as the original, and the swap saves many calories and cuts the fat.

The secret to delicious potato salad

Does your potato salad need some zing? Add vinegar, seasonings, and herbs immediately after draining the potatoes. Hot potatoes are spongier because their cell walls are open, so they absorb flavorings more readily. Add binders like mayonnaise and chopped veggies when the spuds have cooled completely.

RICE

Keep rice water from boiling over

You put a pot of rice on to cook and turned your back for just a moment to chop some veggies—next thing you know, the pot is boiling over. Prevent a sticky, starchy mess in the future by greasing the rim of the pot before putting it on the heat. The fat will form a barrier that'll repel water, preventing it from spilling over the edge.

No more burned rice

Even on the lowest simmer, it's easy to burn the bottom of a pot of rice. Next time, shape a sheet of foil into a 1-inch-thick ring, place on your electric or gas burner, and set the pot on top. The foil "flame tamer" will diffuse the burner's heat output, keeping the rice from scorching.

10 Brilliant Uses for MILK

1 Lift tarnish from silver effortlessly
To get your silver gleaming without the use of strong chemicals, submerge it in a milk-vinegar mixture (1 tablespoon of white vinegar per every 1 cup of milk). Let soak for 15 minutes, then rinse. The combination of acetic acid (in vinegar) and fatty acids (in milk) will dissolve the silver sulfide stains to impart a like-new sheen.

2 Erase hairline cracks in fine china
Oh, no! There's a tiny crack in your favorite china tea cup. Before you look into replacing it, try this: Set the damaged drinkware in a pot and cover it with milk. Bring to a boil, then let simmer over low heat for 45 minutes. (Allow the milk to completely cool before handling the china.) As the milk bubbles, a protein called casein expands to fill in fissures and bond the china back together.

3 Quickly soothe poison ivy itch
The in-a-pinch way to treat a poison ivy rash when you don't have calamine lotion on hand: Dampen a clean cloth with whole milk and place on the affected area for 10 minutes, then rinse with warm water. Compounds in the milk will soothe irritated skin on contact, plus work to calm inflammation. This also works for poison oak and sumac.

4 Tenderize tough corn on the cob
Fresh corn on the cob is the perfect addition to your barbecue menu, but sometimes you end up with tough ears. The way to ensure every cob you cook this summer is tender and delicious: Add a splash of milk and a pinch of sugar to the cooking water. Milk's lactose will help soften the kernels, while the sugar will enhance corn's natural sweetness.

5 Get perfectly shaped drop cookies
An easy secret to drop cookies that look just as amazing as they taste: Dip your spoon into a cup of milk before scooping up the refrigerated cookie dough and dropping it onto your baking sheet. The dairy staple will create a nonstick coating that will allow that dough to slip right off the spoon and onto the sheet in smooth, round lumps. Perfection!

6 Remove ink stains from leather
Oops! You accidently "wrote" on your beautiful leather bag. To remove the mark, saturate a soft cloth in milk, then use it to blot the area. Enzymes in the milk will break down the ink (without harming the fabric) so you can just wipe off the mark with a clean rag. This will remove ink marks on a leather couch, too!

7 Soothe pizza burn in seconds

Mmm . . . pizza! Sometimes a fresh-from-the-oven pie looks and smells so fantastic that we can't wait to take a bite—and we end up scorching the roofs of our mouths. If this ever happens to you, immediately drink a small glass of cold milk (or simply swish the milk around in your mouth). The chilled liquid will soothe the burn on contact. Plus, the milk protein will coat the sore, creating a protective barrier that will help prevent further injury.

8 Add luster to plant leaves

If your greenery has started to look a tad dull, combine equal parts milk and water in a bowl, then dampen a cloth in the mixture and rub the leaves. Milk's fat and protein will restore a healthy gloss to the greens. Bonus: Watering with the leftover solution will infuse the soil with nutrients to help your plant thrive.

9 Boost the flavor of frozen fish

Frozen fish fillets can taste more like the catch of the day with the help of milk. Simply place the fish in a bowl of milk and let sit in the refrigerator until thawed. The protein-rich dairy will seep into the fillets and act as a brine, loosening the cellular bonds in the fish for a fresher flavor.

10 Guarantee Fido smells extra fresh

You love snuggling up with your furry pooch, especially after he receives his weekly bath. But sometimes odors linger on his coat, even after a good washing. To the rescue: milk. The next time you bathe your little buddy, add 1 cup to the water before putting him in the tub. Then massage the treated water into his fur and wash with shampoo as usual. The milk's enzymes will dissolve oils while neutralizing any unpleasant odors. Bonus: Milk's lactic acid will make his fur feel extra silky-smooth.

Easy fix for burned rice

You've got your nose buried in a novel when you realize you were supposed to take the rice off the stove 10 minutes ago! To salvage your side dish, remove it from the heat and place two bread slices on top of the rice, then cover the pot and let sit for 10 minutes. The spongy bread will absorb the bitter taste from the hot rice. (When serving, discard any burned rice bits stuck to the pot.) No one will be any the wiser!

SALADS AND DRESSINGS

Genius way to tote a salad

Packing a salad for lunch can be a hassle: You have to store the dressing separately or end up with soggy greens. To the rescue: a Mason jar! Start by pouring dressing on the bottom, then add sturdy vegetables like chopped cucumbers and peppers. Place the lettuce on top. When it's time to eat, shake and enjoy (or transfer the salad to a bowl if you prefer).

Hot-weather trick for crisp salad

To keep a tossed salad from wilting at your next cookout, freeze your prettiest cast-iron pot for 1 hour and use it as a serving bowl. Cast iron retains cold as well as it does heat, so the pot will keep your salad cool and crisp for up to 2 hours. Bonus: Its handles and lid make transport easy.

Genius use for leftover salad

Use your leftover and often wilted greens to make a delicious gazpacho: In a food processor or blender, pulse 2 cups of salad (including vinaigrette and croutons), 1 small onion, and 1 garlic clove until coarsely chopped. Transfer to a large bowl, stir in 2 cups of vegetable juice, and chill.

Blue cheese dressing—made healthier!

Blue cheese dressing is yummy, but it can turn a healthy salad into a fat bomb. Make it healthier by mashing 2 tablespoons of blue cheese into 2 tablespoons of white wine vinegar and drizzle it on your salad. The cheese adds the creaminess you love and packs a huge flavor punch, but with far less fat than store-bought dressing.

An even healthier vinaigrette

In an effort to up your veggie intake, you've been serving salad with dinner every day. But you'd rather not weigh down your greens with a heavy dressing. Genius idea: Try substituting brewed black, green, or white tea for one-third of the oil when you make vinaigrette. The tea will help balance the acidity of the vinegar without adding calories.

Secret to making a skinny vinaigrette

If you love homemade vinaigrettes but worry about the oil, here's a prep secret that trims calories: Combine all the ingredients in a jar, but cut the amount of oil called for in half. Next, toss in an ice cube, seal the jar, and shake vigorously for 1 minute or until the dressing comes together, then remove and discard the cube. The ice cools the oil and vinegar so they blend easier, but it doesn't melt enough to make the dressing watery. The result: thick, flavorful dressing with half the fat!

Genius use for the last of your jam

There's not enough jam left in your jar to spread on toast, but that last little bit stuck to the sides and bottom of the glass doesn't have to go to waste— you can use it to make a fruity vinaigrette. Simply add equal parts oil and vinegar to the jar, plus salad dressing seasonings like fresh herbs. Close the jar and shake well to loosen the jam and mix everything together. Enjoy on salad or as a glaze for meat. Delicious!

Healthier homemade croutons

You love the crunch that croutons add to salads . . . if only the bread didn't end up so greasy. For light, crisp results every time, coat the cubes in lightly beaten egg whites instead of oil (about two whites for a loaf of bread). The egg whites will crisp up the bread cubes without adding extra fat.

 ## Balance overly tart salad dressing

Lightening up homemade salad dressings by cutting back on the oil sometimes leaves dressing too tart. Try adding a pinch of baking soda to help tame the vinegary bite. Since baking soda is alkaline, it neutralizes the acidic sting but doesn't add any unwanted flavor.

SOUPS AND STEWS

Prevent cream-based soup from curdling

The last time you made your creamy tomato soup, the milk curdled. The fix: Stir 1 teaspoon of baking soda into the tomato base before adding the dairy. The soda will neutralize the acid that causes curdling. (This also works when mixing milk with other acidic ingredients like lemon juice and wine.)

Skim fat off soup in seconds

When you make chicken soup, you don't need to wait for it to cool in order to skim off the grease. Instead, use this trick: Drop several ice cubes into the pot of hot soup. The fat will cling to the frozen cubes, making it easier and faster to skim off with a ladle.

Easily remove fat from stew

If you want to skim the fat off the top of your soup or stew but don't have time to wait for the dish to cool, try this trick: Place a large leaf of tender lettuce, such as romaine, on top of the stew for 30 seconds or until the leaf wilts. Carefully remove and repeat with a fresh leaf if necessary. The leaf will soak up any surface fat so you can enjoy your soup in no time.

Lump-free way to thicken soups

Next time you need to add body to soup, reach for instant potato flakes. Simply stir them into the pot, 1 teaspoon at a time, until the soup reaches the desired consistency. The starchy flakes will plump up and thicken the broth without creating lumps.

Help for a too-thin stew

Grandma's chicken-and-dumplings recipe may be a hit, but the sauce sometimes turns out a bit too soupy. So instead of stirring in flour or cornstarch, which can result in a clumpy mess, add instant potato flakes 1 tablespoon at a time. The flakes quickly absorb the excess liquid as they dissolve into the broth to deliver a thickened, silky texture that's just right.

Fix oversalted stew with this

It's easy to overpour the salt when making soups and stews. As soon as you realize the mistake, toss a few raw, peeled potato quarters into the pot. The potatoes' spongy texture will absorb the excess salt. Remove the potatoes before serving and your recipe will turn out just as delicious as always!

STUFFING

Test Kitchen Tip: Crisp up soggy stuffing

Did your favorite side dish turn out too wet and mushy to serve? Spread the stuffing on a baking sheet and top with a layer of cubed stale bread, unseasoned stuffing cubes, or unseasoned croutons, then put it back in the oven for 15 minutes. The bread will pull the extra moisture from the stuffing and add a contrasting crispy texture as it toasts. Then just stir the mixture, scoop it into a serving dish, and enjoy.

Dry out stuffing before serving

Stuffing cooked inside the turkey has lots of rich flavor, but it may come out dense and heavy. Get the best of both worlds—flavor and crispiness—by removing the cooked stuffing from the turkey, spreading it out on a baking sheet, and baking it uncovered at 375°F for 15 minutes. The stuffing browns and forms a deliciously crunchy crust so everyone gets to share the crunchy topping.

Herb and Spice Advice

It's amazing what a difference a little pinch of rosemary makes in a recipe and how flavorful dill can be. The key to perfect herbs and spices is proper storage and preparation. Refer to these quick tips to ensure your herbs liven up every meal.

Double the life of fresh herbs

You picked an armful of fresh basil from your garden for a pasta salad recipe and used only half the leaves. To keep the rest fresh all week, wrap the bunch in a damp paper towel and store in an unsealed plastic bag in the refrigerator. This method provides just the right level of moisture to keep the herb green, perky, and tasting like it was just picked.

Tip for storing fresh herbs

After making your Super Bowl herb dip, you have handfuls of leftover thyme and rosemary. To preserve them all winter, chop the leaves and add 1 tablespoon to each well of an ice cube tray, then fill the wells with olive oil and freeze. Later, when you need to roast vegetables or season a chicken, you can heat up one of the cubes and use the flavorful oil.

Easy way to preserve summer herbs

If your garden is overflowing with herbs, try chopping and stirring some into softened butter. Use parchment paper to roll the herbed butter into a log, wrap it in plastic, and freeze for up to 3 months. The butterfat will preserve the herbs' fresh flavor, so cut off a slice and enjoy on steak, fish, or bread when you want a taste of summer.

Spices to go!

You love cooking on vacation, but you never know what spices will be available at rental houses. Instead of purchasing a whole set of seasonings, use a daily pill case to store and carry small amounts of your favorite herbs and spices. Each compartment holds about 1 tablespoon of ingredients.

Mince herbs in a flash

Your favorite knife has dulled and turns your fresh herbs into mush. To get a clean chop, put the herbs in a glass, then use kitchen shears to snip them until minced. The glass will keep the herbs contained so they're easy to cut up, while sharp scissor blades will chop the leaves without bruising them.

Neater way to chop herbs

You love flavoring salads and grilled meats with fresh herbs from your garden. But chopping rosemary, thyme, and other small-leaved seasonings can be a pain because the pieces fly around the cutting board as you work. The fix: Tuck smaller herbs into a basil leaf, then roll tightly and slice. All your herbs will stay in one place and get neatly chopped together.

Bring out the flavor of dried herbs

Sure, it's convenient to sprinkle dried herbs into a soup or stew when you don't have fresh on hand, but you barely notice their flavors in the final dish. Next time, try sautéing the herbs in a teaspoon or two of oil before using them in a recipe. The direct heat will release their fragrant essential oils, making their flavors more pronounced.

Drink Delights

Nothing says celebration like a glass of champagne! Drinks, both alcoholic and nonalcoholic, are delightful parts of any meal. Keep reading to learn how to create the smoothest hot chocolate, the tastiest margaritas, and many more favorites.

DRINKS FOR EVERYONE

Add *this* for silky-smooth hot chocolate

If your homemade hot chocolate starts to separate and form a dark skin, stir a bit of cornstarch (about ½ teaspoon per serving) into the mixture as it cooks. The starch is an emulsifier, which will keep the chocolate's cocoa butter from separating and rising (the culprit behind the dark skin). It'll also thicken the hot chocolate into an extra-velvety treat.

Brew tastier iced coffee

The secret: cold brewing. Just mix 4 parts cold water and 1 part coffee grounds in an airtight container. Let sit overnight, then strain. Cold brewing preserves 90 percent of the coffee's flavor compounds, resulting in an extrastrong sip that will stay fresh in the fridge for a week. Dilute with water or milk and serve over ice.

Crystal-clear iced tea every time

After brewing and chilling a pitcher of iced tea, you notice the drink looks unappealingly cloudy instead of clear. Next time, let the tea cool to room temperature before storing it in the fridge. The reason: Cooling tea too fast causes its tannins to separate, resulting in a hazy appearance.

Prevent soda from fizzing over

When you're hosting a barbecue or a birthday party, pouring soda for a crowd can be tricky: The ice-filled glasses often fizz and overflow all over the table. Next time, place the ice cubes in a colander and rinse under cold water for a few seconds before adding them to the glasses. The water will smooth out the ice's surface, causing less friction and fewer bubbles, so you can pour multiple drinks at once without worry.

Quick tip for crystal-clear ice cubes

Freezing plastic spiders, gummy worms, and candy corn inside ice cubes is a great festive touch for a Halloween party. To ensure your ice freezes perfectly clear so the decorations are fully visible, simply boil the water before pouring it into the trays. Boiling will help remove the air bubbles that make ice appear opaque.

DRINKS WITH ALCOHOL

Keep champagne fizzy twice as long

Pouring champagne into a flute can result in a thick head of foam, which quickly kills the bubbles. To preserve the fizz, hold the glass at an angle and gently pour the champagne down the side of the flute (like you'd pour beer). This trick will prevent twice as much carbon dioxide from being released, so it won't create the layer of foam.

Make your tastiest margaritas ever

For the most memorable girls'-night cocktail, soak lime zest in the fresh lime juice for a few hours, then strain and add to the other ingredients. As it sits, the zest will infuse the juice with its flavorful oils, delivering a margarita with a real kick.

Serve mulled wine without stray spices

Your signature mulled wine is a hit every Christmas. The only downside: finding a stray clove in your (or a guest's) cup. This year, insert the cloves into pieces of fruit before adding them to the pot. This will keep the spices contained so your ladle won't pick them up when you're ready to serve.

Make leftover wine last longer

Next time you have half a bottle of wine left over, pour the remainder into a smaller jar or bottle that's just large enough to hold the liquid and seal tightly. This will reduce the headspace so there's less exposure to oxygen, keeping the wine fresh tasting for a few more days.

No more wine drips!

You'd like to use your best white tablecloth for Easter dinner, but the thought of red wine dripping from your decanter gives you pause. Prevent hard-to-remove stains by rubbing a piece of waxed paper around the rim of the decanter. The wax will transfer to the glass surface, where it will repel wine droplets and stop them from dripping.

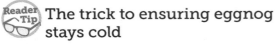

The trick to ensuring eggnog stays cold

"Instead of keeping my eggnog cold with ice cubes, which end up melting and diluting the drink's flavor, I make a larger batch of the nog and freeze some in a plastic container. Right before serving, I place the frozen nog in a punch bowl and pour the rest over the top. The giant 'ice cube' keeps the drink chilled and flavorful all night long."

—*Julianne Rice, Boston, MA*

Decadent Desserts

Everyone loves dessert! From birthday cakes to Christmas cookies, dessert is a fundamental part of entertaining. Discover helpful hints for baking scrumptious desserts to please everyone.

BAKING TIPS

Quick save for dried-out vanilla beans

You discovered a vanilla bean you'd forgotten about in your pantry, but it's become hard and brittle. The fix: Cut it in half crosswise, put it in a bowl with enough milk or cream to cover, and microwave for 1 minute. This will soften the bean so it's easier to split and scrape out the seeds. Add the vanilla-flavored milk to coffee or use it to make whipped cream.

Stop batter splatters

Tired of the mess that comes with mixing batters? Try this: Grab a paper plate and use a skewer to poke two holes that are the same distance apart as the beaters of your mixer. Stick the beaters through the holes before attaching them to the appliance. The plate will act as a shield, catching any wayward batter as you mix.

Clean a gluey pastry brush effortlessly

Even though you wash it after each use, your pastry brush is starting to feel sticky. The fix: Soak the bristles in white vinegar for at least 2 hours, then rinse. The acid in the vinegar will dissolve the residual oil and sugar responsible for the gluey coating.

The trick to measuring sticky ingredients

Whenever a recipe calls for honey or molasses, it seems that more gets left behind in the measuring cup than actually gets into the mixing bowl. The fix: Fill the measuring cup with the hottest tap water, then dump it out before adding the sticky food. The residual heat and moisture in the cup will help the ingredient slide right out.

Easily separate eggs

If the idea of painstakingly separating a half dozen eggs is giving you second thoughts about trying that cake or soufflé recipe, use this technique: Crack each egg into a bowl and gently pour them one by one into a small funnel set over another bowl. The egg white will fall right through, while the yolk will stay in the funnel.

BISCUITS AND PASTRIES

Perfectly puffed pastry

Frozen puff pastry is a great time-saver when making appetizers: Just cut into squares, bake, and add toppings. But the squares often turn out uneven, with some parts puffing while the rest stay flat. The easy fix: Use a pizza wheel to slice the dough. The tool's thin blade will make a cleaner cut than a knife, ensuring pastry that's as lovely as it is delicious!

Bakery trick for the sweetest scones

Our last batch of scones left a bitter taste in our mouths. The culprit: baking powder, which often contains harsh-flavored aluminum. Now we use a DIY leaven of two parts cream of tartar and one part baking soda, a combo that preserves treats' sweet flavor.

Never waste buttermilk again

After making biscuits, you're left with nearly a quart of buttermilk. To save it, pour ½-cup portions into disposable cups, then place them on a tray and freeze until solid. Once frozen, toss the cups into a zipper-lock freezer bag. Next time you need buttermilk, thaw the cups in the refrigerator and use as you normally would.

CAKES AND CUPCAKES

The secret technique for a level cake

We wanted to make a graveyard cake for our Halloween party, but domed, hard-to-frost cake layers kept foiling our plans. Then our baker friend told us to use fridge-cold eggs, which (when beaten) produce smaller air bubbles that decrease the cake's rise.

Perfectly portion a large cake

You'd like to serve that gourmet cheesecake at tonight's get-together, but how to divide the oversize confection without creating giant portions? Just cut a cylinder from the center of the cake (using a small pot lid as a guide), then cut the outside ring into wedges. When the outer slices are gone, you'll be left with a smaller cake to serve for seconds.

Ensure a crack-free cheesecake

To keep your confection from cracking, run a knife around its edge as soon as it comes out of the oven. This will allow the sides to pull away freely from the pan as the cake cools and contracts, leaving the center intact.

The secret to supermoist pound cake

Have you ever waited until the tester comes out clean but found your cake turned out dry? When testing pound cakes, insert the skewer halfway between the center and edge of the pan instead of directly in the middle. Because the center of a pound cake is more moist than the rest of the loaf, it may appear to need more time when it's actually just right. The cake will firm up to the perfect texture as it cools.

Easily tote a dozen cupcakes

How to transport frosted cupcakes to a Valentine's Day party without making a mess? Use a knife or scissors to score Xs into the top of a shirt box, then nestle the cupcakes in the openings. The cardboard flaps will securely hold the cupcakes, ensuring they remain upright.

Easier cream-filled cupcakes

Everyone loves the surprise of biting into a cupcake and discovering a creamy center. But the treats are tricky to make, since it's hard to add the right amount of filling with the traditional pipe-and-squeeze method. Instead, use a melon baller to scoop a hole in each cupcake, then add cream and cover with the scooped-out piece of cake. You'll have uniform holes and perfectly filled cupcakes!

Neater way to cut brownies

Ooey-gooey brownies often look like sloppy squares when you try to cut them. Try this baker's secret: Use a plastic knife. The treat doesn't stick to plastic like it does to metal, so the utensil glides through without causing clumping or crumbling. Your brownies will look as fabulous as they taste!

Save cupcakes from candle wax

The secret to birthday cupcakes that aren't marred by wax drips: Insert each candle into a mini marshmallow, then place on top of the frosting. This technique ensures any melting wax will end up on the marshmallows, which you can then toss. Plus, the little white puffs add a fun, festive look to the confections.

CHOCOLATE TREATS

Perfect chocolate-covered strawberries

If you've made homemade chocolate-dipped strawberries, you may have had the experience of seeing the chocolate slide right off the berries before it could set. The tiny droplets of water on berries can prevent chocolate from adhering to them. To make sure your strawberries are completely free of moisture, try gently blowing them with a hair dryer set on cool before dipping them in melted chocolate.

Melt just a little chocolate

The cookies you made for your sweetie would be even more special with a message written on them in chocolate, but it's a hassle to melt and transfer such a small amount to a piping bag. Instead, place the chocolate pieces in a plastic pastry or zipper-lock bag, seal tightly, and submerge in hot water for 5 minutes, or until the chocolate is soft. Knead the outside of the bag until all the chocolate has melted, then snip the bottom and use to drizzle, decorate, or write.

SOS for clumpy, overheated chocolate

If you've left chocolate melting in the double boiler too long, it may turn clumpy and thick. You'll need to cool it down fast. Immediately turn off the heat; add a few extra pieces of solid, unmelted chocolate; and stir until smooth. This way, the chocolate cools slowly, preventing it from seizing. Pass through a sieve to remove any remaining clumps.

Mess-free chocolate chopping

Chopping chocolate can create a mess of shards all over your cutting board and counter. Make the job neater by warming the chocolate bar in the microwave just until the sides begin to melt (about 1 minute) before chopping. Softened chocolate stays intact better than a room-temperature bar does, so it won't break into tiny pieces as you chop it.

COKIES

 ### Ship baked treats safely every time

Worried your delicate sugar cookies will arrive as a pile of crumbs when you ship them? Check out this easy packing trick: Place the cookies in a zipper-lock bag, tuck it in a box, and surround it with unbuttered, unsalted popcorn. The padding will keep the treats from crumbling.

Pretty cookies in a pinch

A simple way to make cookies look extra special when you don't have decorating tools on hand: Before baking, press down on each cookie with the bottom of a crystal glass to imprint the design from the glass onto the dough. This works best on cookies that don't spread, such as shortbread.

Keep cookie logs round

Freezing cookie dough in slice-and-bake rolls is a great stress-saver during the holidays—but one side of the roll always goes flat in the freezer, resulting in oddly shaped treats. The save: Wrap each log of dough with plastic wrap, then slice an empty paper-towel tube lengthwise and tuck the log inside. The tube will keep the dough perfectly round, ensuring all your cookies turn out beautiful.

 ### Fuss-free cutout cookies

In a hurry with no time to chill your sugar-cookie dough? Trying rolling and cutting out the dough directly on the baking sheet, leaving 1 inch of space between each cookie. Then just peel away the scraps and slide the sheet into the oven. Since you'll barely have to handle the warm dough, the cookies will hold up beautifully.

Prevent cookies from spreading too much

Your aunt finally gave you the recipe for her chocolate chip cookies. But while the taste is spot-on, the treats spread too much in the oven and come out thin and crispy instead of thick and chewy. Next time, sprinkle a bit of flour on the greased baking sheets, which will make them less slick so the cookies won't spread as easily.

Smooth curling parchment paper— without a fight

To prevent parchment paper from rolling up at the corners when you're placing cookie or biscuit dough on a baking sheet, put a small refrigerator magnet on each corner of the pan. The magnets will hold down the paper, making it easy to evenly space the dough. Just remove the magnets before placing the baking sheet in the oven.

DESSERT BREADS

Outsmart bluish walnut bread

Your book-club pals are calling for your banana-walnut bread, but you don't like the way the nuts tint the bread blue. An easy fix: Roast the nuts in a 325°F oven for 10 minutes, or until dark brown, then let cool for 5 minutes before adding to the batter. Roasting causes a chemical change in the nuts that will keep your bread from turning blue.

Guarantee even distribution of raisins in baked goods

When you make soda bread for St. Patrick's Day, do all the raisins sink to the bottom of the loaf? Toss them with some flour from the recipe before stirring them in. This gives the raisins more lift so they stay evenly distributed throughout the treat.

Chop candied ginger sans stickiness

You love the spicy flavor candied ginger adds to banana bread, but chopping the stuff into even slices can be sticky situation. Not so when you nix the knife for a clean garlic press. Simply squeeze the handle for neat, even slivers.

Clever way to speed the rise time of yeasty baked goods

Mmm . . . whether it's waffles or cinnamon buns or bread that you're baking, yeast-based baked goods hit the spot on a cold day! Trouble is, a cold kitchen can slow yeast down. To spur the little guys into activity, try an electric heating pad. Just set it to high, lay a towel over it, and place your bread pan or bowl on top. You'll have fully risen, oven-ready dough in no time.

Your best gingerbread ever!

For the most flavorful gingerbread or spice cake, sauté the spices (like cinnamon, ginger, and cloves) in 1 tablespoon of butter for 1 minute, then add the spiced butter to your cake batter along with the eggs. (Reduce the oil, butter, or shortening in your recipe by 1 tablespoon.) "Blooming" the spices will release their essential oils, and the butterfat will carry their flavor throughout the batter to guarantee a delicious dessert.

FROSTING

 ### Fluffy frosting—with half the fat!

Do you love heavily frosted cakes and cupcakes? No need to give up these goodies! Instead of making frosting with butter, use marshmallow cream—it's fat-free! Sub in the cream for half the butter in the recipe and, since the cream adds sweetness, cut the sugar by about one-sixth. Here's a quick-and-easy frosting recipe: Beat $\frac{1}{2}$ cup of butter, $2\frac{1}{2}$ cups of marshmallow cream, $2\frac{1}{2}$ cups of powdered sugar, and a splash each of vanilla extract and milk until creamy.

Sweet way to frost cupcakes

While icing cupcakes for a birthday, you find that the soft frosting tends to slump down or slide off. For a perfect swirled topping, place a marshmallow on top of each cupcake, then pipe on the icing. The marshmallows provide structure so the icing won't slump, and kids love their sweet flavor. Bonus: You'll need to make only half as much frosting!

 ### Easily transfer frosting to a piping bag

Filling a piping bag with homemade frosting is a messy job—you never seem to have enough hands to hold the bag, spoon in the icing, and ward off squirts and spills. Luckily, a pastry-chef friend tells all: Place the bag upright in a tall drinking glass and fold the edges over the sides, then use a rubber spatula to transfer the frosting into the bag. The glass holds the bag firmly in place, plus makes a great resting place for it while you're decorating cookies or a cake.

 ### The easy way to keep crumbs out of cake frosting

Drop tablespoon-size dollops of frosting onto the cake about 2 inches apart and spread from one dollop to another until the cake is covered. Because you won't have to drag your knife over the entire cake, you'll be able to avoid picking up crumbs.

Silky-smooth frosting in a flash

If cake frosting looks stiff, lackluster, and dull, run a blow-dryer a few inches from the surface of the cake for about 10 seconds, or until the frosting slightly melts. Once it dries, the cake will take on a shiny, polished look with a satiny texture.

FRUIT COBBLERS AND CRUMBLES

 ### Preserve rhubarb's bright color

Raw stalks of rhubarb are a beautiful vivid pink, but sometimes rhubarb cobblers and jams turn out muddy brown. Try using a nonreactive glass, stainless steel, or enameled pan whenever you cook or bake with the fruit. As with tomatoes, rhubarb's acidity combined with reactive metal pans like aluminum, copper, or cast iron causes the fruit to turn brown.

Key to a crispy cobbler top

So much fresh fruit, so little time! That's why quick-and-easy cobbler is such a great choice. The hitch: More often than not, the fruit juices end up making the topping soggy. To prevent this from happening, par-bake the topping and your fruit separately. Simply bake the topping until lightly browned and the fruit until it releases juices. Then combine the two and continue to bake until the topping is browned and the fruit is bubbling. Perfect!

Your best fruit crumble ever!

You love to make crisps and crumbles with all the ripe, juicy fruit at the market, but sometimes peaches and berries can release too much juice, leaving the crumb topping soggy. Here's a 15-minute fix: Spread the crumb topping on a parchment paper–lined baking sheet and cook it in a 325°F oven for about 15 minutes before sprinkling it over the fruit. Prebaking the crumb topping ensures it will stay crisp when the fruit's juices bubble up the sides of the baking dish.

Make your flakiest shortcakes ever!

Your berry dessert came out heavy and dense. Next time, roll out the biscuit dough into a ¾-inch-thick rectangle, sprinkle with flour, and fold into three sections (as if folding a letter). Roll out and repeat twice. Then cut and bake the biscuits as usual. This technique for making croissants and puff pastry, called lamination, creates many layers of dough and butter to encourage flakiness.

Quickly cool down a piping-hot pan

You'd like to bring your straight-from-the-oven apple crisp to your friend's potluck dinner, but the pan is too hot for anyone to hold during transport. To cool it down faster, place ice packs underneath a wire rack and rest the dish on top while you get ready to go. The ice will chill the bottom of the pan, making it easier to carry.

ICE CREAM

No more ice cream cone drips!

To prevent chocolate-stained T-shirts, place a miniature marshmallow or two in the bottom of each cone before filling with ice cream. The marshmallows will form a barrier that stops melting ice cream from leaking out.

Cut through ice cream cake with ease!

Your gang can't wait for you to serve the ice cream cake, but it's too frozen to slice. The simple fix: Run your knife under hot water. This will warm the blade just enough so it slides right through the cake. If you're cutting the cake while outside, bring out a pitcher of hot water so you can dip the blade between slices.

Serving ice cream to a bunch of kids? Try this!

Instead of dishing out ice cream as children are hovering about, anxiously awaiting a scoop, prep your servings before the gang arrives. Simply place cupcake liners in a muffin pan, add a scoop of ice cream to each, and pop the pan in the freezer. When it's time for dessert, just set out the pan and guests can quickly grab their own ice cream cups.

Unstick a stubborn ice cream cake

Having trouble getting your ice cream cake out of the pan? Run a blow-dryer set on cool about 1 inch away from the surface of the pan for 30 seconds, then try inverting the cake again. The cool air will slightly melt the surface of the ice cream so it releases easily.

10 Brilliant Uses
for POTATOES

1 Ensure a floral bouquet holds up perfectly

For an arrangement that looks like it came straight from the florist, enlist the help of a raw potato. Simply cut the spud in half crosswise, then set the flat side of one half in the bottom of a vase. Using a barbecue skewer, carefully poke several holes in the potato and tuck a flower stem into each hole. The potato, then securely hold the stems in place. Bonus: The complex sugars in the spud will provide nutrients that can keep the flowers thriving for up to 5 days longer.

2 Quickly erase food stains from skin

Beets, cherries, blackberries . . . yum! But the stains that highly pigmented foods like these leave on your hands can be tough to remove. To the rescue: a raw potato. Just rub the flesh on the discolored areas for 1 minute, or until the stain dissipates, then rinse with cool water. The vegetable contains a lightening enzyme that gently breaks down the color pigments so your hands will be spotless in no time.

3 Lift muddy footprints from carpet

A simple fix for tracked-in slush and mud stains on your carpet: Let the stains dry, then brush away as much dirt as you can. Next, rub the cut side of a halved raw potato on the marks.

Let dry and brush off the dirt again, then blot the area with a clean, wet cloth. Natural acids in the potato will seep into the material and break up the stain, making removal a cinch.

4 Soothe tense, achy muscles instantly

If a sore back (or neck) is slowing you down, you can feel better fast with a homemade hot compress. To make, pierce a large raw potato several times with a fork, then microwave for 2 to 3 minutes, or until hot. Wrap the spud in a clean hand towel and apply to the achy areas. The vegetable's absorbent starchy compounds will retain heat for up to 45 minutes to relieve tension and loosen tight muscles.

5 Make unsightly warts disappear

The pain-free way to remove a wart: Simply cut a raw potato into several small pieces, then rub one piece on the blemish until it's completely covered in potato juice. (Store the other pieces in a zipper-lock bag in the fridge for future use.) Let air-dry. Repeat daily for 1 week, or until the wart disappears. Compounds in the potato, such as iron, potassium, and natural acids, clear skin by dehydrating the spot (key since warts thrive in moisture) and killing the wart-causing virus.

6 Polish tarnished silverware in a pinch

When dinner guests are due in a few hours and you're out of tarnish remover to polish your silverware, let spuds save the day. Cut a potato into chunks and boil for 10 minutes. Remove the potato and let the water cool, then place your silverware in the pot and let sit for 30 minutes. Rinse the utensils with cool water and buff with a soft, dry cloth. The potato will infuse the water with natural acids that break down tarnish, leaving silverware spotless.

7 Fogproof your windshield

To dodge "defroster is too slow" frustration in the morning, cut a clean raw potato in half and rub the fleshy side over the entire inside surface of your windshield before going to bed. The spud will coat the glass with a starchy, clear film that'll repel vision-impairing condensation for 2 to 5 days.

8 Eliminate under-eye puffiness

An easy way to look bright-eyed even after a late night: Cut two slices from a raw potato and apply over your closed eyes for 10 minutes. Potatoes contain antioxidants that will seep into your skin and neutralize the histamines responsible for under-eye puffiness, instantly reducing swelling.

9 Alleviate your dog's upset stomach

To cure a case of doggy diarrhea, try feeding your pooch plain boiled potatoes (which contain stool-solidifying starches) instead of his regular food. The dose some vets advise: one large spud, peeled and sliced, three or four times a day for larger dogs, or two or three times a day for smaller dogs. (Check with your vet to get a targeted dose.) When your pup starts to feel better, gradually add dog food back into his diet.

10 Safely remove a broken lightbulb

A lightbulb that bursts while still attached to the lamp can be difficult to remove because of the jagged glass left behind. The save: Cut a raw potato in half and press the fleshy side into the broken bulb (make sure the lamp is unplugged), then turn the spud counterclockwise. The sharp pieces of glass will sink into the potato, so the bulb can twist easily and safely out of the socket.

PIES

Secret to a flaky piecrust

It's a measuring mishap every baker has made: adding too much water to the dough and winding up with a tough piecrust. The way to prevent this? Instead of using water, make a mixture of half cold vodka and half cold water. Alcohol stops the formation of gluten, which is what causes toughness, so you'll get a perfect crust even if you overpour. And since the alcohol evaporates out, it doesn't have to be an adults-only dessert.

The secret to flaky pastry in hot weather

Every good baker knows that the key to light, melt-in-your-mouth shortcake or piecrust is cutting the butter into the flour mixture without it melting. But how to do that when it's 95°F out? Try this: Freeze the stick of butter, then grate it into the flour. Since the butter was frozen when you started and grating adds little heat, it will stay cold as you mix it in.

No more sunken apple pie!

You've baked a beautiful apple pie and then . . . you cut into it and notice a big gap between the apples and the top crust. And after the first slice is served, the whole crust collapses! Here's the fix: Sauté the sliced apples in a skillet for 15 minutes, then toss with the spices, sugar, and thickener before adding to the pie shell. This allows the fruit to release some of its water and shrink down, minimizing the amount of steam in the oven, so the crust stays snug against the fruit filling.

Your best pumpkin pie

To prevent that extramoist pumpkin filling from making your piecrust soggy, sprinkle ¾ cup of ground gingersnap cookies into the unbaked pie shell before adding the filling. The cookie crumbs will absorb any excess water, ensuring your crust stays perfectly crisp—and the ginger spice will add a bit of extra flavor to your pie.

Fuss-free way to keep a piecrust from burning

Instead of cutting strips of foil to protect your piecrust, snip the center out of a disposable foil pie plate and place the remaining ring upside down over the pie before baking. The lightweight, reusable foil will cover the crust without crushing it.

Prevent piecrust leaks

After blind baking the crust for your pecan pie, you notice a small crack in the pastry. To keep the pie filling from seeping through, brush a beaten egg white on the cracked area and put the crust back in the oven for 5 minutes. The egg white will harden, creating a barrier that will prevent the filling from leaking out and making the crust soggy.

The key to crumb crusts that won't crumble

The gang flips for your ice cream pie, but your cookie-crumble crust always comes undone when you slice it. The fix: Use ice cream (instead of butter) to bind the crumbs. Melt 2 tablespoons of ice cream in the microwave, combine with 2 cups of crumbs, and press into the pie plate. Freeze until set, then fill.

WHIPPED CREAM

Double the life of whipped cream

To assemble dessert in advance without fear of "weeping" cream, dissolve 1 teaspoon of gelatin in

2 tablespoons of water and drizzle it into the cream, then whip as usual. Thanks to the stabilizing proteins in the gelatin, your confection will stay fresh for an extra day.

Test Kitchen Tip: Top treats with this for a calorie-burning boost

If you love adding a dollop of homemade whipped cream to desserts, you know that it's heavy on empty calories. So for a healthier indulgence, whip up fresh coconut cream. Simply chill a can of coconut milk in the fridge overnight, then remove the solid cream from the top—the liquid can be saved for use in other recipes, like piña coladas. Next, whip the cream with a hand mixer, adding sugar to taste. The result: a delicious, dairy-free topping that's lower in calories and completely free of cholesterol, plus rich in the trace mineral manganese and healthy fats that have been proven to speed metabolism.

Whip up just a little bit of cream

Mmm . . . a dollop of fresh whipped cream would take your slice of cherry pie over the top. But it's hard to whip such a tiny amount of cream with a hand mixer. Try using your blender instead. Since the blades are at the bottom of the blender jar, they'll easily reach the shallow layer of cream, forming peaks in a minute or two.

Test Kitchen Tip: Smart use for leftover whipped cream

If you have leftover homemade whipped cream, pipe or spoon the remainder onto a parchment paper–lined baking sheet and freeze for 1 hour, or until hardened. Transfer the frozen pieces to a zipper-lock bag and store in the freezer to use later in hot chocolate or coffee drinks.

Dip, Spread, and Sauce Solutions

What are chips without salsa? Mashed potatoes without gravy? Here, you'll find handy tips on how to make brilliant spreads, dips, and sauces that perfectly complement your meals.

BUTTER

Easy save for melted butter

You forgot to set out butter to soften for your cookie recipe, so you microwaved it—but now it's a soupy mess! The fix: Put the butter in a bowl with two ice cubes and stir until the butter starts to solidify (which takes less than a minute). Remove the ice and use the butter as usual. The ice will chill the dairy staple, reversing the melting process. And don't worry about any water that gets mixed in—it won't affect your recipe.

Secret to softening cold butter quickly

You started to make a batch of cookies, then realized the butter is still in the fridge and will be too hard to cream. Instead of microwaving it (which can cause the butter to oversoften), fill a bowl with hot water and let sit for 2 minutes. Pour out the water, dry thoroughly, then cream the butter and sugar in the warm bowl.

Create your own spreadable butter

Hate how bread crumbles under cold butter? Instead of buying a tub of margarine, just use an electric mixer to beat 1 stick of butter, ⅓ cup of canola oil, and salt to taste. The mixture will stay soft and fresh in the fridge for up to a month. Bonus: Unlike many store-bought spreads, this butter blend is free of artificial trans fats!

The fastest way to soften butter

You were all ready to bake your cranberry cake, only to find that your butter is too hard. Instead of using the microwave, grate the butter into a bowl using the large holes of a box grater. The small pieces will soften within minutes, so you can get baking.

GRAVY

Quick fix for burned gravy

Oops! The gravy sat on the stove a bit too long, and it burned. The save: Pour it into a different pan (leaving behind any burned stuff that's stuck to the sides of the pan), then whisk a teaspoon at a time of creamy peanut butter into the gravy until it tastes just right. Peanut butter will mask the charred flavor without making the gravy nutty. Serving to someone with a peanut allergy? Use sugar instead.

 **Your most flavorful gravy ever!**

Making pot roast with carrots and onions is a Sunday tradition. But if you don't have the time or energy to prepare a traditional gravy with the meat drippings, pour them into a blender with a few of the cooked vegetables and puree until smooth. The veggies thicken the sauce to a gravy-like consistency, plus add rich, delicious flavor to the dish.

GUACAMOLE

Outsmart watery guacamole

What's guacamole without the great taste of fresh tomatoes? The problem: Adding the red orbs ends up watering down your once-thick dip. To keep your guac thick and creamy, remove the seeds and membranes of the tomatoes you plan to use, then pat the pieces with a paper towel before chopping. Voilà—you can add the tomato pieces (and their refreshing flavor) without fear of watering down your dip.

Fresh cilantro—fast

You love the flavorful punch that a handful of cilantro adds to homemade guacamole. But plucking off the leaves one by one can be frustrating. To streamline the job, hold a bunch of herbs in one hand and use the other hand to comb the tines of a fork through the leaves. Any remaining bits of stem will be easy to locate and remove.

Make-ahead guac that stays green

Your fresh guacamole is always a hit at cookouts . . . until it starts to brown and people stop scooping. To help ensure that your guac stays green even when you prepare it in advance, simply spray the top with cooking spray. This will create an air-blocking barrier that helps prevent the dip from oxidizing and turning brown. Problem solved!

A low-cal twist on guac

Fresh guacamole with chips is a favorite snack—and avocados deliver heart-healthy mono-unsaturated fats. But 1 cup of guac has about 120 calories, and it's easy to overindulge. And when you factor in all the chips you're crunching on, the calories quickly add up. Try replacing half the avocado in your go-to recipe with grated zuc-chini. This low-cal swap doesn't change the flavor, but it does add a nice crunch, plus vitamin C to make the snack even healthier!

PEANUT BUTTER

Store natural peanut butter this way

Leave a new jar of natural peanut butter upside down in your pantry for a couple days before eating. The separated oil will naturally gravitate "up" toward the bottom of the jar, distributing itself evenly throughout. Store in the fridge once opened.

PESTO

Keep pesto bright green for days

The batch of pesto you whipped up just yesterday is already turning muddy brown in the fridge. That's because exposure to air causes the spread to oxidize. Next time, place a piece of plastic wrap directly onto the surface of the pesto to create a seal, then cover the container with an airtight lid. This trick also works great for guacamole.

Prevent pesto from browning

If your fresh pesto looks beautiful right after it's made but turns dark and muddy within minutes, plunge the basil leaves into boiling water for 30 seconds, then place them in ice water before starting the recipe. Blanching the basil inactivates the enzymes that cause the herb to oxidize and turn brown once chopped.

SALSA

Tame too-spicy salsa

If your garden overflows with tomatoes, peppers, and herbs, you probably make salsa from scratch. But the hot peppers can be superspicy. Help neutralize the heat by adding a little sugar or acid to the mix. After stirring in a spoonful of honey and an extra squirt of lime juice, your salsa will mellow and be more balanced. This trick works well for overspiced chili, curry, soup, and pasta sauce, too.

SAUCES

Save for overly simmered sauce

Thin out too-thick pasta sauce without sacrificing flavor by stirring in a bit of pasta cooking water. Threw out the water already? Mix $\frac{1}{4}$ teaspoon of cornstarch with 1 cup of water and microwave until hot. The starchy water will dilute the sauce and add a creamy, silky texture to the dish.

 ## Quick finesse for too-thin pasta sauce

If you don't have time to let tomato sauce simmer and reduce—and the resulting thin sauce ends up in a pool at the bottom of the serving bowl instead of on the pasta itself—toss the hot noodles in grated Parmesan cheese, then add the sauce. This helps the dish come together and adds a touch of extra flavor. Or add two or three whole lasagna noodles to the saucepan for the last 5 to 10 minutes of simmering. The noodles will absorb some of the liquid as they cook, plus release a bit of sauce-thickening starch. When it's time to eat, simply fish out the noodles with tongs.

Stainproof plastic storage containers

Every summer you freeze a big batch of sauce made from the tomatoes in your garden. But the plastic containers you used last year are still stained orange. This time, spray the insides with cooking spray before filling them with sauce, which will provide a thin barrier to protect the plastic from absorbing the food's color.

SOUR CREAM

Keep sour cream fresh

If you won't need that sour cream for a few days, store the container upside down in the fridge. This will create a vacuum seal that will inhibit the growth of bacteria, helping the cream stay fresh for an extra week. (Toss it if it smells bad or looks moldy.)

Fresh-from-the-Farm Breakfasts

Everyone knows that breakfast is the most important meal of the day, but why do people seem to slack off when it comes to morning meals? With these yummy tips and tricks, you'll never want to skip breakfast again.

BREAKFAST PASTRIES

Your best breakfast biscuits ever

If your buttermilk biscuits always crumble when you try to split them for sandwiches, try this: Roll out the dough half as thick as usual, then fold it over once. Cut out the biscuits and bake. The extra fold will ensure the biscuits split open easily when you're ready to serve.

Tender muffin tops—guaranteed

Every time you bake a batch of muffins, the top edges come out hard and crusty. The possible culprit: overgreasing the pan. When a pan is too slick, the batter slides back down as it bakes and forms a hard "lip." Next time, grease the pan only halfway up the sides. This will help the batter cling to the pan, creating tall, tender muffins.

EGGS

Add this for extracreamy omelets

When making egg dishes, skip the milk and stir in a bit of mayonnaise instead. Milk solids burn at low temperatures, causing eggs to turn brown and dry out. But mayo's emulsion of oil, egg yolks, and vinegar will produce creamier, fluffier omelets.

Transport deviled eggs without worry

You promised to bring deviled eggs to your pal's cookout, but you're afraid that by the time you arrive, they'll have made a mess in the container. Simply place each halved egg in a mini-cupcake liner and arrange in a single layer. The liners are the perfect size to hold the eggs intact.

Perfect poached eggs every time

The secret to flawless poached eggs: Use a ceramic coffee mug instead of a ramekin or custard cup to lightly float each egg into the simmering water. The handle will make it easy for you to partially submerge the mug, eliminating the need to drop the eggs from a higher distance and risk breaking the yolks.

Yummy egg-ring alternative

Every time you crack an egg into the pan to make fried eggs, the whites spread all over. You could use an egg ring, but there's no need to buy another gadget when there's a tastier solution: Place a ½-inch-thick onion- or pepper-ring slice in a skillet, then crack the egg inside the veggie ring and cook as usual. The veggie will contain the egg, preventing the whites from running. Plus, the onion adds extra flavor.

Leaner sunny-side-up eggs

A genius trick that will give you the delicious taste of pan-fried eggs with a fraction of the fat: Place a heatproof plate over a pot of boiling water, then crack an egg onto the plate and cook for 8 minutes, or until set. This method is easier than poaching an egg—and since you can serve the meal on the plate that it cooks on, there's less cleanup!

HARD-BOILED EGGS

Easy-peel hard-boiled eggs— guaranteed!

Canadians love to eat hard-boiled eggs for breakfast. To ensure your own hard-boiled eggs aren't difficult to peel, add 1 teaspoon of salt for each quart of water in the pot and cook your eggs as usual. The salt will help separate the eggs from their shells while cooking, making them a cinch to peel later on.

Peel hard-boiled eggs with ease

If you want the shells to come off without taking half the whites with them, crack the eggs on a flat surface before placing them in a bowl filled with cool water for 5 minutes. The water will seep into the cracks, loosening the eggs from their shells.

Perfect hard-cooked eggs every time

To prevent green-tinged yolks, turn off the heat after the water comes to a boil and let the eggs sit for 10 minutes. This gentle cooking process will produce firm-tender eggs and minimize the iron-sulfur reaction that causes that green tint.

PANCAKES AND WAFFLES

The secret to fluffy summer pancakes

Your crew is clamoring for blueberry pancakes, but you feel your go-to recipe is a bit too heavy to serve on a hot, humid morning. The fix: Swap out the recipe's milk or buttermilk for seltzer. The bubbles will help aerate the batter to produce a light and fluffy texture. Add the seltzer last, gently folding it in so you won't lose all that fizz.

Whip up pancakes—without the mess

Sunday morning pancakes get the gang smiling, but you could do without the batter drips that dot your stove as you transfer the batter to the pan. To messproof the meal, make the batter in a large liquid measuring cup. Thanks to the spout, you can pour the mix right into the pan. No drips!

Keep make-ahead waffles crisp

Making waffles for a crowd often results in a mixed bag of soggy and crisp specimens. Next time, lay the finished waffles on a wire rack set on a baking sheet, cover with a towel, and place in a 200°F oven while you cook the rest. Your waffles will stay hot and crunchy until it's time to eat.

QUICHE

No more soggy quiche crust!

To ensure that the crust on your quiche stays crisp, sprinkle 3 tablespoons of grated Parmesan cheese in the bottom of the empty pie shell before adding the filling. While baking, the cheese will melt and become a flavorful barrier between the moist filling and the crisp crust. Bonus: If there are any small tears in your crust, the cheese will create a "seal" to lock in the filling and guard against leaks.

Quiche that's delicious, fast, and lower in calories

Quiche is easy to make—just whip up the egg mixture, add some leftover meat or veggies, combine in a crust, and bake. To save time, you can use a premade piecrust, but it can be a bit too heavy and dense for this dish and may add unnecessary fat and calories. Try phyllo dough, which is much lighter. Coat five sheets of thawed phyllo dough with cooking spray and layer in a pie pan before filling and baking. The result is flaky and tasty.

Easy Cheese Tricks

There are plenty of cheese lovers out there, but storing and preparing cheese can be tricky. Learn how to keep cheese fresh and grate it more easily for a simple, tasty snack or your favorite cheesy recipe.

KEEP IT FRESH

Prevent cheese from drying out

Cheddar was on sale this week, so you bought a huge block. How to keep it fresh until you can use it up? Spread a bit of butter on the cut sides. This will seal in moisture so the cheese won't go dry in the fridge. (This works best with hard cheeses like Cheddar, Edam, and Gouda.)

Keep cheese fresh for twice as long

To ensure your favorite cheese stays mold-free in the fridge, store it in a sealed container with two sugar cubes. The sugar will absorb the moisture released by the cheese, inhibiting the growth of mold spores.

GRATE EASIER

Spray the grater

In terms of flavor, freshly grated mozzarella on pizza is hard to beat—if only the block of cheese didn't stick to the grater and separate into strands or crumble. The save: Lightly spray the grater with nonstick cooking spray first. The extra lubrication will allow the cheese to slide smoothly across the tool for perfect shreds.

Bag the cheese

A genius way to keep your counters clean and your fingers nick-free when grating: Place the grater and block of cheese inside a large zipper-lock bag, then grab the cheese from outside the bag and grate as usual. The cheese will go directly into the bag as you work, and the plastic will help protect your fingers from the grater's sharp edges.

Chill soft cheeses

Mmm... freshly shredded cheese like mozzarella or Gouda makes your dishes even more delicious. The only problem: When you try to grate soft cheeses, you end up with clumpy, crumbly pieces. To prevent this, place the cheese in the freezer for 15 minutes (or until slightly hardened) before you plan to use it. This will firm up the cheese so it drags through the grater holes easily, giving you long, even shreds.

Shred potatoes before cheese

You love potato gratin but could do without the impossible-to-clean cheese residue left on the box grater. Next time, set aside half a raw potato and shred the spud on the dirty grater. This will break up the cheese, making the tool easy to clean.

Bread and Pasta Pointers

Drat—stale bread again? Soggy pizza? Or cracked taco shells? Sidestep mishaps to create the perfect pizzas, tortillas, lasagnas, and more.

BREAD

Bring stale bread back to life

You're packing sandwiches for a brown-bag lunch when you realize the last few pieces of bread have gone hard. To refresh the bread in minutes, stick the slices in a dampened paper bag and place in a 325°F oven. When the bag is dry (after 3 or 4 minutes), the bread will have absorbed the moisture and regained its former softness.

Stale bread? Whip up this

You usually make French toast or bread pudding when you have a stale loaf sitting on your counter, but it's too hot for that today! Instead, toss together an Italian panzanella salad. Simply cube the bread and mix with your favorite cheese, vinaigrette, and chopped veggies (whatever you have on hand). Let sit for 30 minutes so the bread soaks up the vinaigrette, then enjoy. Or make it a meal by adding leftover cooked chicken. Easy!

BREADED FAVORITES

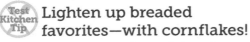 ### Lighten up breaded favorites—with cornflakes!

Breading on chicken tenders or fish sticks turns what would be a lean protein dish into a fat bomb. So instead of store-bought bread crumbs, use crushed cornflakes. Simply dip chicken or fish in egg, then dredge the fillets in cornflakes before pan-frying or baking. Since cornflakes are lower in fat and sodium and absorb less oil, you can cover the meat for a healthy allover crunch. Plus, cornflakes deliver stress-soothing B vitamins.

Keep bread-crumb topping crunchy

Your signature casserole is always a hit at potlucks. The only problem: The crunchy topping becomes soggy during transport. To prevent this, lay a dish towel on top of the pan before covering with foil. Any condensation will be absorbed by the towel instead of dripping back into the dish.

PASTA

Measure out a perfect pasta portion

Whenever you're making less than a whole box of spaghetti, it can be tricky to figure out how much to cook. Try using an empty spice jar with a 1-inch-diameter opening as a guide. The amount that fits in the jar is perfect for two. (Halve this amount when cooking for one or multiply it for a crowd.)

Extra-delicious lasagna leftovers

Your lasagna tastes terrific fresh out of the oven but turns dry when it's reheated the next day. For the tastiest leftovers, use a knife to poke holes about 2 inches apart all over the dish, then pour milk over the top (about 2 teaspoons per serving). Cover with foil and bake at 375°F until warmed through. The milk will rehydrate the lasagna from the inside out.

PIZZA

Make pizza dough behave

Homemade pizza dough tends to shrink into a ball after it's rolled out. The solution: After pressing the dough into a flat circle, place it on a large, inverted bowl until you're ready to top and bake it. Gravity will keep the edges from shrinking back so your dough will stay perfectly shaped.

Sidestep a soggy pizza crust

Using prepackaged pizza dough for deep-dish pies saves time, but the crust can end up soggy. To prevent this, we roll out the dough, brush with olive oil, and bake sans toppings for 8 to 10 minutes. Then we add sauce and cheese and bake for another 2 minutes, or until the cheese melts.

TACO SHELLS AND TORTILLAS

Easily unstick cold tortillas

Ever have tortillas that were stubbornly stuck together? Wrap the stack in a damp cloth and microwave the bundle on medium power for 20 seconds. The cloth will hold in moisture, creating steam that will gently separate the tortillas and keep them moist and delicious.

Crunchy tacos without the mess

Taco night is always a hit with your gang, young and old, but the crispy shells tend to break while you're eating, causing the toppings to spill out. Next time, serve the tacos with coffee filters. Guests can simply tuck their shells in the filters, which are large enough to catch anything that falls out.

Keep taco fixings from falling out

Do your crispy taco shells shatter while you eat, leading to messy drips and spills as the filling tumbles out? Line each taco shell with a large lettuce leaf before filling it with the other ingredients. This way, even if the shell breaks, all the tasty fixings will stay inside the leaf.

Chapter 4

DECORATING AND ENTERTAINING WITH EASE

Everyday Accents

Every home needs a little sprucing up now and then. And don't be afraid to DIY! Keep reading for tons of expert tips and tricks to update every room of the house.

TEXTURE AND COLOR

Add instant cheer with pink gingham

According to feng shui practitioners, beds dressed in pink gingham will encourage a restful night's sleep followed by an energized morning. The reason: Pink has serene "yin energy" that relaxes and soothes, while white has invigorating "yang energy" that motivates and revitalizes. When choosing bed linens, opt for a small-scale pattern (⅛-inch checks), which provides a more streamlined effect because it resembles a textural solid color.

Gaze your way to happy!

Research shows that just looking at the color yellow boosts mood. In a study at the University of Georgia in Athens, 94 percent of people who gazed at this color for 30 seconds reported feeling "happy," "energetic," and "excited." Researchers believe the hue influences mood through learned associations to nature-related imagery like the sun and blooming flowers.

Serve up style with a variety of textures

For place settings that impress, borrow a designer mix-and-match formula: one part shine, one part matte, and one part metallic, all unified by hue and motif (such as a glazed plate, embroidered napkin, and beaded napkin ring).

PRETTY PAPER PLEASERS

Add a hint of happy with paper

Give an old chair new life with an appliquéd effect. First, remove any surface dirt with a brush, then cut pieces of paper to fit each area of the chair. Working in sections, apply a coat of clear decoupage paste and smooth on the paper. Let dry, then apply another coat on top to seal your crazy-quilt chair.

Wake up a tired dresser with patchwork

Give your old dresser a wake-up call with retro-chic floral panels. To do: Remove any surface hardware, then cut paper to fit drawer and door faces and the top surface of the bureau. Brush on a thin coat of clear decoupage paste and smooth on paper. Let dry, then seal with another coat of paste.

Make perky patterned shelves

Traditional paper-lined cabinets will get a refreshing update when tame patterns are traded for sassy scrapbook designs. To do: Measure shelves and cut pieces of scrapbook paper to fit. Using repositionable spray glue, attach the paper to the shelves. If desired, press paper lace trim onto the front of shelves to create a decorative edge.

Be creative with a "quilted" wall

Tacking up squares of scrapbook paper creates an instant accent wall that pops with color, pattern, and charm. To do: To keep the grid pattern straight, start at the top of the wall (in a corner) and use removable glue dots (available at craft stores) to tack up one square of scrapbook paper. Then add squares below it and alongside it, stepping down in a pyramid fashion, until you cover the wall or get the "quilt" to the size you desire. For a more permanent installation, instead of glue dots, coat the back of the paper with decoupage paste and apply to the wall. Then let dry overnight and top with another coat of paste.

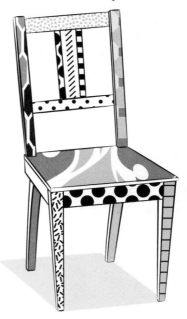

THE PERFECT GALLERY WALL— GUARANTEED!

The key to a cohesive art display: a balanced mix of frames arranged within the borders of a geometric outline. For a well-proportioned look, aim to establish equal visual weight from left to right and top to bottom. An easy trick: Cluster small frames into a grouping that will balance larger pieces.

The ideal placement for your geometric outline is above a piece of furniture or an architectural element (like a sofa or banister), which acts as an anchor to unify the room scheme. One rule of thumb: For the most balanced look, the width of the gallery should be at least half the width of the furniture. To start, use painter's tape to "draw" a rectangle or square on the wall. Then fill in the outline with frames, remove the tape, and enjoy your finished gallery.

Try a practice run with newspaper
Before hanging the frames, trace each one onto a piece of newsprint or brown paper and cut out the shapes. Then use painter's tape to affix the paper to the wall, rearranging until you pinpoint the most pleasing pattern. This helps you visualize your display before breaking out the hammer and nails.

Grab a comb to help hold nails steady
When you're ready to hang a picture, carefully place the nail between the tines of a fine-tooth plastic comb, then hammer as usual. The comb will hold the nail securely in place, ensuring your fingers stay out of harm's way.

Enlist glue dots to keep frames straight
Place a peel-and-stick glue dot (available at craft stores) on the back corners of each frame before hanging. The glue will provide traction to keep the frames from sliding and becoming crooked over time, plus act as a cushion that will guard against wall scratches.

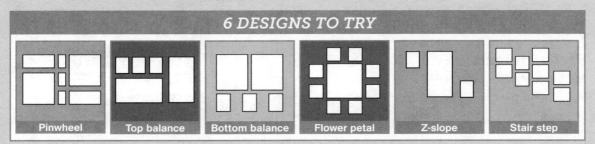

6 DESIGNS TO TRY

Pinwheel · Top balance · Bottom balance · Flower petal · Z-slope · Stair step

PHOTOS AND PICTURES

Unstick a photo from its frame
Transferring a treasured family photograph to a new frame can be tricky when the picture becomes fused to the glass. To remove it without tearing, slide the glass and photo into an open plastic bag and place in the freezer for 24 hours. The frigid temperature will freeze the moisture responsible for bonding the photo to the glass, so the picture can be peeled away unharmed.

The trick to foolproof picture-hanging
To sidestep the struggle of holding up a heavy picture frame while simultaneously marking off where the nail should go, try taping a thumbtack (pointy-side out) to the back of the frame, directly under the mounting bracket. Position the picture and press the frame into the wall to make a small indentation. Then hammer a nail through this impromptu nail marker.

Clever way to hang photos
When you're hanging pictures in your home, the last thing you need is to fuss around trying to find where you set down the nails. To ensure that you always have nails in reach, stick a magnet inside the pocket of your shirt or pants, then place a few nails on the outside of the fabric. The magnet will hold the metal pieces in place while you work so you can easily get to them.

Protect fingers from a hammer oops
You love the picture you bought for the living room but are hesitant to hang it—the last time you wielded a hammer, your fingers ended up suffering some collateral damage. This time, keep your hands safe with the help of a clothespin: Simply clip one onto the nail and hammer away. The clothespin will add a few extra inches of space between your fingers and the nail, so even if the hammer does slip, you'll be out of the "danger zone."

MAKE ANYTHING LOOK BRAND-NEW!

Paint a pretty "potted" étagère
Stack up terra-cotta pots and pine boards to create columns for a sleek étagère that showcases your home accents. Coating hard, porous materials like terra cotta or concrete with deck sealer before painting them protects surfaces and repels moisture that may cause the paint to bubble or peel. To do: Gather four 14-inch-tall terra-cotta pots and two 50-by-16-inch pine boards. Brush on one thin coat of deck sealer. Let dry. Apply one coat of white high-gloss exterior latex paint to the pots and pine boards; let dry. To create the étagère, set two overturned pots on the floor and top them with one board. Then add two upright pots and top with the other pine board.

SPRUCE UP ANY ROOM FOR LESS

Perfect for a breakfast nook: Painted shelves

Open shelves can make displays look like clutter, no matter how carefully arranged. But a bright backdrop fills in the empty space around accessories, so everything looks neatly composed. Use a mini roller to avoid brush marks.

Perfect for the kitchen: Shadow boxes

Kitchen must-haves stay attractively in reach with shallow, wall-hung boxes. But when they're stark white, the effect can be that of unfinished cabinets without doors. Outsmart that "naked" look by adding decorative stripes around each box. Use a foam brush for the straightest lines.

> A fresh coat of paint gives anything a face-lift, and it doesn't have to be a chore. Just make sure to use a tool that's tailored to the job.

Perfect for the entryway: A shutter coatrack

By adding a few screw-on hooks, louvered shutter panels create low-profile catchalls for jackets and more. Feel free to raid your garage, pick up a curbside find, or look in the hardware store's "as is" bin—a fresh coat of paint will hide any surface imperfections. Use a bristle brush to paint the area between the slats of the shutter. Hang the shutter panels on the wall and add decorative coat hooks.

Perfect for the living room: A cherry-red chair

A bright "slipcover" of spray paint turns a wicker chair into an occasional seat that won't look out of place indoors. And since the pigments used to create red paint are more finely milled than any other hue, it sticks to porous wicker best. To cover the nooks and crannies of wicker without unsightly drips, apply several light coats of spray paint.

Transform a rustic crate

Shipping boxes or crates can be refashioned into hanging cubbies with modern-country appeal, ideal for shadow-style storage and display. Sand the wood with medium-grit sandpaper, then apply one coat of spray latex primer; let dry. Then sand again, using fine-grit sandpaper. Spray on a coat or two of satin-finish white latex enamel paint; let dry. Hang crates on the wall with 2- to 3-inch-long screws.

Create a charming suitcase chest

A vintage piece of leather luggage can become a beautiful storage chest—perfect for storing folded linens. To do: Wipe the suitcase with rubbing alcohol to remove the shiny finish so the surface will absorb, rather than repel, paint. Brush on one coat of acrylic paint diluted with one part water. Then apply a coat of full-strength acrylic.

DECOR RIGHT FROM YOUR CLOSET

Showcase your shoes

Racks and shelves make a chic display case, keeping shoes in plain sight so you'll never be left searching for the pair you want to wear. To do: Select the shoes to be displayed, allowing approximately 1 linear foot of shelf space per pair.

Hang up your happy hats

Displaying hats on a wall keeps them from being crushed in closets and dresses up a room. To do: Lay out three to six hats on a bed to compose a compatible grouping. For cohesiveness, allow no more than 4 inches between hats. Next, create paper templates by tracing the bottom of each hat onto a piece of newspaper and cutting around the outline. Use masking tape to arrange the templates on a wall. Then replace the templates with the hats, using adhesive hooks to hang them.

Arrange jewelry for a vogue vignette

Browsing your jewelry collection is easy when all your favorite accessories are presented front and center in a lovely still life. To do: Select a trio of jewelry display pieces—a bust or statue for necklaces, a glass jar for bangles, and a pedestal plate for smaller items like earrings, rings, and pins. For an uncluttered vignette, limit necklaces to three and bangles to five; on the pedestal plate, aim to have 1 inch of space between items. To keep the display interesting, rotate jewelry selections every couple of months.

4 BRIGHT IDEAS FOR BANDANNAS

Sew up perky cushion covers

Bandannas are the ideal size for creating eye-catching cushion covers, which can help unify those thrift shop chairs you've collected. To make: Stitch two bandannas together on three sides, right sides facing. Next, turn the "pocket" inside out and slip in a cushion. Close with Velcro dots along the fourth side to make changing—and laundering—covers a cinch.

DIY picnic and patio caddies

Wrap juice cans in bandannas to make colorful carryalls for flatware and more. To do: Use a sewn edge for the bottom edge of the can, then fold and iron a $1/2$-inch top hem to fit the juice can. Hot glue both edges in place.

Create a patio chair "backpack"

A creative slipcover can perk up a plain chair while keeping outdoor leisure items within reach. For the slipcover, fold one bandanna over the back of the chair. Pin, then stitch the sides together. Next, fold another bandanna to create the pocket. Sew (or use iron-on hem tape) to attach the sides and bottom of the pocket to the slipcover, and add at least one vertical seam to divide the pocket into sections.

Make an instant country canopy

A clever awning made of bright bandannas creates a shaded, private nook—perfect for reading or relaxing. Start by stitching nine bandannas together in three rows of three bandannas each (or sixteen bandannas in four rows of four bandannas each for a larger awning). You may want to reinforce the corners of the awning by stitching a 2-inch square of fabric to each corner—this provides a second, stable layer that's less likely to tear; snip a small hole in the center of the 2-inch square. Or you may choose to use a grommet tool to install a reinforcing grommet rather than snipping the fabrics. Use 6-foot-high wood poles for each corner, and screw an eyehook into the top of each pole. Drive the poles into the turf, leaning them outward slightly. Attach the bandanna awning to the eye-hooks or tie it with string or ribbon.

ADD INSTANT WOW WITH MAPS

Use road maps for drink umbrellas

Ordinary beverages can be transformed into exotic sips when topped with an easy-to make drink umbrella. Set a soup can on a map, then trace around the bottom to create a circle. Cut out the circle, mark a ¼-inch-wide pie-shaped section on it, then cut out the wedge. (Optional: Use scalloped scissors or pinking shears to create a fun outer edge.) Bring the edges of the pie shape together to form a cone. Slightly overlap the edges and glue. With the tip of a scissors, make a slit in the center of the map umbrella, then slide it onto a straw.

Fashion caddies with favorite locales

Turn a tin can into a tabletop caddy, pencil holder, or upcycled vase for a stylish memento of a favorite locale. To do: Measure and cut a piece of map to fit around a recycled can. Affix the map band with hot glue. So that the can caddies wipe clean and last longer, brush a coat of decoupage paste onto the paper. Let dry and repeat for extra durability.

Record memories in a crafty travel diary

To "theme" a journal of a recent vacation, simply fold a map into a rectangle and wrap it around the middle area of the journal cover, tucking in the ends and securing with glue. To get sharp creases on the map, run a ruler or the dull side of a butter knife along the edges to "set" the fold. Then add a label to commemorate the trip.

Savvy shelf face-lift

Covering an old shelf with a map conceals scratches and wear and instantly creates a conversation piece. To do: For a custom fit on each surface, cut a length of map paper that's 1 inch larger on all sides. Then glue down the paper with decoupage medium. Trim the excess with a razor, then coat the map with more decoupage medium (to laminate it for a wipe-clean finish).

10 Brilliant Uses
for CLUB SODA

1 Perk up fading houseplants
If you have a bottle of club soda that's gone flat, set it out on the counter so it comes to room temperature, then use it to water your houseplants. The beverage contains nourishing minerals (like potassium bicarbonate, disodium phosphate, and sodium citrate) that will enrich the soil and help your potted plants flourish.

2 Get a rusty screw to turn
There's no need to waste time struggling with a screw that doesn't want to budge—simply pour club soda on it, then let it sit for 5 minutes before twisting again. The carbon dioxide that makes the beverage fizz will react with the rust and sediment buildup, bubbling it away so you can turn the hardware with ease.

3 Avoid a stuck-on-food nightmare
A hassle-free way to head off a postdinner scrubbing battle with your pots and pans: While the cookware is still warm, pour in just enough club soda to cover the bottom, then let it sit while you eat. The carbon dioxide in the beverage will soften the food particles, keeping the mess from sticking, so washing will be a breeze.

4 Whip up fluffier flapjacks
Make a wow-worthy breakfast by substituting club soda for the water or milk in your favorite pancake and waffle recipes. The soda's bubbles will aerate the batter to produce a light, fluffy stack. Bonus: You'll save 140 calories for every cup of whole milk you cut out.

5 Polish chrome sans streaks or spots
To get bathroom fixtures sparkling, trade your old cleaner for club soda. Simply pour the liquid onto a clean, soft cloth and use to wipe down the metal. The soda's carbonated molecules will fizz away grime without leaving lines or spots in its wake.

6 Erase stubborn mug stains
A daily tea fix can leave your mug with a hard-to-remove brownish tinge. The save: Fill the cup with club soda and let it sit overnight. The soda's carbonic acid will eat away the stains, leaving your cup looking like new.

7 Turn gelatin into a dazzling dessert

The next time you make this classic treat, jazz it up by swapping club soda for cold water when dissolving the powder. The bubbles caused by the carbonation will add eye-catching sparkle to the dessert, plus give it a surprising fizzy kick. Tip: Use a flavored seltzer (like lemon-lime, cherry, or vanilla) to add extra zip.

8 Make old jewelry sparkle like new

Instead of splurging on pricey jewelry cleaners to get your gems gleaming again, place dulled pieces in a cup of club soda. The fizzy beverage will safely loosen dirt and oils. And since the bubbles can seep into every hard-to-reach crack and crevice, you won't even have to scrub with a brush. Simply let them soak overnight, then gently dry them in the morning.

9 Effortlessly remove bird droppings

Hearing the birds chirping on a sunny morning is a treat. Heading out to your car and seeing their droppings on the windshield? Not so much. The easy fix: Pour club soda into a spray bottle and spritz on soiled areas. Let it sit for 1 minute, then wipe with a paper towel. The carbonation will dissolve the grime so it comes off with a single swipe. Bonus: Spritz your wiper blades to reduce streaking on rainy days.

10 Break a pet accident cycle

Even after thoroughly cleaning up your pet's accident, you can still smell traces of urine on the carpet. To neutralize the odor so there won't be a repeat occurrence, saturate the area with club soda and let sit for 5 minutes before blotting with paper towels. The soda minerals will safely deodorize the spot.

CHIC WAYS WITH CHAMPAGNE GLASSES

Dazzling crystal pedestal prisms

A champagne glass filled with clear beads does more than stylishly steady a taper—the shimmering stones reflect the flame and multiply the glow for a truly sparkling effect! To do: Hold a 6-inch taper candle in the center of the bowl, then simply fill the rest of the bowl with clear craft-store beads or gems. Success secret: If candles are toppling, secure the base of the taper to the bottom of the glass with a few drops of hot glue.

Luxe candlelit lassos

Looking for a unique and luxurious tabletop centerpiece? Combine halos of spray roses and snapdragons and twinkling candlelight in gleaming cocktail glasses. To do: Cut a piece of floral wire that's long enough to fit around the rim of the glass plus 2 inches. Thread 15 pink spray roses onto the wire and twist the wire ends together to form a circle. Then place the mini wreath onto the rim of the glass, pop in a votive candle, and add 1 inch of water. Finish by filling the space between the wreath and the candle with sprigs of refreshing white snapdragons.

Lovely layered parfaits

A simple dessert gets elevated to gourmet status when you serve it in a pretty pedestal glass—perfect for any impromptu "looks like you planned it" celebration. To do: Add spoonfuls of vanilla pudding and fresh berries to the glass, creating casual layers, then top the confection with a sprig of fresh mint. Next, set the glass on a saucer or dessert plate. For more flair, add a floral blossom or two and another sprig of mint to the base of the glass. When carrying top-heavy dessert glasses to the table, take a tip from pro servers: Simply place a paper cocktail napkin under each glass to prevent it from slipping off the tray.

CREATIVE IDEAS FOR CORKS

Make a mosaic-style mirror

A frame decorated with sentimental cork "tiles" from anniversary and birthday celebrations will inspire a smile whenever you see it. To do: Cut corks lengthwise and into $1/8$-inch-thick disks, using a razor blade or serrated knife to avoid shredding or crushing. Next, organize the disks as desired and adhere to the frame with hot glue. (To prevent your fingertips from getting burned, use tweezers to position the pieces on the frame.)

THE PURIFYING POWER OF FERNS

Another benefit: According to NASA research, ferns can remove up to 87 percent of indoor pollutants like formaldehyde and benzene from the air every 24 hours through a process called phytoremediation. So keeping a few ferns nearby will boost health and mood. Here, the best varieties for every room!

IN THE BEDROOM: Brake fern
A sneaky source of indoor air pollution is no-iron bedding, which often contains formaldehyde to prevent wrinkling. Unfortunately, this toxin can trigger headaches and sinus pain. But a study in the journal *HortScience* found that brake ferns are "excellent" performers at removing airborne formaldehyde, so you can breathe easy all night.

IN THE OFFICE: Deer fern
Disinfectants, carpeting, plastic products, and other home-office staples contain volatile organic compounds (VOCs) that can trigger headaches and brain fog. Luckily, a NASA study found that low light–requiring houseplants like deer ferns filter out VOCs to drastically improve air quality.

IN THE BATHROOM: Boston fern
Inhaling benzene (a carcinogen found in air fresheners, toilet bowl cleaners, bubble bath, and shampoos) can cause fatigue, dizziness, and eye and throat irritation. The good news: Chinese researchers named Boston ferns one of the most effective plants at removing benzene from the air—so placing one by the tub will nix these ill effects.

Surrounding yourself with greenery is an easy way to feel cooler—and ferns are an especially effective choice. That's because their fine, feathery fronds give off the maximum amount of water vapor during the day, which can lower the indoor temperature by a few degrees.

IN THE KITCHEN: Limpleaf fern
In the summer, open windows allow ozone to drift indoors. And since the throat-irritating gas is formed when UV rays combine with outdoor pollutants, levels tend to be low in the morning and high in the evening, when you're likely to be spending time in the kitchen. Setting an ozone-absorbing limpleaf fern in a kitchen window can keep the toxin at bay.

IN THE LIVING ROOM: Asparagus fern
In a study at the University of Georgia in Athens, asparagus ferns were ranked as "superior" at filtering pollutants like toluene, benzene, and trichloroethylene from the air. Placing one in the living room can remove these toxins, which are found in upholstery, paints, air fresheners, and carpets.

Try a "vintage" trivet

Heat-resistant corks make a perfect trivet. Start with an 8-inch-square cardboard base or tile. Slice corks in half lengthwise, then position and glue them around the edge. Next, slice corks into ⅛-inch-thick circles. Set them inside the border in rows, spacing evenly, then glue into place.

"Beaded" room divider

Strands of cork hung from the ceiling offer an organic take on room dividers. Start with 3 yards of twine per strand. Drive a corkscrew or drill through each cork from end to end to create a hole. Then thread twine through, using a paper clip bent into a needle shape. Knot every 2 inches and alternate corks with beads. Tack strands to the ceiling 3 inches apart.

BUT WHAT ABOUT CANDLE WAX?

The fix for caked-on wax

Removing wax from holiday candlesticks is a cinch with this trick: Pop the candleholders in the freezer for 15 minutes, or until the wax becomes brittle (you'll see little cracks), then use a butter knife to carefully lift the wax. The cool temperature will bind the wax's molecules more tightly so the residue can be chipped away in seconds.

Easily remove wax from candlesticks

After pulling out your fanciest candlesticks for the Easter table, you notice they're marred with stuck-on red wax left over from Christmas dinner. Instead of scraping it off, try this quick and easy save: Point a blow-dryer (set to low) directly at the wax-covered areas for about a minute, then gently peel the wax off. The hot air will slightly melt it, making it a cinch to remove.

Waxproof votive holders

Placing candles throughout the house puts everyone in a festive mood. But who wants to spend time scraping melted wax out of the votive cups? Avoid the hassle by misting the inside of the cups with cooking spray, then adding a few drops of water before inserting the candles. With this trick, the melted wax won't fuse to the cup and will pop out easily.

Outsmart pesky candle drips

Taper candles add a festive touch to your table—but waxy drips left on the tablecloth are a "touch" you can do without. To prevent them, fill a basin with 1 gallon of warm water and 1 cup of salt and stir to combine. Then submerge your candles in the solution for 24 hours before putting them into their holders. The salt water will create a hard but transparent outer shell on the wax's surface that melts more slowly than the candle itself, so drips become trapped within. One dip in the solution will last for the candles' lifetime.

Spring Accents and Celebrations

What's spring without flowers? Or Easter without decorated eggs? Surprise your mom (or pamper yourself) with a casual-chic gathering this Mother's Day. Here, you'll find decorating info for season-long celebrating.

SERVE UP ST. PADDY'S DAY SMILES

Enchant everyone with a sunny, spring-green setting

Though St. Patrick's Day seems like more of an occasion for raising a pint than gathering guests, it's a perfect opportunity for getting back in touch with friends. And you can create a welcoming atmosphere that counters gray skies with glimpses of green. Start by laying two green table runners across a crisp white tablecloth. Then set the table with white dishware. St. Patty's Day decor will get everyone into the party spirit.

Add flair fast with clover coasters

With a little bit of felt (which doesn't fray when cut), you can snip out a whole set of coasters in mere moments. Simply trace a clover shape onto a piece of solid green felt, then cut out.

Dress up napkins with shamrock rings

Party favors are a great, inexpensive way of showing guests that you care. Better yet, these wee shamrocks can be enjoyed now as napkin cinches and later as lucky key rings! Simply snip out a four-leaf-clover shape from felt, then pierce a corner with a hole punch and thread onto a basic key ring (available at hardware stores).

SPECIAL EASTER BRUNCHES

Surprise them with a centerpiece

A sunny collection of dyed eggs nestled in a bed of spring florals creates a lovely low-profile table arrangement. To do: Place an 8-inch soaked foam wreath on a 12-inch round platter. Cut 12 mimosas and 12 daffodils to 5 inches. Press the mimosas into the foam until covered, then insert daffodils around the top of the wreath. Fill the center of the wreath with eggs.

Create a cupcake-inspired bouquet

Silicone baking cups aren't just for cupcakes: They create diminutive containers for mini bouquets. Cut a bloom at the top of the stem and place it in the baking cup so the petals fully rest on the rim (otherwise the bouquet can topple). Add a few drops of water to keep the flowers fresh.

Cultivate charm
with a spring setting

A deceptively easy table starts with a runner snipped from a roll of birthday gift wrap. Gift wrap's perky color will brighten any tablecloth. Just cut a length to fit your table, plus 6 inches on either end to cascade over the table edges. Next, put a new spin on place settings by folding cloth napkins lengthwise, then letting the ends drape over the plates and table's edges by 3 inches. Finish the tabletop decor by topping a salad plate with craft moss and a bunny borrowed from the Easter basket.

Surprise them
with an embellished egg

For a festive favor, cut out a 2-inch floral pattern from gift wrap, then coat a painted wooden (or hollowed out) egg with decoupage paste and smooth on the design. Let dry, then seal with another coat of paste.

Effortlessly beautiful Easter eggs

You want your Easter eggs to stand out but don't have time to painstakingly decorate each one. Just cut out 6-inch-long strips of lace, tightly wrap the eggs once, and secure with a rubber band. (There should be extra lace so you can hold on to the egg.) Dye as usual, then unwrap the eggs and let dry. The dye will seep through the lace's holes, leaving a pretty pattern.

LOVELY MOTHER'S DAY LUNCH

An easy way to arrange flowers

Grab a plain white jug to lend simple country charm to your Mother's Day table. Create an artful floral display by inserting two identical flowers in the center of the jug, then letting them drop to opposite sides. Continue adding opposing pairs of blooms to form a perfectly symmetrical nosegay.

Set an enchanting scene
with French country textures

A color palette of cool hues like blue and white amplifies light, making a room feel more relaxed. The limited palette also puts the focus on casual textures like chambray, vintage tin, and rustic wood. For a low-fuss centerpiece, fill a vase with snippets of common stock flowers. To keep these top-heavy beauties from tipping out, be sure to leave two or three blooms below the rim of the vase. As with all spire-shaped stems, the lower blossoms will buttress the vase, providing invisible support.

Enchant everyone
with floral-filled flutes

A trio of lily of the valley nosegays tucked into champagne glasses clustered together makes a wonderful floral centerpiece. To do: For each glass, cut six lily of the valley stems to 8 inches. Wrap leaves around the stems and set in water-filled flutes.

Inspire smiles
with a mix of old and new

A blend of modern simplicity and heirloom accents creates an effortlessly fresh afternoon table. The key to the perfect balance is to choose one or two antique elements (like vintage salad plates) to mix but not match, and keep the rest of the setting streamlined. A limited color palette keeps mismatched pieces from looking busy, and layering on cozy-chic details (like ribbon-tied napkins and a lush rose bouquet in a simple white pitcher) completes the charming tableau.

Delight guests with a fresh-picked palette

The key to capturing the excitement of a newly sprouted garden: starting with a light and vibrant verdant-green tabletop and adding happy spots of saturated petal pink. For instance, a lime runner placed over a bright white cloth creates vibrancy. Add a polka-dot cachepot, a petite bud vase bursting with spring florals, and other objects with texture and color for seasonal flair.

Garnish place settings with a savory sprig

A napkin will get an unexpected new look with a simple pocket, perfect for holding flatware and a sprig of heavenly scented rosemary. To do: Fold the bottom of the napkin up to its center, then fold the right side under to create a neat pocket. For a no-sew trim, top with a folded band of ribbon. Tuck the napkin under the plate.

Soothe stress with lily of the valley

Simply setting a few stems of this sweet little spring flower on a tabletop will release a fragrance that will subliminally relax everyone, according to aromatherapists.

Add foliage to flatware

Bundling silverware with a knotted length of lush grass gives place settings a snippet of seasonal style. To do: Cut a handful of maiden grass to about 14 inches. Lay a fork, knife, and spoon down on the center of the grass and tie it around the handles, then knot to create the flatware cinch. To accompany the flatware wrap, tie a length of grass around a mini bouquet of buttercups in the same manner and stack them together at each place setting.

Grab some grass for your table

Coiling a handful of grass around blooms floating in a water-filled bowl adds a chic springtime touch—perfect to brighten a coffee table or end table. To do: Fill a glass bowl halfway with water. Cut a handful of lily grass or another ornamental grass and wrap the blades around your hand, then place them in the bowl and release, allowing them to expand to create a grassy halo. Finish the arrangement by cutting two peonies and setting the flowers afloat in the center of the bowl. To prevent the peony from sinking, cut a 3-inch square of bubble wrap and tuck it under the flower to buoy it up to its prettiest height.

10 Brilliant Uses for TENNIS BALLS

1 *Easily sand curves in wood surfaces*

Your wooden patio needs a presummer sprucing—a few spots are worn and splintered. But sanding curved areas (like the railing) can be tough. To do: Wrap a tennis ball in sandpaper when you're ready to work on curved sections. The ball's shape and flexible rubber will mold to bends and curves, and the tennis ball is just the right shape to fit comfortably into your hand for easy sanding.

2 *Create a magnet for gnats*

The gnats and flies that buzz around when you work outside in the garden are more than just annoying—they leave you covered with bites. To fend them off without resorting to toxic chemicals, thickly coat a tennis ball with petroleum jelly and hang it where the bugs can spot it but you can't. (Replace the ball as needed.) The bright yellow color will attract insects. When they get close, they'll get stuck in the gooey petroleum jelly. Bonus: An aphid-infested plant can be saved by hanging a petroleum jelly–covered tennis ball on or near its branches.

3 *Anchor helium-filled party balloons*

The balloons you brought to your niece's outdoor birthday party look bright and festive, but you forgot to bring weights to anchor them. The save: Cut a small X into a tennis ball with a sharp knife, then use a funnel to fill the ball halfway with sand. Tie a cluster of balloons together, then slip the knot into the X. The balloons will stay grounded, plus the tennis ball's bright yellow color will add a festive touch.

4 *Effortlessly clean a kiddie pool*

A plastic swimming pool is a pain to empty and refill, so you usually cover it with a tarp overnight and refill it only a couple times per week. But after a few days, the water develops an oily film. To clean the water without the hassle of having to empty the pool, toss in one or two tennis balls and let them float for an hour. The balls' fuzzy exteriors will sop up the film-causing body oils that build up in the pool, leaving the water pristine. (Throw out the balls after each use.)

5 *Trick your car's interior light*

Your car is desperately in need of a good vacuuming, but you don't want to drain the car battery by keeping the door open (and the interior lights activated) while you do so. The fix: Wedge a tennis ball between the open door and doorjamb. The ball will depress the light switch, so the car will think the door is shut and the lights will stay off.

6 Make your broom do double duty

For a simple way to speed up those tedious household chores, try this: Using a sharp knife, cut an X into a tennis ball and pop it over the end of your broom. As you sweep, you can use the tennis ball to clear away cobwebs in the corners of the ceiling—the webs will cling to the ball's fluffy surface. You can also turn the broom upside down and rub the ball across the floor, where the firm rubber will quickly and safely erase scuff marks left by black shoes.

7 Keep a bicycle steady on soft ground

If you're sick of your bike toppling over when the kickstand sinks into soft sand, mud, or grass, just cut a small slit in a tennis ball and insert it onto the end of the bike's kickstand. The kickstand will close as it normally does, but when the bike needs to be propped up, the ball will provide a wider base, allowing the bike to remain upright—even on the softest surfaces.

8 Quickly remove shower curtain mold

Summer humidity makes cleaning the mildew on your shower curtain liner a never-ending battle. Tennis balls to the rescue! Put the liner in your washing machine with two tennis balls and 1/2 cup of white vinegar, then wash as usual and let air-dry. The vinegar will kill the mold and mildew spores, while the friction from the bouncing balls will scrub them away. Bonus: Toss a couple tennis balls into your dryer to fluff towels and down pillows.

9 Relieve your pet's tummy troubles

Poor Fido often suffers from gas and an upset stomach after eating. Try placing a tennis ball in his dry-food bowl before he eats. The obstruction will force your pup to nose around to reach his kibble, which will slow down his eating. And that will help him swallow less air, a likely cause of his flatulence and indigestion. Just be sure the ball is bigger than your pet's mouth so he doesn't choke or accidentally swallow it.

10 Disguise valuables at the pool

You try to bring as few items as possible with you to the town pool, but some—car keys, MP3 player, cash for snacks—are mandatory. To keep your stuff safe when you take a dip, grab a tennis ball. Make a 2-inch-long slit in one seam, squeeze the sides so it gapes open, and pop your valuables inside. Your goods will be safely disguised and protected from the sun's heat. (This trick works well at the gym, too.)

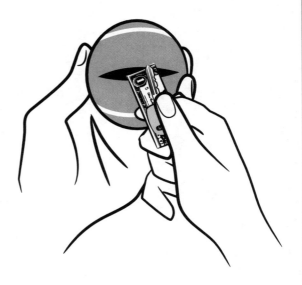

SIMPLY SWEET TEA PARTIES

Dress up drinks with butterfly straws

Silken wings fluttering above the rims of glasses give sips a garden-party flair. To do: For each butterfly straw, cut a 2-inch length of fine floral wire. Twist the wire around the body of a craft-store butterfly, then around the straw (2 to 3 inches from the top).

Fill sweet treat bags for guests

A grab-and-go sampling of cookies, cake, and a pretty posy (or two!) will continue the gal-bonding afterglow long after everyone heads home. To do: Set zipper-lock bags filled with a sampling of cookies, cake, and other goodies in pretty gift bags tied with pink craft-store raffia.

Serve up style with a do-it-yourself lace tray

A cast-off crocheted doily livens up any server! Start by tinting a plain doily with fabric dye, following the manufacturer's instructions; let dry completely. Then drape the doily over an overturned bowl covered in plastic wrap. Brush on a coat of fabric stiffener and let dry, then remove the shapely doily from the bowl. Turn the bowl over and use it to display faux fruit and flowers.

Pamper guests with an herbal tea "buffet"

Edible garnishes transform each teacup into a personalized delight. To do: Tuck tea bags into a wooden display box, then surround them with 2-inch-long herb clippings (like mint and sage) and edible flowers (like rose petals and chamomile blossoms). While the tea bags steep, let guests choose fresh flavor sprigs to add to their cups.

Setting the mood with accessories

Want the secret to creating a backyard tea party? Cover a well-shaded outdoor table with layers of all-out feminine luxury. Pair a soft white tablecloth with patchwork quilt–cloaked benches for an enchanting sitting area. Showcase pretty tabletop touches like mismatched floral china, vintage linen napkins, and fresh-picked blooms to add timeless flair. The whimsical finishing touch: flowering containers nestled around the foot of the table and other plants suspended from shepherd's crooks create a cozy garden canopy feel.

Summer Splashes and Sparklers

Summer is always sizzling—friends, family, picnics, and fun. *First for Women* loves a great party, so look to these tips to create special moments and unforgettable summer parties.

GARDEN PARTY PERFECTION

Surprise them with edible florals

A sprinkling of ready-to-eat blooms from the garden or supermarket (like daisies, pansies, or scented geraniums) turns any salad into an unexpected—and delicious—accent. To do: For the freshest blossoms, remove the stems and float the flowers in a large bowl of ice water for up to an hour before serving. Pat dry and place about a half dozen blooms on the salad.

Magical lanterns in the trees

Candles dropped into small jars make stunning glass luminaries. To do: Twist a 12-inch-long piece of 20-gauge floral wire around the rim of a 12-ounce jar to create a "collar." Place a votive into the jar and hang from a tree branch with two 30-inch-long pieces of wire attached to either side of the collar.

Make it special with sweet petal "ponds"

A tray of clear glass dishes with floating flowers creates a whimsical mini water garden to display on a dining table. To do: Cut the stems of 10 petite flowers to ¾ inch (this length keeps blossoms upright) and set afloat in 1 inch of water in small, shallow bowls.

Dress up napkins with crepe-paper cuffs

A simple wrap secures napkin rolls and creates a festive band to hold seasonal blooms. To do: Fold each napkin in half, then roll. Cut a 6-inch-long piece of crepe paper and secure around the roll with tape. Tuck in an 8-inch-long tulip or freesia stem.

Add paper lantern covers to plain vases

Remember the paper lanterns you made as a child? Here, pretty scrapbook paper helps dress up vases to create a charming lamp base. To do: For a 3-inch-wide vase, fold a piece of 8½-by-11-inch paper in half lengthwise. Cut slits ½ inch apart along the folded edge, stopping 1 inch from the open edges. Unfold the paper, roll into a cylinder, and secure with glue. Slip the paper lantern over the vase, then insert a candle in the vase.

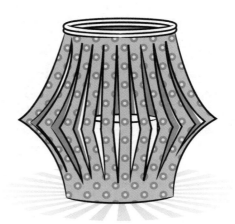

Delight them with a dessert cloche

A glass cake dome adorned with a flower-and-herb garnish instantly upgrades a plain cake—no fancy cake decorating required! To do: Twist 24-gauge craft wire into a 2-inch circle. Next, attach six 4-inch herb sprigs to the circle with a secondary 20-inch piece of wire, overlapping stems as you go. To finish, loop an 8-inch-long satin ribbon through the wreath and drape it from the knob of the cake dome.

A FESTIVE FOURTH OF JULY

Dress things up with a floral flag

Patriotic supermarket bouquets are perfect for a whimsical flag table centerpiece. Just fill a baking pan with floral foam, then alternate red and white blooms (like pom-pom mums) for stripes and use blue flowers (like yellow-centered daisies) for stars. To display upright, lean the pan against a couple of cans filled with sand.

Turn spare blankets into no-sew bolsters

When folded, rolled, and cinched with ribbon, extra throws become neck roll–style pillows that turn even the most humble patch of lawn into a comfortable lounging spot. You can also try this trick with beach towels.

Unfold a cart into an instant bar

"Have bar, will travel"—that'll be your new motto if you purchase one of the new foldable wooden carts on wheels, which are a perfect investment for Independence Day and beyond. Many import stores and bed-and-bath stores carry a variety of tall carts; normally used in kitchens, these high carts allow you to mix drinks with ease.

Keep bottles from clinking together

Sodas and mixers are a must for any bar setup, but transporting them can be a balancing act. Instead, reach for a wine rack. Simply place it on its flat side to create handy compartments that'll prevent bottles from clacking and toppling while traveling.

Spillproof cocktails with Mason jars

Screw-top jars make it so simple to whip up a batch of cocktails the day before your soiree. (And they make slips and spills a nonissue.) Before serving, give 'em a shake to refresh their flavor. This make-ahead party plan means that all you have to do on the Fourth is celebrate.

The safer way to enjoy sparklers

Children love sparklers, so you picked up a box for your Fourth of July celebration. But you're concerned that wee fingers could get burned. To keep them safe, stick the nonburnable end of each sparkler into a tub of Play-Doh, then light the other end as usual. The firm clay will securely hold the sparklers, so you can enjoy the light show worry-free.

Instant star appliqués for your table

Set the scene for a patriotic celebration with bright, no-sew embellishments that easily come off after the party's over. Simply use a large, star-shaped cookie cutter to trace the shapes on white and red construction paper or card stock. Position stars in rows across your tablecloth, adhering with double-sided tape.

Burst of cheer

Liven up your table with a centerpiece that'll have your guests seeing stars—in a good way! Start with

5-inch and 4-inch stars made from red and blue paper. Top each with a white star center that measures $\frac{1}{2}$ inch smaller on all sides and attach with glue. Using a glue gun, affix the two-toned stars to skewers. Once dry, display in a bowl filled with patriotic marbles.

Freedom rings

Spread spirit with star-spangled bands. To do: Cut a length of $1\frac{1}{2}$-inch-wide blue satin ribbon to fit around a rolled napkin. Use hot glue to attach a small 3-inch red star to the center of each ribbon. Top the star with a white button and glue to secure. Let dry, then tape or stitch the ribbon ends together to form a ring.

KICK BACK AT A BARBECUE

Inspire joy with daisy lanterns

Candle-filled jars become lovely luminaries topped with a halo of field flowers. To do: Twist a 12-inch length of floral wire around the rim of a 12-ounce jar to create a collar, then tuck 2-inch daisies, wildflower foliage, and grass cuttings into the wire. Place a tea light inside the jar and attach a 30-inch length of wire to both sides of the collar. Twist an S-hook from a 5-inch-long wire to hang.

Make it magical with milk-bottle lanterns

Slipping taper candles into vintage milk bottles creates makeshift hurricanes that add rustic appeal to an outdoor table. To do: Affix a craft-store glue dot to the bottom of a 6-inch taper candle. Press the candle base into the center of a milk bottle, then set the bottle in a small baking pan and tie a length of ribbon around the neck.

Perfume the air with daytime candles

Delightfully decorated drinking tumblers plus lavender-scented candles serve as wind-resistant lanterns that keep bugs at bay during your barbecue. To do: Drop a lavender-scented tea light in a glass tumbler, then trim the glass rim with a band of patterned washi tape (available at craft stores).

Easy end-of-season grill cleaning

You want to give your grill one last deep-cleaning but dread tackling all that burned-on food residue. Simply fire up the grill, lay a sheet of foil over the grate, and close the lid for 15 minutes. Then turn off the grill, ball up the foil, and use it to scrub away any debris. The foil will intensify the heat on the grate, reducing food particles to a fine, easy-to-remove ash.

No more "cooler hands"

You always set out a cooler filled with beverages at your outdoor gatherings—but when the ice starts to melt, everyone has to reach into freezing water to grab a drink. The easy alternative: Fill several water balloons until they're about the size of a plum and freeze, then pack the coolers with these "ice balloons" instead of ice chunks. When the party's over, you can toss the balloons back into the freezer for future use.

Fire up a charcoal grill in a flash

Everyone's ready to chow down at your backyard bash, but your husband is having trouble getting the coals to burn. The fix: Toss a few spoonfuls of sugar onto the coals and light them again. When exposed to high heat, sugar rapidly decomposes and forms hydroxymethylfurfural, a chemical that will immediately take to the flame.

Ensure all your grilling tools are handy

"During our last cookout, I forgot my tongs in the kitchen, and the steaks ended up burning while I ran in to get them. Then I thought of an easier way to keep my grilling utensils on hand: I put them all in a pocketed pot holder and use the cloth loop to hang it on my grill. Everything stays together, and I don't waste precious minutes running in and out of the house."

—Jessica Kaymen, Columbia, MO

Watermelon centerpiece

Flip the top of a watermelon to the bottom to create a pretty summer "vase." To do: Start by cutting a ¼-inch-thick slice from the bottom of the watermelon to create a level base. Then cut a 2-inch-thick slice from the top of the fruit. Place this slice flat side down on a plate and secure it to the bottom of the melon with toothpicks to create the vase foot. Next, use a large metal spoon to scoop the flesh and seeds out of the melon. Drop in a water-filled, 3-inch-wide drinking glass and insert a bouquet of summer flowers (with stems cut to about 10 inches).

Stop an outdoor tablecloth from slipping

While setting up for your alfresco dinner party, you notice your tablecloth is prone to slipping. To keep cups from tumbling, arrange whatever pieces of nonadhesive shelf liner (or rug pad) you have on hand to cover as much of the table as possible, then lay the cloth on top. The rubbery liner will provide traction, keeping everything in place.

Guarantee that a picnic blanket stays dry

After a rainy morning, the sun is shining and the kids are begging for a picnic in the park. The only problem: The ground is still a bit damp, so you know your picnic blanket will end up getting wet . . . and anyone who sits on it will probably have a damp bottom, too! The save: Lay a plastic or vinyl shower curtain liner on the ground before placing your blanket on the grass. The waterproof barrier will keep your blanket dry and clean, so you can sit back and relax.

Clean a grill with ease

When it's time to shut down the grill for the season, try a scrub-free cleaning trick: Remove the grate and place it in a thick plastic garbage bag, then pour in 3 cups of ammonia (which will break down stuck-on gunk), close the bag with a rubber band, and lay it flat in the yard for 24 hours. Before opening, don a painter's mask and rubber gloves, then grab the grate and hose it off. Done!

Get a bonfire roaring fast

Settling in around a cozy firepit is so relaxing—but getting the fire started is another story. Make the task a breeze with this trick: Scatter the remains of a bag of potato chips or corn chips over the wood, then light as usual. The greasy chip bits will ignite quickly and help keep the fire going longer than kindling alone.

Quick trick for degreasing a grill

Cooking up a batch of barbecued chicken left your grill grate a mess. To make cleanup a cinch, use a two-pronged grill fork to scrub the hot grates with a halved onion dipped in vegetable oil. (If you have a gas grill, reheat the grate as needed.) Onion juice contains alliinase, an enzyme that breaks down grime, while the onion's layers will act as abraders to help scrub away the mess. And the oil will help soften the buildup, plus add a layer of nonstick protection for easy cleanup next time.

So-cute ice bucket—from a melon!

A hollowed-out watermelon makes a wonderfully whimsical beverage cooler. To do: Using a serrated knife, cut a ¼-inch-thick slice from the bottom of a melon to create a flat base for stability. Next, cut a 3-inch-thick slice off the top of the melon, then scoop out the fruit with a large metal spoon. To finish, fill the melon three-quarters of the way with ice and gently insert bottles, using a twisting motion.

Shrivelproof carved melons

When placed in a shady spot, watermelon crafts will last up to a week. To keep yours fresh for twice as long, use a soft cloth to apply a thin coat of petroleum jelly to the inside of the hollowed-out melon and all the cut surfaces. This layer of protection will seal in moisture, keeping the rind from getting dehydrated and mushy.

A SEASIDE SOIREE

Sun-and-sea hues

Assigning each guest a "signature color" with stacked mismatched dinnerware offers a playful alternative to uniform place settings. The trick to ensuring the table looks artfully cohesive: limiting the color palette to saturated blues, greens, and yellows.

Seaside souvenirs

The finishing touch on a coastal table is a variety of nautical accents. Displaying keepsakes like a rustic model boat and wooden lures alongside natural finds like seashells and seagull feathers captures the ambience of a charming fishing village right at your table.

Bring on bliss with blue-tinted glasses

Color studies have shown that cool tones prompt calmness, so gracing the table with cobalt blue wineglasses will add a dose of relaxation to your beach-inspired dinner theme—even before that first refreshing sip!

"Washed up" place cards

Personalized "message in a bottle" place markers make terrific table decorations. Just purchase inexpensive glass apothecary bottles, write the guest's name on a small piece of paper, and slip it inside the bottle. Display the bottle right on top of the table setting for each and every guest.

Slip in tropical flair with raffia mats

So-simple dinner plates are transformed into stunning seaworthy place settings when set on rustic woven raffia mats, available at home-goods stores at great prices.

Inspire *oohs* and *aahs* with a maritime mix

The key to creating a coastal-chic scene is showcasing splashes of saturated sea blue in harmony with light, natural textures. Keep it simple and forgo the tablecloth, allowing your wooden table to serve as the backdrop. Use sun-bleached and raw-to-refined accents like seagrass mats and cork candleholders. Bright blue highlights carry out the serenity-at-sea theme.

10 Brilliant Uses
for TOOTHPICKS

1 Temporarily repair broken glasses
You love dining alfresco. But as you reach into your purse for your sunglasses to reduce the glare, you notice that one side has come loose due to a missing screw. Fix it for the time being by aligning the screw holes of the arm with the frame and inserting the tip of a toothpick; break off the excess. The wooden sliver will fit right into the opening to hold the parts together. (When you're ready to replace the screw, simply remove the toothpick with a pair of tweezers.) Now that your eyes are shielded from the sun, you can focus on the menu!

2 Spice up an ordinary manicure
Instead of applying only the same old shade of polish, add flair to your nails with a trendy swirl accent. First, select two of your favorite colors. Coat an entire nail with one shade, and before it dries, place a drop of the second color on the nail. Then use a toothpick to blend the hues together. The pick's fine point lets you create loops and twists for professional-looking results.

3 Serve perfectly done burgers
You have no problem memorizing how each of your guests wants her burger cooked. But once the patties are lined up on the grill, confusion sets in and you can't remember which is which. To easily keep track of the levels of doneness, color the tips of several toothpicks using three different shades of marker to signify rare, medium, and well done. Just insert the picks into the burgers as they finish cooking. Voilà—a job, er, well done!

4 Support a weakened plant stem
Just because the stem of your favorite plant folded over doesn't mean the bloom is doomed. Brace the stalk by placing a toothpick against the stem and wrapping with transparent tape. Then water the plant as usual. The toothpick will act as a splint to help the stem regain its strength and stand up straight. (Note: Removal time varies depending on how fast the plant grows, but most plants will be back to normal within a week.)

5 Slow quick-to-pour vinaigrettes
Oops! You added too much dressing to your salad . . . again. Blame it on the hard-to-handle, widemouthed bottle that dispenses as if it has a

mind of its own. The solution to your dressing dilemma: toothpicks. Next time you open a new bottle, instead of removing the seal, use a toothpick to poke several small holes in it. The tiny openings will allow you to reduce your dressing intake. As a result, you'll cut calories and your bottle will last twice as long.

6 Ensure sausages brown evenly

Cooking sausages can be challenging—they roll around on the grill, making it difficult to keep track of how long each side has cooked. Guarantee they're always perfectly prepared with this trick: Soak toothpicks in water for 10 minutes, then pop one into each side of the meat. This will prevent the links from moving about, so you can accurately time their flipping.

7 Find the edge of the tape every time

Whenever you use masking tape, you struggle to find where the roll begins. Avoid the hassle for good by placing a toothpick under the free end each time you tear off a piece. This marker will make it a cinch to spot the edge, helping you eliminate wasted time.

8 Quickly plug a leaky garden hose

Oh, no! While watering your thirsty lawn, you realize that your garden hose has sprung a leak. To seal it, insert a toothpick in the hole and break off the excess that's sticking out. Keep the plug securely in place with a piece of duct tape. The toothpick will swell when wet to snugly fill the opening.

9 Clean a pet brush in seconds

Dislodge every last piece of fluff from Kitty's brush with this foolproof technique: Run a toothpick down each row of bristles, pulling up the fur as you go. The pointed tip will easily get under the tightly wound strands, so no fur will get left behind.

10 Decorate a cake like a pro

The last time you attempted to write "Happy Birthday" on your son's cake, you ran out of space and were forced to crowd the letters together as you reached the edge. Not this year! After frosting the cake, use a toothpick to write your message on it. Then trace the lines with the icing bag. You'll be able to map out the design (and smooth away any mistakes) beforehand to ensure a flawless celebratory dessert.

Coastal candlescape

If you ever find a boat-shaped dish, snap it up to use as a centerpiece for beach-inspired parties. To do: Fill a 12-inch to 18-inch crescent, almond, or oval bowl three-quarters of the way with sand. Nestle two 2-inch candle disks into clamshells and set in the sand along with an assortment of starfish and shells, allowing some shell edges to overlap the rim of the bowl for a naturally relaxed composition.

Beach-chic "buoy"

Your shell collection takes center stage when a wreath is paved with these pretty keepsakes. To do: First, gather two bucketfuls of 1-inch to 2-inch clamshells (about 20 dozen). Using a hot-glue gun, attach the shells to a 16-inch foam wreath in an overlapping pattern, starting at the top and working clockwise until the foam is covered. Next, coil

a 36-inch length of thick cotton cording around the top of the wreath and knot in place. Lean the wreath on a tabletop, letting the cord ends drape and puddle on the table's surface.

Fall Festivities and Fun

Savor the season's last warm days with table settings that feel cozy and comfy. From pumpkins and leaves to turkeys and apples, you're bound to find ideas here to get your creative fires going.

GET INDIAN SUMMER STYLE

Celebrate the harvest with leaves

Ornamental leaves nestled around votive cups upcycle everyday candles into seasonally sensational mini lanterns. To do: Wrap a rubber band around the base of each votive cup. Then tuck colorful leaves under the band. Wind and tie tinted raffia around the base and pop in a candle.

A "peeling" harvest wreath

A halo of this mini autumn fruit presented in rows on a natural-twig base offers a happy, hearty "hello" when suspended from any door, porch pillar, or front gate. To do: Hot glue rows of crab apples onto a 12-inch grapevine-wreath base, beginning in the center and working outward and alternating the placement of the apples so they nestle into each other. For a longer-lasting display, slow down decay and seal the crab apples by wiping them with a soft cotton cloth dipped in acrylic floor wax.

Sweeten their cup with a handful of autumn daisies

Filling a teacup with petite sunny-centered asters provides an extra hit of happy when displayed alongside the dessert course. To do: Fill a teacup with soaked floral foam. Snip about 2 dozen asters to 2 inches. Use a skewer to predrill holes, then insert stems into the foam.

Add an extra hit of color with a pretty pileup

Arranging fruit in a country-style trug basket creates a pleasing balance of rustic and fresh. For the perfect stack: Fill the bottom of your basket with larger oranges, leaving a small free space in the center. Place one large orange atop the space, then pack medium-size lemons around it. Finish by adding a few sprigs of lemon leaves for unexpected texture.

HAPPY HALLOWEEN HOW-TOS

Extend the life of a jack-o'-lantern

Here's our Halloween horror: We've taken all the time, discipline, and energy to carve those jack-o'-lanterns, only to watch them slowly rot into a slimy mess on—you got it—October 30. But this year, we're breathing easy because we know this tip (and now you will, too!): Just combine one part water and one part white vinegar in a spray bottle. Then give it a shake and spritz those gourds' exposed areas (their insides and any cuts). Since the acetic acid in vinegar kills more than 90 percent of pumpkin-rotting bacteria on contact, we're confident this move will guarantee our best fright night ever.

Make carved pumpkins last

Here's another idea for keeping pumpkins fresh. You work so hard on your jack-o'-lanterns, so don't let the gourds rot before Halloween. This year, keep Jack smiling by smearing petroleum jelly on the cut areas (eyes, nose, mouth, and lid). The lubricant will keep the exposed areas firm by locking in moisture and keeping out air, ensuring the pumpkin lasts long past your final trick-or-treater.

Make a jack-o'-lantern last twice as long

The only thing scarier than a Freddy mask? Watching your jack-o'lantern become a stinky, slimy mess. This year, try brushing the exposed areas (the inside and any cuts) of the hollowed-out gourd with lemon juice. Lemon's citric acid will inhibit the oxidation that causes pumpkin flesh to soften, plus stop unsightly mold from forming.

Create surprise with a mummy snack bowl

This supersimple mummy will boost the fun factor of your festivities for pennies. To do: Cut off the top and bottom quarter from a gallon milk jug; discard the top section. Cut "teeth" into the bottom section on the front side of the jug. Spray the center section with adhesive and wrap with gauze bandages (use gauze on a roll for best results). To finish, glue the bottom back to the lower edge of the center section and add felt eyes. Fill the top of the jug with popcorn.

Add a dash of flair with a bat garland

Who says bats have to be black? These colorful cuties will add cheer to any room they "fly" through. To make: Glue googly eyes and construction-paper wings, ears, and feet onto each overturned cup. Draw on smiles, then add paper fangs to half. To hang, pierce holes in the cups' sides and thread with yarn.

Inspire smiles with a mini-pumpkin bouquet

A pretty pumpkin nosegay on each place setting offers guests a warm greeting. To do: Slice off the top inch of a 6-inch pumpkin, reserving the lid. Scoop out the flesh and fill the gourd with soaked floral foam. Cut six each of roses, hydrangeas, and berries to 4 inches and press stems into the foam. Gently place the pumpkin lid on top.

Add a hauntingly happy glow with spooky silhouettes

Juice glasses turn into creepy candle cups, thanks to simple Halloween-inspired paper shadows. To do: Cut an orange or yellow tissue-paper band to fit around a juice glass and tape in place. Next, using a piece of chalk, trace a Halloween cookie cutter onto a piece of black paper. Cut out the shape and affix it to the tissue paper with double-stick tape, then pop a tea light into the glass.

Spread festive cheer with etched pumpkins

Engraved pumpkins pay a more sophisticated (and less messy!) tribute to Halloween than jack-o'-lanterns, nodding to the day without shouting it. And since etching removes only the gourds' skin, the results will last up to 2 weeks. Start by drawing leaves on each pumpkin. Then use the tip of a paring knife or vegetable peeler to trace over the designs, being careful not to cut all the way through the pumpkin flesh. Scrape away the orange skin to finish the design as desired.

LOVELY LEAFY ACCENTS

Dress up your gift of wine

Autumn leaves will create a lively gift "wrap" to transform any bottle into a spirited hostess gift. To do: Use dots of hot glue to attach an overlapping row of oak leaves around the middle of a wine bottle. Tie a length of gold cording around the leaf band and tuck a sprig of berries into the knot. Create a matching gift tag with an autumn-leaf feel by cutting a scrap of wine-colored card stock with a pair of decorative-pattern scissors (from the craft store) or just fold and tear the edges by hand for a rustic look. Then tie the tag around the neck of the bottle with gold cord.

Festive foliage hurricane

Brighten a bare tabletop or cast a welcoming glow in a window with a twinkling luminary made from a tall hurricane glass vase and faux autumn accents. To do: For each luminary, pop a votive candle inside a glass tumbler, then place the tumbler inside the hurricane vase. Attach one large maple leaf onto the front of each glass. Next, create a fan with four or five smaller leaves and glue onto the bottom of the larger leaf along with a berry sprig.

Natural "give thanks" note

Create a beautiful autumn card for each guest (or mail to faraway relatives) and let your guests jot down words of gratitude before the Thanksgiving feast. To do: Buy window cards at a craft store. Tape a piece of frosted vellum behind the "window" opening and hot glue a maple leaf onto the front. For a "framed botanical" effect, label the leaf on a piece of ripped masking tape.

HAPPY THANKSGIVING

Create a stunning focal point with a rustic runner

Rich fall colors and abundant produce always make a warm, welcoming Thanksgiving setting. The highlight: a breathtaking reclaimed-wood centerpiece. For a rough-hewn yet elegant look, choose wood with a distinct grain, like oak. Have it cut to 12 inches by 24 inches and treat it with wood oil,

then top with grapes, gourds, and sprigs of wheat. To finish, group at either end candles that match in hue but vary in size.

Maximize table space with this napkin trick

Putting napkins under, not beside, place settings is a stylish way to save on space. Simply fold napkins into thirds and tuck one under each plate so it hangs 4 to 6 inches over the edge or just covers the table's apron. Add Thanksgiving-inspired appliqué patches to give plain napkins a holiday motif.

Brighten up a dark corner with a seasonal "skyline"

Setting candles in a tray of from-the-yard foliage creates a striking autumn display—perfect for an entryway or coffee table. To do: Center three pillar candles (4 inches, 6 inches, and 8 inches tall) on an 18-inch tray with the shortest candle in front. Arrange 12 each of pinecones, prickly seedpods, nuts, and autumn leaves around the base of the candles. Then tuck in 12 Chinese lanterns and two dried sunflowers.

HARVEST PARTY PERFECTION

Secure a tablecloth with playful windproofers

Supersmall apples (real or faux) make fun and effortless weights to help keep your tablecloth in place during outdoor parties. To do: Twist floral wire around each apple's stem, then use a clothespin to attach the wire's other end to the tablecloth. Use thin floral wire (look for 36 gauge) to wind around the skinny stems, so they'll seem to float off the bottom edges of the tablecloth.

Pair organic with graphic for maximum impact

Blending natural shapes (like apple appliqués) with graphic elements (like dots, stripes, and large gingham) creates an inviting contrast of form and style. To make the tablecloth, use pinking shears to cut apple shapes from fabric layered with no-sew fusible web, then iron to a low-cost canvas drop cloth, which acts as a sturdier weatherproof table-cloth.

Winter's Wonderful Wonderland

Filled with evergreen, baubles, and snowflakes, these ideas are perfect when you need a little creative outlet during the hustle and bustle of the holidays. Craft a whole tablescape or just choose a few ideas to bring magic to the season. And then it's on to Valentine's Day!

COZY UP WHEN THE COLD ARRIVES

Warm up with cinnamon-stick candles

Encircling a candle in a simple cinnamon-stick wrap releases a spicy-sweet scent. Simply stretch an elastic band around the candle and slip cinnamon sticks underneath, then hide the band with twine. Place each pillar on a saucer or coaster and display as a warm accent anywhere. And here's a tip: Shorter supermarket cinnamon sticks will cover 3-inch pillars.

Jump-start joy with a snuggly surprise

Slipping treats inside a pair of Christmas slippers creates a wonderfully wearable alternative to a holiday stocking. To do: For the best display, press tissue paper into the toes of each slipper. Then insert and fan out small bags and boxes filled with stocking stuffers.

From shirt backs to plush pillow covers

A pile of irresistibly oversize flannel-covered cushions is the perfect antidote to chilly weather. To do: Place a pillow on the back of a flannel shirt. Cut a square for the front of the pillow that's large enough to cover it plus 2 inches all around. Repeat this process with another shirt for the back of the pillow. With the right sides facing, stitch the two flannel squares together on three sides. Then turn it right side out and tuck a pillow into the pocket. Use a slip stitch to close the remaining open edge.

CHRISTMAS DAY DELIGHTS

Surprise! Candles in daylight add that extra sparkle that warms the heart and brightens the spirit.

BOLD: Planted pillars

Chunky candles resting in mossy beds make eye-catching table accents. To do: For each arrangement, fill a 9-inch bowl with soaked floral foam. Set a 3-by-6-inch pillar candle in a cup and press it into the center of the foam. Cover the foam with sheet moss. Pierce an orchid stem through the moss, then place ornaments, lady apples, and berries on top.

CHARMING: Fresh-picked tapers

Petite taper candles get a sweet seasonal twist when tucked into McIntosh apples. To do: Use a screwdriver to drill a hole into the top of each apple and insert a slim 6-inch taper. Set apples in cupcake liners. Crimp a strip of foil around the base of each candle, forming a drip-catching "collar" for melting wax.

COUNTRY: Floating tea lights

So country, so cute! Flickering tea lights make simple Mason jars more reflective. To do: Place holly sprigs and fresh cranberries in a clear Mason jar, then add a few inches of water. Float a tea light in the water to create a homespun candle.

DELIGHTFUL: Easy battery candles

So kid-friendly, battery candles are perfect for filled-to-the-brim holiday gatherings. To do: Place a large battery-powered candle in the center of a large, shallow dish. Fill the space around the candle with red and green peppermint candies in cellophane.

SUBTLE: Tabletop tea lights

Scattering red and white tea lights on your table is an easy way to bring understated elegance to a holiday gathering. Low-profile candles reflect off simple white dishes and glassware, illuminating the entire setting with a soft glow that will make the meal look even more delicious. Crimson damask linens create a warm backdrop that enhances the cozy-chic ambience.

Fast-and-easy sugar-cube centerpiece

Arrange a row of sugar cubes around the edge of a 7-inch cardboard circle, leaving ¼ inch between each. Mix together 2 egg whites and 3 cups of confectioners' sugar for "mortar" (or use white tube icing). Add another row so each cube straddles the two beneath it, painting their bottoms with "mortar" before stacking. Repeat to make seven rows and let dry. Set the finished "igloo" on a cake stand and top with granulated sugar "snow," then sprinkle shredded coconut around the base and set a tea light inside. To guarantee the sturdiest structure, build five layers, wait an hour for the "mortar" to dry, then build the final two.

Gift-wrapped place settings

Arranging a bow and bauble atop each plate offers friends and family a festive "present." To do: For each setting, cut a 1½-yard length of 1½-inch-wide red satin ribbon. Center the ribbon horizontally under the stacked plates, lift the ends to wrap the plates together, and tie a bow on top. Tuck in two 4-inch sprigs of evergreen and add a 3-inch red ornament.

Instant antidote to stress

Head off holiday overload with a whiff of cinnamon. A recent study found that people who smelled cinnamon while behind the wheel reported less frustration and an increase in alertness—even in high-stress conditions!

SMART WREATH SECRETS

Make a festive wreath for pennies

We love the idea of transforming our front doors with seasonal wreaths, but it can be pricey to do. So we were happy to learn this trick: Create a wreath form by cutting an old pool noodle to the desired size, then attach the ends with duct tape. Cover with ribbon, silk leaves, and seasonal ornaments. It's easy and inexpensive, so you can create a different wreath for each holiday and reuse it year after year!

Stay-fresh tip for a holiday wreath

To prolong the life of your festive garland, mist its entire surface with a generous coating of hair spray. The elastesse in the beauty staple will trap moisture, keeping the evergreen needles perky. Plus, the spray will act as a bonding agent, ensuring any loose needles stay firmly in place.

Effortlessly clean a dusty wreath

You're having a blast decking the halls . . . until you pull your festive faux wreath out of storage and see that it's covered in dust. The simple solution: Place it in a paper bag and add ¼ cup of salt, then gently shake for 30 seconds. The abrasive granules will knock dust and grime off the wreath, leaving you with a lovely—and clean—welcome to greet your holiday visitors.

RING IN THE NEW YEAR

Say "Cheers!" with cocktail flags

A personalized party pennant provides a festive solution to "whose glass is whose?" confusion. To do: For each drink flag, cut a 1½-by-6-inch piece of white paper. Fold the paper in half around the top of a 12-inch-long wooden skewer (available at supermarkets), attaching with glue. Then cut a V shape into the end of the paper and scroll on a name.

Make magic with evening metallics

Gold is a perfectly luxe color palette choice for your New Year's bash. White tablecloths become the canvas on which golden accents—like lengths of lamé, doilies, dessert plates, and repurposed ornaments—simply pop. To further evoke a luxe feel, place pillar candles on a nest of pearl garland, scatter a few gold-painted nuts and pinecones, and place a few ivory amaryllis blooms in brocade-covered vases.

Cast a gorgeous glow with a gilded candlescape

Pillar candles that are painted gold become a simple yet stunning display. Just mix acrylic paint with a paint adhesion medium so it sticks to the wax. To vary the finishes, apply the paint with a brush, dab on with a sponge, or wipe on with a rag. When dry, cluster the candles on a tray and tuck in ornaments and greenery.

Make a shiny stemware "collection"

Single champagne flutes are a common thrift-store score, and clustering mismatched stems makes a delightfully modern statement. Simply set glasses on a shiny tray and add tea lights to boost refractory light.

VALENTINE'S DAY FESTIVITIES

Melt their hearts with a rose-kissed ring

Turn a few tiny tea lights into a lovely centerpiece. To do: Cut two pieces of 24-gauge floral wire to 30 and 20 inches and bend each into a heart shape. Wind on red raffia (available at craft stores) to cover and set the hearts, one within the other, inside a 12-inch-wide shallow bowl. Fill the space between the hearts with tea lights (alternating between pink and red), then pour ½ inch of water into the bowl and set fresh rose petals afloat.

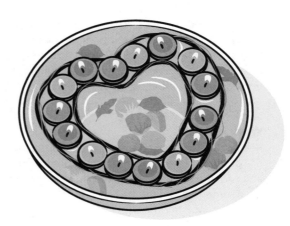

DODGE HOLIDAY LIGHTING DANGERS

Decking the halls can expose you to a surprising array of toxins that cause coughing, eye irritation, brain fog, and more. Luckily, protecting yourself is easy!

WHEN A BULB BREAKS:
Use duct tape

It's easy for any lightbulb to break as you make room for a Christmas tree. But if it's a curlicue-shaped compact fluorescent light (CFL) that shatters, these bulbs start releasing toxic mercury vapors that, even at low levels, can cause tremors, confusion, and weakness.

Do not vacuum up the mess, because it spreads mercury vapor and dust throughout the area. Instead, open a window for at least 15 minutes to let the vapor dissipate. Then, wearing rubber gloves, scoop up the broken pieces with two index cards. Pick up the finest particles with duct tape and wipe the area with a damp paper towel. Put all the waste and cleaning materials into a container, shut it tight, and store it outside until you can take it to your recycling center. Do not place it in the trash.

WHEN HANGING TREE LIGHTS:
Wear gloves

Researchers at Cornell University tested a variety of indoor/outdoor sets of Christmas lights and found that all of them contained lead at levels deemed unsafe by the EPA.

To safely string lights you already own, wash your hands after handling to prevent transferring any lead from your fingers to your mouth, since swallowing lead poses the greatest danger. Buying new lights? Consider purchasing a lead-free product that states on the label that it complies with the Restriction of Hazardous Substances (RoHS) standard used in the European Union. A safe bet: any of the holiday-light chains at IKEA stores.

WHEN CHOOSING CANDLES:
Skip those with paraffin

Conventional candles are made from paraffin, a type of wax that's derived from petroleum by-products and releases harmful gases when burned. It's not just the wax that's worrisome: According to research at the University of South Florida in Tampa, the synthetic fragrances in many candles emit invisible soot that can trigger coughing, burning in the eyes, breathing problems, and skin irritation. The fix? Burn candles made from palm, soy, or vegetable wax or beeswax, which don't release problematic fumes—and choose varieties that are fragrance-free or scented with essential oils.

Sweeten the celebration with sugared flutes

Glasses kissed with a heart motif will inspire smiles with every sip. To do: Using a fine-tip brush, coat each flute's rim with honey, then paint honey hearts onto the glasses. Let sit for 3 minutes so the honey can set, then spoon granulated sugar over the painted areas. To ensure crisp edges on the sugared hearts, paint very thin coats of honey and use a toothpick to refine the shapes' edges.

Show your love with a bouquet

These takeaway nosegays make a pretty addition to a chair back, doorknob, or railing. To do: Roll a piece of 8-by-10-inch gift wrap into a cone and secure with double-stick tape. Trim the open end straight across. Cut the edge off a paper doily and glue inside the rim, then fold it to the outside as a collar. Tuck three roses (cut to 4 inches) and a chocolate heart into the cone. To hang, staple two 18-inch-long gingham ribbons to either side of the rim and tie. For the longest-lasting blooms, take a cue from the pros and pop each stem into a floral pick.

Kick-start the fun with foil favors

Traditional British cracker rolls will be the sweethearts of your Valentine's Day party. To do: Cut a paper-towel tube into thirds. Fill the center portion of each tube with candy. Set the rolls in a line and tape on a 9-by-15-inch piece of silver foil paper. Pinch the foil between the rolls to secure and cut halfway between the tubes. Cut a 3-inch band out of pink foil and wrap it around the cracker roll, securing it with tape or glue. Write names with a glitter pen or write them with glue and sprinkle glitter on top.

Chapter 5

MONEY MATTERS

Smart Ways to Slash Energy Costs

In both summer and winter, the costs of heating and cooling a house can become a financial burden. Check out these clever tips and no-stress suggestions for cutting energy costs and save hundreds.

CUT HEATING AND COOLING BILLS

Seal leaky windows with foam tape

"A few weeks ago, I noticed air was leaking in at the bottom of my living room windows," says Joanie Demer, cofounder of TheKrazyCouponLady.com. "My solution? Foam tape, which I bought at the hardware store. The tape is barely noticeable and so easy to use. I opened the window, snipped the tape, and stuck it to the frame. It blocks all the cold air from coming in."

Warm up floors with an "insulated" rug

"Our laundry room is on a cement slab and the floor is vinyl, so there's a constant chill in the winter," says Brittany Bailey, founder of PrettyHandy Girl.com. "Since putting new flooring down wasn't an option, I got creative. I ordered two 6-by-9-foot rug pads at Overstock.com, stacked them on top of each other, and put them on the floor for double insulation. Then I topped the pads with a throw rug. It was the perfect fix, and now my feet stay warm when I'm sorting and folding clothes."

Check for attic door leaks this way

"My handyman neighbor always shares the best home-improvement secrets. Last month he told me our pull-down attic door was most likely leaking cold air into our top floor. His trick: Turn on the attic light, then step back down the stairs and close the door. If you see light shining around the perimeter of the door, chilly air is escaping into the house. Sure enough, there was plenty of light coming through. It only took a few minutes and a roll of weather stripping from Walmart to seal the door's border."

—*Mary Lauer, Dickinson, ND*

Plug up pipe drafts with expandable sealant

"You'd be surprised at how much cold air gets in from openings around pipes, especially in the water supply lines under the sink," says Brittany Bailey. "So when I realized there were gaps surrounding the pipes that lead outdoors from my kitchen and bathroom, I picked up a can of expandable foam sealant for $4 at the Home Depot, then sprayed until each gap was filled halfway; the foam expanded to fill the rest. A tweak like this knocks a few bucks off my bill each month and $20 a season."

Block cold winds with thermal curtains

"We have glass French doors that lead to the back deck from our living room, and boy, are they drafty! After years of avoiding the 'chilly section' of this room, I did some research and learned that thermal curtains can block up to 60 percent of cold air. After hanging them, the room felt warmer right away. There was no more chilly airflow near the door, which meant fewer thermostat crank-ups and up to $10 off my bill each month."

—*Cynthia Burke, South Plainfield, NJ*

End chimney chill with a DIY fireplace cover

"I had read that drafty fireplaces raise energy use by up to 30 percent, so in our last house, we put a plywood cover in front of the fireplace opening to keep cold air out," says Brittany Bailey. "When we moved, I wanted something similar but more attractive and not as heavy. So I bought a piece of dense insulated sheathing from the home-improvement store and had it cut to size. Next, I used duct tape to secure fabric around the insulation. It's so easy to move when I want to start a fire, and it adds a homey touch to the room."

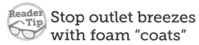

Stop outlet breezes with foam "coats"

"Last winter a friend gave me a great tip: Place your hand over the electrical outlets around the house to check for drafts. I tried it and felt cold air flowing through several outlets. I assumed filling the gaps with caulk would be the best fix, but my friend suggested I try foam gasket covers. I bought a 12-pack of the covers at the hardware store, unscrewed the cover plate, put the foam in place, and screwed the plate back on. With so many outlets sealed, I'm saving myself cash and I'm a lot toastier."

—Bobbie Caldwell, Albany, NY

FREE YOURSELF FROM AC

Feel frosty on contact with aloe vera

Most people reach for aloe vera lotion only when they get sunburned. But smoothing it on anytime you feel overheated is smart, say Australian researchers: The cream lowers skin and subdermal temperature on contact by as much as 5°F. Plus, a study at North Texas Research Laboratory in Grand Prairie found that aloe penetrates skin four times faster than water and reaches seven skin layers deep (while water reaches only the outer layer), so the cooling effect will last longer than taking a cold shower.

Fool yourself cool with mint

The protein TRPM8 is responsible for making humans feel coldness. When it's chilly out, this protein sends an "It's cold" signal to your brain, which makes you react physically by shivering and getting goose bumps. A team of researchers at the Scripps Research Institute in La Jolla, California, found that the TRPM8 receptor is also triggered by menthol. So if you need relief, chew a stick of peppermint gum or rub on some mint-scented lotion to fool your brain into sending cooling signals to your skin.

Ward off UV heat with blue

We generally think of white as the most light-reflective—and therefore coolest—clothing color. But New York University researchers found that dying a white cotton shirt blue boosts the garment's UV light protection by 544 percent, ensuring better defense against overheating and sunburn. Plus, color studies have shown that viewing the color blue causes body temperature to instantly drop by a few degrees, so looking at yourself in the mirror will boost the cooling effect.

Drop room temperature with houseplants

According to USDA estimates, a room full of indoor plants can lower air temperature by up to 10°F. The reason: Plants go through a process called transpiration, in which they absorb warming carbon dioxide from the air and emit cooling water vapor. Even placing just a few potted plants in sunny or oft-used rooms can lower the temperature by up to 3°F. Tip: Desert plants, which are used to offset arid conditions, conserve water during sunny hours and transpire only at night, so keep cacti or other desert plants in your bedroom.

2-MINUTE ENERGY TWEAKS

Switch your TV to "home mode"
Manufacturers ship televisions that are set to the "vivid mode" used in store displays. But that level of brightness isn't necessary to get superior image quality in your home, so consider switching to "standard mode," which uses 25 percent less power. To do, click on the "change mode" option in the menu settings or check the manual.

Annual savings: $90 to $150

Fix even little drips
A leaky faucet may not seem like a big problem, but even tiny drips add up: If hot water is trickling out at the rate of one drop per second, you will lose up to 1,600 gallons of water over the course of a year. That's like flushing $35 in electricity or natural gas and $3 in water costs down the drain.

Annual savings: $38

Stop rinsing dishes
Skip the prerinse step on your dishwasher and you'll save 6,500 gallons of water (plus the energy to heat it) and get cleaner dishes. The reason: Soap needs something to cling to, so food particles actually enhance detergent's cleaning action.

Annual savings: $75

Clean the lint trap
To trim the cost of running the dryer, clean the lint trap after every load. The appliance works by moving hot air through wet clothes and venting water vapor outside, so a clear screen will improve the machine's efficiency.

Annual savings: $34

Hook up entertainment devices this way
Even when you think your cable box, DVD player, stereo, and TV are off, their standby settings consume the energy equivalent of a 100-watt lightbulb running continuously—enough to increase your electric bill by $10 per month. The fix: Plug all your electronics into a power strip and flick the switch whenever they are not in use.

Annual savings: $120

Use less soap
Dishwashers and laundry machines manufactured after 1994 are designed to use less water—and in turn less soap—than older models. But out of habit, most people use more detergent than necessary. This wastes up to $154 in supplies each year, plus the extra soap creates buildup that can cost $100 in repairs. Instead, use half the amount specified on the detergent container.

Annual savings: $254

Dial the thermostat down 1 degree
Studies by the nonprofit American Council for an Energy-Efficient Economy found that for every degree you lower the thermostat, you can reduce your heating bill by 3 percent. For optimal savings, set the temperature to 68°F when you're home and 65°F or lower before leaving the house or going to bed.

Annual savings: $74

Swap out lightbulbs

Compact fluorescent lightbulbs (CFLs) use 75 percent less electricity, so each bulb cuts $11.16 from utility bills over 12 months. And they last 10 times longer than standard bulbs. So if you spend $50 on CFLs for 20 light fixtures, you can save $223 every year for the next 10 years.

Annual savings: $223

Run fans in reverse

Most ceiling fan units come with a switch to rotate the blades clockwise, which helps pull down warm air that pools near the ceiling. This cuts heating costs by 10 percent. No ceiling fans? Run any freestanding fan pointed straight up toward the ceiling to force warm air back down.

Annual savings: $104

Close the door to the guest bedroom

Closing off rooms that aren't in immediate use (like a guest room) is an easy way to slash heating costs by 20 percent. Just shut off the heat vents (or turn down the radiator) inside the room before closing the door. This saves up to $25 per 100-square-foot room each year in homes with forced air furnaces.

Annual savings: $25 per room

Activate the computer's "power save" function

You can shave $90 per year off your energy bill thanks to your computer's power save function. Just click on the control panel and find the power save options—Windows users will find this under "Power Options" and Mac users will find it under "Energy Saver."

Annual savings: $90

Set your water heater to this temperature

Setting your water heater too high (140°F) can waste as much as $61 annually in heat lost into the surrounding basement area and more than $400 in hot-water demands, cautions Evan Mills, PhD, a staff scientist at the US Department of Energy. Instead, set the thermostat at 120°F or lower. Mills assures us this will generate water that is warm enough to safely clean and comfortably bathe.

Annual savings: $461

Choose a pot that fits

Be sure to use the right size saucepan on the stove: A 6-inch pot on an 8-inch burner wastes more than 40 percent of expended heat. By fitting the pot to the burner, you can conserve enough energy to save $36 annually on an electric range or $18 on a gas range.

Annual savings: $36

Modify curtains

Did you know that 20 percent of household heat loss can be attributed to your windows? Partly to blame: drapes, which trap indoor air that cools quickly beside the cold window. The fix for long drapes: Slip a butter knife in the center of the bottom hem. The weight will bring the material flush with the wall so air can't get behind it. The fix for sill-length curtains: Attach them to the wall with Velcro.

Annual savings: up to $10 per window

Place foil behind radiators

When radiators are positioned next to an exterior wall, there's a risk that heat is escaping outside. To remedy, tape aluminum foil behind the heater, shiny side facing the room, so heat reflects off the foil and back into the room. Make sure your HVAC ductwork is sealed tightly. Use mastic (about $4 at home-improvement stores) to plug any gaps or leaks.

Annual savings: up to $65

Trigger evaporative cooling with spicy foods

Though a bowl of ice cream may be tempting on a summer day, consider reaching for chips and salsa instead. "Eating hot peppers causes gustatory facial sweating, which produces an evaporative cooling effect," explains Luke LaBorde, PhD, an associate professor of food science at Pennsylvania State University. "That may be why spicy foods are so popular in tropical climates." Conversely, researchers at Purdue University in West Lafayette, Indiana, found that eating sugary foods forces your metabolism to speed up, causing a spike in body temperature.

Lowering Food Expenses

Yikes! The average American family spends $771 a month on groceries. To the rescue: *First for Women* polled savvy shoppers for tips and tricks that can save you hundreds.

 ### Click for supermarket gift-card deals

"If I'm planning ahead for a big grocery trip, whether it's to prepare for houseguests, a dinner party, or a holiday, I'll make it a point to buy a discounted gift card to a chain like Costco, Target, Kroger, or A&P at GiftCardGranny.com. My husband says it's my 'genius grocery trick,' since most people assume sites like this are for cards to restaurants or retail stores. Last week, I scored a $75 gift card to Target for $60 and had the card shipped to me for free. My local Target has a huge grocery and produce department, so that's like getting $15 worth of free food."

—*Barb Janson, Richmond, VA*

Mail-order local coupons

"When I heard I could buy coupons at sites like TheCouponClippers.com, I didn't think it would be worth it, but I was wrong," says Sarah Roe, founder of MoneySavingQueen.com. "I can visit the site and get regional coupons that aren't in my newspaper.

The best part: Many of the coupons are worth $1 or more and cost as little as 5 cents!"

 ### Shop the drugstore for eggs and milk

"When my sister-in-law mentioned to me that she stocks up on eggs and milk at the drugstore rather than the supermarket, I was stunned. She said she was surprised herself when she noticed drugstore chains selling fresh staples like these at impressively low prices. I stopped into my local Rite Aid to check it out and saw that the store's prices were 25 percent lower than supermarket prices."

—*Rita Simpson, Cleveland, OH*

Score big with smart substitutions

"I always step into the grocery store with a few recipes in mind for the week—then I implement my 'substitution rule,' which saves me up to $30 a month," says Richard Ingraham, chef and recipe blogger at ChefRLI.com. "Last week I was picking up ingredients for a veggie pasta dish that called for portobello mushrooms ($3.60 per pound) and yellow tomatoes ($4.99 per pound). But instead I bought white mushrooms and plum tomatoes, which were each selling for $1.99 a pound—saving $4.61 on one meal. Multiply that by every meal I cook and that's a lot of cash saved!"

Reader Tip — ID the one day you can double up on savings

"I signed up for cooking classes at my local community center. It's a great way to learn new recipes and get cooking tips, plus the teacher tells us where she buys her ingredients and how much she spends on them. This often leads to insights on grocery savings. Her most helpful hint: Shop the local grocery store on Fridays. It's when all the new coupons for that weekly cycle are released—plus you can take advantage of last week's sales for double the savings. The same rule applies to many supermarkets—you just need to find out which day new coupons are released."

—Anne Shelton, Denville, NJ

Stick to the dairy aisle for specialty cheeses

"Every store has an artisanal cheese table filled with cheeses like Gouda and Gorgonzola, but they can cost 30 percent more than varieties in the dairy aisle," says Phil Lempert, founder of SupermarketGuru.com. "The only difference: the packaging, presentation, and location. The other day, I picked up Cabot Cheddar in the dairy aisle—it was the same as the brand in the fancy food case but cost $5 less a pound."

Reader Tip — Get food delivered to your doorstep

"At first I was hesitant about ordering groceries online, but when my neighbor mentioned that Stop & Shop's Peapod service was available in our town, I gave it a try. I browsed the aisles digitally and stocked up on produce, snacks, meat—everything! As I added items to my cart, I could see a running tally of my bill, so I could budget more effectively. And there were no impulse buys—my usual downfall at the supermarket. I could sort items based on price, use my loyalty card, and apply coupons. Just like at my local store, manufacturers' coupons are doubled. For me, the $6 to $10 fee is well worth the money, hassle, and time I save. Plus, the store will even reduce the fee if I schedule delivery at 'off' times."

—Valerie Amato, Wall, NJ

CUT COOLING COSTS IN HALF

Yikes! Running the AC accounts for 70 percent of a homeowner's utility bill in the summer. To the rescue: We polled savvy women for tricks to help you stay cool for less.

Block 70 percent of solar heat with shades

"I covered the windows on the side of the house that gets direct sunlight with thermal curtains, which cost about $20 each at Target. During the day, I close those windows and open the ones in the shaded part of the house. This routine has cut my electric bill in half. Plus, the curtains keep cold air out in the winter, so we save year-round."

—Jen Carl, Lehigh Valley, PA

Leave your AC on all day

"Shutting off the air when I left for the day didn't lower my utility bill—the system had to work so hard to recool the house each evening that it ended up using more energy than I saved by turning it off. Now I just set the temperature to 77°F and leave it on all day. Since I started doing this, my electric bill has gone down by $14 per month."

—Lynn Smith, North Wales, PA

Stay cool all night with rice "pillows"

"My kids find it hard to sleep in the heat, but rather than turn up the air-conditioning at night, I make cooling packs to lower their body temperature. I just fill old clean socks with raw rice and tie them closed with rubber bands. The rice-filled socks go in the freezer for an hour before bedtime, then I place them inside the kids' pillows. The rice retains the cold long enough for them to drift off."

—Sandra DeTerno, Tulsa, OK

Opt for a washable air filter

"I'd read that regularly replacing your air conditioner's filter can lower summer energy consumption by 15 percent or more, since a dirty filter makes the unit work much harder to cool the air. But I found that I was spending $10 or more every month or two on a new air filter—more than the amount I was actually saving on my utility bill. So I decided to invest in a permanent washable air filter for about $25 at the hardware store. Now I just pull out the filter, quickly give it a good rinse outside with my garden hose once a month, and it's as good as new! It's saved me tons on replacement filters—and my utility bill has gone down by $15 a month!"

—Amy Green, Portland, ME

Get cross ventilation with box fans

"A few years ago, I bought cheap 20-inch box fans at a discount store after reading up on cross ventilation. Every morning I open all the windows and doors in the house. Next, I set these fans in the windows on the hottest side of the house, aimed to blow the warm air outside. This draws air from the cooler side of the house and sets up a nice breeze throughout. Then at night, I place the fans in our bedroom windows, aimed to blow cool evening air into the room. This has kept the house cool enough the past three summers so that we haven't even turned on the air."

—*Cynthia Pratt, Avon, IN*

Try a "swamp" cooler

"On hot desert nights, my grandparents used to dampen their sheets and sleep on the porch—the breeze blowing over the sheets kept them cool. To get the same effect, we use an evaporative, or "swamp," cooler, which pulls warm air over a moist pad and cools it using evaporation. Window units start at $72, but they use 40 percent less energy than air conditioners, so it's worth the cost if you live in a hot, dry climate. Ours saves us $35 per month! One caveat: The cooler can't be used when it's humid out, since it would bring too much moisture into the house."

—*Margie Carnahan, Phoenix, AZ*

Funnel hot air down and out

"When the temperature soars, the first thing I do is change the direction of the ceiling fan so it spins counterclockwise. That way the blades blow air from the ceiling down toward the ground, creating a breeze that pushes hot and humid air away from the body. This air movement allows me to keep the thermostat on 78°F instead of 74°F, which saves me $11 a month on my electric bill."

—*Amy Green*

Run appliances only after sunset

"My family has a rule to run appliances like the washing machine, dryer, and dishwasher only in the evening, after the sun has set. That way we aren't generating extra heat from the machines when the air-conditioning is pumping during the day. I love having a good excuse to not tackle chores in the hottest part of the day, and it saves us about 10 percent on our utility bill each month."

—*Amy Green*

Managing Medical Costs

Doctors and health-care professionals share the secrets that can cut medical costs by $2,000 or more. And even if you aren't able to save big bucks right away, you can keep these tips handy in case you need medical care in the future.

Bring the Rx list

Your insurance company's drug-pricing system will determine your co-pay, so it's smart to print out this list from your provider's Web site before your appointment, says Julie T. Chen, MD, a physician at the Integrative Health Clinic in San Jose, California: "If you need a prescription, ask your doctor for the best option with the lowest cost to you."

Don't hesitate to negotiate

Three out of five adults who request a lower price from a doctor succeed, according to a Harris Interactive Poll. "We realize many people have fewer insurance benefits, and we're glad to help," assures Abbie Leibowitz, MD, coauthor of *The Healthcare Survival Guide*. To negotiate a lower visit cost, ask your insurer about the rate it pays local physicians, then see if your doctor will accept that price. Offering to pay the bill in full before leaving the office can also be an incentive for doctors to give you a discount.

Write off weight loss

If you shed pounds under a doctor's orders, any expenses that exceed 7.5 percent of your adjusted gross income (AGI) are tax deductible. For example, if your AGI is $65,000, you can deduct fees for Weight Watchers, nutrition counseling, and FDA-approved drugs in excess of $4,875—as long as you have a doctor's statement noting your medical need to lose weight. Log on to IRS.gov for details on filing a claim.

Stock up on samples

If your doctor writes you a prescription, ask if she has free samples for the first month. "We get these samples from pharmaceutical reps for the sole purpose of giving them away," says Dr. Leibowitz. "So we're always happy to give them out." You can also find promotional coupons for drugs or even skin cleansers in waiting rooms or on pharmaceutical companies' Web sites.

Try the dental school

A college dental clinic, where third- or fourth-year students perform services under the supervision of a faculty member, can be a great place to get quality dental care for less if you have to pay out of pocket, says Peter K. Krimsky, DDS, a dentist in Plantation, Florida. For instance, having a cavity filled at the Boston University Henry M. Goldman School of Dental Medicine costs $60—that's 70 percent cheaper than what you'd pay at a dentist's office. To find a school near you, visit ADA.org.

Check on alternative health coverage

Almost 90 percent of insurance plans cover alternative medicine, but many customers don't realize that. For example, Horizon offers members 25 percent off chiropractic services and 40 percent off supplements. Plus, Dr. Chen notes, alternative therapies like massage and chiropractic care may help you avoid costly surgeries.

Score discounts on eye exams

Your AAA or AARP card can net you savings on eye care. For instance, AAA members get 30 percent off exams and glasses at Pearle Vision and LensCrafters. But present your health insurance card, too—even if you don't have vision coverage. Many insurers offer better discount programs.

Cash in on Rx rewards

Many pharmacies offer gift cards of $20 to $30 for transferring a prescription to them. For example, having a medication refilled at CVS or Rite Aid gets you up to a $25 reward card to use on store purchases. One caveat: Check to make sure your co-pay won't go up, or you may not reap savings long-term.

Shop around for lower-priced diagnostic tests

"When a doctor orders a lab test or MRI, think of it like a prescription you're free to fill anywhere," notes Howard Podolsky, MD, chief medical officer of NextCare Urgent Care centers. "I always tell my own family members to check around for prices." He suggests calling independent facilities first since they don't incur huge overhead costs and can charge less. (The average in-network cost of an MRI at a hospital is $1,145, compared with $560 at an independent radiology facility.) But don't be swayed by price alone, warns Dr. Podolsky: "Check with your physician about quality of care before visiting any testing facility."

Examine your bill

The Medical Billing Advocates of America report that 8 out of 10 hospital bills contain errors that increase costs by 25 percent. To avoid overpaying, keep a log of tests and medications, then look over the invoice for discrepancies. If you spot an error, send a certified letter requesting a corrected bill.

10 Brilliant Uses
for RICE

1 *Get glowing skin for pennies*
To enjoy the perks of a facial without the cost, try this spa-inspired mask: Using a blender, grind 2 tablespoons of rice for 5 seconds, then add water to make a paste. Apply to your face. Let sit until it begins to dry and crack (about 30 minutes), then rinse with warm water. The rice mask will gently cleanse while providing nourishing vitamins to help clarify and tighten your skin.

2 *End Buster's barking habit*
Your furry pal has started yapping at everything from the neighbor's cat to dinner guests. To break him of the habit, fill a clean, dry can one-third of the way with rice, then cover the opening with foil and secure with a rubber band. Next time the barking begins, shake the can. The loud noise will startle your pet, and he'll soon associate the sound with his behavior and learn to stay quiet.

3 *Bake up the perfect piecrust*
That coconut cream pie recipe you found sounds delish. But it calls for prebaking the crust, which always causes the dough to bubble up. The fix: Top the crust with parchment paper and a layer of rice. After prebaking, remove the paper and rice and add pie filling. The weight of the rice will keep air pockets from forming. Perfection!

4 *Test cooking oil temperature*
Heating oil for deep-frying when you don't have a thermometer doesn't have to be a gamble. To test the oil, drop in a grain of rice. If it pops to the surface and starts cooking, you're ready to fry.

5 *Create a soothing heating pad*
Sore muscles? Get fast relief with a homemade heating pad. Simply fill an old tube sock with rice and tie the end shut, then microwave it for 2 minutes. (Be careful when handling—the sock will be hot.) Because rice has a dense mass, it will retain heat for up to 45 minutes. And there's no need to toss it after it cools—you can use the pad for years without having to replace the rice.

6 Quickly clear spice grinder buildup

Your spice grinder is one of your go-to kitchen gadgets, but you've started to notice that your seasonings taste a little off—probably because there's a buildup of residue from different spices. To clean the grinder, fill it halfway with rice and grind until fine. The rice will gently lift residue and absorb odors. This easy trick can be used to clean coffee grinders, too.

7 Add volume to limp hair

For full, bouncy tresses, combine ¼ cup of uncooked rice and 1 cup of warm water in a spray bottle and let sit overnight. In the morning, spritz onto damp hair and style as usual. The rice's starch will cling to each hair shaft, giving you a mane that's full of body. Bonus: The water will be infused with hair-nourishing B-complex vitamins.

8 Effortlessly clean a bud vase

The scrub-free way to wash a narrow-necked vase: Pour 1 tablespoon of uncooked rice, a drop of dish detergent, and some warm water into the container. Cover the top with your hand and shake. The abrasive rice will remove stuck-on grime, leaving the vase sparkling clean.

9 Save a soaked cell phone

Oops! You accidentally dropped your phone in the sink, and now it won't turn on. The save: Remove the battery and SIM card, dry with a soft cloth, and set aside. Then cover the phone's SIM card slot with a small piece of tape and submerge the device in a bowl of uncooked rice for 24 hours. The absorbent grains will draw out any trapped moisture to get your phone functioning properly again.

10 Protect gardening tools from rust

Excess moisture in the springtime air can cause metal pruning shears, shovels, and trowels to rust—even when they're safely tucked away in a toolbox. But you can outsmart Mother Nature by sprinkling a handful of uncooked rice in the bottom of your toolbox. The grains will absorb any dampness in the air and prevent rust from forming on the metal.

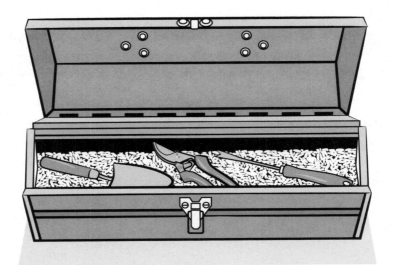

Curbing Car Costs

Between fuel and repairs, car costs can really add up. Find out how to slash car costs and save money so you can keep more cash in your budget for fun!

Nix fuel-sapping clogs

When a clogged air filter keeps air from the engine, gas burns more easily. To improve fuel economy by up to 14 percent, have your filter replaced once every 12 months or 12,000 miles. This $25 service can save you 50 cents per gallon.

Pump up "spring" tires

Tire pressure falls approximately 1 pound per square inch for every 10°F drop in temperature. So by winter's end, most tires have low pressure, which increases friction on the road and creates drag. By inflating tires to the pressure recommended in your owner's manual, you'll save 12 cents per gallon on gas and reduce the risk of a blowout.

Drive at this speed

A *Consumer Reports* study found that every 10 miles per hour (mph) increase in speed above 55 mph reduces fuel economy by an average of 5 miles per gallon. That's the equivalent of spending an extra three cents per mile if you travel at 75 mph.

Lighten the load

Every 100 pounds of added weight (think strollers and sports equipment) reduces fuel economy by 2 percent. The US Department of Energy estimates that drivers can save 14 cents per gallon by removing unnecessary items.

Streamline stops

If you have several errands to run, always begin with the farthest one. When you start with the farthest trip, you allow your engine to rev up to its most efficient temperature, which decreases fuel usage throughout the day.

Get a free repair diagnostic

Many mechanics charge $20 to $100 to determine the cause of a check engine light, plus use the opportunity to up-sell you on services you don't need. A better bet: Go to an auto parts store like AutoZone to have a store technician hook up the car to a mini computer for a free diagnostic. Oftentimes, it's as simple as a loosened gas cap setting off the check engine light. For more complicated issues, the tech can advise you on how to fix it yourself or provide a printout to give to your mechanic.

Top off your tank on Wednesdays

In the summer, people fill their tanks for weekend trips, then have to refuel at the start of the week for their commutes. Because stations raise prices during these times to capitalize on demand, midweek yields the cheapest prices.

Reader Tip — Score low-cost tires online

"Last year an irreparable flat tire was going to cost me $137 to replace at the Honda dealer. It seemed like a steep price to pay for just one tire, so I started doing some digging online and stumbled on DiscountTireDirect.com, which offered a better-rated tire than the one at the dealer and cost just $83 with free shipping and a lifetime warranty. Even with an installation fee of $20 at a local mechanic, I saved $34. And because the site also offers instant rebates for buying multiple tires, my savings will be even bigger when it comes time to replace the other tires."

—Laura Harper, Racine, WI

Click on cruise control

A study conducted by Edmunds.com found that when cruise control was set for a long-distance drive, fuel economy improved by 14 percent. That's enough to save you 51 cents per gallon. Curbing habits like rapid acceleration and hard braking in stop-and-go traffic is also smart.

Have your mechanic "eBay it"

You can save up to 60 percent by asking your mechanic about used parts for your repairs. Typically, mechanics will give you price quotes for different options. The most reliable choice is usually rebuilt parts, which have been disassembled, cleaned, and fitted with fresh parts like bearings so they perform like new.

Don't be swayed by brand-name gas

Big oil companies advertise chemical innovations designed to make their gas better for your car. But a study at the Maryland State Motor Fuel Lab found that brand-name gas isn't any cleaner or more efficient in the engine than generic gas— even though it costs an average of 20 cents more per gallon.

Cut back oil changes

Thanks to updated engine technology and improved oil chemistry, most cars bought in the past 8 years can go 5,000 to 7,500 miles between tune-ups. Scale back oil changes to every 6 months or 6,000 miles and you could save $60 a year.

Reader Tip: Fill up at the warehouse

"Gas prices at my local Costco are typically 10 to 15 cents cheaper than at other gas stations. For instance, last week, regular unleaded was $3.60 per gallon versus $3.75 per gallon at a nearby Hess. That means every time I fill up my 13-gallon tank, I save $2 or more. It doesn't sound like much, but since I fill up six times a month, I'm saving nearly $150 a year. That pays for the $55 membership nearly three times over!"

—Leigh Adler, East Rutherford, NJ

Scout the right shop

Independent technicians aren't always trained to deal with technology in newer cars, so the dealer is your best bet for problems with the electrical, fuel injection, or computer systems. But stick with a local mechanic or a franchise like Pep Boys for routine maintenance (oil changes, brakes, tires). These stores do a high volume of service that allows them to cut prices by more than 50 percent.

10 Brilliant Uses
for PENCIL ERASERS

1 Polish jewelry in a pinch

The gold necklace you put on before running out the door really complements your outfit . . . but while en route to your appointment, you notice the metal is a tad lackluster. The super-quick fix: Rub a pencil eraser over the dull areas. The tool's rubber particles will absorb oil and grime, so your accessory will look flawless.

2 Prevent a mealtime mess

Your adorable dog eats with such gusto that his dish slides across the floor, causing quite the mess! The solution: Pull the erasers off three pencils and glue them to the bottom of his dish, forming a large triangle. The rubber will grip the floor so the bowl won't budge as Fido chows down.

3 Wipe out landline static

Your cordless phone has started to chirp and buzz in the middle of your chats. To remedy, rub a pencil eraser over the metal squares on the bottom of the handset and the charger. The rubber will clear away any dust buildup that's interrupting the flow of electricity between the metal contacts. The result: crystal-clear calls.

4 Remove price tag residue with ease

Success! You were able to easily peel away most of the price tag from your new vase . . . there's just a stubborn bit of white residue left behind. To the rescue: Grab a pencil eraser and glide it back and forth over the remnants. The rubber shavings will absorb the adhesive, so you can simply rinse it off with warm water.

5 Plant seeds in half the time

To make planting seeds as easy as can be: Insert a pencil, eraser side down, into the soil until the metal part is no longer visible. Then drop a seed into the depression. The hole will be the perfect size and depth for your seedling—and you won't get dirt on your hands!

6 Buff away keyboard grime

To spiffy up your keyboard (no liquid cleaner required!), rub a pencil eraser across the keys, then blow on the surface to remove any debris. The eraser's abrasives will easily dislodge grime, while the rubber absorbs dirt and oil.

7 Keep frames from scratching walls

The success secret that's guaranteed to make your artwork and framed photos look fabulous on your walls: Pluck the erasers from a few pencils and glue them to the bottom corners on the back of each frame. The soft rubber will provide traction that will keep the frames from sliding and becoming crooked over time, plus it will act as a cushion that protects against scratches in your walls' paint.

8 Make a scuff mark vanish—in seconds

For a quick way to banish scuff marks on laminate flooring, rub the offending marks with a pencil eraser, then wipe clean with a damp cloth. The rubber contains pumice, a slightly abrasive mineral that will gently loosen the residue without scratching the floor's surface.

9 Lift an ink stain from suede

Oops! You accidentally "wrote" on your new suede handbag with pen. The fix: Rub the stain with a pencil eraser, following the direction of the suede's grain. The tiny, crumblike particles that break off from the eraser will work their way into the fabric and lift the ink mark—plus, the gentle buffing action will "fluff up" the suede fibers. Beautiful!

10 Repair a scratched LCD screen

If the screen on your tablet, cell phone, or TV gets scratched, grab a pencil eraser and gently rub it down the length of the mark. The rubber will smooth jagged edges and serve as an invisible filler for the small gash.

Check your phone before filling your tank

Free price-tracking smartphone apps like "Cheap Gas!" pinpoint your location and provide prices at the 100 nearest gas stations. A recent search for Knoxville, Tennessee, showed a station selling unleaded regular gas for 13 cents less per gallon than a station just 2 miles away.

Want to save even more? Don't hesitate to check (and top off) your own oil. For a complete how-to, log on to CarsforGirls.com and check out the maintenance section under "Guides."

Perfect your tire pressure

Instead of inflating tires to the number printed on the tire, use the number printed on the driver's side door of your car. Perfecting tire pressure decreases friction while driving, then decreases fuel usage. Money saved: up to $1.63 per tank

Roll up the windows

It's counterintuitive, but closing your windows and running the AC can boost fuel economy by 5 percent, according to an Edmunds.com study. That's because open windows create aerodynamic drag. Money saved: up to $2.46 per tank

Reader Tip — Follow the "half tank" rule

"My mechanic warned me that gas evaporates when it's exposed to air—the more empty space in the tank, the faster gas disappears. Now I fill up when the ticker reaches the halfway mark, so I know I'm getting the most miles per gallon from my gas."

—Elizabeth Cogliati, Idaho Falls, ID

Map out errands like the pros

"UPS drivers use a 'mapping' system that minimizes the number of left turns made in their daily route," says Lauren Fix, the Car Coach at LaurenFix.com. "This helps them avoid idling at red lights and wasting tons of gas. To use that principle when I have to grocery shop, pick up my prescription, and stop into BJ's, I take 2 extra minutes to 'Google Map' my route. Then I use the map generated to plan out a course that avoids main traffic lights and prioritizes right turns. This little bit of planning saves me a lot of time and fuel consumption."

Reader Tip — Turn groceries into gas rewards

"My local Kroger offers points toward cents off at the pump, and the savings really add up. I recently nabbed extra gas points for buying three listed items I buy anyway, like dish soap and laundry detergent. With coupons, I saved $8 on those items and 20 cents per gallon on my next gas purchase. That day I spent $3.40 less filling up my 17-gallon tank!"

—Joyce Baki, Prince Frederick, MD

Yard Sale Savvy

Having a yard sale is a great way to both free up your closets and make a profit! And don't forget, cashing in on yard sale deals yourself is the perfect way to pick up basics for a steal. Read on for the inside scoop on how to be a yard sale genius.

DOUBLE YOUR GARAGE SALE TAKE

Create clothing sets

Brand-name clothes from stores like Justice or Gap attract customers quickly. The key is to use safety pins to pair pants and shirts together as outfits, which allows you to sell more clothes at a faster rate.

Stagger online ads

To drum up business, start online with an ad that lists specifics about big-ticket items. (Instead of "old sewing machine," try "Singer sewing machine circa 1950.") Promote sales $2\frac{1}{2}$ weeks in advance on GarageSaleHunter.com and BackPage.com, then update the free ads a day before the sale. Also, post your yard sale information on your Facebook page, another form of free advertising.

 ### Spread the word with free advertising

"I'm so thankful that the days of pricey newspaper ads are over! Of course I post on Facebook to notify nearby friends, but I also announce my sale at YardSaleSearch.com and GarageSaleHunter. com. The former site is very popular with the yard sale pros because there's a mobile version, too. At my last sale, a woman stopped by after she saw the ad pop up on her phone—and I'm so glad she did: She spent $25!"

—*Donna Lennox, Ann Arbor, MI*

Be smart about signage

Post signs no more than a week in advance. Any earlier and people will begin to mentally block the signs out. Also, use neon poster board with the word "Sale" boldfaced, an arrow, and your address. Cover with clear packing tape to make the signs waterproof.

TO SELL OR NOT TO SELL?

Half the battle of planning a yard sale is deciding what's worth selling and what to donate, since displaying your most appealing goods is the key to drawing in drive-by customers and boosting profit. To eliminate the guesswork, follow this handy guide.

TOYS

Cash in on . . . plastic items, toy cars, and figurines, since germ-conscious parents know they're easy to clean. And to draw in parents and kids alike, group items in sets and price them together. Displaying a toy dump truck with a shovel and bucket or a fairy wand with a tiara and jewelry makes it easy for customers to visualize how the toys can be used.

Help others with . . . stuffed animals, which are hard to deep clean. Instead, mail items to Loving Hugs (go to LovingHugs.org for more information), a charity that has toys professionally cleaned and sent to kids in need.

HOME ACCESSORIES

Cash in on . . . larger, higher-quality items like furniture and light fixtures. Quality wooden furniture and nice upholstered pieces will definitely bring crowds. You may not get top dollar for valuable antiques, but buyers are looking for furnishings in good condition.

Help others with . . . fixtures and furniture from your remodel. It may not suit your décor any longer, but house rehab enthusiasts will appreciate your pass-alongs.

SPORTS EQUIPMENT

Cash in on . . . larger or more expensive goods like golf clubs, basketball hoops, bicycles, and complete game sets (such as bocce ball or croquet). Since sports equipment is built to last, people generally have fewer qualms about picking it up secondhand. Place bigger or heavier items closest to the street. This will attract attention from people driving by—plus make it easier for buyers to cart away goods.

Help others with . . . any type of sports ball or smaller accessory like baseball tees, Wiffle Ball bats, padding, cleats, and uniforms. These generally only sell for pennies, if at all. Another poor seller: old exercise equipment like treadmills and stationary bicycles. Try calling Goodwill, the Salvation Army, or a school or church and ask if these items are needed.

CLOTHING

Cash in on . . . children's clothes. Children outgrow clothing quickly, often leaving them in a nearly unused condition. The most popular sellers? Sizes worn from infancy through the elementary school years. Other sought-after items include handbags and men's blue jeans.

Help others with . . . plain women's clothing, suits (male or female), and shoes with obvious wear—these items can be brought to a local clothing drop-off box. Also on the "don't sell" list: baby or toddler clothing with hoods or drawstrings. Since these items are frequently recalled, many parents pass right over them at sales. Before donating, check the items against the Recalls.gov database. If they come up clean, charities would love them.

BOOKS

Cash in on . . . both paperback and hardcover books, as long as you don't want much for them. Sell paperbacks three or four for a dollar and hardcovers for 50 cents or a dollar each. And, if your buyers know you read a lot, they'll visit your yard sale early in the day to see the bestsellers you're offering.

Help others with . . . brand-new books that can be donated to schools, libraries, and children's charities. There are plenty of organizations that accept new books around holiday time, too.

LAWN AND GARDEN TOOLS

Cash in on . . . trowels, shovels, pots and starter pots, hoes, rakes, and even knee pads that are in good shape. To maximize profit, try sprucing up metal tools before setting them out for sale. Simply soak them in strong brewed black tea for a few hours, then rinse with water and let dry. The tea's tannins will dissolve any rust and grime—sans scrubbing. (Just don't soak wooden handles or parts, as the tea can stain and discolor wood.)

Help others with . . . large or expensive items like lawn mowers, Weedwackers, or leaf blowers. Save yourself the hassle and contact the Boys & Girls Clubs of America (go to BGCA.org to find a club near you). Many have gardening or camp programs that can use the equipment. If not, call your city hall and ask if they do a lawn mower roundup—you may be able to drop yours off for recycling. Another option: Visit Earth911.com and type in the name of your item. The database will bring up all the nearby donation centers that will accept it.

Make prices obvious

People respond best when 75 percent of merchandise is marked. But since marking each item can be labor-intensive, try this: Arrange similar items in boxes, then post prices for each group—like 50 cents for books or $1 per toy—on poster board.

Start low to move more merchandise

Deal seekers can be turned off by high prices, so be mindful of this when pricing your items. For example, price a toolbox at $75 if you want at least $50—then you have some flexibility if people want to haggle.

Designate a kids' zone

Parents who come with kids won't be able to browse if they're trying to keep Junior from touching everything. The fix: creating a kids' area where they can color while parents shop. Bonus: If the wee ones like a toy, it might result in a sale.

Have a test strip handy

When selling electrical items like a toaster or blender, have an extension cord and power strip attached to a nearby outlet so shoppers can test the items. Also, put new batteries in games like Nintendo DS and charge a couple extra bucks—buyers will appreciate the favor.

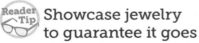 Showcase jewelry to guarantee it goes

"In my experience, jewelry often gets lost in the shuffle at a yard sale. So rather than piling a bunch of accessories into a bin that people have to dig through, I display rings, cuff links, and brooches in ice cube trays—the tiny crevices are perfect for tucking the jewelry in, and each item gets its own spotlight. I also hang earrings through the holes of a clean cheese grater. At my last sale, this strategy helped me make more than $40 on jewelry in 2 days."

—*Fran Conway, Phoenix, AZ*

Show items' value

If you're selling used tech gear, providing proof of what the item is currently selling for can help you get top dollar. If you can use your smartphone to pull up the prices for electronics, you can assure your customers they are getting true bargains.

Set up a "department store" floor plan

"When I have a garage sale, I try to think like a retail-store manager would," says Joanie Demer, cofounder of TheKrazyCouponLady.com. "I organize my items into different departments so it's easy for shoppers to find what they're looking for: housewares, women's clothing, kids' stuff, and electronics. I even create a 'pay station' and add an impulse-buy section filled with jewelry, nail polish, and small toys next to the register to tempt people to grab one more item as they go. Then at the end of the day, I have 'sales.' I start slashing prices and have a sign ready to go to advertise the price cuts. This method has allowed me to rake in hundreds!"

Draw in crowds by offering freebies

"I've tried so many nontraditional sales strategies to attract customers and keep my stuff moving," says Heather Wheeler, cofounder of TheKrazy CouponLady.com. "My favorite one: filling a 'free' box with lower-priced but good-quality items like CDs or kids' books for people to rummage through. I allow one free item per customer, and I always make sure to mention it in my ad. You'd be amazed at how many people will show up when they know there's free stuff available. The proof is in my pocket at the end of the day!"

Appeal to men

Guys are more likely to object to perusing a sale if they perceive it to be filled with "kids' stuff." But they will be more inclined to stop if you place items that pique their interest (think power tools and game consoles) closer to the street.

Kick off your sale a day early

"Most people host yard sales on Saturday, but I usually start mine early on Friday morning and run it all the way until the evening," says Lynda Hammond, founder of GarageSaleGal.com. "This attracts the yard sale pros and people on their way to and from work. The best part is that I have no competition. I've made up to $400 opening on a Friday—that's $200 more than what I've made starting on a Saturday."

Try this end-of-day strategy

"Handing out bags to shoppers—or having your little one do it—is a smart way to influence people to buy more," says Christina Heiska, founder of YardSaleQueen.com. "Plus, it helps speed up the end-of-day clean-out process. We all have a drawer or closet filled with extra grocery bags, and this is a fantastic way to put them to use. I've even used the bags as a selling pitch for the last hour or so, by declaring: 'Fill up the bag for $5!' This turns shopping into a fun game for customers, and it's an easy-on-you way to clean out the sale."

Display clothes like this

Reader Tip

"After a recent closet clean-out, I had piles of jackets, dresses, and blouses to sell—but nowhere to display them. I wanted one of those pro garment racks, but they run about $80 online. So I was thrilled to find that big-box stores carry racks for much less. I purchased two clothing racks at Walmart.com for $14 each. It made my entire sale look more professional, and shoppers were able to thumb through garments quickly. I earned my money back—and then some—on the first day when I sold $45 worth of clothing. And now I use the garment racks to dry clothes in my laundry room."

—*Debbie Miller, Salt Lake City, UT*

Make a moving display

Hang jewelry on a jewelry tree and place it on a lazy Susan, giving it a spin every so often. Research shows that kinetic displays boost sales by up to 317 percent. Also, try arranging merchandise at eye level rather than low to the ground—this is shown to increase sales by 83 percent. The exception: toys, which should be at a kid-friendly height.

YARD SALE SAFETY: PASS OR PURCHASE?

Comfortable sneakers? Check. A mapped-out route? Check. Small bills? Check. A list of recalled products? Huh? A recent law passed by the US Consumer Product Safety Commission (CPSC) has called out a slew of secondhand finds for being unsafe. Don't let a lack of recall knowledge slow down a fun day of bargain hunting. Instead, use our cheat sheet to confidently shop the sales.

PASS: DIY furniture

Be wary of those ready-to-assemble bookshelves, chairs, and tables. No matter how perfect they might look on the outside, you have no idea what the condition of the separate parts is. You could have collapsing furniture on your hands if there's been a recall of a specific part in the package you bought.

PASS: Water-stained items

Water is notorious for carrying harmful bacteria into your household. If you can't disinfect the object (for example, cushions, stuffed toys, or particleboard furniture), don't buy it. If it's salvageable, toss the damaged box or packaging and clean the item.

PURCHASE: Clothing

Load up on tees, jeans, and dresses—they're usually priced to move. But opt for plain garments rather than embellished articles. Rhinestones, snaps, zippers, grommets, and appliqués could contain lead or be a choking hazard.

PURCHASE: Lighting

Lamps, especially halogen ones, get a bad rap for being fire hazards. But with a few stipulations, they're fine to buy. To meet updated safety requirements, a lamp needs to have a polarized plug (one prong that's larger than the other), and the shade should be checked for loose fabric or a damaged protective lining. Also, halogen lamps need a wire guard. (Find out how to request one for free at CPSC.gov.)

PURCHASE: Toys

Most hard plastic toys like action figures, old dolls, or toy trucks (which can easily be sanitized in the dishwasher) are safe bets. But skip soft, flexible plastic items such as bath toys and inflatable objects (especially if the toys will be put in the child's mouth)—they may contain harmful phthalates.

PURCHASE: Books

Reading materials are a given at yard sales. Just quickly flip through the pages to make sure there's no water damage. The one exception? Metal-bound children's books—the CPSC banned their resale after numerous recalls due to lead.

PASS: Chipped cookware

Buying used cookware is typically fine (who doesn't dream of unearthing a Le Creuset cast-iron skillet?), but don't purchase warped pots or pans or anything with cracked enamel. Some older pans can become toxic as their finish wears off. Also, check labels: If you come across non-anodized aluminum, don't buy it—the metal can leach into your food.

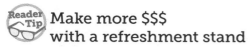

Make more $$$ with a refreshment stand

"Offering bottles of water and baked goods to shoppers is an easy way to boost sales—plus, it's the perfect way to get the whole family involved. I typically buy a case or two of water from the supermarket for $3 or $4, throw it over ice, and have the kids set up a small refreshment stand where they sell bottles for 75 cents each. Since it's usually so hot and sunny, the water goes like hotcakes. I also whip up a few batches of simple-to-make slice-and-bake chocolate chip cookies and charge 25 cents per cookie. You'd be surprised how much these extras can rake in!"

—*Sarah Hogan, Atlanta, GA*

Choose this background music

In one study, people listening to classical music spent an average of $40, compared with $37 with pop and $35 without any. Classical music makes people feel more affluent, so they spend more.

Arrange items counterclockwise

Put an eye-catching display to the right of where people will enter your sale and use arrows to create a counterclockwise path. According to the market research firm TNS Sorensen, shoppers who stroll counterclockwise spend $2 more than clockwise shoppers. (That's why supermarkets put produce to the right of their entrances.)

Serve free snacks

Offering coffee or fruit encourages shoppers to linger, and studies show that the longer customers shop, the more money they spend.

TIPS FOR BUYING SECONDHAND

Watch out for packaging

Check exactly what you're getting, because sometimes older items will be placed in boxes that appear new. And be wary of discolored boxes, which may indicate water damage.

Double-check the pricing

To make sure you're getting the best deal on unfamiliar merchandise, send a text to Google at 466453 with the item's make and model and the words "price" and "used." The site will respond via text with a list of current prices, which you can use as leverage when bargaining. Aim for markdowns of at least 60 percent.

Use this haggling clue

When negotiating for a lower price, keep your cash in your hand. A study in the journal *Psychological Science* found that seeing and touching money causes the brain to release endorphins, resulting in a feeling of camaraderie. The feel-good boost the seller gets from the visual cue will make her more willing to give you a bargain.

Cut the Clutter and Save

Wouldn't it be nice to get rid of clutter and earn money back? *First for Women* readers and experts agree. Keep reading for pro tips and tricks on how to cash in on your clutter.

SELLING AND RECYCLING

Recyclables with a reward

You already recycle—why not get something for it? Go to RecycleBank.com for a program that weighs your recyclables and awards you points toward gift certificates at 2,400 retailers (including CVS, McDonald's, and Omaha Steaks). No location near you? You can earn points for green actions, like sending in old electronics. A sample reward: 2,500 points gets you a $10 gift card.

Reader Tip — Offering antiques to "friends"

"My favorite site for selling fragile or big items like fine china and furniture: Facebook. I created a 'garage sale' group and invited 25 local friends—then they invited some friends, and the group quickly reached 120 members. I simply upload a picture of the item, the asking price, and any other details, then post it on the wall. Last month, I listed our gently used sectional and quickly sold it for $400!"

—*Janice Roberts, Phoenix, AZ*

Sell your unused gift cards

Once you find all of your unused gift cards, visit CardCash.com. The site will buy unused gift cards from most well-known retailers, from department stores to restaurants and cinemas.

Cosmetics—what's old is new

Estée Lauder's Origins stores accept tubes, bottles, and jars from any cosmetic manufacturer at their retail counters for recycling. In return, you'll get a free sample of an Origins skin-care product. And if you return six MAC Cosmetics containers to the store, you'll receive a free lipstick in return.

Reader Tip — You can even sell craft supplies

"I'm a big fan of shopping on Etsy.com for hand-made home accents, gifts, craft supplies, and jewelry. Then the other day I found out that I could sell my crafting supplies on the site as well! The listing process is so easy—you just have to follow a few short steps to sign up for an account. If you're overloaded with yarn, string, glitter, buttons, beads, or any other art supply, it's supersimple to resell them here."

—*Jamie Novak, founder of JamieNovak.com*

Selling (or scrapping) appliances

Unwanted-but-working appliances like washers, dryers, and refrigerators can earn you quick cash when you put them up for sale on Craigslist.org. And since the site connects you with local buyers, you can have machines picked up rather than moving them yourself. If you need to unload appliances that don't work, consider selling them as scrap metal. At press time, Alter Metal Recycling in Lincoln, Nebraska, was accepting fridges and stoves for 8 cents per pound—which means a 250-pound refrigerator would yield about $20 (though you usually have to drop goods off at the facility).

A new game for sporting goods

"Paddleboards, baseball bats, mountain bikes. . . . the list of sporting gear accumulating in my garage is neverending. I used to sell items individually on Craigslist, but it ended up being more work than I had time for. Then my friend, who has four sons, filled me in on her solution: Play It Again Sports, a chain with stores all over the country [Go to PlayItAgainSports.com for details.] Over the past few months, I've sold a gently used baseball bat, golf clubs, and an elliptical and made well over $150. The most helpful aspect: I can choose to receive the payment as cash or store credit to stock up on items I actually need—it's so easy!"

—*Diane Ballard, Austin, TX*

CLEAR AWAY CLOTHING CLUTTER

Choose consignment for clothing

Reselling clothes at a consignment shop can earn you triple what you'd get at a garage sale. Oftentimes, a storefront makes people more inclined to spend. Even better, you get to reap the cash or store-credit rewards, while the store takes care of selling your clothes. Google your town and "consignment shops" for local stores.

Online selling made easier

"My closet is filled with old clothes, shoes, and purses. Instead of hopping between eBay and secondhand stores, I did some research and found Tradesy.com. You just post your item, and when it sells, Tradesy sends a prepaid shipping kit. And they take only 9 percent of the final sale—some sites take 20 percent. Recently I listed a $120 Banana Republic dress and it sold for $75!"

—*Jamie Novak, founder of JamieNovak.com*

10 Brilliant Uses
for BANANA PEELS

1 Rid your garden of aphids for good

After noticing some insect damage in your garden, you decide that it's time to nip the problem in the bud. Just cut up two or three banana peels, then dig a 1-inch-deep hole in the ground at the base of your plants and place the peels inside. Aphids and ants find the high potassium concentration in banana peels unappealing, so this little trick will make the pesky bugs retreat.

2 Make a natural fruit-fly trap

Even though the oranges and apples in your fruit bowl are nowhere near expiration, you often find little flies buzzing around your kitchen. Catch the pests once and for all by crafting a trap. First gather a large yogurt container, a banana peel, a hammer, and a nail. Using the nail and hammer, poke holes in the lid of the yogurt container. Place the banana peel inside, snap on the lid, and leave it where the flies tend to gather. The sweet smell of banana will attract the fruit flies, leading them to crawl inside—but they won't be able to fly back out through the tiny holes. Dispose of the trap after a day or when most of the flies have been caught.

3 Stop a scratched CD or DVD from skipping

If your favorite disc just won't play smoothly, fix it with a banana peel. To do: Rub the back of the disc in a gentle circular motion with the inside of the peel. Wipe off any residue with a soft cloth, then lightly spray the disc with glass cleaner and buff it until it looks clean. The wax in the peel will fill in scratches without harming the plastic finish, so the disc can play sans skips.

4 Swiftly lift ink stains from skin

Thanks to an exploded pen, your teenage son came home from school with ink-covered hands—and soap and water aren't doing the trick. To the rescue: banana peels! Rub the white side onto the discolored areas and watch the stains disappear. The natural oils in the peel will attract the oils in the ink, weakening the pigment's bond with the skin for easy removal.

5 Whiten teeth on the cheap

No need to spend a fortune on professional whitening strips—let banana peels do the job instead. Simply rub the inner white side of a peel against your freshly brushed teeth for about 2 minutes every day. The combination of plaque-busting, astringent salicylic acid and gently bleaching citric acid in banana peels will effectively lighten surface stains on teeth without wearing down the enamel. With this trick, you'll have bright pearly whites within a week!

6 Grill a juicier piece of chicken

Your husband is a grill master ... except when it comes to skinless chicken breasts. They're so lean that they dry out faster than he can flip them. Next time, have him place a banana peel on top of each breast while cooking. The peel will create a barrier that acts like skin, helping the meat retain its natural juices.

7 Soothe an itchy bug bite—stat!

Summer is coming to a close, but it seems the mosquitoes have yet to get the memo—the critters are still biting you. For fast, chemical-free relief from an itchy bite, rub the inside of a banana peel against the inflamed area. The peels are full of polysaccharides, which will seep into skin cells to halt swelling and inflammation within minutes.

8 Buff away scuffs on leather shoes

Last year's sling-backs are still in great condition, except for a few scuffs on the toes. The fix: Lightly rub the spots with the white side of a banana peel, then wipe with a clean cloth. The peel's potassium (a key ingredient in leather polish) will be absorbed into the leather and diminish the marks, leaving your shoes looking brand-new.

9 Perk up dull, dreary houseplants

If your potted ferns, cacti, and spider plants look like they need a little pick-me-up, give them a quick rubdown with the white side of a banana peel. The skin's rough texture will gently buff away dust, while its natural oils will add a nice polished sheen. Bonus: Banana peels contain nutrients like potassium that feed plants to keep them healthy and flourishing.

10 Remove a splinter painlessly

While playing on the deck, your daughter got a splinter in her finger. Make removal of the tiny wood sliver a cinch with this trick: Tape a piece of banana peel, white side down, over the wound and leave it on for 30 minutes. The enzymes in the peel will seep into the skin and encourage the splinter to move toward the surface for easy plucking. The result: a tear-free extraction your child will appreciate.

Sell kids' clothing without the work

"There's a big opportunity to make money on children's clothes," says Stephanie Nelson, founder of CouponMom.com. "Most of the time, the outfits are only gently used, since kids outgrow them so fast. Going to consignment shops works, but selling them online is even easier. My go-to Web site? ThredUp.com. You simply sign up for a free account and they send you free 'clean out bags,' which you can fill with clothing and shoes. Then just place it in the mail and they'll do all the work for you! They'll inspect your goods and pay you via check or PayPal for every item that sells."

Jewelry deals that pay

The popularity of stores specializing in cash back for used jewelry has given consumers the upper hand in such transactions. The dealer will offer you a percentage of the retail value for undamaged jewelry that can be resold. Any damaged pieces will be evaluated to determine the value of metal and gems that can be salvaged with resetting. For example, a 24-inch 14-karat gold chain weighing 6.5 grams could net you $85 to $95. Log on to AmericanGemSociety.org to find a certified jeweler in your area.

EXPERT ELECTRONICS RECYCLING

Sell your cell for cash

With the ongoing advances in technology, a cell phone's average life span is now less than 18 months. But your outdated phones can make you money. Search the Internet for sites that offer cases for your phone. Just log on and type in the manufacturer and model number (found on the back of the phone) to learn its value, then ship the phone according to the instructions on the site. Once the company receives and processes the phone, they'll send a payment to you.

Web Sites for gadgets and cash

"We're always upgrading our laptops, cell phones, cameras, and tablets. So I sell my old gear through sites like Gazelle.com and NextWorth.com. You type in information about your gadget and receive an instant quote. Then you mail in your product (for free!) and wait for your cash. Right now my old iPod Touch would net me $50."

—*Jamie Novak, founder of JamieNovak.com*

Trade your video games

Is your smart little gamer always mastering his video games and asking for a new challenge? Trade his used games for store credit at your local GameStop store. Check GameStop.com for the latest trade-in bonus offers.

FREE ELECTRONICS UPGRADE

To get a crisper TV image

Enhancing the picture on your TV takes just one simple tweak: Go into the "picture settings" menu with your remote and set the "brightness" and "picture" to about half their maximum, then continue to tweak as needed. TVs are often preset to deliver a sharp picture in store showrooms, where the lighting is bright and harsh. To get a better fit for your living room, just recalibrate picture settings to fit your needs.

To guarantee sharper printouts

Printing a Web page or PowerPoint slide from your home printer can result in difficult-to-read, distorted, or obscured text. The common culprit: background graphics. The excess ink needed to print images and backgrounds clouds your printout. Just be sure to unselect "print background colors" when it comes time to print.

To capture more colorful photos

It's easy to make your digital camera's snapshots as bright, bold, and crisp as the images you see in a magazine: Turn your iOS setting to the lowest level. Set it to 50 to 100 for shots taken in bright light, 200 if shooting in overcast conditions, and 400 for indoor or action shots. Slightly increase the "saturation" setting in the "color mode" menu for better pictures.

These days a new cell phone, camera, or computer comes out every week. Rather than trying to keep up with the onslaught, improve the quality of your existing electronics—without spending a dime! Here, the simple "upgrades" that will keep you on top of the tech game.

To ensure better GPS navigation

Since GPS navigators run on software, they need occasional map updates to stay current. But many updates can cost $70 or more. The way to sidestep pricey fees: Next time you're heading out someplace unfamiliar, connect your GPS to your computer, go to Maps.Google.com, type in your destination, and click on "Send to GPS." Your directions will never fail you, because Google Maps is constantly updated.

CDs, DVDs, and video games

"Whenever I want to sell any of our music, movies, or video games, I head over to CashForCDs.com and SecondSpin.com, both of which accept all of the above. SecondSpin is currently paying up to $12 for all Nintendo Wii games. When you bundle these items in bulk to sell, you can easily make a quick $100 or more."

—*Dawn Voorhees, mom of five, Topeka, KS*

Memorabilia makes money

After Michael Jackson's passing, Jackson-related collector's items went for five times their original price. (One dealer sold a sealed *Thriller* album for $1,000.) Even collectible VHS tapes can be hot sellers. For best results, package them in bundles—21 Disney tapes recently sold for $30. For hassle-free online selling, try one of eBay's new registered drop-off locations. These stores take a photo of each item, write a description, set up a PayPal account, and ship the items to buyers for a small fee and commission of the sale.

Double your take with the right username

"Whenever you sell anything online, you're required to create a username for the Web site that you're selling through," says Jamie Novak, author of *Stop Throwing Money Away*. "So after a lot of research—and trial and error—I discovered a username secret that increases the likelihood that my items will sell quickly. The trick: I start my name with the letter *A* or the number 1 and tailor it to the items being sold. For example, if I'm selling a bundle of classic books, I'll create a username like 'ABookworm' or '1BookEnthusiast.' Here's why it works: First, it shows buyers that you're passionate about what you're selling, so they'll assume your items are in good shape—that makes them feel confident buying from you as opposed to another seller. Second, starting the username with an *A* or a 1 guarantees that your listing comes up first when potential buyers search for books. This method always works out great for me!"

Chapter 6

SMART SHOPPING AND SAVINGS

Clever Ways to Save on Clothes

Shopping for clothes can really put a dent in your budget. But lucky for you, *First for Women* readers and experts alike are happy to chime in with quick tips and savvy solutions on how to score great styles at low prices.

SCORE BIG AT THE MALL

Receive tailored-to-you coupons via text

"My top way to save: text coupons," says Dia Adams, founder of TheDealMommy.com. Stores like Macy's and Bath & Body Works send regular texts alerting you to sales and coupons. You can sign up at each store's Web site. The best part: Once you start using the coupons, the alerts are tailored to your purchase patterns!

Visit the "concierge" for unexpected deals

"As soon as I step foot in the mall, I head to the customer service desk," says Joanie Demer, cofounder of TheKrazyCouponLady.com. "It's like the mall's version of a concierge. When I stopped by last month, the attendant handed me a bunch of coupons and flyers for current sales. They even offer freebies from time to time: I've scored Aveda beauty samples, department store portraits, and BOGO coupons for hot pretzels and drinks at the food court."

Get "cash" back at top stores

"A few months ago my sister told me about 'cash back' programs at stores like Gymboree and Old Navy. My favorite: the Sears Shop Your Way rewards card. I show the card anytime I shop at Sears, Land's End, or Kmart and earn points for every dollar I spend. Last week I realized I had 30,000 points, or $30 in rewards. I was able to put that toward my husband's new work shirts—it was like shopping with free cash!"

—*Maria Smith, Omaha, NE*

 ### Stock up on kids' clothes in an "adult store"

"I'm always in a rush at the mall, but last week I had extra time to shop. As I was thumbing through blouses at H&M, I spotted a kids' section tucked in the back corner. I'd never noticed it before, so I headed over to take a look. And I'm glad I did! I picked up leggings (two for $10) and sweaters for $10 for my daughter. And I scored $5 tees for my son and pants for $10."

—*Laurie Donovan, Atlanta, GA*

Speak up to cash in on sneaky sales

"It seems like whenever I buy something at full price, the price drops a day or two later. So last month, when I had my eye on a pair of adorable leather flats that cost a bit more than I wanted to spend, I asked the sales associate if there were any coupons I could put toward the shoes. She replied with a smile: 'I have a 10 percent off coupon today, but if you come back tomorrow those shoes will be marked down by 30 percent.' So I put the flats on hold and swung by the next day. Simply speaking up took my bill from $50 to $35. I've tried this tactic at other stores, and it's worked again and again!"

—*Colleen Smith, Ann Arbor, MI*

 ### Use this app to make the most of coupons

"The number of coupons mailed to my house each month is crazy! I can never keep track of them or squeeze them all in my wallet. So I was thrilled to find a free mobile app that does the work for me. I downloaded SnipSnap and scanned my coupons with my smartphone before tossing them in the trash. Now when I'm at the mall, I scroll through to find the coupons I need. The app even alerts me to active coupons when I enter certain stores. It's made saving—and organizing—so much easier."

—*Caroline Donahue, Greenville, NC*

 ### Buy "summer jeans" in September

"Every fall I dedicate one shopping trip to buying jeans—and it's always a pricey purchase. Recently, I was browsing designer jeans in the department store, but at $80—or more—per pair, they were out of my budget. Then I noticed a 'blowout sale' rack off to the side. It was filled with 'summer' jeans that were practically identical to the full-price denim, except that they came in lighter, faded washes. And since the store was trying to make room for new merchandise, these jeans were a fraction of the price of the 'fall' styles. I picked up two pairs of faded straight-leg jeans for $30 each—less than the cost of one fall pair."

—*Pamela Samson, Brighton, MI*

KNOW WHAT TO BUY WHERE

 ## Warehouse stores for basics

"Bulk-buy stores like Sam's Club and Costco are my go-to spots when I need to stock up on basics like underwear and socks for my family. My husband and sons all wear Burlington cotton socks from Sam's—a six-pack is $6, versus $11 at a big-box store. And I scored a two-pack of women's camisoles with built-in bras for $10—a big savings, compared with $15 for one camisole at a department store."

—Heidi Johnson, Harrisburg, PA

Outlet stores for jeans

"I always scour the outlet mall for deals on denim," says Stephanie Nelson, founder of CouponMom.com. "I can use a coupon from the discount book provided at the mall's customer service center on top of the discounted price. Last week my daughter found an $80 pair of jeans on sale for 25 percent off at the Levi's outlet store. With a 25-percent-off coupon, the total came to $45!"

 ## Online discount stores for suits

"I've found that liquidation sites like Bluefly.com and Overstock.com are my best bet when my husband and I need dressy outfits for a wedding or other special event. The deals just can't be beat. For my niece's upcoming wedding, I got myself a BCBGMaxAzria dress for $90 at Bluefly.com (retail price $400) and ordered my husband a Ralph Lauren suit (originally $499) for $150 at Overstock.com. We saved $659!"

—Donna Fulco, Orlando, FL

Big-box stores for T-shirts

"Every August I stock up on T-shirts for the whole family at Target," says Melea Johnson, founder of Freebies2Deals.com. The summer tees are always in the clearance section, marked down to $3 to $4 apiece—and even the full-price shirts are really reasonable. Plus, I can usually find extra discounts at Coupons.Target.com. For instance, this week I printed out three coupons for $3 off Merona T-shirts and used them to buy scoop-neck tees that were on sale for $6 each. For a total of $9, I got three supercute shirts that I'll wear forever—what a steal."

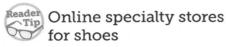 Online specialty stores for shoes

"I order my family's shoes from Web sites like Zappos.com and 6pm.com. It's the easiest way to compare lots of brands and prices at once. I'll simply enter the type of shoe or brand I'm looking for, then click on the 'sort by lowest price' tab to see the cheapest options first. I just nabbed a pair of Western Chief rain boots for $28 at 6pm.com—that's $22 off the retail price."

—Heidi Johnson

Thrift stores for accessories

"I save an unbelievable amount on vintage necklaces, hats, and belts by shopping at local secondhand stores. My teenage kids and I have taken to calling it treasure hunting because the items we find are truly unique. The other day we found an old gold locket and chain for $4. It was a real bargain, considering my daughter had been eyeing a similar $50 necklace at J.Crew for a week!"

—Margie Carnahan, Phoenix, AZ

Yard sales for kids' clothes

"My secret to getting high-quality children's clothes at rock-bottom prices is to hit the yard sales. Every August I spend two Saturdays combing through the classified ads for keywords like *name brands* and *unworn children's clothes*, then I head to those sales first. Two weeks ago I found a children's Gap windbreaker, a pair of OshKosh B'gosh jeans, a J.Crew long-sleeved dress, and a jacket from the North Face on a rack for $3 each—and many of the items still had tags on them. Even better, when I offered the seller $2 per item instead, she happily accepted. For $15 I was able to get back-to-school essentials that would've cost me at least $300 in department stores."

—Nadine Bartlett, Green Lake, WI

Discount retail stores for lingerie

"I love the confidence boost I get from wearing pretty bra-and-panty sets, but I don't love how much they cost at department stores. So I was thrilled to discover that discount stores like T.J. Maxx, Ross, and Marshalls carry all my favorite designer brands—including Calvin Klein, DKNY, and Maidenform—for up to 50 percent less than the suggested retail price. At T.J.Maxx I found two Calvin Klein bras for $10 each (retail price: $40) and five pairs of Maidenform panties for $3 apiece (originally $8). To save even more, I signed up for e-mail newsletters from T.J.Maxx. Now I regularly get $10-off coupons in my in-box that make my undergarments an even bigger steal."

—Lois Tullman, Manasquan, NJ

Cut Personal-Care Costs

The average family spends more than $500 each year on shampoo, conditioner, and other grooming goods—that's a lot of soaping and sudsing! Now you can look great and spend less by trying out these tips.

 ### Click for the best prices on fragrances

"I love experimenting with different perfumes. What I don't like: shelling out lots of money for them. My go-to source for savings? Overstock.com. I recently got a Vera Wang fragrance for $42—that's $50 less than the department store's price!"

—Rose Orrico, Ann Arbor, MI

 ### Name your price with alerts

"When I was shopping for a new blow-dryer, my tech-savvy son taught me how to set up a Google alert. I visited Google.com/alerts and entered the name of the hair dryer, a minimum price, three periods, and my maximum price: Chi Pro Hair Dryer $50 . . . $75. Then I clicked 'create alert' and got an e-mail when any Web site dropped the price to within that range. I got the dryer for $25 less than retail!"

—Diane Goodman, Omaha, NE

Triple your savings with the 4-week rule

"When it's time to stock up on items like lotion, deodorant, and soap, I make sure to time my purchases right,' says Teri Gault, founder of TheGroceryGame.com. Every 4 weeks, national drugstores offer impressive sales on personal items through their 'instant rewards' programs—I keep up-to-date by checking out their weekly circulars. By combining sales with coupons and my instant rewards, I get triple the savings."

 ### Save up to 50 percent by choosing men's products

"I recently read that women's grooming products are often more expensive than men's, solely because of the pretty packaging and presentation. So the last time I went to the drugstore, I looked more closely and found that it was true! The male and female deodorants had the same active ingredients, but the men's varieties were about $3 cheaper. Since then, I've been buying unscented men's deodorant and saving plenty of cash."

—Catherine Lyons, Norfolk, VA

 ### Score favorites in bulk online

"My sister is constantly sharing her savings tricks. And last month when I was about to restock my favorite Olay products, she suggested I log on to eBay and use her 'lot' secret. She explained that when you type the name of a product followed by the word 'lot' into the search bar, it brings up items sold in bulk. For instance, I found a 'lot' of four Olay lotions for $10—that's $2.50 per lotion, compared with $8 each at the supermarket."

—Jessica Smith, Phoenix, AZ

Sign up for free loot

Swing by a Sephora store or visit Sephora.com to register for their Beauty Insider club. The no-cost membership nets you a gift (like a lip-gloss set worth $12) on your birthday, plus allows you to accrue points for free products and entitles you to three samples at checkout.

Nab brand names for a buck

"Shopping for things like shampoo, soap, and toothpaste for my family used to be one of my pricier errands, especially since I can never find time to clip coupons. Then a couple of months ago, I stopped into our local Dollar General for some gift wrap and a few other items I needed and was stunned at the variety of brand-name personal-care products. I picked up four full-size tubes of Colgate toothpaste for $1 each—I usually pay nearly $4 per tube at the drugstore!"

—*Barb Meyers, Shark River Hills, NJ*

Get a customized beauty kit at your doorstep

"While scouring the Internet looking for beauty bargains, I stumbled upon the Web site BeautyFix.com. After I answered questions about my skin, eyes, and hair, the site's panel of 25 experts, ranging from aestheticians to makeup artists, recommended a customized selection of 100 products from high-end brands like Murad, Perricone, and Jane Iredale. I was able to choose any eight products for $49, which is $6.50 per item—what a steal! The box was shipped to my door for free and was worth more than $300."

—*Joan Davis, Fairfield, CT*

Hit the baby aisle for makeup remover

"The beauty necessity I used to spend too much cash on: makeup-remover wipes," says Richelle Shaw, president of the National Association for Moms in Business. "For years I spent $15 for a package of 30 specialty wipes—eek! Then one day while running errands at Target, I overheard another shopper say she uses baby wipes to remove her makeup. When I realized I could get a 56-count box of unscented baby wipes for $2, I was sold. They're essentially the same product as my fancy makeup-remover wipes—at a fraction of the price. They gently remove mascara and eyeliner and stay moist for just as long!"

Whip up high-end skin care at home

Before you shell out for "all natural" scrubs or moisturizers, consider making your own. Try this simple body scrub: Combine 2 cups of sea salt and ½ cup of olive oil in a shallow plastic container and keep it in the shower. This mixture will leave your skin just as soft and dewy as a similar $24 scrub from a high-end spa store, but the ingredients cost less than $8 at the supermarket.

Ask about off-peak salon rates

When it comes to booking hair appointments, it can pay to wait until the last minute. Salons often offer discounts up to 25 percent on slow days. Simply call the salon ahead of time and ask if discounts are available. Hint: Mondays and weekday afternoons are typically salons' slowest times.

Extend hair color with a glaze

To refresh or extend the life of your hair color without spending a fortune, consider a glaze treatment, like John Frieda Clear Shine Luminous Color Glaze ($9), which instantly enhances hair color and fades slowly over time. That lets you go even longer—often 3 more weeks—before your next color treatment, helping you eliminate up to four salon color treatments a year. In fact, since each one can cost about $75, you'll save $300 annually.

Home Goods Happiness

You don't have to spend a fortune to update your home decor. By making small decorating changes and finding deals at discount stores, you can freshen up your home for practically pennies. Try these clever ways to score discounts on fabulous furniture, bedding, kitchenware, and more!

SAVE ON HOME UPDATES

Upgrade cabinets with new knobs

"My kitchen cabinets were looking outdated, but I didn't want to pay $1,100 to have them refaced," says Kristl Story, founder of TheBudgetDiet.com. "Instead, I perused the Home Depot and found oil-rubbed bronze knobs for $3 each. The modern hardware gave my kitchen a whole new look—and it only cost me $30!"

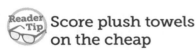 Score plush towels on the cheap

"Last fall I decided to splurge on new bath towels and started reading up on towel fabrics to make sure I got the most bang for my buck. It turns out that a U.S.-grown cotton called pima offers the luxe look and feel of Egyptian cotton for much less. Rather than spend $20 per towel, I nabbed pima towels for $9 each at Sears. The bright hues updated both bathrooms—and the soft fabric makes guests feel like they're at a four-star hotel!"

—*Karen Hart, Cape Coral, FL*

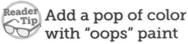 Add a pop of color with "oops" paint

"I love to paint an accent wall or molding to revitalize a room. And since I need only a gallon of paint to complete the job, I can get 'oops' paint—that is, unsold custom-blended colors—for just $5 to $10 per gallon, compared with $25 for a regular gallon. Recently I scored a pretty sage green for $10 that I used to paint one wall in our living room, and I was flooded with compliments on the color!"

—*Katherine Finney, Bridgeport, CT*

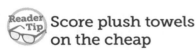 Find bedding deals online

"I wanted to buy new sheets before my houseguests arrived, but I didn't want to spend hundreds. Then my money-savvy friend clued me in to her inexpensive bedding source: Overstock.com. Sure enough, when I logged on, I found a gorgeous 300-thread-count sheet set for $32 and a queen-size comforter and sham set for $37—I saved $150, compared with what I would have spent on similar bedding at the department store!"

—*Patricia Williams, Austin, TX*

Snag an "as is" rug at the decor outlet

"Warming up the hardwood floors in our bedroom should've been easy, but I couldn't seem to find a rug that made a style statement for less than $1,000," says Sherry Petersik, cofounder of Young HouseLove.com. "That's when my husband and I decided to check our favorite lighting outlet, which also sells new rugs that are deeply discounted. We were able to score a $1,287 rug for $250 simply because it had a small tear in one corner. The hole isn't even visible when the rug is laid out flat—and the floor cover enhances the room beautifully."

10 Brilliant Uses
for BUBBLE WRAP

1 Prolong the life of produce

To help keep your fruit and vegetables blemish-free in the fridge, line the crisper drawer with bubble wrap. The air pockets in the packaging staple will provide cushioning for thin-skinned produce such as pears and apples to prevent bruising. When the lining gets dirty, just throw it away and replace with fresh wrap.

2 Pop away stress in seconds

Love popping bubble wrap? Us, too—and science proves it's good for you. The activity has been shown to lower blood pressure and heart rate, plus decrease levels of the stress hormone cortisol and increase levels of feel-good serotonin. Keep a sheet in your drawer or purse, and when you need to blow off steam, get poppin'!

3 Outsmart suitcase-induced wrinkles

Whenever you pack for a trip, you leave extra space for souvenirs or gifts you might buy along the way. But the breathing room causes belongings to shift around en route, making freshly pressed garments a wrinkled mess. To help everything stay put, stuff bubble wrap into the empty areas of your bag. It will keep your possessions in place, so your garments will come out as neat as they were when they went in. And when it's time to pack for home, you can use the wrap to encase fragile souvenirs.

4 Eliminate pet food messes for good

Sometimes it seems as though more food ends up on the floor than in your pet's mouth—resulting in you having to wipe up the area around his bowl multiple times a day. The solution: Lay down a small sheet of bubble wrap and place your pet's dish on top. Stray food particles will be caught in the wrap's nooks and crannies, so your floor will stay spotless. For cleanup, simply replace the wrap.

5 Make a sleeping bag extra comfy

The more the merrier—that's always your philosophy when it comes to the holidays. But all those extra kids and teens in the house means you have to rely on sleeping bags. To ensure everyone snoozes in comfort, try this easy trick: Tape pieces of bubble wrap together to form a mat about the size and shape of each sleeping bag, then lay the "mattress pad" on the floor and place the sleeping bag on top. The bubbles will act as cushions, creating a softer surface that will guarantee a pleasant night's rest.

6 Fashion a cushiony bath pillow

When you want to take a relaxing soak in the tub but your bath pillow is nowhere to be found, grab a few sheets of bubble wrap. Fold them into a pillow shape and secure with duct or packing tape, then place the makeshift pillow behind your head. The air-filled bubbles will comfortably support your head and neck.

7 Put an end to "hanger creases"

Hanging freshly ironed dress pants often results in unsightly creases across the knees. Avoid the problem by circling the horizontal bar of the hanger with bubble wrap and securing with clear packing tape. The wrap will provide a padded cushion that prevents the dreaded creases, ensuring you look extra sharp.

8 Keep ice and snow off your windshield

The next time the weatherman predicts snow, lay a large sheet of bubble wrap across the front windshield of your car before you go to bed. (Secure with your windshield wipers if necessary.) Rather than freezing to the glass, the snow will settle on top of the bubble wrap. All you'll have to do in the a.m. is slide the plastic sheet off the windshield, making cleanup a cinch.

9 Insulate drafty windows

If chilly air is seeping through thin-paned windows (like those in the basement) and making the room too cold for comfort, try this: Press pieces of bubble wrap against the inside of each window, then seal the edges using packing tape. The bubble wrap will create a barrier that keeps warm air in and blocks wind gusts.

10 Reshape squished shoes

After rooting through dozens of shoes in your closet, you finally found your go-to pumps. Unfortunately, they are crushed beyond recognition. Repair the damage by cutting two pieces of bubble wrap so they are the same length as the shoes and three times the width. Roll each piece into a tube shape, wrap masking tape around one end (so it is narrow enough to fit into the toe box), and tuck one tube into each shoe. Let sit for 20 minutes. The plastic will push the leather back into its original, like-new shape.

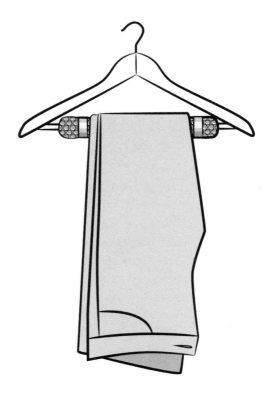

Pick up candles at the dollar store

"Nothing adds ambience to a room like candles—the soft illumination, sweet scents, and pops of color can make any space feel more festive," says Laura Oliver, founder of AFrugalChick.com. "But buying a bunch of decorative candles can get expensive fast. To my surprise, I found really pretty scented pillar candles for 98 cents each at the dollar store—a steal, considering similar candles cost $12 each at the home store. I bought 10 and put them on display on simple platters in the living room, entryway, and bathrooms. For less than $10, I was able to add lighting that makes my home look like a million bucks!"

Nab outdoor pieces now—and use them inside

"If I'm looking to replace a piece of furniture, I wait to shop until late October, when most stores mark down their outdoor pieces. Last year I had my heart set on a mahogany kitchen table—and scored an outdoor version for $174 at Overstock.com. It cost $426 less than a similar table I was eyeing at Crate & Barrel—and it works perfectly in my kitchen!"

—Debbie Collins, Mt. Pleasant, MI

Turn discount fabric into throw pillows

"When shopping at discount stores, I often find great fabric that can add a unique touch to my decor in a pinch," says Kathy Woodward, founder of TheBudgetDecorator.com. "For instance, last holiday season, I wanted to punch up the blue accents in my guest room before houseguests arrived. So I grabbed a large, royal blue tablecloth I'd gotten at a thrift store for $3, then used iron-on hem tape I bought at the craft store for $2 to turn the tablecloth into covers for the throw pillows on the bed. It took me only an hour to cut and iron the seams for four pillow covers—and I had enough fabric left over to create a table runner for the dining room, too! My 'new' pillows immediately brightened up the guest room for just $5."

Get discount artisan ware here

Buyers from T.J.Maxx and Marshalls are able to deal directly with local artisans from Italy, Mexico, and Poland to negotiate steep discounts on handmade vases, platters, and glassware. Artisan glassware can be expensive at department stores, but T.J. Maxx and Marshalls offer sets of glassware for much cheaper.

Buy kitchenware like the pros do

For quality yet affordable kitchenware, look no further than a restaurant supply store. To find a store, search "restaurant supply" and your city online.

Rack up rewards on exotic textiles

Home decor stores like Pier 1 Imports and World Market offer free rewards programs that can net you discounts, like $10 off a $30 purchase. Just enter your e-mail address at their Web sites or fill out an in-store application to get the perks. World Market will give you a coupon for 10 percent off your first purchase just for joining their Explorer Rewards program.

Use mirrors as art

Mirrors can liven up any room—for 50 percent less than you'd spend on artwork. You can find large, framed mirrors for under $50 at Marshalls or small ones for $20 or less at Walmart. Use a big one to reflect light in an entryway, or hang clusters of smaller mirrors in smaller rooms.

Save big on cabinets

You can get quality kitchen cabinets for less by asking a salesperson at the cabinet store to direct you to discontinued models or floor samples. Or check out closeout or overstock sites like CloseoutCabinets.com for great deals online.

Snag unexpected steals at the hardware store

Because stores like the Home Depot manufacture the home goods they sell, they are usually much less expensive than home goods found at department stores. *First for Women* found an Adesso swivel floor lamp for $18 with free shipping at HomeDepot.com—a $36 savings off the Walmart price.

SPRUCE UP YOUR BACKYARD FOR LESS

Buy flowers in bulk

To save big on plants, be sure to buy many at once. For example, the Home Depot sells single pansy plants for $2 each, but a flat of 12 plants goes for $12. If you aren't in the market for that many plants, split the purchase with family and friends to share the savings.

Score landscaping leftovers on Craigslist

It can pay to check the free sections on Web sites like Craigslist.org and Freecycle.org. People often list surplus rocks and other materials left over from landscaping projects at no cost.

Find garden art at the flea market

Instead of spending a fortune on a new garden fountain, scout out a flea market for a good deal. For example, one *First for Women* editor scored a vintage wood garden bench at a local flea market for $15—a $235 savings, compared with a similar garden bench at LogCabinRustics.com.

Click for half-price plants

Don't be afraid to look online for flower deals. Check out the daily deals, huge clearance sales, and selection of plants for $10 or less at GreatGardenPlants.com. Or head to BluestonePerennials.com, a site that discounts select flowers and plants by 50 percent every day.

Nab free mulch from the parks department

There's no reason to pay a bundle for mulch—most parks and recreation or forestry departments will give out wood chips or shredded bark at no cost. Just call your local city service office and request "clean chips" (which means they're free of weeds and other material)—some cities will even deliver the chips to your home. One *First for Women* editor saved $168 by using pinewood chips obtained from her community's parks department to cover her 500-square-foot garden.

Shop the warehouse for patio sets

Wholesale retailers like Costco, BJ's, and Sam's Club offer unbeatable prices on outdoor furniture. And you don't have to hit the stores—many deals are also available online with free shipping.

Rack up rewards on gardening goods

Chain hardware stores like the Home Depot and Lowe's offer free gardening rewards programs that can net you huge discounts, like 40-percent-off coupons and buy-one-get-one-free plant deals. Just fill out an in-store application or enter your e-mail address at the store's Web site to get the perks. The Home Depot Garden Club even offers free 24-hour access to garden experts.

Scout out free trees

Trees can cost more than $150 each at nurseries—but you can often get them for free. Just call your Department of Public Works to see whether your community hands out trees for free. Or sign up for a $10 membership at ArborDay.org, and the Arbor Day Foundation will ship you 10 flowering or evergreen tree saplings at no cost.

Advice for Appliances and Gadgets

Appliances and electronics eat up a large portion of every family's budget. Read on for expert tips and tricks for cutting costs and saving big on refrigerators, cell phones, cameras, and more!

GREAT WAYS TO SAVE ON ELECTRONICS

Keep an eye out for entertainment bundles

Manufacturers trying to introduce consumers to new technology (which they often do at the start of the year) will offer "free gift with purchase" deals or "bundles." For example, you can find amazing deals like this bundle once offered at Sears.com: a free 3-D Blu-ray player with the purchase of an LG 3-D TV. Savings on these types of twofer deals can be amazing.

Take advantage of credit card perks

If you purchase items with certain credit cards (including American Express and some cards from Chase and Citibank), you'll double the warranty at no cost. For example, if you buy a digital camera that comes with a 1-year warranty from the store or manufacturer, American Express will automatically extend the warranty to cover the camera for another year.

Know where to go for quality "refurbs"

It's smart to buy refurbished tech items through the manufacturer's Web site, since gadgets often come with the best prices and a 1-year warranty. At Apple.com, *First for Women* found a refurbished iPad for $100 less than the same version would cost new.

Buy cell phones online

For the best selection and steepest bargains, go to Amazon.com and Wirefly.com, where you're still allowed to use main carriers like Verizon.

Hit the outlets for small appliances

Factory outlets offer unbeatable prices on appliances like mixers and juicers. And you don't have to hit the store—deals are also available at outlet sites like SearsOutlet.com and Overstock.com. *First for Women* found a Keurig B60 single-serve coffeemaker with free shipping at Overstock—a savings of almost $50 off the retail price.

Put deal hunters to work for you

Surf to TechBargains.com, CrazyTownDeals.com, or DealNews.com, all of which have pro bargain hunters who browse forums and other resources to scout out savings. Then click the "hottest deals" for dramatic price reductions—like the Sony Bravia LED 55-inch HDTV that *First for Women* found through TechBargains.com for $425 less than the price at Sony.com.

Click for cash back

When shopping for big-ticket items, it pays to use cash-back portals like Ebates.com and ShopAtHome.com. These sites allow you to earn up to 15 percent back on purchases from manufacturers like HP and Apple. (Rebate checks are mailed out every 3 months.)

Negotiate a lower price

According to *Consumer Reports*, only 33 percent of people who bought major appliances haggled over prices, but 75 percent of those who did haggle saved a median of $100. To make bargaining even easier, use your phone to show salespeople ads for the same product at a lower price elsewhere.

Say no to premium accessories

Many retailers push accessories like HD video cables for a TV or ultra-high-speed memory cards for a camera. But often these add-ons aren't necessary. Before purchasing any accessories, be sure to research whether you actually need it.

Search "hidden" prices

Web sites like Amazon.com and Overstock.com often have items marked "add to cart to see price." That's usually code for "deep discount." The reason: Online stores can't post prices that are less than the manufacturers' advertised price. They get around this by requiring that you add the item to your cart to see the deal. And don't worry—you don't have to purchase it. After you see the price, you can simply take it out of your cart.

Cash in on price guarantees

If you buy tech goods at large retailers like Walmart and the price drops within 2 weeks, you can bring your receipt and get a refund of the difference. Sometimes you can even get a rebate if the item goes on sale at another store, as long as you bring the other store's ad and show a salesperson.

Ask for open-box items

People often return tech items without using them—but if the box has been opened, those items won't sell for top dollar. That's why it pays to ask if any open-box items are available. Just make sure to find out why the item was returned, and ensure you have the same refund policy and warranty as the original buyer.

MAKE APPLIANCES LAST YEARS LONGER

CLOTHES DRYER:
Average life span = 12 years
As dryers get older, they tend to take much longer to dry clothes. To blame: obstructions in the venting system that block air flow. To fix this, unplug the dryer, move it away from the wall, and detach the hose, then use a vacuum to clear out lint and dust. (If your vacuum hose is short, home centers sell attachments designed for cleaning vents.) When reattaching the dryer hose, avoid kinking it, as this can speed future buildup. Also try gently scrubbing the lint filter with hot water and a clean toothbrush every 6 months to remove dust.

Added life = up to 3 years

REFRIGERATOR:
Average life span = 14 years
The refrigerator's condenser coils are responsible for releasing the heat that the machine generates, but these coils can easily become covered with dust, pet hair, and other debris. This causes the refrigerator to use more energy to stay cold, decreasing its life expectancy. Twice a year (three or four times for pet owners), turn off the fridge, remove the grate protecting the coils (behind the fridge on older models; at the bottom on newer models), and use a vacuum brush attachment to remove dust and grime. Also try relubricating the rubber door seal, which can be weakened by food buildup. Just wash it with warm, soapy water; let dry; and buff on a thin layer of petroleum jelly to soften the rubber and repel future food splashes.

Added life = up to 4 years

DISHWASHER:
Average life span = 10 years
Prolonging your dishwasher's life is simple—just run hot water through the garbage disposal for 30 seconds before turning on the machine. The water flushes out any debris that could otherwise be sucked into the dishwasher's drain line, leading to clogs. And even if you don't have a disposal, running the tap gives the water a chance to heat up, so it's already hot when you start the dishwasher. This helps dissolve the dish soap faster, preventing machine-harming residue. Also try using powder soaps, which leave behind less soap buildup.

Added life = 4 to 8 years

WASHING MACHINE:
Average life span = 11 years
A common problem: When the clothes washer isn't level, the drum or tub grates against the frame during the spin cycle, causing damage. Lay a level on top of your machine to make sure it's sitting relatively flat. If it's uneven, most newer models have front-leveling legs that can easily be adjusted—just move the legs up or down. To level older machines, use small pieces of plywood, cork rounds, or furniture pads instead. Also try using less detergent, which decreases soap buildup and clogs. Use just 2 tablespoons of detergent for front-loading washers and about a quarter capful for top-loading machines.

Added life = up to 3 years

GET YOUR MONEY BACK—STAT!

Get out of a cell phone contract

Canceling a cell phone contract can be pricey—some providers charge more than $200 in early termination fees. But you can sidestep charges if you know the loopholes. Whenever the provider changes the contract, they are obligated to let you opt out. Since major carriers often change their "terms and conditions" once or twice a year, you'll have a handful of opportunities to free yourself from a 2-year contract. But contract-change notices are often buried in fine print on your bill or other mailings. The save: Type "[carrier name] change of contract terms" into Google.com/alerts to automatically receive an e-mail whenever a change is mentioned online. Then call your provider and say, "You changed my contract terms. According to FCC rules, you have to let me opt out without an early termination fee."

Another out: If service gets significantly worse at home, or if you move to a no-service area, providers will generally let you out of your contract—though they aren't required by law to do so. To build your case, look at a coverage map to see if reception in your area is weak. If they don't agree to release you, tell them you'll be filing a complaint with the Better Business Bureau.

Get out of a costly warranty

If you decide the extended warranty you purchased with a big-ticket item such as a dishwasher or laptop isn't worth the price, don't bother heading back to the store to cancel it. Salespeople often get commissions for selling warranties, and that's why they will often try to talk you out of a refund—they'll lose their commission if you stand your ground.

The better bet: Call the warranty provider directly. (Find their contact information in the warranty paperwork.) If you cancel within the trial period (usually 30 days), you'll receive a full refund. After 30 days, if you paid for the warranty in full, you should request a pro rata reimbursement—that means you'll receive a percentage of your payment based on how much time is left on your coverage period. If you are making monthly payments, simply state that you want the payments stopped.

Get out of a "mystery charge"

It's a familiar frustration: A small charge from a vaguely named company begins appearing on your credit card statement. Almost always, this means you've accidentally enrolled in a membership or loyalty program—usually by redeeming a coupon or rebate online that sneakily opts you in.

The fix: Start by searching online for complaints against the company. Then contact your credit card provider—most allow between 30 and 90 days to file disputes. Unfortunately, it takes people a few months to catch on to these charges, but most credit card companies just need to know when you first noticed the charges, not when they began. Just say, "I never authorized these charges, and I'd like them removed." If the credit card company only offers to refund the past month or two, strengthen your case by saying that other people are complaining about the same scam. Most important: Ask that they decline all charges from that merchant going forward.

Family Fun at a Lower Price

Vacations and local activities don't have to cost a bundle! Discover how cash-savvy readers find great deals, save money, and keep everyone in the family happy.

ENTERTAINMENT ON THE CHEAP

 ### "Flash" for local entertainment discounts

"I love the idea of coupons, but I always forget them at home. Then I heard about the free Yowza!! app, which offers tons of deals you can use on the go. Now when I'm at a restaurant or attraction, I just flash the coupon on my phone for instant savings. Recently, my husband and I scored a $20 deal for an all-day bike rental, followed by free appetizers at a restaurant. It was great!"

—Karen Francis, Rutherford, NJ

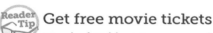 ### Get free movie tickets

"I've had Cablevision as my cable provider for a while but was unaware of my movie-theater rewards until a few months ago. Through the company's Optimum Rewards program, we get two free tickets to Clearview Cinemas every Tuesday. It's become a regular date night for my husband and me, and if we're busy, I just offer up the tickets to my teenagers."

—Tracy King, Cherry Hill, NJ

"Like" and "follow" your town online

"When spring arrives, I'm instantly in the mood to plan outings with my husband and kids. I've found that 'liking' local city or town pages on Facebook and following my town's community center on Twitter are the ultimate activity resources. Just last Friday, I was browsing my newsfeed and saw an update for the upcoming Family Kite Festival at Veterans Park, with free admission, free parking, live music, and more."

—Danielle Watts, Milwaukee, WI

 ### Strike a deal on bowling

"My husband and I are avid bowlers, and we love taking along our kids, nieces, and nephews, so I'm always searching for deals. Last year I discovered that the national chain Brunswick Zone offers impressive prices. The best specials: Every Sunday between 9 a.m. and noon it's just 99 cents per game, and on Thursday nights it costs just $8 for unlimited bowling and $1 per shoe rental.

Usually, it's $4 per game and $4 per shoe rental, so these specials easily save us $35 or more!"

—*Claudia Griffin, North Ridgeville, OH*

 Hit these stores for free arts and crafts

"Our kids always look forward to the first Saturday of the month, when the Home Depot hosts a free kids' workshop. Whether it's building a fire truck or an herb planter, my little ones always have a blast. Also fun: Lakeshore Learning, a chain of educational stores that hosts free educational crafts every Saturday."

—*Mackenzie Rollins, founder of CheeriosAndLattes.com*

 Enjoy big-name concerts on the cheap

"Every spring my family gets together for one big night, like a concert or sporting event. After hunting down tickets for years, I've found that sites like SeatGeek.com are the best options, since they pool prices from hundreds of ticket sites. We wanted to see Jason Aldean, Kelly Clarkson, and Jake Owen at Wrigley Field, and I got tickets for $68 each—a savings of $40 per ticket. This is going to be a night to remember!"

—*Ann Voorhees, Chicago, IL*

 Snag free museum admission

"I regularly take advantage of my credit card's point perks. Then the other day I received an e-mail listing my card's other rewards. Turns out, most credit cards offer extra programs filled with freebies—and you don't have to buy anything to enjoy them. For example, my Bank of America card has a 'Museums on Us' program that grants us free admission to a variety of science centers, museums, aquariums, and planetariums on the first full weekend of every month. BankOfAmerica.com has a full list of participating venues—it's so fun to pick and choose!"

—*Shelly Robinson, Fort Lauderdale, FL*

 Slash $40 off a day at the zoo

"My brood always has a blast at the zoo. But individual passes are a little on the pricey side ($22 per person), and we don't venture there enough to take advantage of the yearly membership savings. Then when I was checking out the Atlanta Zoo Web site, I saw a link for group rates. I'd always figured that these were for very large groups, but it turns out you need only 10 people to qualify, and it slashes individual ticket prices by $4 each. So I gathered my extended family for a day at the zoo. Collectively, we saved $40 by choosing this rate, and I soon learned that most big zoos offer similar group pricings on their Web sites—I'll definitely be taking advantage of this deal again!"

—*Sheila Goddard, Atlanta, GA*

BEST WAYS TO BEAT CABIN FEVER

Pick up the classics at your local library

Many libraries offer more than just good reads. According to a survey by the Online Computer Library Center, US public libraries lend out an average of 2.1 million videos and DVDs per day. Classic films, TV shows, and even new releases in Blu-ray and DVD are available for a small charge (around $1) or free, with a library card.

Sign up for group discounts

Register your city and e-mail address at Groupon.com and LivingSocial.com, deal-of-the-day Web sites that can net you steep group discounts to local spas, events, and dining establishments. At press time, we found half-price tickets to the Greensboro Symphony Masterworks Series in North Carolina on Groupon.com.

Leverage your memberships

Don't overlook your memberships with AAA, AARP, credit unions, alumni groups, or professional organizations. Associations like these often provide coupons or discounted tickets for local entertainment attractions. For instance, AAA offers a "buy one, get one free" game of bowling at Brunswick Zone in Minnesota.

Join the fan "club"

Many singers, comedians, and up-and-coming bands use their Web sites or Facebook pages to alert fans to new shows, presale events, and ticket discount codes. So consider registering as a fan on your favorite artist's Web site to ensure access to the best seats at the best price. One *First for Women* editor recently scored presale tickets to see her favorite comedian at a $15 discount per seat just for signing up on the fan site.

Enjoy the arts on campus

Check out the nearby college for discounted music performances, theater productions, dance recitals, and author lectures. Event tickets are often free or inexpensive because the performance costs are supplemented by the university or the show is put on by students. One such offering: Cleveland's Case Western Reserve University offers free live jazz music at Arts Collinwood Café every Wednesday night.

Volunteer as an usher

To net free admission to the performing arts center, consider volunteering. In exchange for passing out playbills and helping people find their seats for an hour before a show, most theaters will let you stay for the performance. To get involved, inquire about the usher program at your local theater's box office or customer service desk.

Buy film tickets in bulk

If your family enjoys going to the local cinema to catch the latest flicks, consider buying tickets in bulk. Costco sells a set of four Regal Entertainment Group tickets for $30—that's a $4 savings per ticket on a regular price admission of $11.50. Or search CheapMovieTicketsOnline.com, where

First for Women found a set of 10 AMC Silver Theatre Passes with free shipping for just $70 (a $45 savings).

Pinpoint the best ticket price

To find the lowest price for sports and concert tickets, search the event at Ticketwood.com, a site that allows you to compare costs at different online vendors. At press time, a Brad Paisley concert at Amway Center in Orlando was showing a $22 price difference between sellers for seats in the same section and row.

Try free in-store events

Crafting lessons at Michael's, readings at the local bookstore, cooking demos at Williams-Sonoma . . . Such in-store events can be fun (and free!) for kids. Check store bulletins or the community calendar for local events.

Net game-day deals

Resellers are motivated to lower prices on the day of an event. To score last-minute deals, log on to Craiglist.org on game day. There, you can scope out tickets and starting prices from locals who may be willing to meet at a public place to exchange tickets and payment. Or check StubHub.com, which offers electronic tickets that can be instantly downloaded and printed.

DINING FOR (FEWER) DOLLARS

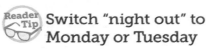 ### Skip the children's menu

"Parents assume that kids' meals are a good deal, but often it's cheaper to split one adult entrée between their children. That's why I always tell parents at IHOP to order the $10 breakfast, which comes with three large buttermilk pancakes, a large serving of hash browns, and three strips of bacon, instead of two or three $6 kids' meals that come with one buttermilk pancake, hash browns, and one strip of bacon each. It saves them up to $8 per check and keeps their little ones happy."

—*Anonymous server at IHOP, Wayne, NJ*

Switch "night out" to Monday or Tuesday

"My husband and I do date night early in the week because most restaurants offer discounts to get customers in the door. Last Monday we found an Asian fusion place offering 50 percent off the entire bill. We were able to get $88 worth of food and drinks for $44—what a steal!"

—*Barbara Seymour, Tinton Falls, NJ*

Score double deals on gift certificates

"At Restaurant.com, you can get a $25 gift certificate for $10," says Stephanie Nelson, founder of CouponMom.com. "I thought that was a great deal, but then I found out that if you type 'restaurant.com coupon codes' into Google, codes for an extra 50 percent off will pop up. I just scored a $25 certificate to India Chef in Atlanta for $4 using a coupon code. That's like the restaurant giving me $21 to spend for free."

10 Brilliant Uses
for VEGETABLE OIL

1 Shine wood floors for pennies
You'd like to spruce up your floors before your guests arrive, but you're out of polish and there's no time to run to the store for more. Create your own wood polish by pouring equal parts white vinegar and vegetable oil into a spray bottle. Spritz the solution onto the floor and rub it in with a cotton cloth, then wipe clean. The vinegar's acetic acid will dissolve dirt, while the oil will moisturize the wood, leaving it with a radiant shine.

2 Safely separate stuck glasses
While setting the table for a Sunday brunch with your friends, you reached for your favorite antique juice glasses—only to find a stack of two stubbornly stuck together. To pry them apart without chipping the delicate glassware, pour a little vegetable oil around the inside rim of the bottom glass and let sit for 15 seconds, then gently wiggle the glassware. The oil will seep between the glasses, creating a slippery surface that will allow you to pull them apart with ease.

3 Effortlessly lift paint from skin
In an attempt to avoid the mess of carving pumpkins, you reached for oil-based paints to create jack-o'-lantern faces. But now you're dealing with the mess. For a no-fuss cleanup, apply a drop of vegetable oil to painted skin, then rub with a damp sponge and rinse with soapy water. The oil will break down the paint pigments so they come off sans scrubbing.

4 Revive a lackluster strand of pearls
Your grandma's vintage pearls are the perfect addition to your flapper costume, but they're looking a little dull. Vegetable oil to the rescue! Simply dip a soft cotton cloth in oil and use it to clean each pearl individually. Let dry overnight, then buff with a clean cloth in the morning. The oil will cut through accumulated dust and grime and restore the pearls' moisture level, leaving them looking luminous.

5 Season cast-iron cookware
You haven't used your big cast-iron skillet since last holiday season, and when you pulled the pan out of storage the other day, you discovered that it was rusted. To restore its finish, first use a nonmetallic scrubber to remove the rust, then wash with mild dish soap, rinse, and dry. Next, wipe the inside of the skillet with a vegetable oil–soaked paper towel, making sure to leave a very thin layer of oil behind. The oil will provide a protective coating that will prevent rust from forming.

6 Unstick stubborn oven racks

It's getting harder to slide out your oven racks when removing baked goods. The fix: Take out the racks and rub the tracks in the oven wall with steel wool, then wipe clean with a damp rag and dry. Next, wipe the tracks with a vegetable oil–soaked paper towel. The steel wool will eliminate grime, while the oil will lubricate the tracks so the racks move smoothly.

7 Keep cooking wine tasting fresh longer

Whenever you have a bit of wine left over, you like to save it to use for cooking later in the week. But sometimes the wine goes stale and loses its flavor before you get to it. To prevent this, add 1 teaspoon of vegetable oil to the bottle before you store it in the fridge. The oil will sit on top of the liquid, providing an airtight seal that will delay flavor-sapping oxidation.

8 Swallow large pills with ease

The antibiotics you were prescribed to clear up an infection are so huge, you're having trouble swallowing them whole. To make the task less stressful, lightly roll each capsule in vegetable oil before taking it. The slick coating will help the bulky pill glide down your throat.

9 Solve Snowball's hair ball problem

There's nothing worse than discovering hair balls scattered throughout your house . . . *yuck!* For a homemade cure, try adding 1 teaspoon of vegetable oil to your cat's food once a week. The tasteless oil will lubricate her digestive tract, making it easy for any ingested hairs to pass through instead of accumulating into hair balls.

10 Eliminate sticky adhesive residue

You're always thrilled when you score a great piece of furniture or cookware for a song at a local flea market or garage sale. But it's frustrating when you peel the price sticker off your goods and pesky glue residue gets left behind. To remove it, dip a paper towel in vegetable oil and use it to gently rub the sticky spots. The vegetable oil will dissolve the adhesive's bond, allowing it to come off without damaging wood, metal, porcelain, and plastic surfaces.

Flip to the middle of the menu

"National chains like Olive Garden, TGI Friday's, and Chili's tend to design their menus so mouth-watering photos and bold typography draw your eye to the most expensive and profitable dishes," says William Poundstone, author of *Priceless: The Myth of Fair Value (and How to Take Advantage of It)*. "Meanwhile, cheaper items are listed in menu Siberia. At Chili's, for instance, the more expensive petite sirloin and salmon dish are listed first, while the less expensive sandwiches are buried toward the middle. So when I get to a restaurant, I flip to the middle or back page to find the most reasonably priced items, then make my selection from there."

Be wary of menu buzzwords

"Menu writers have a flair for making dishes sound extra special with words like *artisanal* and *pan-roasted* that allows them to charge 50 percent more for very basic food," says William Poundstone. "Recently I've seen a lot of 'beet root' listed on menus as a pricey vegetable option—but beets are generally very inexpensive at the market. Just avoiding these buzzwords can save you enough cash to splurge on dessert!"

"Book" hundreds of discounts

"Buying an Entertainment Book at Entertainment.com is one of the best financial decisions I've ever made," says Stephanie Nelson. "For $35 I got a book filled with buy-one-get-one-free coupons for local restaurants and national chains. Mine paid for itself in just two dinners out. We keep the book in the car so we have coupons on hand whenever hunger strikes, but the site also offers an app for $25 per year that lets you access coupons from your smartphone. Just last week we went out to a local steak house, and our Entertainment Book app had a coupon that took $19 off the bill!"

Go for wine #3

"Bar and restaurant managers have clued in to the fact that most of us looking for a deal order the second-cheapest option on the wine list, so they're marking that wine up by nearly as much as their house wine," says William Poundstone. "That means in order to get the best quality for the best price, it's smart to consider the third-cheapest wine on the menu—the markup can be up to 50 percent lower!"

Start with a side dish instead of a salad

"If I'm out to dinner and looking to get in an extra serving of greens for the day, I'll choose a vegetable side dish from the a la carte menu instead of a salad starter or appetizer," says Kate Edwards, restaurant consultant and owner of Kate Edwards Consulting LLC. "Restaurants usually offer an option such as sautéed spinach, steamed broccoli, or mixed veggies that costs as little as $4 per plate—that's a big savings, compared with the $10 or $14 that I'd spend on a Caesar salad or an order of spinach-artichoke dip. Even better, the plate of vegetables fills me up just as much as any appetizer would, but it's more nutritious and saves me hundreds of calories!"

Value-Packed Family Vacations

Planning a family vacation doesn't have to break the bank! Try these savvy tips to help you save on everything from gas to lodging, flights, food, and more.

WALLET-FRIENDLY ROAD TRIPS

 ### Enlist the help of a free tour guide

"Every summer, my husband and I take a road trip to a big city. We love sightseeing, but rather than paying for a guided tour, I Google 'podcast walking tour' and the city we're visiting so I can download a free podcast on my phone. Last year I picked up a $2 headphone splitter at a big-box store before the trip, and we were ready to explore."

—*Doreen Davis, Cherry Hill, NJ*

 ### Slash breakfast costs in half

"I find that it's easiest to save cash on breakfast, so I always pack tons of nonperishable foods like muffins, fruit, instant oatmeal, and instant coffee. Last month we started our drive to Virginia Beach at 5 a.m., and when we made our first pit stop at 9, we were desperate for breakfast and coffee. We would've easily spent $20 on rest-stop food, but instead, I dashed into the quick mart and filled a few cups with hot water, then set up a picnic-style breakfast outside. We all enjoyed the fresh air—plus my husband and I got our caffeine fix for the rest of the drive!"

—*Samantha Menkin, Lexington, KY*

So long "Are we there yet?"

"Last year before our 11-hour car trip, I was looking for an inexpensive way to keep the kids occupied, so I stopped at the dollar store," says Natalie Lesnefsky, founder of TheBusyBudgetingMama.com. "I was surprised to find a big selection of coloring books, crayons, and toys. I wrapped each one and packed them in the kids' backpacks, then whenever they got restless, I let them open a toy. They loved it. My $10 'investment' kept them busy the whole time!"

Make the most out of every pit stop

"Road trips are more about the journey than the destination, so I always research our route before we go," says Jennifer Close, founder of TwoKidsandaMap.com. "Most major highways have rest areas with something special. Last year we stopped at one in Elkmont, Tennessee, that has a rocket ship memorial. The kids went crazy for it, so we're going again this year."

HIDDEN SAVINGS ON DREAM VACATIONS

Search out packages

When you book a room and airfare together on a discount site (like Kayak.com), you'll often spend less than you would on the airfare alone. *First for Women* found a trip from Omaha to Los Angeles that included two plane tickets and a 7-night stay for $1,517 at Orbitz.com—$357 less than the cost of booking each separately.

Clear your cookies

Travel sites can track searches through "cookies" on your Web browser and raise price quotes as a result. According to a *Consumer Reports* study, even checking flights more than once prompted the cheaper fare to disappear. To outsmart these tactics, click "preferences" in your browser options and select to clear or remove cookies.

Friend your favorites

Southwest, AirTran, JetBlue, and other smaller airlines don't always post sale airfares on search engines, so it can pay to sign up for Twitter, Facebook, or e-mail alerts from any airlines that travel to places you want to go.

Check the visitors bureau

If you're heading to a tourist destination, scope out the visitors bureau's Web site for deals on hotels, car rentals, and more. You may find discount passes for many of the area's attractions.

Take a chance on Mother Nature

Though hurricane season in the Caribbean technically starts in mid-June, most storms don't hit until early fall. Take advantage of off-season prices at the beginning of the summer for a gorgeous vacation at an affordable price for the family.

Book flights on Tuesday

Industry experts reveal that most airlines post sales Monday night, and by the next morning, the competition has usually matched these fares. That means on Tuesday afternoon, you'll have the best selection of flights at the lowest price.

Rent a campsite complete with RV

Renting an RV can be an affordable way to vacation with your family, and you don't even have to drive it if you don't want to. Do a Web search for "on-site RV rentals" near an area you'd like to visit. *First for Women* found a weekly rental at an on-site RV park in Oregon, near the Umatilla National Forest, for $420. Or check out CruiseAmerica.com and ElMonteRV.com, which offer rentals in locations like the Grand Canyon, Key West, and more.

Fly out on these days

Monday, Friday, and Sunday are busy days for business travel, so rates are usually higher. There's less demand for flights on Tuesday, Wednesday, and Saturday, so traveling on these days can save you as much as 50 percent.

Bargain with the source

It's smart to check for hotel deals online, but always phone the hotel and ask for a discount before booking. Find the best rate online and then ask if the hotel can match that price.

Prepay to save

Many hotels offer "advance purchase" rates for travelers who pay for their vacations ahead of time. Just be careful—these deals are often nonrefundable, so wait until you know your vacation plans for sure.

Make travel agents compete

Log on to the site Compete4YourSeat.com and input your flight, hotel, and car rental requirements to receive deal offers from travel agencies.

Get a rebate on already-purchased airfare

To ensure you get the best ticket price even after you've bought a ticket, enter your flight itinerary and what you paid on Yapta.com. If the same seat class becomes available for less, the Web site will send you instructions for calling the airline to claim your refund. (Note: This applies only to tickets purchased directly from the airline.) One recent Yapta customer saved $128 on a ticket from Seattle to San Diego.

Score last-minute deals on condo rentals

When it gets to be about 30 days out, time-share resorts and homeowners with vacation rentals start offering huge discounts to fill unused units. For great deals, log on to SkyAuction.com (bonus: you never have to sit through any time-share sales pitches!) or log on to Wyndham-Vacation.com and click on "Last Minute Vacations" for discounted units at Wyndham Resorts.

Find cheap airport parking

If you plan to leave your car at the airport, check BestParking.com, a site that directs customers to discount lots near 79 North American airports. Just allow an extra half hour to catch a shuttle bus to the airport prior to your flight.

Slash rental car costs

There are great deals to be found on car rentals at warehouse clubs. At Costco, you can receive offers for 30 percent off car rentals. And through BJ's, you can get a free upgrade on car rentals, plus 25 percent off from companies like Hertz and Budget. Just go to your warehouse club's Web site or call the customer service line to get the discounts. Also smart: Look into deals through your college alumni association, your AAA membership, and the Entertainment Book.

Ask about "positioning flights"

Most airlines have daily flights that are scheduled for logistical purposes—often to transport a plane from Airport A to Airport B—rather than to bring in revenue. While these flights aren't listed online, you can score hugely discounted airfares if you call the airline and ask about positioning flight deals.

Cut out the middleman on vacation rentals

There's no need to pay huge broker's fees when booking a vacation rental—sites like FlipKey.com, FamilyVacationCritic.com, and HomeAway.com connect potential renters directly to property owners. This eliminates booking charges and allows you to negotiate lower weekly rates with the owner. Hint: Many time-share resorts and homeowners offer bigger discounts on units that remain unfilled about 30 days out, so it can pay to schedule your rental last-minute.

Save 50 percent by taking the train

Trains can be a much more affordable option than planes. While you may spend a few more hours in transit, you can get up to half off on tickets and save another $150 on baggage fees, parking, and taxi costs. Plus, you'll have more leg room and be able to use your cell phone the entire ride.

EAT ON THE GO AND SAVE

 Bring along a dozen incredible edibles

"When my friend and I took our six kids on a road trip in Arizona last spring, we agreed to eat breakfasts and lunches from our picnic baskets to save money. So I filled a cooler with a dozen hard-boiled eggs, and we'd munch on them with salt and pepper or over lettuce from the cooler for a healthy snack. While my friend's premade turkey and tuna sandwiches got soggy, my eggs stayed fresh and delicious."

—Margie Carnahan, Phoenix, AZ

Eat out for "linner"

"If we're going to dine at a restaurant, we eat a really late lunch. It's more like an early dinner, but we're paying lunch prices. For example, on a trip to Orlando, we ate around 4:30 p.m. at this cute bistro where chicken sandwich platters were $8 on the lunch menu. If we'd waited an hour longer, the same meal would have cost $13 for dinner. Usually, our 'linner' keeps us full for the rest of the night, but I stock the room fridge with cheese, fruit, and deli meat so we can snack if we get hungry later."

—Jennifer Close, mom and founder of TwoKidsandaMap.com

Carry on oatmeal

"I always pack instant oatmeal for flights. A handful of packets and a baggie of almonds and dried fruit take up almost no room in my carry-on—and when we get hungry, I just ask the flight attendant for a cup of hot water and an extra cup. It's a great healthy option—and saves me from having to buy the $10 airline snack boxes."

—Alexandra Oppenheimer, registered dietician and mom

Make your own snow cones

"I love taking my grandchildren to the local fair every summer, but it's tricky finding treats to pack that are exciting enough to satisfy kids screaming for expensive cotton candy and snow cones. So last year I filled two plastic bags with ice that I had crushed in a blender. Then I stashed the bags inside a cooler with a $2 package of insulated cups, some plastic spoons, and a bottle of cherry-flavored syrup. When I surprised the kids with the DIY snow cones at the fairgrounds, they were so excited that they forgot all about the treats selling for $6 or more apiece."

—Sara Pellechia, Old Bridge, NJ

Play "spot the farm stand"

"When packing for a road trip, I stash a good knife (in an empty paper-towel tube for safety), cutting board, and colander into the truck. That way we can buy fruit and veggies from farm stands for next to nothing. I tell the kids to watch out the window for the next roadside market. It's a fun game that keeps them occupied for hours and gets them excited about eating a healthy snack. I'm a stickler about rinsing produce, so once we make our purchases, I'll put the fresh goods into the colander and run a bit of water from a water bottle over them. It makes for supercheap and fun snacking."

—Margie Carnahan

Whip up personal snack bags

"We used to go through two or three $5 bags of trail mix in just a couple of hours on a road trip. To cut costs, I started making my own snack mix with my family's favorite munchies. The supersimple recipe: In a large bowl, combine 3 cups of Cheerios, 4 cups of popcorn, 1 cup of raisins,

1 cup of nuts, and 1 cup of M&M's, then portion into five or six plastic sandwich bags. One batch will last us through a 1-week vacation, and it costs me less than $7 to make. Plus, the kids love it!"

—Jennifer Close

Stay cool with double-duty water bottles

"When we took a family trip to Disney World last summer, we didn't want to spend a fortune on food and beverages, but water bottles alone cost $3 or more per bottle. Luckily, Disney allows groups to bring in soft-sided coolers, so we froze water bottles at our condo beforehand and used them as ice packs. They kept our food cool through lunch, then kept us hydrated after they thawed. Plus, we refilled them at water fountains the rest of the day. This trick saved us more than $75 on food and drinks."

—Jennifer Close

Score Savings on Entertaining

You love hosting get-togethers for friends and family, but between food and decorations, costs can really add up. Discover these tips from entertaining pros to cut the cost of hosting festive gatherings by 50 percent or more!

HOLIDAYS FOR LESS

Serve a "gourmet" appetizer for less

"I love butternut squash soup—I always order it when we go out to eat in the fall, but I assumed it was pricey or difficult to prepare," says Tracey Doull, founder of KitchenMoxie.net. "So when my chef friend told me I could make it for six people for $7, I decided to serve it on Thanksgiving. I bought three packages of frozen squash for $1.50 each, and I already had the other ingredients, like oil, spices, and broth, on hand. My guests were so impressed with my 'gourmet' soup!"

Time your turkey purchase to save big

"Everyone knows frozen turkeys are cheaper, but prices drop even more the week of Thanksgiving," says Stephanie Nelson, founder of CouponMom.com. "Right before Turkey Day last year, I scored one bird for 69 cents per pound and got a second one free. I thawed one for Thanksgiving and froze the other!"

Know where to pick up table decor

"Party stores tend to overprice place cards, and that's something I never want to splurge on. So last year I came up with an easy DIY option: I went to the dollar store and picked up a pack of 50 gift tags and a pack of 50 fall-themed napkins. Then I wrote each guest's name on the gift tag and tied it around a napkin with ribbon. For $2, my table looked picture-perfect!"

—Tracy Sandoval, Mount Holly, NJ

Try this shopping strategy

"I host Thanksgiving every year, and I always make an easy three-part list before I hit the grocery store," says Cynthia Ewer, founder of Organized Christmas.com and OrganizedHome.com. "Two weeks before, I stock up on nonperishables. This is when items like canned gravy, cranberry sauce, and brown sugar first go on sale for the holiday. The next week, when supermarkets tend to run crazy sales on store-brand frozen goods, I pick up the frozen veggies. Then I save the fresh goods for the week of Thanksgiving. I've found that I'm able to get fantastic prices for a fresh turkey, yams, and rolls when I buy a day or two before the dinner. Best of all, this strategy allows me to plan ahead and spread the burden of costs over a 3-week period."

 ## Snag delicious desserts on the cheap

"Last year I had my heart set on serving pies and pumpkin cheesecake, but it would have cost me $30 or more at the bakery, and I had no time to bake. So when a friend told me Trader Joe's has superaffordable seasonal pies, I headed over to check it out—and I was surprised by the great selection. I snapped up a pumpkin pie for $5, a pumpkin cheesecake for $7, and a box of four mini pumpkin soufflés for $2. I stocked up on dessert for my feast for just $14, and it was just as fresh and delicious as if it came from the bakery."

—*Jen Watson, Atlanta, GA*

 ## Discover the best local deals with this app

"Comparing supermarket circulars to find the lowest prices can get overwhelming—especially before Thanksgiving. But the other day my sister mentioned a free app that saves her money and time at the store. With Grocery Pal, you plug in

items on your list and it tells you which stores offer the deepest discounts. Over the past few weeks, I've saved at least $25 on groceries. It's really going to come in handy for my Turkey Day shopping trip!"

—*Carla Winston, Grand Rapids, MI*

 ## Spend $5 or less on crowd-pleasing sides

"My friend, who always brings delicious dishes to parties, recently shared her secret: Her recipes come from frugal food blogs like 5DollarDinners.com and MommyHatesCooking.com. I decided to try it for Thanksgiving, since I usually cook a new side each year. I chose a recipe for roasted green beans. It cost just $5, and the crowd kept coming back for more!"

—*Doreen Smith, Miami, FL*

Buy beer and wine at the last minute

"Liquor stores always have big sales the week before the holiday, but I wait until the day before Thanksgiving to stock up," says Jennifer Davidson, cofounder of SaveOnBrew.com. "In my experience, that's when prices hit rock bottom. To save even more cash, I bypass the seasonal and specialty liquor and beer, which are pricier and more in demand, and purchase the classic brews like Budweiser and Heineken. My family prefers them, and they're always marked down at this time."

Try food as decor

Holiday displays can cost $50 or more. But pretty arrangements of winter squash, fruit, and herbs can be had for less than $5. Just create piles of winter vegetables and add a few candles for a gorgeous table topper. Want something even lower priced? Try drying apple and orange slices on a luxe platter for an extra accent.

Check for farmers' market closeouts

You can find great end-of-season deals at farmers' markets in late October. Because fall vegetables can store well in the fridge for at least a month, feel free to stock up at the end of the season. Last fall *First for Women* spied 5 pounds of Brussels sprouts for $5 and two-for-one squash at a New Jersey farm stand.

Get quality for less with these store brands

You don't have to sacrifice flavor for lower prices. In a *Consumer Reports* test, canned vegetables, spices, and baking staples from Costco's Kirkland, Target's Archer Farms, and Walmart's Great Value labels rated better than name brands and cost 27 percent less. Kirkland's vanilla extract sells for 35 cents per ounce, for example, while it's $2.25 per ounce for Nielsen-Massey.

Mix fresh greenery with faux

Intertwining artificial foliage with the real thing allows you to create custom holiday decor at a fraction of the price of designer wreaths. To get the effect, drape artificial garland over door frames, sideboards, and mantels. Then add a splash of color by attaching holly berries, fresh mums, or dried pinecones with floral wire or a hot-glue gun.

Go for a frozen turkey

Turkeys found in the grocer's freezer cost up to 50 percent less than fresh birds—and taste just as good. To determine when the bird was frozen, check the weight tag for the lot number: Ignore the first three digits (which represent the plant) and skip to the next five numbers—the "Julian" date (a three-digit code in which 001 is January 1 and 365 is December 31) and year of processing.

Visit the day-old aisle

Hit the supermarket in the a.m. to snap up lightly bruised apples and overripe mushrooms, which are perfect for baked casseroles and desserts, for pennies on the dollar. Day-old bread can be found for 50 cents per loaf and used for stuffing or bread pudding—a big savings, compared with $3 fresh loaves.

Discover exactly what you'll need

To avoid overspending on food and drinks, consult a servings calculator like the one at WholeFoods Market.com. Just type in the number of guests you're expecting and get a breakdown of exactly how much cheese, turkey, pie, or wine you'll need per guest.

Arrange a buffet like the pros do

Hosting a big soiree? Place low-cost dishes like rolls and potatoes at the front of the buffet table. Guests often take more food at the beginning of the table, so you'll save on the more expensive foods placed at the end.

Get creative with dishes

Instead of spending $25 and up on serving platters, pick up wall mirrors for $10 at HomeGoods stores to make elegant platters for crudités. Wooden cutting boards make practical trays for cookies or meats and cheeses.

Pick up a ready-made meal here

A holiday spread prepared by a grocer can cost 50 percent more than a meal made from scratch. But there's still a way to save if you have a time crunch (or hate to cook!). Boston Market offers a holiday meal to go that includes enough turkey, spinach-artichoke dip, cranberry relish, stuffing, mashed potatoes, gravy, dinner rolls, and pie to feed 12 guests for $90—up to 30 percent less than a similar-quality ready-made feast from the supermarket.

Serve up a signature cocktail

Offering one festive drink to 20 guests will cost as little as $35—that's $65 less than wine and beer for the same group. Two crowd-pleasers: Top off Prosecco with cranberry juice for a pretty "Poinsettia" cocktail. Or simmer low-cost vino with orange peels, cloves, and cinnamon sticks to make a tasty mulled wine.

Bake one recipe in bulk

"Holiday baking can get expensive fast, so I make one specialty sweet—a family recipe for homemade candy that costs almost nothing to make. I'll whip up a big batch and bring it to all my holiday events. Everyone loves it! Friends of mine do the same with one favorite cookie or cupcake recipe, and we all save a lot of time and stress—not to mention money on ingredients."

—Cynthia Ewer

Score plastic cutlery at a warehouse store

"When I'm hosting, the last thing I want to do at the end of the night is wash dishes, but I couldn't justify spending $4 on 30 plastic forks to save a little time scrubbing. Luckily, I stumbled on surprisingly good-quality cutlery at Costco. I was able to get 100-count boxes of Dixie Heavy Weight forks, knives, and spoons for $3.59 each. I even found 100 plastic plates for $11. That's more than enough to get me through this holiday season and the next—and now I can spend time with my family instead of cleaning up."

—Liz Scott

Nab decor accents at the dollar store

"When I host my annual holiday party, I keep the decorations simple by filling a few glass vases with pine-branch clippings, holly, and pinecones from my backyard. For any other decorations, I hit the dollar store. Most of the time, the decorative holiday items are the same quality as those sold at party stores but are priced much lower. Last year I bought red napkins, crimson candles, ribbon, and a pretty golden wreath for the fireplace mantel—my entire party was decorated for less than $10!"

—Stephanie Nelson

GREAT GIFTS AT GREAT PRICES!

Net huge savings on DVDs

"It's hard to find discounted movies and music at brick-and-mortar stores, so I stock up at clearance sites like DeepDiscount.com," says Mary Hunt, author of *Debt-Proof Your Christmas*. "They have a huge variety, and the prices are up to 94 percent lower than at big-box stores. Last week I got a popular movie on DVD for $5.50 and an album for $8."

Nab free shipping on online purchases

"I was spending over $100 to ship gifts to relatives—until I learned that more than 1,000 online retailers offer free delivery by Christmas Eve through FreeShippingDay.com. You just have to do all your shopping on the designated day. With stores like Kohl's and Best Buy participating last year, I sent gifts across the country at no extra cost. I've already got my calendar marked for the big day on December 17 this year!"

—Debbie Calvin, North Wales, PA

Score wrapping supplies at the dollar store

"My go-to place to pick up everything I need for wrapping gifts is my local dollar store. It usually carries paper in various colors and patterns starting at $1 per 10-square-foot roll. Many dollar stores also have a big selection of tape, bows, and ribbon

for less than $1 each. I scored five rolls of pretty silver and gold paper, red bows, and tape for $6.50—this was enough to wrap all the presents under the tree, and they looked professionally wrapped!"

—Brenda Hansen, East Rutherford, NJ

Give luxe gift certificates for 50 percent less

"I've always wanted to gift the half-off spa treatments and prix-fixe meals that pop up on daily deal sites like Groupon.com, but wrapping up a paper printout code never seemed special enough. Then I heard about Presentify.me—a free site that turns these codes into gift certificates. I bought my mom a $50 certificate to a steak house for $25, and when I converted it into a gift certificate, only the retail value showed up. Now I'm on the lookout for deals that my husband and friends might enjoy. I could save $300 this season."

—Patricia Douglas, Shrewsbury, NJ

Snag gift cards for up to 20 percent off

"Gift cards are the most requested present from the teens in our extended family, and I finally found a way to save: I shop online sites that sell gift cards for up to 20 percent off—like a $30 Old Navy gift card for $25," says Joanie Demer, cofounder of TheKrazyCouponLady.com. "If I give gift cards to four people, I save $20. I even buy gift cards for myself to use when I'm holiday shopping. By stacking a sale with a coupon and paying with a discounted gift card, I've gotten items for more than 60 percent off the retail price."

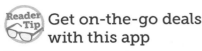 ## Get on-the-go deals with this app

"I never seem to have department store coupons with me when I spot the perfect gift. So I was thrilled to learn about the free coupon app for my smartphone at RetailMeNot.com. Its database of available in-store and online coupons lets me download discounts for up to 80 percent off that can be redeemed at the register. Last week I found a purse for my sister at Macy's, so I typed the store name into the search box and a coupon for 40 percent off popped up. The clerk scanned it from my phone and the $50 Nine West tote came to $30. I can't wait for my sister to open it!"

—*Samantha Nixon, Ann Arbor, MI*

 ## Buy hostess gifts in bulk

"With all the holiday parties I have to attend, buying a bottle of wine or a plant for each hostess can get expensive. So I started picking up gifts in bulk at warehouse stores. It makes the price per unit so much lower—and once I wrap the present, it looks like I spent much more than I did. For example, last year at Costco, I found a set of 20 individually wrapped scented pillar candles for about $20. If I'd gone to a candle store, I would've paid that much for just one. They were such a hit that I might do it again this year."

—*Mary Hunt*

Create custom gift baskets on the cheap

"Last year I wanted to buy a gourmet gift basket for my best friend, but the ones I priced online cost up to $100—so I decided to make my own basket filled with her favorite goodies. I picked up a nice selection of fruit, meats, cheese, and crackers from Trader Joe's ($20) and a cute cutting board and knife set from HomeGoods (on sale for $12). Then I placed everything in a brown wicker basket from the dollar store and wrapped it up beautifully. My friend adored the gift, and it looked just like one of those $90 baskets—but I paid only $33."

—*Kimberly Carillo, Durham, NC*

Ship packages for less

Before mailing holiday packages, compare rates at ShipGooder.com. Just input the beginning and destination zip codes to see price estimates for FedEx, DHL, UPS, and USPS. For instance, shipping a 10-pound box from Grand Rapids Michigan, to Memphis will cost $10.95 at the post office—a $20 savings, compared with $31.05 at UPS and $31.18 at FedEx.

Post holiday greetings for 35 percent less

Mail out holiday postcards instead of traditional greeting cards this year and you'll save on overall cost and postage fees. You can buy traditional holiday postcards at a card store or online or make your own using online photo sites.

SUPER SNACK SAVINGS

Score snacks at the drugstore

"Last February I found the steepest discounts for chips at the drugstore," says Heather Wheeler, cofounder of TheKrazyCouponLady.com. "People often forget that chain stores like Rite Aid and Walgreens have impressive sales for the Super Bowl, too. Last year I stocked up on jumbo bags of Chex Mix, Lay's, and Pringles for less than 99 cents each. I also picked up two boxes of Nabisco crackers for 50 cents each. For $14, we had more than enough snacks to go around."

Serve three dishes for the price of one

"Every year our family and friends work up a mighty appetite while watching the game, so I always stick to a meal that's easy, filling, and affordable," says Sarah Roe, founder of Money SavingQueen.com. "The key to getting the most for my dollar: whipping up one dish in bulk and serving it in a few interesting ways. Last year, for example, I made a big batch of chili and offered it as three different serve-yourself meals: chili dogs, nachos, and chili fries. Everything came together so easily, and the chili cost me only 63 cents per serving. Best of all, everyone was thrilled with the variety of dishes."

Pick up stylish serveware here

"We were all set for our party when I realized I needed more serving dishes," says Heather Wheeler. "A friend suggested I check out the selection at IKEA, but I was hesitant. I didn't think a furniture store would have much in the party department. Boy, was I wrong. I picked up a glass serving bowl for $2, a bread basket for $8, and a set of four stainless-steel serving bowls for $5. For just $15 I now have chic serveware to use year-round."

Stock up on beer on these days

"Everyone knows the liquor store has sales on beer the week before a holiday, but my secret is to wait for the 'weekend only' sales," says Jennifer Davidson, cofounder of SaveOnBrew.com. "They start the Friday before Super Bowl Sunday and run until game day. Last year I had my eye on 24-packs of Bud Light, which were marked down to $20 during the week, but I waited until the day before the game and got them for $14 per case. I spent $28 on beer for the entire party—what a steal!"

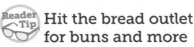 ## Hit the bread outlet for buns and more

"I was planning to serve hot dogs, hamburgers, and chili at my party, so I was determined to find the best deal on buns and rolls. That's when my savvy friend shared her best-kept secret: the bread outlet. She told me to go to BimboBakeriesUSA.com, where I clicked on 'Our Brands' and saw a list of outlets. I stopped by the nearest store and picked up name-brand hamburger buns and dinner rolls for next to nothing. They also had great prices on dessert items like cupcakes and doughnuts."

—*Beth O'Riley, Madison, WI*

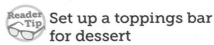 ## Set up a toppings bar for dessert

"The last item on my Super Bowl party shopping list was dessert, and purchasing pricey cakes or baking something were both out of the question. While scouring the grocery store for an answer, I spotted premium-brand ice cream on sale for $5 for 2 gallons. So I added two tubs of vanilla, one strawberry, and one chocolate to my cart. Then when my friends asked what they should bring, I replied, 'Your favorite ice-cream toppings.' We had a variety of offerings, from chocolate chips to fresh fruit, and the kids and adults loved this DIY dessert. It was such a hit and required no work from me. I'll most certainly do it again this year."

—*Olivia Lauer, Cherry Hill, NJ*

10 Brilliant Uses
for PLASTIC STRAWS

1 Core strawberries in half the time
You offered to bring a berry tart to your family reunion, but now you're regretting it—coring strawberries with a knife can be so tedious. An easier way: Clean and stem the fruit, then cut the end of a straw at an angle. Press the pointed tip through the top of each berry, twist the straw, and pull it back out. The sharpened hollow tube will instantly dislodge the strawberries' cores, so you'll be finished prepping in no time.

2 Get more life out of stubby crayons
Thanks to your kids' constant coloring habit, their crayons always seem to be breaking or getting so worn down that they're too small to get a good grip on. To make the art supplies last a little longer, slide each too-short nub as far as possible inside a plastic straw, leaving just the tip exposed. The straw will give your kids more length to grab on to, so they can keep drawing—and you can save a few bucks!

3 Put an end to clothesline pileups
When you're hanging heavy items like rugs and sheets to dry, the line sometimes sags under the weight. This causes the items to slide into one another, slowing drying time and leading to wrinkles. To prevent this, cut a few straws into 4-inch-long pieces and slit them lengthwise with scissors. When you hang laundry, clamp a length of straw over the line between each piece. The plastic tubes will help the rope stay taut to prevent linens from overlapping.

4 Quickly organize embroidery thread
The plastic container where you keep your embroidery thread is a tangled, unorganized mess. To add some order, cut a plastic straw into three or four pieces and cut a small slit into one end of each piece. Take a roll of embroidery thread and stick one end into the slit, then start wrapping the thread around the length of the straw. When you're done, tuck the other end into the slit, too. This trick will keep the thread from tangling and take up less space in your sewing basket.

5 Fix a running toilet for pennies
If your toilet runs too long after every flush, the flapper chain may be getting tangled and holding the valve open, keeping the water from shutting off. The save: Thread the chain through a 6-inch-long piece of straw. The straw will keep the chain from tangling so the valve can close properly when it's done flushing.

6 Reseal peeling tabletop veneer

The veneer on your porch table is starting to peel up in one corner, and you're worried that lifting it to apply glue will cause the thin surface to bubble or tear. Try filling one half of a flattened straw with glue and slipping it under the peeling corner. Lightly blow out the desired amount. The thin straw will fit under the veneer without causing further damage.

7 Keep necklaces from tangling in transit

You wanted to pack your favorite necklace to wear on your vacation next week, but the long chain tends to get hopelessly tangled, especially after being tossed around inside a suitcase. To ensure the necklace is ready to wear as soon as you unpack, unhook the clasp and thread the chain through a plastic straw, then refasten and pack as usual. The long, sturdy straw will keep the chain knot-free.

8 Ensure cake layers stay in place

The three-layer cake you baked for your honey's birthday looks lovely, but the whipped-cream filling is so slippery that the layers are starting to slide. The fix: Cut four straws so they're just shorter than the cake and insert them at evenly spaced intervals into the dessert, pushing them in so they're no longer visible. Cover the holes on top with frosting or whipped cream. Voilà—a beautiful (and stabilized) confection!

9 Arrange blooms with too-short stems

Oops! You accidentally trimmed some of your tulip stems too short. Even out the blooms by inserting each short stem into a plastic straw. Hold the flowers in a bunch and trim the straws so they're the same length, then arrange the bouquet as usual. The straws will invisibly correct the height differences for a picture-perfect floral arrangement. Bonus: Slide weak, drooping steams through straws for extra support.

10 Clogproof your caulk tube

When your husband finished resealing the bathtub this weekend, the tube of caulk he used was still half full. To keep the paste from hardening and forming clogs, insert a plastic straw into the tip of the tube and trim it so 1 to 2 inches remain. Fold the outside end over and secure with tape. The straw will seal out air, ensuring the opened product won't dry out.

BUCK SAVERS
FOR YOUR BBQ BASH

Get gourmet burgers on the cheap

Purchase a chuck roast on sale at the meat counter and have the butcher grind it—you'll save $1 per pound over prepackaged ground beef. Bonus: This lean cut packs more flavor than ground beef, which is made from trimmings that can leave burgers dry or tough.

Pick up a tablecloth at the fabric store

Consider topping outdoor tables with oilcloth. This polyvinyl material costs $5 to $7 per yard at fabric stores (and FabricDepot.com), so you can get a 60-inch covering for as low as $10, which is about 50 percent less than a same-size store-bought tablecloth. Even better, the waterproof surface ensures any messes can be easily cleaned with soapy water.

Consider bone-in cuts

Bone-in meats require less processing and therefore cost less to produce, so you can save big. *First for Women* spotted bone-in chicken breasts on sale for 99 cents a pound at a Food Lion in Florida—that's a 55 percent savings over the boneless, skinless breasts priced at $1.79 a pound.

Snag bargain utensils

"The best place to stock up on plastic cutlery is the dollar store," says money-saving guru Kristl Story, creator of TheBudgetDiet.com. A bag of 48 forks, spoons, or knives costs $1—a $5 savings, compared with the $8 box of 150 pieces (50 of each utensil) at superstores.

Upgrade inexpensive meat for pennies

To make low-cost cuts of meats tender and juicy, whip up your own marinade: In a bowl, combine 1 cup of orange juice, 1 tablespoon of minced onion, 1 teaspoon of minced garlic, 1 teaspoon of chili powder, and 1 teaspoon of soy sauce, then pour it over the meat and let marinate overnight. The orange juice helpfully breaks down a cheap cut. Better yet, this mix costs less than $2—a $4 savings, compared with a $6 bottle of Lawry's Herb & Garlic Marinade.

Make hot dogs a star

Frankfurters, typically priced at less than $2 per package of eight, can easily feed a crew of 20 for $10 or less. To add flair to this classic fare, create a "bar" of gourmet yet low-cost fixings. Set out plates of cheese ($1), grilled onions (25 cents), roasted peppers ($2), and chili ($1.50 for a can of Hormel) so guests can craft their creations. Even with a $10 spread of toppings, you can keep your food budget under $20!

Shop for day-old buns

Bakery outlets (go to BakeryOutlets.com to find a local shop) sell buns that are close to or past their "sell by" date for as little as $1 per bag, which is a big savings over the $3 retail price. If you happen to get a few stale buns, just toast them on the grill to improve the taste.

Hit the deli counter for your favorite sides

Potato salad, macaroni salad, and coleslaw are backyard crowd-pleasers. To get them for less, swing by your supermarket deli counter and ask about weekly salad specials, which are often cheaper per pound than the prepackaged selections in the refrigerator section.

Save 30 percent on condiments

Choosing generic brands for staples like salsa, Dijon mustard, and steak sauce can save you up to 30 percent—and your guests will never notice the difference. In a blind taste test conducted by *Consumer Reports,* store brands of these products tied with or tasted better than name brands. Hint: To disguise the generic bottle, serve condiments in pretty candy bowls or Mason jars adorned with ribbons.

Decorate on a dime

Rather than buying pricey lanterns or tiki torches to light up an outdoor bash, try luminaries. Pick up tea lights ($3 for 50) and white paper bags ($4 for 40; both at Walmart stores), then fill the bags with a quarter inch of sand, set a candle on top, and place one on each table.

Save on grilling fuel

Lighter fluid can be costly and leave meat tasting

like chemicals. Instead, use paraffin wax starters, which heat faster and burn clean, to cut charcoal costs without affecting the taste of grilled food.

Stock up on free ice

There's no need to spend a bunch on ice every time you have a soiree. Instead, clean out empty soda or water bottles, add tap water until they're three-quarters full, and stash in the freezer. Nestle the bottles in a cooler to chill drinks; refreeze as needed.

Fitness and Finances

Looking and feeling your best doesn't need to cost a bundle! *First for Women* polled cash-savvy women for their best money-saving tips when it comes to staying fit.

SLIMMING ON A SHOESTRING

 Flip the channel for free fitness classes

"A few months ago, I was flipping channels and saw that Cablevision, my cable provider, offers On Demand workouts that change frequently, so I always have a new routine to try. (Many other cable companies offer similar options.) I love that I can do these workouts without buying DVDs or paying for a gym membership. I've been exercising for 30 minutes a day in the comfort of my living room—this easy routine has inspired me to get fit by summer!"

—*Liz Marone, Omaha, NE*

Score personal training sessions for a song

"I'd heard that a few women in my town were nabbing group discounts on in-home personal trainers for $15 an hour. So I got my hands on the trainer's number and called her. Typically, 1 hour costs $60, but group sessions of three to four people cut the price significantly. So my three friends and I signed up for a trial. Dishing out $15 for a training session is such a steal, and the workouts are so much fun!"

—*Jill Swanson, Nashville, TN*

 ### Juice without a juicer this way

"I wanted to kick off the new season by juicing more regularly. I considered investing in a juicer, but it just wasn't in my budget. Then my chef friend told me how to make my own juices using my blender and a paint-strainer bag ($2, at hardware stores). For example, to make carrot-orange juice, I place $\frac{1}{2}$ cup of water, 2 chopped carrots, and 2 chopped oranges in the blender and hit 'blend' until smooth. Then I pour the juice through the strainer into a glass and enjoy. When I'm done, I rinse the bag so I can reuse it."

—*Janna Elrich, Topeka, KS*

 ### Shop here for fitness gear

"The other day at Marshalls I spotted a huge bin filled with yoga mats, weights, bands, and more. I'd been putting off buying new gear because I couldn't find low-enough prices, but when I saw a stability ball for $10 and a set of weights for $8, I had to snatch them up!"

—*Janet D'Agnese, Belmar, NJ*

 ### Save on fresh produce at a grocery outlet

"My favorite veggies cost a pretty penny at the supermarket, so I was thrilled when I discovered grocery outlets. These stores get overstocked items from regular grocers and sell them at rock-bottom prices. I Googled 'MN + grocery outlets' and a list of stores in my state popped up. Last week I got a bag of baby carrots for 99 cents and organic greens for $1.99!"

—*Sue Roberts, St. Paul, MN*

Go à la carte at the gym

If you're joining a gym, opt for a month-to-month membership. Though it can cost more per month, you can "quit" when it gets nice enough for outdoor exercise.

Score a free pedometer

Pedometer wearers automatically up their daily activity by at least 2,000 steps (more than a mile), which translates to an extra pound lost per month. To start stepping for free, Google "free pedometer." *First for Women* found a coupon for a free gadget from Kmart and an offer for a pedometer from Tylenol if you register for well-being e-mails at JustKeepMoving.com. Or download a free pedometer app (like StepTrakLite) on your smartphone.

Tap in to tax rebates.

Ask your doctor to prescribe a weight-loss regimen and you may be able to write off some expenses on your taxes. The IRS allows families to claim costs of treatment or prevention of obesity-related diseases (including diabetes, hypertension, and heart disease) that exceed a percentage of your adjusted gross income. This includes supplements if recommended by your doctor for a specific condition, as well as fees for membership in groups like NutriSystem and Weight Watchers. While the cost of food for these programs and membership fees at health clubs can't be deducted, you may be able to deduct nutritional counseling. To net the benefits, save receipts that document weight-loss expenses, then include as itemized deductions on your tax forms or consult your tax preparer.

Create DIY snack packs

Those 100-calorie packs of your favorite snacks can short-circuit mindless eating to make budgeting calories a breeze, says Christine Gerbstadt, MD, RD, a spokeswoman for the American Dietetic Association. But they'll also lighten your wallet. A study at the Center for Science in the Public Interest in Washington, DC, found that the mini packages cost up to 279 percent more per ounce than the full-size ones. A better bet: Portion out 100-calorie servings at home. We load snack-size zipper-lock bags with healthy munchies like 1 ounce of cheese, $\frac{1}{4}$ cup of dried fruit, 1 cup of fresh fruit, 15 almonds, 5 small pieces of chocolate (like Hershey's Kisses), 18 mini pretzels, 25 jelly beans, or 40 Goldfish crackers.

Turn kitchen items into hand weights

Replacing 1 pound of fat with 1 pound of muscle can trim $\frac{3}{4}$ inch from trouble spots, plus increase metabolic rate by 3 percent. To firm up for less, use bottles filled with water or sand, as well as a 5-pound bag of rice, in place of dumbbells. Use the bottles to do biceps curls, shoulder presses, and triceps presses, and hold the bag of rice during squats and ab exercises. You can adjust the weight by increasing the amount of water or sand in the container.

Get brand-name fitness gear for half price

More than 60 percent of members at the weight-loss forum SparkPeople.com say new workout clothes motivate them to exercise. But you don't have to spend a lot to get great gear. Check out the discount Danskin line at your local Walmart or Target. These stores offer the same quality and flattering designs as their parent brands but cost up to 50 percent less. And there's something for everyone. Log on to Target.com to find petite and long versions of their fitted pants and plus sizes up to 3X. Or go to Walmart.com to find plus sizes up to 4X.

Fill up on free fluids

Sip 16 ounces of water before meals and you could lose 22 pounds a year, report researchers at Virginia Tech University in Blacksburg. That's because the fluid revs metabolism by 30 percent for up to 40 minutes, plus dampens appetite, helping dieters cut 75 calories per meal. And according to the Environmental Working Group, drinking tap water instead of soda and sports drinks can save consumers more than $1,000 a year. To hydrate on the go, consider a reusable bottle with a built-in filter. We love the Power Bottle USA 20-ounce Filter Water Bottle ($10, at Amazon.com). It's made with BPA-free plastic and has a wide opening so you can add ice or fruit.

Take a generic multi

Women in one study who took a multivitamin daily for 6 months lost 7 pounds more fat (especially from the belly) than multi skippers. And generic will do: When *Consumer Reports* tested 21 multis for nutrient levels and contaminants, store brands rated just as well as name brands. Two top picks: Costco Kirkland Signature Daily Multi (90 cents per month) and Walmart Equate Complete Multivitamin (92 cents a month). That's big savings over One A Day Maximum's $2.51 a month.

DETOX YOUR LIFE FOR LESS

Save 50 percent on spa services

To sweat out toxins in a sauna or flush fat with a lymph massage on the cheap, check out SpaWeek. com. This site offers ongoing deals.

Consider online food sources

Studies show that some food additives (including trans fat, HFCS, and MSG) can contribute to health problems like obesity, heart disease, and diabetes. But you can stock up on prepackaged foods without these chemicals by searching "organic food" at Amazon.com. You'll receive results for bulk buys on natural brands like Annie's Homegrown, Organic Valley, and Bob's Red Mill, which can save you 30 to 50 percent, compared with health-food store prices.

Whip up a homemade all-purpose cleaner

You've likely heard that chemicals in household cleaners can aggravate asthma and allergies, but the price of nontoxic brands can be steep. The solution: Fill a spray bottle with equal parts water and white vinegar, then use to clean almost anything. One $3 gallon bottle of white vinegar provides eight times more cleaner than a 32-ounce bottle at the same price, saving you nearly $24!

Grow your own greens

Leafy vegetables (like lettuce, spinach, and kale) are nature's best source of potassium, calcium, and chlorophyll. These alkalinizing nutrients work to neutralize acidic waste known to cause fatigue, headaches, and weight gain. To enjoy these veggies for a steal, try growing them yourself. One bag of greens can cost $3.50 or more, whereas a $2 pouch of seeds will keep you stocked in produce for months. The seeds sprout quickly, so plant some now to enjoy greens in 2 to 3 weeks.

Scout out organic dairy discounts

Organic milk contains 68 percent more slimming omega-3 fatty acids than conventional milk. But it also costs $1.62 more per half gallon. Luckily, brands like Stonyfield Farm and Horizon offer cost-curbing coupons on their Web sites. If you pair manufacturer coupons with an in-store sale, you can often score organic dairy for a lower price than conventional milk. When you do spot a deal, take advantage—organic milk lasts twice as long, so you can stock up for 5 to 6 weeks.

Create your own air freshener

Researchers at the Natural Resources Defense Council found that 86 percent of household air fresheners—even some bearing an "all natural" label—contain phthalates. These chemicals can disrupt the body's endocrine system, triggering hormonal imbalances, as well as reproductive and neurological damage. Sidestep these health problems (and save $48 on a year's supply of air freshener) with this DIY odor neutralizer: In a spray bottle, combine 1 teaspoon of baking soda, 1 teaspoon of lemon juice, and 2 cups of water, then spritz as needed.

Chapter 7

BRILLIANT LITTLE BEAUTY SECRETS

Secrets to Salon Beautiful

If there's one thing that delivers an instant boost of confidence, it's having a perfect hair day. To guarantee you always look like you just stepped out of the salon, we asked hair experts for the simple steps that make a real difference in achieving beautiful, long-lasting style.

STYLE LIKE A PRO

Cut drying time in half

Because hair is fragile when wet, you can prevent damage and dry your hair faster by drying your hair sans brush at the beginning of the styling process. After showering, gently blot hair with a towel. (Rubbing ruffles the cuticle, which can lead to frizz.) Then, on medium heat, rough-dry strands by tousling hair and lifting small sections with your fingers. When hair is 30 percent dry (wet but not dripping), comb in a dollop of volumizing mousse that contains heat-protecting emollients and continue rough-drying. When locks are slightly damp, begin styling with a round brush—you'll notice that hair feels stronger and more manageable and dries in no time!

For maximum hair volume

The secret to creating face-flattering lift (no teasing required) is to "prop up" roots with Velcro rollers. To do: After blow-drying a 2-inch section, immediately place a large roller at the roots, letting the rest of the hair drape over the top. (The Velcro's tiny teeth will grip strands, keeping the curler in place.) Repeat on each section, then remove the rollers and tousle. Hair takes on shape as it cools, so the rollers force strands to cool in a lifted position, locking in bouncy volume.

Get a smooth, frizz-free result

Using a flatiron is one of the easiest ways to get sleek, frizz-free hair. However, dragging the appliance downward can cause tresses to go limp against the scalp. The quick trick to adding oomph with a straightener (on both long and short styles): Clamp the appliance at the roots of a 1-inch section and hold for 3 seconds. Then glide the flatiron up toward the ceiling, twisting under as you reach the ends. This easy flick of the wrist lifts strands off the scalp so hair appears fuller, while turning the iron at the ends curls the section under slightly, which hides any split ends and create a softer, healthier look.

Hair Tool Tips and Tricks

A little pro know-how can convert old-faithful irons and rollers into styling superstars. The results? Hair that makes you happy, at a price that's just right. We love how a few swipes of a trusty hot styling tool can save a bad hair day—despite annoying April showers! And whether you prefer flatirons, curling irons, or hot rollers, these gadgets can do a lot more than just iron, curl, and roll, giving you even more styles to try.

TWO EASY THERMAL STYLING RULES

Rule number one

Always use a heat-protectant spray. It helps distribute heat evenly and prevent dehydration, allowing you to crank up the temperature to get longer-lasting styles without damage. Just be sure to spray the product on a brush to comb through your hair instead of directly on the hair itself. This way, your hair won't become weighed down by excess product.

Rule number two

Use the size of your tool as a guide for how large to separate hair sections. For instance, a 3-inch curling iron should be used on 3-inch sections of hair.

INSTA-VOLUME WITH A FLATIRON

Flippy moments

Nothing looks more youthful than flippy ends, and this can be done easily with a flatiron. Here's how:

After blow-drying, straighten 2-inch sections beginning halfway down the hair, then gently flip your wrist out as you pull through the last 3 inches.

Create angelic curls

Getting curls from a straightener seems counterintuitive, but it can actually be easier than using a curling iron. Just clamp a 1-inch segment of hair in the iron and loop the section around the outside of the tool once. Holding the end straight down, slowly slide the clamped iron down the segment—like curling a ribbon.

A pixie with polish

Afraid of the all-too-common tangles characteristic of short cuts? The fast fix: Help a crop stay sophisticated and smooth by redirecting and retraining hair's natural direction with a flatiron. Simply lift at the roots (to maintain volume), then drag the iron down in the direction you'd like hair to fall.

Bed-head waves

Loosely braid 2-inch and 3-inch sections of hair, then slowly run a flatiron from roots to ends, rolling the iron the last 2 inches along each braid. Allow the braids to cool, then separate sections. Don't be afraid to make braids of different sizes—this creates a variety of waves for a more natural look.

A SOFTER LOOK WITH A CURLING IRON

Soft, stretchy corkscrews

For naturally curly girls: Wrap 1-inch sections around the outside of a 1-inch curling iron. Then slip the iron out of the spiral and pull the coil downward, stretching it as it cools.

Irregular waves and curls

Use a "broken" curl technique to achieve effortless, uneven waves. Starting even with your cheekbones, wrap the middle of a 2-inch segment around a large-barreled curling iron, leaving 2 inches loose at the ends. Repeat, curling all sections in the same direction.

Make a sleek flip

Think curling irons can be used only for curling hair? Think again—a 2-inch curling iron can be used as a straightener to give your hair plenty of life and body. Starting at the roots, loosely clamp a 2-inch section of hair in the curling iron, then slowly drag the iron in a C shape, arching up from the scalp, then curving under at the ends (which will flip as hair falls).

Get relaxed ringlets

To create big, bouncy curls, wrap hair around a large-barreled curling iron without clamping down on the hair. Then alternate the direction of each spiral but wrap front sections away from the face.

HIGH PRAISE FOR HOT ROLLERS

Create rolled-in lift

For serious volume, hot rollers are a must. To do: After drying, lift 2-inch segments along the crown and spritz a root lifter underneath. Then place the roller at the roots, allowing the section to drape over it. Remove after 2 minutes. Voilà—an instant boost!

Go for beach waves

For tousled "fresh off the beach" locks, roll hair using medium rollers on top layers and jumbo rollers on lower layers. Let cool, remove curlers, flip head over, and mist the ends of curls with hair spray as you simultaneously ruffle hair at the roots with your fingers. This will relax the curl and add airy volume.

Twist for springy spirals

For a bouncy, no-frizz bob (in mere minutes), roll 1-inch sections in medium rollers, alternating directions. Let cool, then remove each roller by holding the bottom end and gently sliding it out of the curl vertically to create a spiral shape. Separate curls, twist into ringlets, and anchor with hair spray.

Throwback to retro waves

To achieve smooth, old-Hollywood curls, create a deep part, then spritz hair lightly with a heat memory spray. Next, roll small sections in large curlers parallel to the part. Once cool, mist fingers with hair spray and run them through hair to soften the curls.

QUICK HAIR HINTS

Get gorgeous, second-day hair—for less

Dry shampoo is a lifesaver on sweltering mornings when you don't want to blow hot air at your head. But the products can be pricey. The kitchen staple that works just as well: cornstarch. Simply stand on a towel, sprinkle a tablespoon of cornstarch onto dry hair, and massage it into your scalp. Wait 5 minutes, then brush out. The powdery substance absorbs oils and product residue (without leaving behind white traces, even in dark hair), so you'll have gorgeous, bouncy tresses!
Money saved: $7 for dry shampoo

Get a lift with hair spray

Nothing beats tools with a little heat action, but when you're short on time, Velcro rollers can also give you a bit of lift while you multitask. The trick: Lift a 2-inch segment of dry hair, spritz with hair spray, and use the roller's Velcro texture to gently back-comb at the roots, then roll the section. After 10 to 15 minutes, blast with a hair dryer, then remove the rollers and ruffle with your fingers for fabulous all-day volume.

Deep-conditioning hair for pennies

Olive oil can transform locks from dry and dull to healthy and shiny. Just work a few tablespoons into hair from root to tip and let sit for 30 minutes, then shampoo as usual. The oil's fatty acids and vitamin E will hydrate hair and seal in moisture. For best results, repeat every 2 weeks. *Money saved: $10 for a deep-conditioning mask*

The hat trick that ends flyaways

Prevent your winter cap from making hair staticky by pinning a dryer sheet to the inside. The sheet will diffuse the electrical charge that makes hair stand on end—and if static does set in, you can eliminate it by rubbing the dryer sheet along your hair from root to tip.

The secret to shiny, bouncy hair

Long hours under the sun have stripped the moisture from your tresses—and adding shine spray leaves your do limp and flat. For light, lustrous locks, spritz the product onto a blush brush, then gently sweep it all over your hair. The soft bristles will evenly distribute the spray's heavy silicone so it won't weigh down your hair. Plus, the brush allows you to apply precise, targeted shine right where you need it.

SOS for "pool hair"

Reader Tip

"I always find that my hair takes on a greenish tint after a few trips to the pool. Luckily, my stylist taught me that soaking my hair in tomato juice helps remove chlorine and neutralize the green color. After 10 minutes, I simply rinse out the juice in the shower."

—*Sara Mason, Pine Hills, FL*

Brighten dull hair for pennies

We love golden highlights as much as the next woman. To keep our summer streaks bright through fall, we try this once a week: Mix a capful of sparkling wine with a squirt of shampoo and wash as usual. The wine contains tartaric acid, an ingredient in many home highlighting kits, which lightens and adds extra shine to strands. *Money saved: $50 for a salon hair-glaze treatment*

Cool trick for detangling hair

Reader Tip

"Trying to run a brush through my thick, curly hair used to be such a nightmare that I'd skip styling altogether. Luckily, my new curly-haired stylist taught me how to detangle without the pain: When I come across a big knot, I just blast it with cold air from my blow-dryer. The cool temperature constricts hair cuticles, so I can loosen trouble spots easily with my fingers or a comb. My hair has never looked better!"

—*Abby Frank, Amherst, MA*

Keep bobby pins in place

Tonight's party is the perfect occasion for that pretty braided updo you've been wanting to try, but bobby pins always seem to slip out of your hair. The way to keep them in place all night: Lay the pins on a paper towel and spritz them with hair spray. The spray will coat each pin with a tacky texture that will ensure it stays put—even in straight or fine hair.

Shiny hair . . . all summer

A little fun in the sun is great for your well-being—but air pollution, UV rays, and chlorine aren't so kind to your hair. The fix: Store baking soda in an old pill bottle in the shower. Then, twice a week, add a pinch to your dollop of shampoo and suds up. The slightly abrasive particles will scrub away hair-dulling chemical buildup, while the sodium bicarbonate will smooth UV-damaged cuticles to restore luster.

The secret to salon-quality bang trims

Your new bangs are superflattering, but frequent trips to the stylist to have them snipped take time and money. For an at-home job that looks just as polished: Use your scissors to cut a folded piece of foil into strips before you trim. This will sharpen the blades, which is key to a clean cut. *Money saved: $7 for a bang trim*

The kitchen fix for shiny, healthy hair

If you don't have time for a trim but split ends are making your locks look drab, try this: Whisk 1 egg yolk, 2 tablespoons of olive oil, and 1 tablespoon of honey and apply to damp hair. Wrap tresses in plastic wrap and let sit for 30 minutes, then shampoo. The honey will moisturize strands while the oil's squalene and egg's lecithin will "seal" ends, giving hair a fresh-cut look for 3 days.

 Make your own leave-in conditioner

"My long, thick hair is prone to rats' nests, so I go through bottles of leave-in conditioner. When I confessed my addiction to a pal, she told me she just mixes 1 part conditioner with 10 parts water in a spray bottle and spritzes it on trouble spots. This homemade detangler works just as well as store brands and saves me a few bucks every month. Plus, it doesn't leave my hair greasy."

—*Angela Monroe, Blaine, MN*

Smart Hair Solutions

Looking to update your hairstyle? Here, you'll find tips that will help you decide which cut is right for you, plus how to choose a new hair color and how to properly style your new 'do. You deserve it!

FOUND: THE BEST CUT FOR YOU

Your face is round if . . . the measurement from your hairline to the bottom of your chin divided by three is larger than the measurement from beneath your nose to your chin.

Your face is square if . . . the width of your forehead from temple to temple is equal to the width of your jaw from ear to ear.

Your face is oval if . . . the measurement from your hairline to the bottom of your chin divided by three is smaller than the measurement from your nose to your chin.

Your face is heart if . . . the width of your jaw from ear to ear is smaller than the width of your forehead from temple to temple.

Styles for Oval/Long Faces

The darling

How it flatters: A chic crop with a tousled, templelength fringe conceals a tall forehead, which balances a long face and directs the focus straight to gorgeous eyes and cheekbones.

What to ask for: A pixie with very short layers in the back and longer layers through the crown and over the ears, plus razored, asymmetrical bangs that graduate in length from below the brows to the temples.

Tousled pageboy

How it flatters: Layers concentrated between the temple and jawline add volume at the cheekbones to balance length, while razored bangs minimize the forehead.

What to ask for: A bob with layers concentrated between the temple and jawline, plus a full fringe that skims the eyebrow, blending seamlessly into the cut.

Pro styling tip: After drying, work a few drops of silicone-based serum from ends to roots to add youthful shine.

The sweetheart

How it flatters: To add movement and life to your hair, opt for defined layers that open up at the cheekbones.

What to ask for: Shaggy, texturized layers down-cut from the temple to sweep away from the face, with very long, blended layers in the back.

Pro styling trick: Work a lightweight styling foam through wet hair, then blow-dry on high using a large paddle brush, sweeping layers outward for just the right amount of flip.

Razored bob

How it flatters: Texturizing the bottom third of the cut relieves hair's weight and positions volume at the center of the face. This highlights cheekbones so they appear slightly broader, instantly balancing the face's length.

What to ask for: A classic bob with long layers texturized from jaw to shoulders.

Styles for Round Faces

The breeze

How it flatters: Side bangs create an elegant, angular look on an otherwise round face.

What to ask for: A "wedge" cut that's tapered around the back and sides, with cheekbone-length, asymmetrical bangs.

Blunt with diagonal bangs

How it flatters: A blunt cut pulls the eye up and down for an elongating effect, while asymmetrical bangs add angles to help a round face appear more defined.

What to ask for: An architecturally blunt, collarbone-length cut with wispy, diagonal bangs that start at the highest point of one eyebrow and extend across the forehead, graduating in length toward the opposite temple.

Pro styling tip: Blow-dry with a flat brush, lifting at the roots. Then, to help fine hair appear thicker, create a side part that points down the center of the head.

The full shag

How it flatters: Flirty, flipped-out layers give hair airy volume that frames the face and helps it appear slimmer by comparison. And feathery bangs draw attention straight to pretty eyes.

What to ask for: A collarbone-skimming cut that's heavily layered from the chin down and texturized on the ends to flip out, plus a full fringe that blends into face-framing layers.

Pro styling trick: Using a 2-inch round brush, blow-dry hair in sections, directing air first above, then below, each segment. When dry, flip hair forward and rub the ends with a dime-size dollop of finishing balm to defrizz, define layers, and lock in style.

The structured shell

How it flatters: A gorgeous bob that's texturized from the chin down positions the volume toward the top of the crown, which draws the eye vertically for a face-slimming effect.

What to ask for: A graduated bob that's longer in the front and texturized at the ends, plus a diagonal fringe.

Styles for Square Faces

The bombshell

How it flatters: A modern bob with side-swept bangs creates feminine curves and softens a square face.

What to ask for: A jaw-length bob with long, almost-blunt layers and wispy, side-sweeping bangs.

The new "Aniston"

How it flatters: A part that's just off-center rounds off a square forehead, while long, face-framing layers blur the sharp edges of a strong jawline.

What to ask for: A collarbone-length cut with long, angled layers that are texturized at the ends.

Swing bob

How it flatters: Flippy layers maintain movement (to prevent the cut from appearing bottom heavy) and direct the focus up to the cheekbones, plus face-framing pieces soften a strong jaw.

What to ask for: A shoulder-length bob heavily texturized at the ends (rather than all the way through) to impart weightless movement, with the shortest layer skimming just below the jawline.

Pro styling tip: Blow-dry 2-inch sections with a round brush. After finishing a section (while it's still warm), loosely roll hair under with your fingers and clip it at the scalp so it cools. Repeat on all sections to ensure youthful movement.

The tip-top

How it flatters: Longer, tousled layers through the crown give a perky pixie a slightly rounded silhouette that counteracts the angles of a square jawline.

What to ask for: A crop with longer, razored layers on top and short, graduated layers on the sides and in the back.

Pro styling trick: Dab a pea-size amount of texturizing cream onto fingertips, then ruffle through dry hair starting at the back and moving forward.

Styles for Heart Faces

The romantic

How it flatters: Center parts make a wide forehead appear less broad, and coupled with layers, this balances out a smaller chin.

What to ask for: Long, blended layers that fall from the jaw to just below the collarbone.

Stacked bob

How it flatters: Shorter layers at the crown add volume around the upper two-thirds of the head, pulling the focus up to the eyes, and tapered-in lower layers curve under the jaw to fill in a slim chin.

What to ask for: A bob with short-over-long tapered layers with texturized ends that fall just under the chin, and heavy, temple-length swing bangs that can be parted and worn on either side.

Pro styling tip: After blow-drying, run a flatiron just around the bottom half of the hair, along the perimeter of the cut, so the lower layers subtly hug in toward the face with a shiny touch.

The polished pixie

How it flatters: A crop with bangs that "cut across" the forehead helps it appear less broad. Also, blended layers at the crown create a rounded silhouette that counteracts a sharp chin.

What to ask for: A pixie cut with short, asymmetrical bangs and stacked, blended layers that are longer in the crown.

Pro styling tip: Apply a nickel-size amount of smoothing serum to wet hair. Make a deep part, sweeping bangs across the forehead, and secure with an alligator clip. Next, blow-dry hair at the crown with a flat brush, closely following the hair shaft in the direction you'd like the hair to fall. When dry, unclip bangs.

The beachy keen

How it flatters: To call attention to a pretty face, opt for an off-center part with lots of layers.

What to ask for: A collarbone-length cut with visible layers from the jawline down.

Hair Color Confidential

Get salon-spectacular color at home with these DIY secrets that salons don't want you to know!

COLORING FOR BEST RESULTS

If you've never colored your hair before and . . .

. . . you want to go lighter, try a shade darker at the roots. Applying a permanent box color is the easiest way to lighten virgin hair, but there's one caveat: Heat from your scalp can cause it to lighten faster at the roots, making them appear too bright. The fix: Choose a box of your goal hue (like "lightest natural blond") and one that's a shade darker (like "natural blond") in the same brand and tone family—ash, natural, or golden. Mix the colors separately, then apply the darker hue to your roots and the lighter hue to the rest of your hair.

. . . you want to go darker, try a protein treatment. Caution: Exposure to sun and styling can make ends more sensitive, which can result in them looking much darker than the rest of your hair. The secret to rich, even-all-over color: a protein "filler." This hydrating pretreatment patches microscopic holes in the hair shaft so the color absorbs uniformly from root to tip.

Another way to get a deep, glistening shade on virgin hair: Opt for an ammonia-free, semipermanent color. These formulas don't open the cuticle like permanent ones do, so they wash out in 4 to 6 weeks. This lets you experiment with different tones and shades to find your most flattering color.

. . . you want to go red, try nylon bristles. Contrary to popular belief, red may be the easiest color to achieve at home. The reason: When going blond, you remove the hair's pigments; when going brunette, you add color on top of similarly colored pigments. But to go red, you add color molecules that are different from those in the hair (unless you're a true redhead), so the pigments stand out more and the shade better matches the hue on the box.

One drawback: Because it's more distinguishable, red fades faster. To keep reds fiery longer, apply the hue with a nylon-bristled tint brush, which coaxes the cuticle open so more pigments penetrate.

. . . you want highlights, try a flatiron technique. For fast and foolproof first-time highlights, swap the messy bleach mix for a spray-on solution. To do: Spritz the lightening spray onto a 1/4-inch section of hair and run a hot flatiron down the segment five to seven times, or until the hair brightens to the color you want. Then repeat on six to eight other sections framing your face. The result: glowing, natural-looking highlights with no risk of overprocessing or drips.

If you've colored before and . . .

. . . you want to go lighter, try a dual kit. One common oops is to use a box color to lighten previously colored hair, which isn't powerful enough to entirely color over previous treatments.

The two-step solution: First, strip the previous hue using a color corrector, which will shrink the dye molecules in the hair cortex so they wash away, lightening hair by two shades. Then try a kit that contains both a permanent base color and paint-on highlights. Removing the old color, then applying this combo, helps hair appear up to four shades lighter—without looking muddy.

. . . *you want to go darker, try a two-shade tweak*. Unlike virgin strands, hair that's been colored before has had the cuticle opened multiple times, which makes it harder to close with each process. This may cause strands to absorb darker pigments faster and wind up much deeper than expected. The shade-perfect solution: Apply your goal color, then go one shade lighter with the same brand. This should deepen hair to the rich color you're hoping for without making strands overly inky.

One thing to keep in mind: When layering a darker hue over hair that's been previously colored, the old pigments will still be in the hair shaft. For the loveliest look, you'll want the tone of your new color to blend with the tone of your current color. In order to achieve this, stay away from box colors that are labeled "ash" or "cool." When these tones (which contain blue pigments) are layered over lighter hues (especially warm or golden blonds, which contain yellow pigments), hair can end up looking lackluster or—worst-case scenario—green.

. . . *you want to refresh highlights, try a toothbrush*. The secret weapon for touching up highlights: a toothbrush with a triangular head. Using a toothbrush gives you plenty of control, which is essential for professional-looking highlights. To do: Mix a highlighting kit and discard the cap. If your hair is long, gather it straight back into a tight ponytail; if it's short, push it back off your face with a headband. Then dip the pointed tip of the toothbrush into the mix and paint small streaks around your face that "reconnect" your grown-out streaks to your hairline (essentially highlighting the roots). Next, take down your hair and repeat along your natural part. Let process

according to the box instructions and voilà—glowing highlights without the fuss!

If you want to cover gray . . .

. . . *with a light shade on virgin hair, try neutral tones*. Although grays appear ashy or silver (which read as blue undertones), they actually occur when the hair cortex loses both the cool (blue) and warm (yellow and red) color pigments. That explains why attempting to blend away grays using a lighter color that has predominantly cool undertones (labeled "cool" or "ash" on the box) can cause hair to appear dull (because of the lack of warm pigments). On the other hand, if you cover grays with a lighter formula that's mostly warm undertones (labeled "warm" or "golden" on the box), hair can appear brassy (because there are no cool pigments). For the best results, celebrity hairstylist Joel Warren advises using a color labeled "neutral" or "natural" on the box. "These formulas deposit a combination of yellow, red, and blue pigments into the hair," he explains. "This replaces all of the lost tones in the grays, so they blend beautifully and have loads of shine."

. . . *with a dark shade on virgin hair, try "streaking."* Pesky grays can really stick out on dark virgin hair, but if you have just a touch of gray, you can use it to your advantage. In fact, grays and natural color can mix beautifully and even brighten your skin.

Best advice: Mix one-third of the developer with one-third of the dye from a permanent color kit that's one shade lighter than your natural hue. (Keep leftovers in separate containers and store in a cool, dry place for the next time you need a touch-up.) Then take a cotton swab or eyebrow brush, paint the solution over just the gray hairs, and let the color process according to the directions on the box, which helps you to blend color easily.

LOOK 10 YEARS YOUNGER—WITH THE RIGHT BROWS!

Long face = Medium-thick and straight

Brows with a low arch that gets higher at the outer edge of the irises draw attention to the sides of the face, making it appear less narrow. To do: Tweeze one row from the middle of the brows to the outer edges.

Heart face = High and rounded

Brows with a high, round arch visually soften a pointy chin while minimizing a wide forehead. To do: Tweeze one row at the center of the brows right under the arch.

Round face = Full with high arches

Brows with a high, pointed arch cause the eye to scan vertically, which visually elongates the face and slims cheeks. To do: Tweeze one row from the inner corners of the brows up to the arches.

Square face = Thin and slightly angled

Wide, thin brows with a slight arch help balance and soften a broad jaw. To do: Tweeze one row from the inner corner of the brows to just outside the irises.

To take the ouch out of tweezing, turn to chamomile tea. Steep a bag in warm water for 5 minutes, then dip a cotton ball in the brew and apply to skin pre-plucking. The heat will dilate pores, making it easier for hairs to slide out. After tweezing, dab skin with another tea-saturated cotton ball—the flavonoids in the chamomile will help soothe sore skin.

. . . and you've colored before but the color won't take, try presoftening. Those of us who are more than 50 percent gray and have colored at home know firsthand how difficult it can be to actually get dye to absorb into the stubborn white strands. That's because the cuticle on gray hair is extremely compact, making it hard to open and deposit the color pigments.

The gray-be-gone fix: Try a technique called presoftening, using the solution from a perm kit, which is made with ammonium thioglycolate, a chemical that "breaks open" the cuticle so more color can be absorbed. To do: Simply smear a thick layer of petroleum jelly along the hairline to protect skin, then apply the perm solution to gray roots (or any gray areas that you've noticed are extra stubborn) and let sit for 1 minute. Then shampoo, blow-dry, and use your favorite permanent hair color.

10 YEARS YOUNGER— WITH HAIR COLOR

Comb in a rich ombré

Do you have sallow skin? Overbleaching can strip blue pigments from hair, causing it to take on an orangey cast that intensifies yellow undertones in the skin for a dull, tired look. But a neutral brunette restores just enough blue pigments to tone down brass and bring out skin's rosy radiance. And using an ombré technique brightens the face to enhance that glow.

To do: Apply color to dry hair from roots to cheekbones. After half the processing time, wet hair from the cheekbones down, then comb the color through to the ends and finish processing.

Opt for a soft chestnut

Are you a bit pale? The solution: Choose a color that's darker than your skin tone. Try a chestnut hue with red and gold pigments that add warmth and contrast to your complexion, restoring its youthful luminance.

To do: Apply a semipermanent strawberry blond (which bridges the light and dark hues so the brunette doesn't appear muddy), then rinse and blow-dry. Follow with a semipermanent roasted chestnut.

Add lowlights to the roots

If you have thinning hair and your gray roots are lighter than the rest of the hair, they can be visually mistaken for the scalp, making locks appear even sparser. For full hair, incorporate soft lowlights at the roots to add a layer of dimension to your style.

To do: Purchase a permanent hair color that's two shades lighter than your current hue and a permanent cream color that's one shade darker. Apply the lighter hue all over (to even out tone); let process, then rinse and blow-dry. Using a toothbrush, paint the slightly darker color onto the roots in small, 1/4-inch-long streaks (like applying tiny highlights) with 1/2 inch of space between each.

Lighten to a luminous shade

Do you have under-eye circles? If a hair color is more than two shades darker than a woman's natural hue, it can cast shadows under the eyes and enhance hollowing under the cheeks, creating a drawn, tired look. Opt for a lighter shade to lighten the face so you appear more youthful.

To do: Use a kit with an allover color (two shades lighter than your current hue) and separate highlights, which dramatically brighten without damaging hair.

Try a silvering technique

Is your hair a lackluster gray? No one has to settle for frizzy, gray hair. Instead, consider "silvering" your hair, which involves bleaching the hair until white and then adding in a silver hue, which adds shine and softness.

To do: Apply a permanent platinum blond dye that contains the bleach and toner. Tip: Halfway through processing, take small sections of hair and massage the color upward (from tips to roots) to help open the cuticle.

Weave in honey highlights

Is your skin red and ruddy? After a while, golden blond single-process dyes tend to cause a buildup of red and orange pigments in the hair, which can cause the complexion to appear ruddy. Instead, frame your face with honey-toned highlights, which are still in the warm or golden family but are much brighter and contain fewer red pigments, so your skin appears less ruddy. The highlights also draw the eye to lovely features and break up the monotone color, causing the old hue to fade into the background.

To do: Highlight ½-inch sections around the hairline and through the part using a kit.

Simple Skin Secrets

Sick of chapped lips and sunburned foreheads? It's not easy to keep your skin blemish-free when you're contending with hormones, stress, and weather damage. Read on for helpful tips that will make your skin positively radiant.

INSTANTLY COOL

To refresh feet, try a minty mojito scrub

When balmy weather (or hours traveling by car or plane) leaves your feet swollen and sore, try this cooling "cocktail": Combine ¼ cup of sugar, ⅓ cup of olive oil, 2 tablespoons of lime juice, and 5 drops of peppermint oil. Gently massage the mixture into each foot for 2 minutes, then rinse with cool water. The chilly sensation of the peppermint's "active" compounds, menthol and menthane, will invigorate tired toes and constrict blood vessels to reduce puffiness. Plus, the lime juice's citric acid and the abrasive sugar crystals will remove dead skin, allowing the olive oil's nourishing oleic acid to penetrate and hydrate.

10 Brilliant Uses for CLEAR LIP BALM

1 Protect a pet's paws from ice
Fido's not all that concerned about the wintry conditions outside—he just wants to take his daily stroll! But since walking on ice, snow, and salt can cause irritation, coat his paw pads with clear lip balm before heading out the door. The balm will serve as a barrier to safeguard his sensitive tootsies.

2 Rustproof an outdoor lightbulb
Your porch light burned out, but it's tough to twist out because moisture from rain and snow caused it to rust in the socket. Next time, coat the threads of a new bulb with lip balm before twisting it into place. The film will act as a sealant to stop water from seeping in and oxidizing the metal. When it comes time to change the bulb again, you'll be able to unscrew it with ease.

3 Head off a hangnail
Ouch! You have a cracked cuticle that needs attention but no cuticle cream on hand to treat it. The in-a-pinch remedy: Dampen the affected area with lukewarm water, then apply a layer of clear lip balm. The beauty staple will soothe irritation while sealing in moisture—and that's key to warding off a painful hangnail.

4 Remove price sticker residue
You love the new photo frames you picked up on sale—but the clearance stickers that were slapped on the glass aren't peeling off neatly. The save: Smear clear lip balm over the stickers and let sit for 10 minutes. The oils in the salve will disintegrate the adhesives, making removal a cinch.

5 Unstick a zipper—quick!
Argh! The zipper on your winter coat has gotten stubbornly stuck. To loosen it without damaging the coat's fabric, rub clear lip balm over the zipper's teeth. The slick wax will lubricate the metal so the hardware can move along without snagging.

6 Save a scratched disc in seconds
If your favorite disc starts skipping, rub clear lip balm over any scratches, then buff with a soft, clean cloth. The waxy balm will fill in imperfections, while the gentle buffing will clear off dirt and oil. Problem solved!

7 Prevent nails from splitting wood

While you were hammering a nail into a wood shelf, you ended up splitting the lumber. To avoid this in the future, rub clear lip balm over the hardware before starting any job. The slick coating will help the nails slide into the wood without incident.

8 Lift mascara smudges

You had so much fun over holiday cocktails that you laughed till you cried—and now you've got smudges beneath each eye. No worries: Simply grab a tube of clear lip balm from your purse, rub your finger over the tip, and apply it to the smudges. The oils in the balm will gently dissolve and lift away the mascara without affecting the rest of your makeup, so you'll be looking gorgeous for the rest of the night!

9 Fix flyaways in a pinch

It's too cold to go out without your hat and scarf, but when you get inside and take off your cozy gear, your hair is a staticky mess. To quickly tame those wayward strands, rub a bit of clear lip balm on your fingertips, then "pinch" along the affected strands. The moisturizing ingredients in the balm will hydrate thirsty locks so they lie flat. Bad hair day averted!

10 Stop shoelaces from coming untied

Your new sneakers are supercute and fit perfectly—but the laces keep coming undone halfway through your workout. The save: Coat the strings with clear lip balm where you knot the loop. The wax will create a bit of sticky friction between the laces, making them less likely to unravel.

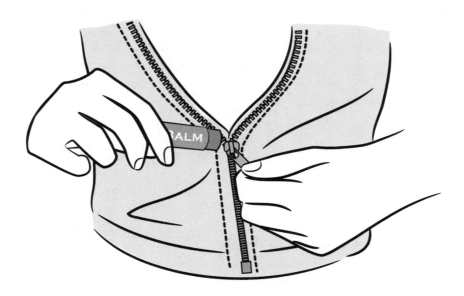

To nix dark circles, dab on yogurt

The biggest culprit of under-eye circles isn't sleepless nights or allergies—it's the summer sun! Exposure to the sun damages under-eye skin, making the veins in that area appear darker. The fix for these summer shiners: Cut a cotton pad in half, dip each piece in plain refrigerated yogurt, and place them under your eyes. After 10 minutes, remove the pads and rinse. The cool yogurt will shrink veins to stop pooling, while its hydrating lipids will plump the skin to conceal dark vessels. Plus, the yogurt's lactic acid will stimulate collagen production to thicken skin and eliminate circles.

To ease redness, spritz on coconut water

Caribbean beauties mist on the mineral-packed juice from the center of a coconut—aka coconut water—to soothe and hydrate flushed, heat-irritated skin. For the same cooling spritzer, pour 2 ounces of coconut water into a travel-size spray bottle and stash it in your handbag. Then mist the water onto your face, décolleté, or back when needed. As the liquid evaporates, it will quickly bring down your body temperature, while the water's potassium and magnesium will reduce inflammation. Bonus: Coconut water is the richest source of cytokinins, compounds that encourage collagen growth to help skin stay youthful and radiant.

BABY-SOFT SKIN FOR PENNIES

Dry skin?

For velvety-smooth, hydrated skin, mix 1 cup of Cheerios (crushed in a baggie), 1 teaspoon of honey, and a few drops of lemon juice into a paste. Gently massage the mixture into clean skin, then rinse. The mineral silica in the cereal's oat flour gently buffs away dead cells, and the oats' vitamin E nourishes skin. Plus, honey's humectant properties help skin retain moisture, while the citric acid in lemon juice brightens dullness.

Oily skin?

In response to the dead skin that builds up during the summer, oil glands go into overdrive to keep skin supple. This can lead to an excess of pore-clogging oiliness. To smooth skin and dry up oil, combine 1/2 cup of orange juice, 1 tablespoon of cornstarch, and 1 teaspoon of salt. Massage it over the face and leave on for 10 minutes, then rinse. Repeat twice a week.

Sensitive skin?

Exfoliating can be touchy for those of us prone to redness and irritation. The secret to achieving silky-smooth without sensitivity: Combine 1 cup of apple juice, 1 teaspoon of baking soda, and 2 teaspoons of plain yogurt and blend until creamy. Massage the mixture over the face and leave on for 5 minutes, then rinse. Repeat twice a week. Apple juice exfoliates skin, while yogurt's lactic acid and lipids help hydrate and soothe. In addition, baking soda instantly balances skin's pH to prevent further irritation.

TRAVEL TOILETRIES

Travel-size toiletries for pennies

Buying mini versions of lotions and shampoos you already own seems like a waste. But if your daughter wants her favorite formula for her class trip, try filling empty pill bottles (the kind with childproof caps) with the desired toiletries. Just make sure the seal is watertight before packing.

Since standard-size pill bottles hold less than 3 ounces of liquid, they're safe to take on flights. Money saved: $3 per travel-size toiletry

 Spillproof packed toiletries

"Last year, en route to my beach vacation, the top of my sunscreen managed to flip open, and lotion leaked all over my clothing. Determined not to ruin a suitcase full of clothes again, I came up with this packing trick: Unscrew the top of each flip-top bottle and cover the opening with plastic wrap, then screw on the top over the plastic. No more messes!"

—*Melissa Jardot, King of Prussia, PA*

SAVVY SKIN TIPS

An easy blotting-paper substitute

"While out to dinner with my husband, I went to the ladies' room to freshen up and realized I was out of oil-blotting paper. The woman at the sink next to me offered a solution: paper toilet-seat covers. They're made with the same rice paper as blotting paper and are found in nearly every public restroom. Now I keep a big piece folded in my purse and tear off sections as needed."

—*Dani Green, Decatur, AL*

Smooth your skin for pennies

For a homemade scrub that will have you glowing, combine ¼ cup of brown sugar, ¼ cup of olive oil, and 1 tablespoon of honey. Massage into skin, then rinse. The brown sugar will gently slough off dead cells, while the honey softens skin and fades scars and the olive oil locks in moisture. *Money saved: $6 for a tube of facial scrub*

Soothing postsunburn skin care

That patch of sunburn on your nose has started peeling, and no amount of moisturizer is helping to end the flakes. What will: fresh papaya. Simply peel, seed, and chop the fruit, then place in the blender and blend on high until a smooth paste forms. Gently rub the paste onto irritated patches of skin and let sit for 15 to 20 minutes before rinsing with cool water and patting dry. Papaya contains an enzyme (papain) that will gently dissolve dead skin cells and put an end to peeling, and the fruit's vitamins will speed skin-cell renewal.

The kitchen fix for radiant skin

To avoid the dry, flaky skin that comes with fall's drop in temperature, try this spa-inspired homemade mask: Mix 1 tablespoon of canned pumpkin, 1 teaspoon of honey, and ½ teaspoon of milk and apply to clean skin. Let sit for 15 minutes, then rinse. Pumpkin's vitamins A and C will gently exfoliate and plump up skin, while the honey will moisturize and work to eliminate blemishes.

Fast relief for sunburned skin

"I try to be good about applying sunscreen, but I still spend half the summer looking like a lobster. Needless to say, I buy aloe vera gel in bulk—it's a lifesaver. And I recently found a way to make aloe even more effective: I fill an ice cube tray with the gel and freeze. When needed, I just pop out a cube and soothe my skin!"

—*Lyn Miller, Durham, NC*

LOOK GREAT—NO MATTER WHAT

When cold-and-allergy season is in full swing, we're bound to feel blah from time to time. But the "side effects" of all the sneezing and stuffiness can make us look blah, too. Here are tips to heal and conceal sniffle-season beauty woes so you'll be radiant all spring long!

Raw, red nose?

Ouch! Even the softest tissues can feel like sandpaper when nostrils are inflamed from excessive blowing.

To heal it: Dab a petrolatum balm around nostrils to seal in moisture and form a protective barrier against friction.

To conceal it: Apply a green aloe–infused concealer. The hue will counteract redness, while the aloe works to ease inflammation.

Dark circles?

Congestion increases pressure on vessels under the eyes, which causes blood to pool and show through delicate skin.

To heal it: Wet two chamomile tea bags and lay them over closed eyes for 15 minutes. The tea's azulene will constrict blood vessels, while its coumarin increases lymph drainage to brighten skin, so you'll look better rested.

To conceal it: Dot on talc-free cover-up in a yellow hue to neutralize bluish circles.

Chapped lips?

When painful cracks appear on your lips (thanks to a stuffed-up nose that forces you to breathe through your mouth), slathering on a balm can seem like the best fix. But be careful—balms that contain alcohol only cause more chapping in the long run.

To heal and conceal it: First, remove flaky skin by massaging lips with one part water and two parts sugar, then sweep on an alcohol- and preservative-free shimmer balm infused with coconut oil. The oil's lauric add will nourish skin and lock in moisture, plus act as an antibacterial to speed healing. What's more, one of the ingredients in shimmer is titanium dioxide, an anti-inflammatory that calms irritation.

The herb that clears blemishes

For a gentle yet effective way to nix summer break-outs, try this trick: Add a handful of fresh basil leaves to 1 cup of boiling water, let simmer for 10 minutes, and let cool. Use a cotton ball to dab the liquid onto problem spots, and wait 10 minutes before rinsing. The eugenol oil in basil kills acne-causing bacteria. *Money saved: $6 for acne treatment*

Mile-high legs—in an instant!

For a no-sweat-required way to look extrafabulous in your summer fashions, smooth a thin layer of body oil down the front of your freshly shaven legs, along the shins. Light will reflect off the oil, producing an optical illusion that will makes legs seem longer—so you'll look leaner from head to toe.

Say "so long" to dull winter skin

Freshen up a flaky complexion with this simple mask: Mix a pinch of turmeric with a dollop of yogurt and apply all over your face, arms, and legs. Let sit for 10 minutes, then rinse. The yogurt's lactic acid will soften and exfoliate, while the spice's anti-inflammatory properties ease puffiness and give your skin a soft glow.

The throwaway that softens skin

An easy way to rejuvenate dull winter skin: Save the peels from limes, lemons, or oranges and store them in an airtight container in the fridge so they won't dry out. Then at bath time, toss a handful of peels into a tub of warm water. The citrus zest will infuse the bathwater with natural oils and acids that will help slough off dead skin cells and nourish the healthy skin underneath. Plus, heat from the water will release the citrus scent, which is proven to invigorate.

The sweet soak that relieves dry skin

Your secret weapon against scaly winter skin: Combine 6 cups of Epsom salts and 2 tablespoons of unsweetened cocoa powder in a jar. Add 3 to 4 tablespoons of the mixture to a warm bath and save the rest to use as needed. (It will keep indefinitely in an airtight container.) The coarse Epsom salts will gently exfoliate dead skin cells, while the flavanols in the cocoa powder will promote new cell growth for a radiant glow. Bonus: Breathing in the chocolaty scent has been shown to make people feel more relaxed.

Soften dry skin for a song

Chilly temperatures force you to stay indoors more often, and the inside air is wreaking havoc on your skin. To rejuvenate it, try this scrub: Combine 1/2 cup of kosher salt, 1 tablespoon of grated ginger, 1 cup of olive oil, and the zest of a grapefruit. Rub on the mixture in the shower, concentrating on dry areas, then rinse off. The coarse salt crystals will help slough off dead skin, while the oil's vitamin E will moisturize. Plus, the zest will improve circulation for a healthy glow. Stored in an airtight container, the scrub will last for up to 3 weeks.

Quick fix for a greasy scalp

In an effort to shave off a few minutes from your morning routine, you've been shampooing every other day. But by 2 p.m. on day 2, your strands start feeling greasy. To erase the excess oil stat, soak a cotton ball in witch hazel and dab it on your roots, then blow-dry on the cool setting. Witch hazel is a natural astringent that will dissolve oil and grease on contact, plus reduce the amount of oil the scalp produces. *Money saved: $10 to $15 for dry shampoo*

Smooth rough skin fast

When it's finally warm enough to move your sundresses to the front of your closet, those scaly elbows need to go. Just mix 1 cup of cornmeal and 1 cup of olive oil, then rub the mixture into rough patches and rinse off. The grainy texture of the cornmeal will exfoliate skin, while the olive oil will infuse it with moisture. *Money saved: $8 for a container of exfoliating body scrub*

Instant relief for razor burn

Thanks to the kids rushing you out of the shower this morning, your quickie shaving job left you with a few unpleasant splotchy spots. To soothe them, try this trick: Soak a black tea bag in water and microwave it for 10 to 15 seconds. Then gently press the tea bag over any spots that are irritated. The tannins in the tea will reduce redness and inflammation in no time.

The slice that softens skin

A long, hot shower seemed like the perfect antidote to a chilly evening, but now your skin is parched. The natural cure: Rub Fuji apple slices in a circular motion on extra-dry spots. Fuji apples contain malic acid, an alpha hydroxy acid that exfoliates and hydrates skin. Plus, the fruit's semi-rough texture will gently slough off dead skin cells. *Money saved: $7 for an exfoliating scrub*

Soft, smooth skin in minutes

No matter how often you moisturize, the dry, flaky patches on your cheeks just won't quit. Nix the scaly look by exfoliating with this easy DIY mask: Mix 1 tablespoon of plain yogurt with a splash of orange juice, then spread the mixture evenly over your face and wait 5 minutes before rinsing off. The alpha hydroxy acids in yogurt and OJ will help slough off flaky dead skin cells and boost the production of skin-plumping collagen. Plus, yogurt is packed with zinc, a mineral proven to eliminate blemishes. *Money saved: $15 for an at-home exfoliating mask*

Heal a blister in half the time

Dancing the night away in stilettos at your New Year's Eve party left a painful blister on your heel. To remedy, moisten a cotton ball with a minty antibacterial mouthwash and gently dab the tender spot. Repeat as needed until the blister disappears. The thymol in most mouthwashes is a powerful antiseptic that will shorten healing time by a couple days. Plus, the mouthwash's menthol will temporarily numb the pain.

Eliminate blackheads for pennies

After looking in a magnifying mirror while primping, you can't stop thinking about those blackheads on your nose—and you're out of pore strips. Make your own by mixing 1 tablespoon each unflavored gelatin and milk and microwaving for 10 seconds. Use a makeup brush to apply the mixture to the problem area, let dry for 10 minutes, then peel it off. The gelatin will cling to and remove the skin's oils and dead cells that leave behind blackheads—without irritating skin. *Money saved: $8 per box of pore strips*

Eliminate pesky underarm "shadow"

Stubborn ingrown hairs can make it look like you're in need of a shave even though you just took a razor to the area. The surefire fix: Twice a week while you're in the shower, gently massage a dollop of exfoliating facial scrub into your underarms. The grainy scrub will slough away the dead cells and deodorant residue that cause hairs to become trapped under the skin's surface, so you can get a superclose, smooth shave.

Smooth rough calluses fast

To soften the cracked heels and calluses that set in after months of tucking tootsies into boots, try this before-bed treatment: Soak a cotton ball or pad in castor oil, then secure over trouble spots with first-aid tape. Leave on overnight. (Wear socks to protect your sheets.) The extra-moisturizing ricinoleic acid in castor oil will penetrate deep into rough skin, leaving you with sandal-ready feet after just 1 week.

The mask that reveals your true radiance

To pamper dull, winter-worn skin, combine ½ cup of oatmeal, 1 tablespoon of honey, 1 tablespoon of olive oil, and 1 egg white. Apply a thin layer of the mixture to your face and let sit for 10 minutes, then rinse with warm water. The oatmeal exfoliates, while the honey and oil moisturize and the egg shrinks pores to tighten skin. The result: a soft, glowing complexion. *Money saved: $15 for a facial-mask kit*

The kitchen mix for younger skin

To rejuvenate a dull complexion, mash 6 red grapes with 2 teaspoons of olive oil, then stir in 2 tablespoons of flour until it forms a paste.

Smooth on the mask, leave on for 10 minutes, then rinse off. The antioxidant resveratrol in red grapes will help minimize wrinkles, while olive oil's oleic acid will restore skin's natural lipid balance. *Money saved: $6 for an age-defying face mask*

 ## Quick fix for "self-tanner hands"

"I love using self-tanner before donning a bathing suit, but I hate how the cream leaves my palms orange. Luckily, my pal gave me some advice: Apply a dab of whitening toothpaste, let it sit for a few minutes, then rinse. The excess color comes right off!"

—*Betsy Kates, Laurel, MD*

Sandal-ready feet in minutes

You've been coveting a pair of strappy sandals at the mall, but you first need to smooth out dry skin and cracked heels. Try this DIY foot mask: In a blender, puree 2 cucumbers, 2 tablespoons of lemon juice, and 2 tablespoons of olive oil. Divide the mixture evenly between two plastic bags, then put a foot in each one (securing the top) and massage it all over. Leave the bags on for 5 minutes before rinsing. The acid in the lemon juice will slough off dead skin, while the high water content of cucumbers and oleic acid in olive oil will moisturize your feet. *Money saved: $20 for a pedicure*

Professional Makeup Pointers

Are you longing for flawless, radiant skin? Striking, dramatic eyes? Look no further—here are expert tips designed to update and effortlessly enhance your makeup routine.

FLATTERING MAKEUP FOR EVERY FACE SHAPE

Slim a round face

To "chisel" a fuller face, apply blush (one shade darker than usual) in an upward-sweeping diagonal in the hollows under your cheekbones. Next, add a light layer of bronzer at the hairline on either side of your forehead, then blend down and around the perimeter of your face for a slimming effect. Tip: For flawless application and blending, try a Kabuki brush with a wide, 1½-inch head.

Soften a square face

To highlight the natural curve of your face: Smile, then apply blush in a circular motion onto the apples of your cheeks. Next, lightly dust your temples with bronzer and sweep upward, blending it into the corners of your forehead. Then apply bronzer on both sides of your jaw, blending down toward your chin to soften a sharp jawline. Finish with a very light swirl over the bridge of your nose. Darkening the center of the face forces the eye to focus on the lighter shades, creating the illusion of soft, rounded cheeks.

Shorten a long face

The secret to widening a long face? Apply blush and bronzer in horizontal strokes for a balancing effect. How-to: Starting high on the apples of your cheeks, sweep blush out toward your ears. Finish by lightly dusting bronzer horizontally across your chin, the bridge of your nose, and the top of your forehead and blend well for a natural, lit-from-within look.

Balance a heart face

The secret to enhancing a heart-shaped face: Sweep a light layer of blush beneath each cheekbone and blend downward. Then, starting at the middle of your forehead (at the hairline), dust bronzer in an outward diagonal toward both sides of your temple to narrow the forehead. Finally, dot a little bronzer on the tip of your chin to optically soften its sharp point.

To narrow a wide face

Bye-bye, cherub cheeks! Placing bronzer diagonally in the hollow beneath each cheekbone creates a more chiseled look and draws the eye up and down to visually narrow the face. Tip: Opt for a cream bronzer for a matte look. Creams are easier to apply, plus they won't accentuate fine lines.

HAS YOUR MAKEUP CLOCK STOPPED?

Some old-faithful cosmetic habits not only look outdated, they can add years to a woman's face. Here, fresh techniques that will help you look younger—in more ways than one!

FOUNDATION

So 1980s: Makeup mask
So now: Sheer coverage

Too-thick makeup makes skin dried out and aged. For luminous coverage that won't smother skin, apply liquid makeup with a slightly dewy finish, using a damp sponge for sheer, flawless color and foolproof blending.

EYELINER

So 1980s: Raccoon eyes
So now: Bare inner corners

Intense eyeliner coating the entire perimeter of the eye showcases any darkness and wrinkles around the eye. The fix: Apply a neutral liner (in a soft brown, gray, or taupe) across the top lash line, sweeping up and outward at the corner. Then smudge liner on the lower lash line, one-third of the way in from the outer corner, leaving the inner corner bare, which illuminates the eyes.

BLUSH

So 1980s: High and heavy
So now: Midcheek and light

Electric blush applied to the top of the cheekbones amplifies and draws attention to crow's-feet. Instead, layer a soft-hued satin blush on the outside of the cheeks' apples (beginning even with the iris) in upward strokes, going no higher than the middle of the cheekbone to avoid calling attention to any lines and wrinkles.

To outsmart puffiness

If you're like us, you don't always puff up in just one spot—your entire face gets rounder! The fix: Darken the outsides of your face to appear thinner.

To do: Starting at the curve of your hairline above your right temple, lightly sweep bronzer down along your hairline to your jaw, then blend inward toward the center of your face. Repeat on the other side. Then use a mirror to look at yourself in profile to make sure you've blended well and there's no distinctive line. Tip: To enhance the effect, dab a bit of highlighter under your eyebrow arches and on the tops of your cheekbones to bring out your bone structure.

To elongate the neck

We may not automatically think to apply makeup to our necks, but a little bit of color can go a long way toward optically erasing sudden throat bloat. The key is to subtly darken both sides of the neck, which directs the eye inward and vertically for a longer, leaner look.

To do: Using a brush, apply a cream bronzer to the right side of your neck, blending down from behind your ear to the top of your collarbone. Repeat on the left side. To enhance the elongating effect, dab highlighter on your finger and draw a line from the top of your neck vertically down your throat to your collarbone, then blend it outward.

To hide a double chin

No need to put on that itchy, confining turtleneck or oversize scarf to disguise an extra chin. Simply sweeping bronzer right below the jawline creates a shadowlike effect that helps the chin appear more angular. Bonus: This clever contour works beautifully to help hide that dreaded turkey wattle in holiday photos, too!

To do: Tilt your head back and apply bronzer right under your chin, blending outward along your jawline and down onto your neck. Tip: To ensure a more natural look, after blending, switch to a clean brush and blend a bit more.

UH-OH! CORRECT MAKEUP SLIPUPS

Oops: too much pressed powder

Layering powder around the eyes and mouth causes it to cake into wrinkles, making them more pronounced. The fix: Use a wide, soft brush to lightly sweep powder over the nose and forehead. Then, without reloading the brush, dust it around the eyes and mouth to cut shine without accentuating lines.

Oops: dark, matte lipstick

Lips naturally lose fullness with age, and dark lipsticks make them appear even thinner. Plus, waxy matte formulas settle into fine lines. A more flattering choice: a sheer, neutral lipstick that moisturizes and plumps lips to blur wrinkles.

Oops: shimmer shadow on lids

Sure, too much light-reflecting shadow can enhance wrinkles. But rather than tossing the sparkle, simply sweep a matte shadow on the lid and dot shimmer only under the arches of the brows for an uplifted look.

FOUND! YOUR PERFECT MASCARA

Short lashes?

To instantly elongate stubby, brittle lashes (which can be brought on by age, excessive sun exposure, or even harsh makeup removers), sweep on a polymer-based mascara that contains tiny silk fibers. With each swipe, the mascara "glues" the fibers to the tips of lashes, extending the hair so it appears longer—like microscopic falsies. And because it's infused with pliable polymers, lashes stay soft to prevent breakage.

Sensitive eyes?

A waterproof mascara can seem like the best option if you're prone to itchy, watery eyes, but it may actually be what's causing the irritation. The reason: Mascaras containing isododecane, a water-resistant solvent, are more likely to flake (which can scratch and inflame the eyes). For lovely lashes sans irritation, opt for a natural isododecane-free formula made with flake- and smudgeproof plant waxes.

Thinning lashes?

Healthy, thick lashes call attention to beautiful eyes. But as we age, the three rows of lashes we're born with naturally dwindle to a single row and lose their lush appearance. To amp up the volume, opt for a mascara that's infused with biotin (a B-complex vitamin that repairs and stimulates the cells responsible for hair growth) and procapil (a derivative of olive oil's oleanolic acid that's commonly used in hair-loss treatments to slow follicle aging by increasing circulation). This potent ingredient combination encourages new lash growth and strengthens the roots of the lashes you already have, so fewer fall out. The amazing result: Lashes can appear 25 percent thicker after 1 month.

 ### The secret to lush lashes

"I love to play up my eyes for holiday parties, but I'm not too keen on wearing false lashes. Instead, I dip a cotton swab in baby powder and tap off any excess. Then I apply a coat of mascara to my lashes, and while they're still wet, I close my eyes and lightly sweep the baby powder over the mascara before finishing with another coat. The powder provides extra particles for the mascara to stick to, so my lashes are thick and full."

—*Charlotte Warwick, Albany, NY*

Quick save for dried-out mascara

"I don't like to waste anything, so it bothers me when my mascara starts to dry out and there's still plenty left in the tube. But I recently came up with a fix: Add a few drops of saline solution, eyedrops, or distilled water to the bottle, then pump the wand a couple of times to mix it up. It works like a charm!"

—*Allison DeMarco, San Diego, CA*

LOOK STUNNING IN SECONDS

15 seconds for perfect brows

Why is it that your brows always decide to look extra unruly when you don't have the time to painstakingly pluck? To guarantee they always look polished, simply dampen an old toothbrush, stroke it over a dry bar of soap, and comb through each brow. The soap molds brows into a defined shape, nixing any wild hairs. But only brush through your eyebrows once—otherwise too much soap can make eyebrows sticky.

40 seconds for youthful skin

Sure, the right moisturizer is key to erasing fine lines, but we've found a way to double its wrinkle-fighting power—without adding time to your daily routine. To do: Before showering, wash your face and pat dry. Then slather a thick layer of moisturizer on your face, gently massaging it into your skin for 30 seconds. Next, shower as usual, but rinse your face last. The shower's steam will open pores so they can absorb the moisturizer's nourishing ingredients, which will plump wrinkles for smooth, dewy skin.

34 seconds for eyes that pop

As lashes thin out as we get older, eyes can seem to recede. Eyeliner is the perfect fix, but it can take forever to get it to go on straight. For liner in a flash, try this foolproof trick: Thickly line your bottom lashes with black, gray, or purple kohl liner. Then close your eye tightly and gently run your clean pinkie or a cotton swab that's angled on one end back and forth along your lashes, rubbing the liner up onto your top lid. Finish by opening your eye and smudging up and outward at the corners to create a little lift.

50 seconds for whiter teeth

To get a gleaming smile without expensive in-office procedures or time-consuming strips, simply sprinkle a pinch of kosher salt and a pinch of baking soda on top of your regular toothpaste each time you brush. The gently abrasive salt crystals and the sodium bicarbonate in baking soda work together to buff away surface stains—just like the polishing paste used in professional cleanings. For extra whitening power, move the toothbrush in slow circles to ensure the entire surface of each tooth is scrubbed to a sparkling white.

59 seconds for silky hair

For a beautiful updo, twist air-dried hair into a messy bun, leaving a few long pieces down to frame the face. Rub a drop of olive oil between your palms and lightly apply to the loose strands, then run a flatiron down each of the small sections, lifting at the roots and flicking the ends under. The iron's heat will help emulsify and evenly distribute the oil's hydrating fatty acids, so hair will look smoother and shinier. Finish by gently ruffling the sections to separate, and voilà—an effortlessly chic look!

10 seconds for undetectable roots

Roots are notorious for being invisible one day and all you see the next. So for brunette beauties whose roots seem to pop up overnight, try this remedy until it's time for a touch-up: After styling, use the wand to sweep black or brown smudge-proof mascara over new growth along the part and hairline, then set the color with a cool blast from a blow-dryer. One caution: Avoid waterproof formulas—they can make strands appear stiff.

58 seconds for shimmering highlights

During the winter, blond highlights can start to appear lackluster and brassy. The culprits: dry indoor heat and hot showers that open the hair cuticle and wash away pigment. To restore shine and amp up color, try this insider secret: Using a puff, pat a shimmering body powder onto strands, then flip your head over and blow-dry for 20 seconds to get rid of any excess to nix brassy color and create a natural shine. Bonus: The powder will also soak up oil and refresh your hair, so you can go longer between washes, which extends the life of your color.

35 seconds for lush lips

There are two ingredients for perfectly plump lips: honey and a toothbrush. Dab honey onto your lips and gently rub the bristles against your lips in a circular motion, then wipe with a wet washcloth. The toothbrush will whisk away dry skin, and the honey will lock in moisture while healing and protecting chapped lips. Afterward, lips will look naturally rosy, so all you need is a swipe of alcohol-free lip balm for a sweet, kissable pucker.

7 seconds to lighten eye shadow

If a dark eye shadow ends up looking "raccoon," simply dust loose translucent face powder generously over the eyelid. Then use a clean blush brush to dust the powder off the lid. The dark pigments of the shadow will cling to the powder, making it easy to whisk it away. Finish with a sweep of a light, shimmering eye shadow to further brighten the eyes.

10 seconds to smooth polish

To stymie air bubbles that crop up in the middle of a manicure, dip the pad of your index finger into remover and run it over the bumps in the lacquer. The acetone will dilute and redistribute the polish to smooth the bubbles instantly. When dry, finish with a second coat of polish if needed.

15 seconds to thin heavy concealer

To fix under-eye concealer overload, pat moisturizer from the center of the eye to the outer corner. This will dilute the concentrated pigments but keep the inner corner bright for a refreshed look.

13 seconds for smooth cuticles

Frigid temperatures and harsh hand sanitizers take a toll on cuticles. But if your schedule is too manic for a full manicure, try this on-the-go tip to keep them supple: Puncture a vitamin E caplet, squeeze the oil onto your cuticles, and massage it into the base of your nail bed to ensure moisture. Plus, the oil will moisturize longer than regular hand creams and give nails a light, healthy, just-buffed sheen.

45 seconds for longer, thicker lashes

To create lush, beautiful eyelashes with any mascara, the trick is to apply it in strategic sections. First, place the wand at your lash line and squiggle it back and forth (without sweeping upward) so lashes settle into the fibers of the wand and mascara coats the base of the lashes only. Do the same to your other eye, allowing both coats to dry. Then swipe mascara in a zigzag motion from the base of each lash to the tip.

27 seconds for a slimmer face

Just a few dabs of strategically placed concealer are all you need to make your face appear thinner. Just be sure to choose a light-reflecting concealer that's a bit lighter than your skin. Dab three dots evenly under each eye and one dot on the very top of each cheekbone, then blend well.

10 Brilliant Uses
for MAKEUP
SPONGES

1 Hydrate plants effortlessly
Watering your plants can seem like a gamble—you think you're adding the right amount, but the pot overflows. The fix? Next time you repot, line the bottom of the planter with flat makeup sponges. The absorbent sponges will soak up excess water and hold it until the roots draw it out, ensuring your greenery never gets too much or too little.

2 Make a cushier ice pack
When you need to soothe bumps and bruises, skip bulky ice packs (which tend to freeze in awkward shapes and have pointy edges) and try this: Cut a sponge in half and soak in a 50:50 solution of water and rubbing alcohol. Place in a resealable plastic bag and freeze until needed. Since alcohol doesn't freeze solid, the sponge will stay soft and flexible, making it more comfortable to hold against sore spots.

3 Repel insects—sans chemicals
A natural option for nixing any creepy-crawlies that try to invade your home: Place five drops of peppermint oil on a makeup sponge and leave it where you've spotted pests. Flies, fleas, and ants detest the strong scent, and since the sponge won't dry out as quickly as a cotton ball or cloth rag, the bug-repelling benefits will last for days.

4 Entertain Whiskers for hours
For a low-cost kitty toy, super-glue two flat makeup sponges together along the edges, filling the space between with catnip before gluing shut. The sponge's air pockets will allow the scent to escape, but the material is durable enough to withstand clawed attacks.

5 Nix refrigerator odors for pennies
A space-saving way to freshen up the fridge: Coat a damp makeup sponge with baking soda, then set it inside. The porous sponge will absorb odors. When the freshness fades, rinse the sponge and reapply baking soda.

6 Safeguard glasses in the dishwasher

To avoid the disappointment of opening the dishwasher and realizing your stemware has cracked, try wedging sponges between the most breakable items before starting the cycle. The layer of padding will prevent glasses from clinking into each other, ensuring your fragile items stay flawless.

7 Effortlessly soften laundry

Adding fabric softener to a load of clothes when your machine doesn't have a dispenser can be a major time drain—who wants to sit around waiting for the rinse cycle? The save: Moisten a sponge with softener, then toss it in once the machine fills with water at the start of the load. The sponge will slowly release the liquid, so you can go about your day.

8 Blisterproof new shoes

Those pumps you scored look terrific but they're a tad loose, so they shift and rub against your heels with each step, causing blisters. The solution: Cut a circular makeup sponge in half, then insert each half-moon between your heel and the back of the shoe. The foamy material will improve the shoes' fit and cushion your skin while being flexible enough to adjust as you walk. Ah, that's better!

9 Lengthen the life of bar soap

It happens every time: Your soap turns into a slimy mess after just a few days, thanks to that little pool of water that always forms at the bottom of the soap dish. End this problem for good by swapping your dish for a sponge. When you place the bar on top, the sponge's porous material will absorb excess liquid, preventing the soap from getting slimy, so it will last longer.

10 Help veggies stay crisp for weeks

Humidity in your fridge can cause produce to soften within days. The remedy: Place a sponge in the crisper drawer alongside the fruit and veggies. The sponge will absorb dampness from the air, keeping produce fresher longer.

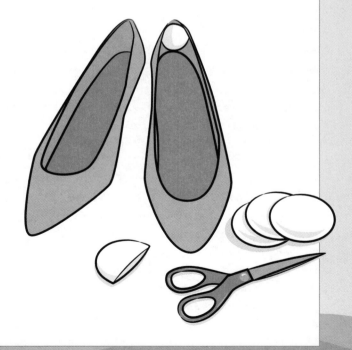

Clever Clothing Fixes

Everyone needs a wardrobe update every now and then. If you're looking for fashions that are figure flattering and provide instant slimming, you're in luck. Read on to discover styles that perfectly complement your body type to keep you looking fit and fabulous.

DROP THREE SIZES— INSTANTLY!

Apple? Opt for ruching

Here's a style secret: Slip on a dark V-neck top with a ruched center seam that instantly creates curves. Plus, a ruffled V that connects to the vertical seam helps draw the eye inward and up and down, creating a longer, leaner torso.

To enhance the middle-whittling effect, wear khakis that show off the curves of the legs. The result: a sexy silhouette.

Petite and busty? Choose a flowing floral

A flowing sleeveless blouse with a hem that falls just below the hips beautifully elongates the torso. Plus, a soft fabric with a large floral pattern helps distract from an ample chest for a more balanced look. Slip into sleek white cigarette jeans with enough stretch to help legs look firmer and a slight crop to show off slim ankles.

Tall and busty? Slip on a cowl-neck

A flattering fix for the busty woman: a top in an eye-catching solid color that's fitted through the hips and waist and has a subtly scooping cowl-neck, which complements yet controls curves. Pair the top with tailored, cropped khaki capris and a light-hued cardigan with a diagonal design across the front. The neutral capris help the sweater's

asymmetrical pattern stand out, which draws the gaze downward (away from the bust) while also subtly accentuating hips to balance the upper body. Bonus: Leaving the cardi unbuttoned draws the eye inward to the vertical line of the bright blouse for a beautifully elongating effect.

Pear-shaped? Add detail at the shoulders

Minimizing hips can be as easy as adding interest up top. Cap sleeves and ruffled shoulders call attention to your shoulders, balancing out wide hips. The pear-perfect pick, which can be dressed up or down: a solid, jewel-toned faux wrap in a jersey fabric with ruffled sleeves and ruching down one side. The look works because it guides the eye to the tiniest part of your waist while draping beautifully over problem areas. Plus, a knee-length, "bias-cut" hem (which drops straight down from the hips) prevents the skirt from clinging, making thighs appear smoother.

Plus size? Try a patterned wrap

Want a beautiful hourglass shape? Look no further than a wrap dress, which calls attention to the thinnest part of your waist. Plus, wrap styles create a deep V at the neck, which instantly draws the eye vertically down the center of the torso for a body-trimming effect. To make a wrap even more wonderful, choose a vibrant, knee-length dress with elbow-length sleeves and a tiny print, which camouflages any problem areas.

YOUR MOST FLATTERING JEANS EVER!

Lower belly bulge? Try tummy panels

Whether we're troubled by a postbaby pooch or those last few hard-to-lose pounds, we've all wished for a way to flatten the lower belly. Wish granted! To make your stomach appear smaller, choose jeans with spandex control panels that go unnoticed by others but work just like Spanx. For the most belly-firming power, opt for a pair with a high-rise cut that hits at the navel (so the panel covers the entire lower abdomen), a 2-inch waistband (which won't roll like 1-inch bands), and "crosshatch" or crisscross textured denim (to help hide any bulges).

Full bottom? Try "over riser" detail

Those of us with voluptuous bottoms know that a pair of jeans that fits the waist often becomes "plumber's pants" when we sit down. To the rescue: midrise jeans with "over riser" detail, which means the yoke is cut in a deeper V. This gives the backside more coverage and allows the pockets to be sewn higher, creating a lifted look. For an even slimmer rear view, opt for jeans that boast sleek, angled pockets with subtle embellishments (bulky pockets have a widening effect) and a boot-cut leg that begins to flare at the knee instead of midcalf (a dramatic flare balances the rear so it appears smaller).

Hourglass curves? Try shaper denim

For women with curvaceous figures, the wrong jeans can create multiple trouble spots—pinching in some areas and sagging in others. But scientists have created a new generation of denim that works like a shaper by comfortably conforming to the body while minimizing lumps and bumps. The best part? The thicker fabric (made of 35 percent polyester, 64 percent cotton, and 1 percent spandex) slims the thighs, hips, rear, and waist at the same time—while still allowing you to breathe. For the smoothest silhouette, try shaper jeans with a high-rise cut that hits at or slightly above the belly button, which simultaneously adds height and minimizes hips.

Muffin top? Try a contoured midrise

Low-rise jeans (that sit more than 2 inches below the navel) are designed to stay in place by pinching and pushing up on the tummy, which can result in belly spillover. To head off a muffin top and help the waist look tiny, choose a midrise style (which falls less than an inch below the belly button) with a contoured waistband. Waistbands are usually one piece of fabric, which doesn't always flatter natural curves. But contoured waistbands are made from pieces of denim that are tailored to complement curves. To recognize a contoured waist, simply look for vertical seams along the band.

Broad hips? Try off-center side seams

One of the newest figure-flattering techniques used by jeans designers: sewing side seams slightly off-center (toward the front of the leg), which allows more hip movement while maintaining a flattering fit. One caveat: This detail may not be listed in the jeans' description, so to identify off center seams, simply hold up the jeans and look at them from the front—if you can see the seams, they've been repositioned. To enhance the hip-slimming effect, choose an indigo wash with a very subtle fade down the center of the thigh, which calls attention away from the hips.

Tall? Try a 38-inch inseam

Until recently, most jeans manufacturers only offered inseams of up to 34 inches, which meant that taller women had to wear shorter, unflattering hems that made their legs appear stumpy. Now, though, specialty brands and major retail stores have taken note of the demand and started offering jeans with inseams all the way up to 38 inches—most of which can be easily found online. Not sure of your perfect length? Determine your inseam by slipping on the shoes you wear most often with jeans, then place a tape measure at the top of your inner thigh and measure from that point to about ¼ inch off the floor.

WHAT A DIFFERENCE THE RIGHT BRA MAKES!

Enhance a small bust with shallow cups

The trick to creating cleavage on a smaller bust is to opt for a bra with demi cups (which cover only three-quarters of the breast) and graduated padding on the sides, which subtly lift and enhance small breasts.

Boost a saggy bust with contour cups

Due to hormonal changes, breast-feeding, and age, our breasts naturally lose volume. A sag-free solution: an underwire bra with broad straps and full-coverage, contoured cups that lift breasts into a rounded shape. Plus, giving breasts a youthful boost exposes the smallest part of the waist for a slimming effect.

D cup or higher? How to find bras that fit

A decade ago the average woman's bra size was 36C, but today it's 36DD, making it harder than ever for women to find the right fit. The reason: Different brands designate cup sizes larger than D in different ways, which leads many women to unknowingly buy ill-fitting bras. To help women pinpoint a just-right bra, HerRoom.com offers two online tools: The Universal Cup Sizing system asks for the size and brand of the bra that currently fits you well, then provides a code (such as 3601, 3602, and so forth) that directs you to the right size in any brand sold on the site. The Know Your Breasts Bra Finder features a quick quiz about breast characteristics, from fullness to shape, then suggests the bra style that will flatter you most.

Contain spillage with a "balconette" base

When you first put on a bra, you likely settle your breasts into the cups perfectly, and the fit can seem right. But breast tissue shifts as the day wears on, and if you're wearing a bra with stiff or too-small cups, your breasts can spill over the top for a lumpy look. To stop the "quad boob" effect, opt for a bra with a "balconette" base (made of sturdy fabric sewn in panels along the bottom and sides of the cups) and stretchy panels across the top. The balconette simultaneously lifts and controls breasts throughout the day. The result: a streamlined silhouette.

Stop strapless droop with a bustier

Strapless bras, while flattering for women with smaller breasts, can have a droopy effect on large-breasted women. The fix: a classic "long line" bra made of lace and boning. Bustiers are supported by your waist, lifting the breasts and filling out your figure.

QUICK CLOTHING FIXES

Foil static cling for good

"Not again," you think as you get up from your desk with your dress clinging to your thighs. (We've been there!) To outsmart pesky static, next time you do laundry, ball up a piece of aluminum foil into a smooth sphere and toss it into the dryer with your clothes. Normally, the friction created by tumbling clothes gives some items a positive charge and others a negative charge, resulting in static cling. But the aluminum foil will act as a conductor that forces electricity to move quickly through fabric and neutralizes the opposite charges. *Money saved: $6 per bottle of fabric softener*

Quick fix for a sweater snag

"I practically live in my blue cashmere cardigan, so I was upset when a coworker pointed out a snag in the sleeve. Luckily, she showed me how to hide it: Just use a crochet hook to pull the loose yarn through to the underside of the garment, then turn the sweater inside out and make a small knot with the extra string. Next, dab the spot with clear nail polish to secure the knot and prevent the snag from showing. Now my cardi looks as good as new!"

—Kim Praxter, Newberry, SC

Quick fix for a fallen hem

Oops! Your pants got caught on your heel, so you're walking around with a slipped hem. The fix: Fold the hem back in place and attach a small binder clip to secure it, then remove the metal handles. The clip won't distort the fabric like a pin would—plus, no one will notice it on dark pants. Stash one in your purse for emergencies!

De-pill a sweater in seconds

"When I need to get rid of pesky fuzz balls on my favorite sweaters, I just spread the garment across a tabletop and use a disposable razor to very gently shave the pillings. The thin razor blade loosens the pills without damaging the fabric. Just be careful around buttons or seams."

—Cassie Bartmer, Saco, ME

Reshape stretched-out sweater cuffs

"When the sleeve openings of my favorite sweaters start to stretch out, I return them to their original shape by spritzing the cuffs with a spray bottle filled with hot water, then blow-drying them on the hot setting. The combination of hot water and air causes the fabric to shrink back to normal, leaving my sweaters ready to wear without a trip to the dry cleaner."

—Pamela Kutcher, Apex, NC

Lift a food stain in seconds

For a stain remover that works just as effectively as stain sticks on oil-based stains like dressing, sauce, and gravy—and costs a fraction of the price—stash some artificial sweetener in your purse. If you have a food "oops," simply sprinkle sweetener on the spot and let sit 10 minutes, then blot. The powdery granules will absorb oil to lighten the stain, which will come out in the wash. (Any artificial sweetener will do, but some experts prefer Splenda since it's thicker.) *Money saved: $4 for on-the-go stain remover*

Spiff up suede instantly!

It's finally cool enough to wear that suede skirt that flatters your figure perfectly—but after months in storage, it's looking a bit shabby. The save: Use a pair of clean panty hose to rub the fabric thoroughly in a circular motion. The positively charged nylon fibers will attract and lift away negatively charged dust particles, while the gentle rubbing will revive suede's velvety texture. The result: Your skirt will look brand new—and you'll look stunning! *Money saved: $10 on dry cleaning*

Slim your face in seconds

For an easy strategy that will help you look even more beautiful, try wearing bold, contrasting colors near your neckline. Stylists say that pairing a dark cardigan with a white blouse makes your jawline appear more angular and adds flattering definition to the face. Gorgeous!

Reader Tip: No iron? No problem!

"Last month while I was on vacation, I pulled out a button-down shirt and noticed the collar was wrinkled from being smashed in my suitcase. Since I hadn't packed an iron, I used my flatiron to press the collar. Well, wouldn't you know, it worked like a dream! Now I use my flatiron for all my small ironing jobs—it's so much easier than lugging out the iron and ironing board."

—*Mary Freeman, Milwaukee, WI*

FAST ADVICE FOR ACCESSORIES

Stretch too-tight shoes in minutes

The leather pumps you found online look fabulous with your party dress, but they're a little too snug for comfort. Before taking them to the shoe repair shop for stretching, try this easy trick: Put on a pair of socks and slip on the shoes, then turn your blow-dryer on high and aim it at the tight areas while wiggling and stretching your feet. Wear the shoes until they cool, then remove your socks and walk around in the shoes to see how they feel. Heat makes leather more pliable, so the shoes will mold to your feet. If they're still snug, try repeating the process. *Money saved: $10 for a trip to a cobbler*

Polish dull leather shoes in a pinch

After pulling out your best pumps for a holiday party, you see they're dusty and dingy—and you're all out of shoe polish. The fix: Rub your shoes with a soft cloth dipped in about a tablespoon of castor oil. The leather will look healthier and give off a glow. There's nothing like "new" shoes for a party.

Remove oily suede stains

Oops! While prepping for your dinner party, you spilled a drop of oil on your favorite suede boots. To the rescue: cornstarch. Sprinkle some onto the soiled area and dab with your finger. Let it sit for an hour, then brush it off with a clean toothbrush. The cornstarch will absorb and lift off the oil, leaving your boots blemish-free.

Fast fix for scuffed leather shoes

You've been wearing your favorite leather peep-toes all summer—and it shows. To erase unsightly scuff marks and make the shoes look new, squirt a dab of hand lotion on the offending spot and rub it in with your fingers. Lotion's moisturizing ingredients will help you buff away superficial marks while keeping the leather soft and supple to prevent future wear and tear.

Get your diamond jewelry glistening

To turn a grungy ring from blah to brilliant, soak it in a mixture of 1 tablespoon of ammonia, 1 cup of warm water, and a squirt of dish-washing detergent for 10 minutes. The ammonia and soapy water will dissolve grease and dirt to restore the jewelry's shine. One caveat: This works for hard metals and clear stones like diamonds but isn't recommended for costume jewelry or colored stones. *Money saved: $40 per ultrasonic jewelry cleaner*

Quick fix for bent shades

"The other day I pulled out my plastic sunglasses for a trip to the park and realized the frames had gotten bent while stored away. Instead of wearing slightly crooked shades, I blasted the frames with warm air from my hair dryer for 20 seconds, then put them on and reshaped the plastic so they fit my face perfectly. It was easy!"

—Julie Shepherd, Tampa, FL

Scratchproof your shades

Ugh—you can't find your sunglasses case and don't want to buy a new one this late in the season. To the rescue: an old necktie. Simply measure about 8 inches up from the wide tip (using your glasses as a guide), then cut off the remainder and glue or stitch the cut end shut. Slide your shades into the open end of the pouch and you're all set. Bonus: The fabric is great for cleaning lenses. *Money saved: $5 for a case*

Freshen up a dingy leather bag

When you retrieve your favorite leather tote from your closet, you notice it looks a bit dirty. The fix: Dip a clean cloth in a beaten egg white and lightly scrub the outside of the bag for a few minutes, then wipe with a paper towel. The ovalbumin in egg whites will remove dirt and dust while bringing out the leather's natural shine. (Test on an inconspicuous area first.) *Money saved: $7 for leather cleaner*

Nix small scratches on sunglasses

After a summer of constant wear, your shades look smudgy and scratched. To erase the little imperfections, moisten the lenses with water, then squeeze a pea-size glob of white (nongel) toothpaste onto a soft cloth and rub gently all over. Rinse and wipe the lenses dry with a soft, lint-free cloth. The paste's gentle abrasives will remove smudges and small scratches, leaving your sunglasses looking like new.

A slimmer face in seconds

Put your best face forward for holiday parties (and all those flashing cameras) by skipping the studs and opting for dangling earrings—ideally, at least 2 inches in length. The danglers will draw the eye vertically, creating the illusion of a longer neck and slimmer cheeks.

No more belt-flap frustration!

"I love the look of wearing belts over sweaters and dresses. But since those garments don't have belt loops, the end of the belt ends up sticking out and looking sloppy. Luckily, my friend shared this smart trick: Apply a strip of double-sided tape to the underside of the belt's tip, then press down to secure. It will stay put all day!"

—Susan Hiller, Plano, TX

Body Beautiful

Let's admit it—sometimes it can be difficult to feel comfortable in your own skin. From rosacea to rough heels, you worry about plenty of bothersome beauty woes. In addition, it's hard to feel like your best when you're dealing with life's little aches and pains. Here, learn how to combat all kinds of body discomforts to feel and look beautiful and confident.

BEAT SUMMER BEAUTY WOES

Beauty argh: Sun spots

Disguise and diminish discoloration with this trick: Dip a cotton swab in mineral foundation with an SPF of at least 30 and dab it on sun spots. The minerals will diffuse light, making skin appear more even and youthful, while the titanium dioxide will protect from further UV damage.

Beauty argh: Stretch marks

"Self-tanner conceals 'stripes' on any complexion," says Hollywood aesthetician Mindi Walters. Also, researchers found that applying collagen-stimulating vitamin C serum each morning and elasticity-boosting glycolic acid cream each night fades marks completely in just 12 weeks.

Beauty argh: Razor burn

Those trails of red dots are often caused by applying pressure to compensate for a dull razor, coarse hair, or dry skin, says Jeannette Graf, MD, a dermatologist in New York City. The Rx: Apply an aloe-infused shave lotion and wait at least 2 minutes before shaving. Dr. Graf explains, "Letting the lotion sit hydrates skin and softens hair so it's easier to remove, eliminating the need to apply irritating pressure."

Beauty argh: Pit pudge

High temperatures can make the lymph system sluggish, causing underarm fluid retention. To rev lymph drainage and ease swelling, try this: With your hands on each side of your neck, stroke toward your shoulders five times. Next, place your hands on the outside of your shoulders and sweep inward along your collarbone five times. Finish by pressing your armpits in a circular motion.

Beauty argh: Cleavage acne

Perspiration pooling between the breasts creates the ideal environment for acne-causing bacteria. But the pimple-zapping treatments we use on our face can irritate the skin along the décolletage. To banish bust-line blemishes, wash with soap containing 2 percent pyrithione zinc and let sit for 2 minutes before rinsing. Zinc acts as a powerful antibacterial yet is gentle on skin.

Beauty argh: Yellow toenails

Whiten the yellowish tinge on your toenails (caused by UV rays and nail polish) with a paste made of juice from 1 lemon and 1 teaspoon each of baking soda and hydrogen peroxide. Let the paste sit for 5 minutes, then rinse. The lemon's citric acid will bleach nails, the baking soda will scour stains, and the peroxide will oxidize the pigments deposited by dark polish.

Beauty argh: Rosacea

If high temperatures have you "seeing red," you're not alone—81 percent of rosacea sufferers name heat as a trigger. "Heat dilates vessels and increases blood flow, which leads to flare-ups," explains Jeanine Downie, MD, a dermatologist in Montclair, New Jersey. She suggests soothing skin with anti-inflammatory licorice extract in a glycerin base, which delivers the extract deep into the skin. One that fits the bill: Eucerin Redness Relief Daily Perfecting Lotion, which has a light green tint to conceal redness.

Beauty argh: Heat rash

In places where sweat and pressure from fabric meet—like under the edges of a swimsuit—the resulting friction can create microscopic tears in the skin. This allows candida yeast to enter, causing an itchy heat rash. To fight fungus and soothe skin: After showering, blast the affected area with a blow-dryer set on cool until skin is completely dry (since yeast multiplies in a moist environment). Then dust the area with an antifungal powder containing miconazole nitrate, advises Cynthia Bailey, MD, a dermatologist in Sebastopol, California. She recommends Zeasorb-AF Antifungal Powder. One warning: Avoid powders with cornstarch, which feeds fungus.

Beauty argh: Thigh chafing

Contrary to popular belief, dusting on powder to halt skin-on-skin chafing can actually amplify inflammation. Sure, powder helps temporarily, but it can end up drying out the skin's surface so it feels even rougher. To soothe chafing long-term, apply a hydrating product that contains dimethicone, a silicone-based oil that creates a barrier to lock moisture into skin and helps thighs glide smoothly past each other, cutting down on friction and pain.

Beauty argh: Summer rash

If you've noticed irregularly shaped, slightly pink or scaly blotches on your back, it may be a common fungal infection called tinea versicolor. This condition is caused by an overgrowth of a type of yeast called malassezia that naturally lives on skin and feasts on sebum. During the hotter months, excess oil helps the little guys flourish. To remedy an outbreak, spray an antifungal foot spray on your back. The formula's active ingredient, miconazole nitrate, kills any tenacious yeast, dries to a fine powder to soak up oil and sweat, and feels cool on contact.

Beauty argh: Cellulite

To win the war on dimples in seconds, whip up this "no wiggle" serum: Combine 1 tablespoon of unflavored powdered gelatin, 1 tablespoon of water, and 2 drops of olive oil. Rub a pearl-size amount of the mixture into your palms and apply to cellulite-prone areas.

Beauty argh: Rough heels

If sandpapery skin is keeping you from kicking up your heels, dermatologist Natasha Sandy, MD, suggests this trick favored by her Caribbean grandmother: "Mix a handful of sand with a little milk—it's a great exfoliating scrub." Or try 1 teaspoon of powdered milk mixed with sand and water. The milk's lactic acids will melt dead cells, while the fine grains of sand will whisk them away, better enabling skin to retain moisture. Then apply a lotion with alpha hydroxy acids to help keep heels smooth.

BEAUTY IN THE BATH (AND TUB!)

Fighting a cold? Soak in orange peels

To stifle the sniffles, tear the peel from one orange into small pieces and toss them into a warm, steamy bath.

Why it works: The oil in the peel is full of vitamin C, which is absorbed into the skin and stimulates the production of lymphocytes, white blood cells that serve as the immune system's front line against viruses and bacteria. Bonus: The vitamin is also an antioxidant that fights cell-damaging free radicals to guarantee luminous skin.

Swollen ankles? Try a seaweed soak

Being cooped up indoors can slow circulation, so the lymph system becomes clogged and blood begins to pool. To reduce puffiness, snip the feet off a pair of panty hose and add 4 tablespoons of powdered seaweed (available at eFoodDepot.com). Tie a knot in the top and hang the stocking over the faucet as the tub fills.

Why it works: Seaweed has phytochemicals that stimulate the lymph system and help flush clogged lymph nodes to reduce water retention. Plus, this soak has the same firming effects as a spa seaweed wrap—minus the price.

Congested? Try a rosemary-and-eucalyptus scrub

If a winter cold—of the wheezy and sneezy variety—has you down, perk up with a decadent sinus-opening concoction. To make: In a resealable jar, combine 1 cup of coarse kosher salt and 1 cup of grape-seed oil, then add 10 drops each of rosemary essential oil and eucalyptus essential oil. Before a steamy shower, massage the mixture into dry skin—inhaling deeply all the while—then step in and rinse off.

Why it works: The cineol in the eucalyptus and the camphor in both essential oils help clear mucus, while their antiseptic properties kill harboring bacteria. Plus, the oils' active ingredients promote circulation and create a warming sensation, which opens pores so skin-healing antioxidants in the grape-seed oil are quickly absorbed.

Tired? Mix in Epsom salts

Dodging fatigue can be as easy as dissolving ½ cup of Epsom salts, ½ cup of baking soda (which balances the pH of the water to prevent the salts from drying out skin), and 5 drops of vanilla extract (studies show the scent lifts your mood) in hot bathwater.

Why it works: Epsom salts are packed with magnesium, a mineral that helps cells produce energy. For women who are magnesium deficient (and that's most of us!), this bath is an efficient way to absorb the mineral through the skin—and boost energy fast.

Cold hands and feet? Relax in a ginger bath

Cold weather causes blood vessels to constrict, decreasing circulation to the parts of the body farthest from the heart. To keep fingers and toes toasty warm, pour ½ cup of freshly grated ginger or 2 tablespoons of powdered ginger into a steamy bath.

Why it works: Active compounds in ginger called gingerols have dilating effects on arteries, increasing bloodflow to fingers and toes. And the temperature increase won't stop once you've dried off—you'll feel the warming effect for up to 4 hours.

Foggy? Try a ginger lotion

Hazy skies have you feeling gloomy? Slather on this pick-me-up lotion: Combine 1 cup of unscented lotion or sweet almond oil, the contents of 3 vitamin E capsules, and 5 drops of ginger essential oil. After showering (or throughout the day to soften), massage the mixture into skin, focusing on the décolletage and parched areas.

Why it works: As you inhale ginger's sharp, fruity notes, the compound zingerone helps improve mental alertness and memory and relieve headaches, while its "active" compound gingerol (a relative of capsaicin, the compound that gives peppers their heat) warms skin and revs circulation.

Achy? Try a cinnamon bath

Wintry weather can be a pain in the neck—literally. To ease those aches (and pamper parched skin) blend 2 cups of powdered milk, $\frac{1}{2}$ cup of old-fashioned oats, and 1 teaspoon of ground cinnamon in a food processor until it becomes a fine powder. Pour $\frac{1}{4}$ cup of the mixture into a warm bath, then sit back in the water.

Why it works: The cinnamon's comforting, spicy aroma boosts mood and memory-boosting brain chemicals, while the spice's anticoagulant properties help relieve muscle spasms, menstrual cramps, and rheumatic pain. Plus, the inflammation-soothing silica in the oats and the exfoliating properties of the milk's lactic acid leave skin feeling soft and looking radiant.

Fabulous from Hands to Feet

Sometimes your hands and feet could use a little TLC. Pamper yourself pretty with these expert tips on how to beautify your hands and feet.

BEAUTIFUL HANDS IN A BLINK

Cracked skin?

Because hands contain very few oil glands and skin produces less oil as we age, exposure to winter air can cause hands to become so dry, they crack. A two-part remedy: First, apply a daily lotion that contains urea, a humectant that locks in moisture and has antibacterial properties to ward off infection without stinging. Then, twice a week, combine 2 tablespoons of plain yogurt, 1 teaspoon of castor oil, and $\frac{1}{2}$ teaspoon of vitamin E oil; slather on hands, slip on cotton gloves, and leave on overnight. As you sleep, the yogurt's lactic acid will stimulate new cell growth, the castor oil's ricinoleic acid will ease pain, and the antioxidants in vitamin E will repair skin.

BEAT-THE-HEAT SECRETS

HOT SPOT: Feet
Stick-on gels
If you've ever dangled your feet in cool water on a hot summer day, you know that when your feet are cool, the rest of you is, too! But this time of year, it seems like nothing can prevent your tootsies from becoming hot, sweaty, and stinky. Enter Be Koool Soft Gel Sheets. Simply stick one to the bottom of your foot (or in your sandal) and allow the self-cooling strip—invented to bring down a fever—to keep your feet refreshed for 8 wonderful hours.

HOT SPOT: Underarms
Deodorant cooldown
Deodorant seems to fail at the worst times—at the company picnic or your cousin's wedding (where everyone wants a hug!). The secret to staying protected? Opt for an antiperspirant that keeps you dry and has a cooling effect.

Also key: making sure skin is dry when applying antiperspirant. The active ingredient, aluminum zirconium, clogs sweat glands, so if the skin is wet, the chemical reaction happens on skin's surface rather than in the pores, preventing the glands from being blocked. And for high-sweat situations, try "pit pads," which stick on the inside of your top and absorb sweat.

It's difficult to look and feel your best when you're sweaty, red, and puffy from high temperatures, but we've uncovered no-sweat tricks and gadgets guaranteed to help you keep your cool all summer—so you can look and feel stunning no matter how high the mercury rises!

HOT SPOT: Red Cheeks
Yogurt mask
When you're seeing red—on your face, that is—try this ultrasoothing mask: Mix $1/4$ cup of yogurt (lactic acid exfoliates and soothes redness), 3 tablespoons of aloe vera gel (an anti-inflammatory and humectant), and 2 tablespoons of wheatgrass juice (revs lymphatic drainage to reduce bloat). Apply to your face and wait 10 minutes, then rinse for soft, glowing skin.

HOT SPOT: Thighs
Antifriction stick
We've all been there: One minute you feel beautiful and flirty in that gorgeous new sundress, and the next minute uncomfortable friction between your thighs has you wishing you'd worn pants. Many women use baby powder as their rub rescue, but it works only temporarily (and is a mess to reapply on the go). Instead, try a soothing, go-anywhere anti-chafe stick infused with comfrey root. The sweatproof gel immediately stops thigh friction, while the comfrey relieves pain and irritation.

HOT SPOT: Back
Mint-tea spritz
When oil glands on the back kick into overdrive, causing sweat spots and bacne, try this chilled tonic: In 1 cup of boiling water, steep 1 bag of peppermint tea (containing cooling menthol that acts as an antibacterial agent) and 1 bag of chamomile tea (which has chamazulene, a powerful anti-inflammatory). Once the tea cools, pour it into a small spray bottle and pop it into the fridge. On steamy days, spritz on your back to cool off, control oil, and stay blemish-free.

HOT SPOT: Legs
Postsun lotions
Getting a flawless shave is tricky enough, but add in salty sweat and irritating heat and you have the perfect recipe for angry red bumps. The secret to silky, soft legs every time: Swap your regular lotion (which feels thick and sticky in the humidity) for a hydrating "after sun" gel infused with aloe and lidocaine. It's not only great for sunburns, it also soothes any heat-related irritation—the lidocaine takes out the sting, while the aloe heals the skin and restores moisture.

HOT SPOT: Neck
Frozen "pearls"
Thanks to its many pulse points, the neck is one of the key cooling spots on the body. In fact, lowering the blood temperature in that area can carry the cooling effect from head to toe in seconds. And we've discovered an icy accessory that cools you down while dressing up your look: Hot Girls Pearls. The pearls are filled with the same non-toxic cooling gel used in ice packs but rest right on your pulse points! And they can be frozen over and over for an all-summer *aah*.

HOT SPOT: Bosom
Bra AC pads
Ugh! Have you ever had one of those days when it gets so hot outside that you're sweating not only on your back and underarms but also beneath your underwire? Talk about uncomfortable! To the rescue: sweatproof cooling inserts. Each gel sheet contains a high percentage of water, as well as menthol and camphor, which work with your body's natural cooling system to bring down your body temperature. And the higher the temperatures rise, the more powerful these bosom buddies become—heat from your skin causes water to evaporate within the gel sheet, creating a long-lasting cooling sensation.

Protruding veins?

During menopause, hormone fluctuations can cause hands' delicate skin to become crepey, making veins more visible, says Peyman Ghasri, MD, of Castle Dermatology Institute in Encino, California. Compounding the problem: winter's chill, which causes hands' muscle fibers to contract and veins to appear more pronounced. To hydrate hands and ward off UV rays that can further thin the skin, Dr. Ghasri suggests applying a hand cream with an SPF of 15 or higher throughout the day. Then, each night, use a hand cream with retinol, which triggers collagen production to firm skin and better conceal veins.

Ridged nails?

The key to strong, smooth nails is biotin, a B-complex vitamin that stimulates the production of keratin, the protein that makes up the nail plate. "Unfortunately, as women age, more biotin is rerouted to support vital organs like the heart, and the resulting shortfall shows up as ridges," says Dr. Ghasri. In addition, winter's low humidity can dry out the nail plate, highlighting the uneven texture. Dr. Ghasri's advice: Supplement with 2.5 milligrams of biotin daily, a step that's study proven to increase nail thickness by 25 percent in 2 weeks. And instead of vigorously buffing to smooth out ridges—which only weakens nails—fill with a nail strengthener that contains fortifying microfibers and silica.

SANDAL SPOILERS SOLVED

Smooth calluses with coconut and honey

You don't need rough foot files and pumice stones—the most effective way to soften tough calluses is to unwind with a coconut milk–and-honey footbath. "Coconut's fatty acids gently melt away the hard layers of skin that form calluses, while honey's humectants lock in moisture," explains Dr. Oliver Zong, DPM, a podiatrist in New York City. To do: Pour a 14-ounce can of coconut milk and 3 tablespoons of honey into a basin of warm water and soak feet for 10 minutes.

Soften rough heels with powdered milk

"Because the skin on our heels doesn't produce any oil, it can dry out in a few hours when exposed to air," cautions Dr. Zong. And although many people use Epsom salt soaks to pamper their tootsies, in this case, salt actually draws moisture out of the skin, making it feel even drier. His swap for oh-so-soft feet: powdered milk. "Milk's lactic acid dissolves rough skin, while its lipids instantly moisturize," he says. To do: Mix $\frac{1}{4}$ cup of powdered milk in a basin of warm water and soak feet for 10 minutes.

Heal fungus with "sangria"

"Nail fungus—the culprit behind yellowed or white-spotted toenails—thrives in warm, moist environments, which is why it can be difficult to cure in the summer," says Dr. Zong. To the rescue: a festive, sangria-inspired footbath. Made by combining white wine and citrus juices, this soak can heal stubborn fungus fast, asserts Dr. Zong: "The alcohol content in the wine dries out the excess moisture that enables fungus to thrive. And citric acid is a natural antiseptic with powerful antifungal properties." To do: First, remove any nail polish from your toenails. Then, in a large basin, combine half a bottle of inexpensive (or leftover) room-temperature white wine and ¼ cup each of lemon, lime, and orange juice. Soak feet for 15 minutes, then rinse. Repeat daily until nails return to their natural healthy color. Bonus: This soothing soak also helps heal athlete's foot.

EFFORTLESS ADVICE FOR NAILS

The easy key to stronger nails

Last year all the holiday cooking and cleaning left our nails a mess just when we wanted them to be party-pretty. So this season we're fortifying them with an easy recipe: Mix 2 egg yolks with 1 teaspoon of olive oil; soak nails for 5 to 10 minutes twice a week. The biotin in egg yolk and the triglycerides in olive oil penetrate the nail bed and work to nourish and strengthen nails.

Simple sudsing for cleaning nails

The leaves are all raked and the mums you planted look amazing, but now your nails are caked with dirt. The way to prevent this next time: Before you head outside, scratch your nails along a bar of soap. The soap will get lodged underneath, leaving no room for dirt to slide in. When it's time to wash your hands, simply suds up.

Reader Tip — Messproof your manicure

"I love doing my own nails. I find it relaxing, plus it saves me money. But because my hand isn't as steady as a pro's, I'm always getting polish on my skin. Luckily, my sister shared a trick: Use a cotton swab to dab petroleum jelly around nails before applying polish. Now any slipups wipe right off. Since I started doing this, I've gotten tons of compliments on my manis!"

—*Julie Shriver, Bend, OR*

Brighten yellowed nails in seconds

That pastel polish you picked out is perfect for spring—but the dark, saturated shades you favored all winter have left yellowish stains on your nails that the new hue is too light to mask. To the rescue: lemon. Simply cut one in half and microwave it for 15 seconds. Next, twist each finger around in the center of the fruit. Lemon's natural acids have a gentle bleaching action, and its pulp will buff away stains. (For extra-stubborn spots, rub nails with lemon, then scrub with a nailbrush.)

Reader Tip — The secret to perfect French manicures

"I was tired of spending money on French manicures, but my at-home attempts always looked messy. Then a friend shared this tip: Apply a base coat and let dry, then place a paper reinforcement ring on each nail, leaving the tips exposed. Paint a contrasting color on the tips and remove the stickers. The rings create an even crescent shape, so my nails look flawless!"

—*Cathy Getz, Hays, KS*

Bye-bye, ragged cuticles!

If an afternoon of nitty-gritty chores left you with rough cuticles, simply rub a slice of fresh pineapple around your nail beds and let sit for 1 minute before wiping off. This tropical fruit contains bromelain, a potent enzyme that will help slough off dead skin cells, plus brighten nails. *Money saved: $15 for a manicure*

Help for dry cuticles

To make dry, ragged cuticles healthy and smooth (and ward off hangnails in the bargain), try this: Warm up a small dish of olive oil in the microwave for 15 to 30 seconds, then gently massage into your cuticles. The oil's oleic acid and vitamin E will nourish dry skin and protect it from future moisture loss. *Money saved: $6 for cuticle cream*

Strengthen nails with this

If hand washing dries out your nails (even though they're polished), try adding ⅛ teaspoon of chopped garlic to your bottle of clear base coat. This pungent bulb is actually an ingredient in many store-bought nail hardeners, thanks to the nail-strengthening manganese, calcium, selenium, and vitamin C it contains. And don't worry about the smell: Applying the middle and top coats will cover up any garlicky odor.

Help for rough, dried-out cuticles

Oops! You forgot your gloves this morning, and now your cuticles are cracked and dry. To revive them, whisk together ½ teaspoon of lemon juice and 2 tablespoons of petroleum jelly and massage the mixture into your cuticles. Acids from the lemon juice will help dissolve damaged cuticles, while the petroleum jelly will act as an emollient to restore lost moisture. Bonus: Add ½ teaspoon of sunflower oil to the mixture to protect cracked cuticles against infection.

The secret to a beautiful manicure

That trendy pink nail polish looked superbright in the bottle. Replicating the vivid color on your fingers, however, requires several coats of polish, which take forever to dry. The easy fix: First, brush on a coat of white polish (the kind used for a French manicure). Let dry completely, then apply the brighter hue. White polish adds a base layer of opacity that allows even sheer shades to shine—without multiple applications. Plus, it helps prevent dark polishes from staining your nails.

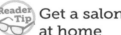 ## Get a salon-perfect manicure at home

"I always used a cotton swab dipped in nail polish remover to clean up the edges of my at-home manicures. But the swab's blunt tip often took off too much polish or left bits of lint behind. Then my friend told me she uses a clean eyeliner brush instead. Its precise edge is perfect for removing tiny bits of polish. Now my manicures look great!"

—*Margaret Hass, Lafayette, IN*

Natural Beauty Recipes

During months of chilly temperatures, chafing winds, and dry indoor heat, you deserve a little extra TLC. That's why *First for Women* scoured beauty blogs, polled spa experts, and asked real women for their favorite feel-good solutions. These 14 recipes (made from ingredients found in your kitchen) guarantee you'll look and feel fabulous all winter!

Complexion-brightening mint facial mask

This creamy mask illuminates sallow, dull skin and makes you look and feel fresh faced instantly.

2 tablespoons mint leaves, crushed
½ cup full-fat yogurt
½ cup cooked oatmeal

Combine the ingredients and apply liberally to the face. After 20 minutes, rinse with warm water.

Why it works: Yogurt's fat hydrates as its lactic acid melts dead skin and the oats gently whisk it away. Bonus: The menthol released by crushing the mint boosts circulation for a gorgeous glow.

Cold sore–calming peppermint balm

Since pesky cold sores pop up when the immune system is weakened, cold and flu season is prime time for them to strike. To stop a sore in its tracks in just 1 day, try this tasty, lip-tingling balm.

1 teaspoon coconut oil
10 drops peppermint essential oil

Mix the ingredients together in a small, resealable container (like an old lip gloss pot or makeup jar) and use a cotton swab to dab the balm directly on the sore twice a day.

Why it works: Peppermint oil has powerful antiviral and antimicrobial properties, while its active ingredient, menthone, has a cooling effect that soothes skin plus revs bloodflow to the sore so it heals faster. In addition, coconut oil's hydrating lipids prevent painful cracking.

Under-eye lightening salve

Winter can cause the skin under the eyes to dry out, making dark blood vessels more visible. This mixture can lighten shadows—fast.

1 teaspoon turmeric
1 teaspoon tomato juice
½ teaspoon lime juice

Combine the ingredients to create a paste, then dot some under each eye. After 5 minutes, rinse.

Why it works: The vitamin C in tomatoes and the curcumin in turmeric act as powerful antioxidants to repair and thicken skin so pooling is less apparent. Plus, the citric acid in limes gently exfoliates for a brighter, healthier look.

10 Brilliant Uses
for BABY POWDER

1 Remove stubborn sand from your scalp

You may be a beach bunny, but you hate the feeling of sand in your hair. Shampooing it out takes forever, and the little granules irritate your scalp. Instead, massage 1 tablespoon of baby powder into your roots, brush thoroughly, then shampoo as usual. The astringent powder will absorb the natural hair oils that bind the sand to your locks, so the stubborn grains can be washed right out. Bonus: A sprinkle of baby powder also helps you brush sand off your skin.

2 Stay cooler on hot summer nights

There's nothing worse than waking up sweaty and sticky. To stay dry all night, lightly sprinkle 1 to 2 teaspoons of baby powder on your sheets before turning in. The granules are so small and silky, you won't even notice them, but the absorbent ingredients—like silica, talc, and cornstarch—will wick away nighttime perspiration for a sound, restful sleep. (Just toss your sheets in the wash the next day.)

3 Protect a summer top from sweat stains

According to this morning's weather report, your company picnic is going to be a scorcher. To prevent stubborn sweat stains from developing on your favorite shirt, turn it inside out and sprinkle the underarms, collar, and other perspiration-prone areas with baby powder. Press with an iron set on medium for 3 seconds. The powder will form an invisible barrier that will absorb moisture before it seeps into the fabric, so the day's sweat will easily wash out.

4 Keep pool inflatables from sticking

Whenever you hit the town pool, you bring along a couple inflatable toys for the kids. The problem: After they're deflated and folded up for next time, the plastic ends up sticking to itself—you once ripped a water wing while trying to pry it apart again. For easier unpacking in the future, dust the plastic with baby powder before folding. The powder will absorb any remaining moisture and create a thin, slippery barrier that will keep the plastic from sticking to itself. This trick also works for pool covers and inflatable pools.

5 Take the "ouch" out of waxing

Sure, waxing is the quickest way to smooth your bikini line, but the last time you used an at-home kit, you shrieked so loudly that the neighbors called! To sidestep the pain, dust the area with baby powder before applying the wax. The powder will absorb moisture and body oils so the wax can properly adhere to each hair, plus it will create a barrier to protect your skin. The result: weeks of smooth skin with much less pain. Dusting on a little powder before shaving protects against razor burn, too.

6 Ensure your picnic stays ant-free

You love eating outdoors in the summer, but the inevitable ant infestation is enough to make you stay inside. To keep the pests away, sprinkle baby powder around the perimeter of your picnic table or blanket. The powder will stick to the pads of the ants' feet, inhibiting their ability to move, so you can enjoy your picnic in peace.

7 Prevent an iron from snagging delicates

Your silk tank desperately needs to be pressed, but you're worried that your sticky iron will snag the fabric. The solution: Sprinkle baby powder on a soft cloth and rub it over the bottom of the cool iron. Then heat the iron until the white residue disappears and iron as usual. The powder will leave behind a smooth, slippery layer that will help the iron glide over delicate fabrics. (Test on an inconspicuous area first.)

8 Silence squeaky wooden floorboards

Forget sneaking downstairs for a midnight treat—one of your wooden steps squeaks so loudly, it would wake the whole house. Silence it with baby powder. Use a clean turkey baster to apply the powder to the crevices between the boards of the step. The fine granules will work their way under the wood, filling in gaps to keep the boards from shifting and making noise.

9 Clean Fido's coat without the work

If your dog's fur could use a pick-me-up but you don't have the patience for the usual bath-time struggle, rub one or two handfuls of baby powder into his coat and let sit for a couple minutes before thoroughly brushing it out. The powder will sop up the built-up body oils that make your pup's fur look dingy, and it won't harm his skin. Plus, he'll smell extra fresh.

10 Rescue a book from water damage

Less-than-ideal storage conditions in the basement left your treasured photo albums, which weren't encased in plastic, with mold and water damage. The fix: Liberally sprinkle each page with baby powder, then place the book inside a paper bag, seal, and leave in a cool place for 3 to 7 days. Remove the album and dust off the powder. The absorbent baby powder particles will dry out the mold and sop up some of the more recent water damage, leaving the albums almost as good as new.

Static-taming spritz

Don't let static undo your pretty do! For tamed tresses in seconds, try this fresh-smelling mist.

8 ounces filtered water
1 teaspoon liquid fabric softener
1 teaspoon conditioner

Pour the liquids into a small spray bottle and shake well. Mist a light coating of the mixture onto a brush and comb it through wet or dry hair.

Why it works: Any hair that's already collected in the brush can exacerbate static, but spraying on this solution balances the overabundance of negative ions that make hair stand on end. The result: soft, silky locks.

Skin-hydrating oatmeal scrub

Restoring baby-soft skin is as easy as applying this ultramoisturizing exfoliator.

$1/2$ cup cooked oatmeal
$1/2$ banana, mashed

Combine the ingredients in a bowl. Before showering, gently massage the scrub in a circular motion onto dry areas (like elbows and knees), then rinse.

Why it works: The oatmeal gently sloughs away dead skin, while its vitamin E, amino acids, and silica alleviate irritation for a healthy glow. In addition, the banana contains potassium and polysaccharides to deliver moisture to parched skin, plus vitamins A, B_6, B_{12}, and C to promote cell turnover.

Cuticle-softening balm

This tropical-inspired treatment helps cuticles stay soft and supple—and, in turn, better able to protect nails from the elements.

2 tablespoons crushed pineapple
1 egg yolk

Combine the ingredients in a small bowl. Massage the mix into the cuticles and leave on for 5 minutes, then rinse with warm water.

Why it works: Pineapple's bromelain enzymes break down the proteins that hold tough, dead skin cells together, allowing them to be easily washed away, while the yolk's rich fatty acids (oleic, linoleic, and palmitoleic) and fat-soluble vitamins (A, D, E, and K) moisturize and condition the skin.

Blemish-banishing lemon ointment

Reach for this easy aspirin "spot" treatment to restore a flawless complexion overnight.

3 aspirin tablets
$1/2$ teaspoon lemon juice
$1/2$ teaspoon water

Combine the ingredients until the aspirin dissolves, creating a paste. Dot the solution on the blemish. Let sit 10 minutes before wiping away with a damp cloth.

Why it works: Aspirin calms inflammation and cuts the production of prostaglandins (chemicals in the skin that promote irritation), plus increases circulation to flush out bacteria. In addition, lemon's alpha hydroxy acids loosen dead skin for faster healing.

Under-eye de-puffing "cream"

Get rid of under-eye bags for good with a salve that feels almost as amazing as it works.

¼ cup whole milk
4 tablespoons baking soda

In a small bowl, mix the ingredients until they reach a pastelike consistency, then place the bowl in the fridge. When cool, apply the paste under the eyes. After 15 minutes, rinse with cool water.

Why it works: Baking soda has mild antiseptic properties that stimulate the lymphatic system to reduce swelling, while milk's rich proteins and lipids cool and calm the skin so bags are less pronounced and skin appears taut and refreshed.

Eye-soothing cucumber compress

Kick back and relax as this refreshing remedy cools eyes, reducing redness and irritation in 5 minutes.

1 teaspoon castor oil
½ cucumber, cut into ¼-inch-thick disks

Rub the castor oil on 1 side of 2 cucumber slices and place them (oil side down) over each eye. After 5 minutes, rinse with cool water.

Why it works: Dry air from indoor heaters triggers the release of "reflex" tears, which lack the lubricating quality of the "basal" tears that normally coat the eyes. This can cause eyes to become red and inflamed. But cucumbers have a high water content that cools and constricts blood vessels to calm irritation, while castor oil has the same pH as basal tears, so it lubricates and soothes tired eyes.

Hangnail-preventing cuticle oil blend

Pulling gloves on and off can snag skin, creating painful hangnails. But a dab of this miracle mix can prevent ripping.

3 drops sweet almond oil
1 vitamin E capsule, split

Combine the ingredients and apply the mixture to the hangnail, then clip the excess skin and cover the cuticle area with a bandage.

Why it works: Almond oil's omega-6 and omega-9 fatty acids hydrate skin (so it's less likely to snag), while vitamin E works as an antioxidant to repair the damaged skin around the cuticle.

Rosacea-healing herb facial tonic

Going from frigid outdoor temperatures to dry indoor heat can cause irritation and trigger skin conditions like rosacea. This solution soothes red skin and reduces flare-ups in minutes.

5 chamomile tea bags
2 green tea bags
3 cups boiling water

Steep the tea bags in the boiling water for 10 minutes, then refrigerate. When cool, dip a cotton cloth into the tea and dab it onto red areas (or lay the compress across the face) until ruddiness is gone.

Why it works: Chamomile's active ingredients terpenoids (bisoprolol, matricin, and chamazulene) and flavonoids (apigenin and luteolin) constrict blood vessels and deliver powerful anti-inflammatory effects, while green tea's antioxidants (polyphenols and catechins) help repair and strengthen skin to ward off future flare-ups.

Lip-soothing sugar scrub

Prevent and eliminate chapping with this citrus balm.

4 drops jojoba oil (or 1 vitamin E capsule, split)
1 tablespoon sugar
$^1/_2$ orange

Mix the oil, sugar, and a few squirts of orange juice in a small bowl. Dampen lips and gently apply the scrub using a circular motion. Then dab with a wet cloth and immediately apply a rich, hydrating balm while lips are still damp.

Why it works: The juice's citric acid melts dead layers of skin, while the sugar crystals painlessly whisk them away. Plus, jojoba oil contains wax esters, which closely match the chemical structure of sebum (skin's natural oil) so it's easily absorbed deep into skin to infuse lips with much-needed moisture.

Nail-strengthening protein soak

Pampering nails in this warm cream feels fantastic—and helps fortify the nail bed to prevent cracking and splitting.

$^1/_2$ cup whole milk
$^1/_2$ ounce ($^1/_2$ packet) plain gelatin

Pour the milk into a bowl and microwave until warm but not hot to the touch, then mix in the gelatin. When the gelatin is completely dissolved, soak nails for 10 minutes before rinsing.

Why it works: Nail plates are made from the protein keratin, so soaking nails in gelatin (made from similar proteins) helps "fill in" damaged areas and seal splits to strengthen the plate. Plus, the milk's lipids hydrate to ward off brittleness.

Hair-nourishing aloe mask

No matter how far the mercury falls, this replenishing treatment is the secret to achieving silky, soft hair with tons of body and shine.

$^1/_4$ cup aloe vera gel
$^1/_4$ cup olive oil
1 egg
5 drops rosemary essential oil

Combine the ingredients, comb the mixture through damp hair, and wrap hair in plastic wrap. After 10 minutes, shampoo and condition as usual.

Why it works: Aloe vera's mucopolysaccharides and olive oil's polysaccharides instantly restore moisture to parched strands, while the egg's proteins fill in any damaged areas. In addition, rosemary stimulates circulation to the scalp for healthier, thicker locks.

Bright-Eyed and Beautiful

When you're feeling under the weather or just plain tired, it's hard to look like your usual perky self. But we're here to help. Just follow these quick tips and you'll look more awake and sparkly in no time.

Brighten up "allergy eyes"

When seasonal sniffles make your eyes red and puffy, hide the irritation by sweeping gold or bronze eye shadow across your lids. The warm yellow hue will counteract the redness, while the metallic shimmer will reflect light, making your eyes look brighter and taking attention away from any under-eye bags.

Wake up tired eyes this way

The next time a late night leaves you puffy-eyed, try this quick morning fix: Dip two cotton balls in a bowl of ice-cold whole milk or cream. Squeeze the cotton balls out slightly and hold one over each closed eye for 5 minutes. The cold temperature will constrict blood vessels to reduce swelling, while the milk fat will soothe delicate under-eye skin. *Money saved: $17 for de-puffing eye serum*

Look more awake in a blink

Try this quick and simple makeup trick to appear refreshed after a late night: Dot a shimmery highlighter on the inner corner of each eye, under your lower lids, and on the outer corners of your brows. The strategic locations of the dots help catch light, so your eyes will look brighter and more awake, taking attention away from under-eye bags or redness.

Look more awake in seconds

Worries about today's big meeting kept you up all night—and thanks to your puffy eyes, everyone will know it. To reduce the swelling, use your index finger to find the lower eye-socket ridge below your pupil, then slowly slide your finger down to your cheekbone. Switch sides; repeat several times. This will release the trapped fluid under the eyes that causes puffiness, smoothing and firming the area for a bright-eyed appearance. *Money saved: $17 for a de-puffing eye serum*

Look bright-eyed even when you're tired

With all that's on your plate during the holidays, a late night or two is a given. If you wake up with puffy eyelids or dark circles, simply mash ½ banana and apply generously under each eye. Let sit for 20 minutes, then rinse with cool water. The fruit's rich stores of potassium will draw excess fluid from skin, reducing swelling so you look stunning. *Money saved: $8 for de-puffing eye cream*

Chapter 8

PET PERFECT

Pet Grooming Guide

As much as your love your pet, sometimes the brushing, shedding, and nail clipping gets out of hand. Discover easy ways to keep your cat or dog looking great.

Curb Fluffy's spring shedding

With the weather starting to warm up, your feline pal has been shedding her winter coat all over your furniture, the floor, and you! To minimize the mess, try using a fine-tooth comb to groom her. The comb's narrowly spaced teeth will effectively remove dead skin cells and hair from Fluffy's undercoat—unlike regular pet brushes, which may reach only the top coat. Combing your cat once a day will keep her coat healthy and reduce the amount of hair she sheds, plus it will help ward off hair balls.

Nix flaky skin during seasonal shedding

In the spring, many cats and dogs "blow coat"— that is, shed their heavy winter coats to lighter ones for summer. To spare your fluffy buddy the itching and flaking that can be part of this process, try supplementing her diet with omega-3 fatty acids, which will nourish her skin and coat. The strategy some vets recommend (but check with yours first): Mix 20 milligrams of liquid omega-3s per pound of body weight into your pet's food daily. And as a welcome bonus for cat owners, omega-3s also help prevent excess shedding, which means fewer fur balls for you to contend with.

The spray that slows summer shedding

Cats tend to lose large amounts of hair with every heat wave—and with 130,000 hairs per square inch of your kitty's body, it's no wonder mounds of fluff accumulate around the house! To help curb her shedding, pour 1 cup of water into a spray bottle and add ¼ teaspoon of pure almond or olive oil. Shake well and spritz over your cat's coat after a good brushing twice a week, rubbing your fingers through her fur to evenly distribute the solution. The oil will help replace lost moisture in her skin and coat to reduce shedding. Bonus: The oil is not only safe for cats to ingest, it will also help ease hair balls through her digestive tract. This spray works for shedding-prone dogs, too.

Fast fix for a nail-clipping oops

No matter how careful you try to be, it's easy to cut your pet's nails just a little too short. If you accidentally nick the fleshy part of the nail and blood starts to flow, try the trick some vets recommend: First, distract your pet with a tasty treat, then press the bleeding nail into a wet bar of hand soap. The soap creates a film that tells blood vessels to stop the bleeding—stat.

Avoid ouches and messes with a winter "peticure"

Walking on slushy sidewalks can cause water and ice to cling to the fur on your dog's paws, and that can lead to discomfort for him—and a mess on your floors for you to clean. To minimize the problem, trim his paw hair with this easy how-to: Start by caressing your dog's legs, then slowly move down to one paw. Gently pull all the hair on the paw upward through his toes, making sure to catch all the strands underneath, and carefully clip the fur with scissors. Then work your way around the paw, snipping any long strands. Give your pal a treat between paws so he'll be content and less likely to fuss as you work.

Make bath time a breeze

Cuddling your freshly washed pup is a joy . . . but actually bathing him? Not so much. Prevent squirming and splashing with a three-towel trick: First, lay a towel in the tub before filling it with water so your pal has a comfy, nonskid surface to stand on. Then drape one towel over his neck and head immediately after washing. This will help delay his impulse to shake (and soak you in the process), so you'll have extra time to use the third towel to dry him off.

Help fur stay static-free

Ouch! Whenever you stroke your furry friend, sparks fly due to static electricity caused by dry indoor air. To reduce static and restore shine to her dried-out coat, make your own pet-friendly leave-in conditioner by pouring 2 tablespoons of melted coconut oil into an 8-ounce spray bottle, then filling the rest of the bottle with water. Shake well and spray over your pet's coat before brushing. The coconut oil will reduce the buildup of the electric ions that cause static. And don't worry if she licks her fur—coconut oil's nutrients help promote digestive health.

Rx for bald spots

If you notice a few bald patches around your pal's face, he may have an overpopulation of *Demodex* mites. These small parasites naturally live on the skin of mammals, but if the immune system is depressed (which can occur in the winter), mites can multiply, causing bald spots. The remedy some vets recommend: immunity-bolstering vitamin E. Pop open one 100-IU capsule per 10 pounds of body weight and squeeze the oil into his food once daily. (If he has bald spots all over, consult a vet.)

Brush Kitty with ease

If you're having trouble grooming Tiger without him trying to bite or swipe at the brush, try this clever trick: Introduce the brush again during cuddle time, but don't use it. Simply let your cat sniff it and rub his head against it as you pet him. Cats have special scent glands in their faces, so if you let your furry pal "mark" the tool, he will think of the brush as his. The next time you groom him, he'll recognize his scent and be more receptive to brushing.

Use cornstarch for matted fur

Your little buddy has been rolling around in the grass again, and now his fur is all tangled. To get his coat silky smooth, sprinkle cornstarch on the matted area and massage it in, then gently lift the hair upward and use a fine-tooth comb to work out the tangles. The cornstarch will absorb any dirt or grease that might be trapped in your pup's fur, so the hair will untangle with ease.

Ward off hair balls

No matter how well you groom her, Mittens still coughs up hair balls. The fix: Once a week, rub a dime-size dab of butter on one of her front paws. She'll lick it right off, and the butter's lipids will coat the ingested fur and lubricate her GI tract, so hair moves through her system more easily.

Fast fix for Fido's tear stains

Bright winter sunlight reflecting off snow can cause dogs' eyes to tear, and that can make the fur under their eyes stick together uncomfortably. It can also leave behind noticeable stains, which are the result of iron-containing molecules in tears. To remedy this, soak a clean cloth with contact lens solution and wipe the fur under your pet's eyes. Vets say the diluted boric acid in the contact solution safely oxidizes the iron that causes the stains, effectively lightening them and easing discomfort. Your pal will be bright-eyed in no time.

Spray away pet dander

Lately, while brushing your furry friend, you've noticed white flakes in her fur. To cut down on dandruff, fill a spray bottle with 8 ounces of water and 1 tablespoon of mouthwash (like Listerine). Lightly spritz the mixture on her fur, then brush as usual. Repeat every other day until she is flake-free. Why it works: The active ingredients in mouthwash (like thymol and eucalyptol) have antifungal properties that enable them to kill the yeast that causes flaky skin.

10 Brilliant Uses
for ORANGE PEELS

1 Keep Fluffy out of your plants
You set your new plant on a shelf but still worry your cat might jump up and try to munch on the leaves, which are mildly toxic and could give him a stomachache. To help prevent this, dice the peels of two oranges and sprinkle them onto the plant's dirt. Cats dislike the strong scent of citrus, so your pal will stay away.

2 Get a fire roaring with ease
A trick that will help you spend more time enjoying the warmth of your cozy fire—and less time trying to get the logs to catch: Let the peels from a few oranges sit out overnight so they dry, then throw them into the fireplace and carefully light. Orange oils are flammable, so the peels will burn longer than paper kindling. Plus, you'll get a citrus scent wafting through the house.

3 Remove tough microwave stains
The no-sweat way to clean stubborn tomato-soup splatters in the microwave: Place a few orange peels in a heatproof bowl and cover with water, then zap on high for 5 minutes. The steam from the water will loosen buildup, while the orange peels' citric acid works to kill bacteria. Even the most caked-on food will wipe away with a damp cloth.

4 Freshen musty closets naturally
When you reached into your guest closet for linens, you got a whiff of a musty odor. To nix the smell, place the rinds from an orange inside the foot of an old pair of panty hose, then tie the end and set the sachet on a shelf. The pith will absorb and neutralize odors, while the fruit's oils give off a fresh fragrance.

5 Stop brown sugar from hardening
Ensure your brown sugar stays soft for all your holiday baking by placing a slice of orange peel in the box. The rind will slowly release oil that keeps the sugar moist. Replace once a month.

6 Take salad from bland to grand
For a delicious way to wow holiday guests, make your own orange-infused olive oil. To do: Add one orange rind and a handful of cranberries to 2 cups of olive oil and let simmer on low for 5 minutes. Allow to cool, then strain the fruit and keep the oil in a sealed container. The fruit acids released into the oil will add tart-sweet pizzazz to your side salads and hors d'oeuvres.

7 Clean counters sans chemicals

Sidestep the headaches that can come from using harsh cleaning products with this all-natural—and wonderfully effective—cleaner: In a spray bottle, combine the peel from 1 orange and 1½ cups of white vinegar. Keep tightly closed for 2 weeks, then add 1 cup of water to the spray bottle. The orange peel's citric acid will break down grease, while the vinegar disinfects to get your home sparkling.

8 Deodorize a garbage disposal

Uh-oh—guests are due to arrive soon and you just noticed a funky stench coming from the garbage disposal. The fix: Toss the peel of an orange down the drain and run the appliance for 30 seconds. The fruit's acids will neutralize odors, while the coarse rind scours away food-particle buildup on the blade. Repeat once a week or as needed.

9 Lift soap scum from glassware

Dingy glasses will sparkle, thanks to this trick: Soak them in a sink filled with warm water and a handful of orange peels for 5 minutes, then wash as usual. The peels' citric acid will power through the soap scum and mineral deposits that cause cloudiness.

10 Prevent an aphid attack in your garden

Last summer, aphids destroyed your roses, tomatoes, and sunflowers. But not this year, thanks to this trick: Steep ¼ to ½ cup of citrus peel in 3 to 4 cups of hot water for 10 minutes. When the solution cools, pour it into a spray bottle and spritz your plants once a week. Aphids love citrus scents, but the peels' citric acid will weaken their soft bodies, eventually killing them—without harming your plants. (This will work for any soft-bodied insects, including slugs.)

Save on pet wipes

Spring showers mean muddy fur and paws—and when you have no time to bathe your buddy, wet wipes are a lifesaver. Instead of shelling out for wipes at the pet store, make your own for a third of the cost. To do: Bring 1 cup of water to a boil, let cool, then combine with 2 tablespoons each of aloe vera gel and liquid castile soap. Place a roll of heavy-duty paper towels in a large pan and pour the aloe mixture on top. Let soak for an hour, then turn the roll over and let sit for another hour. When the wipes are saturated, store in a plastic container and use as needed.

Healthy, Happy Pets

It's awful when your doggy or kitty isn't feeling her best. Follow these quick suggestions on how to ward off illnesses, fix minor ailments, and keep your pet feeling 100 percent.

Quickly gauge Fluffy's health

Your cat just isn't herself—she's sleeping more and eating less than usual—but you don't have a pet thermometer to check for a fever. Instead, take her pulse: Press two fingers on the inside of her upper hind leg where it meets the body. Count the pulses for 15 seconds and multiply by 4 to get the beats per minute. A heartbeat of 100 to 180 is normal—anything outside of that range might warrant a trip to the vet.

Ward off fleas naturally

Spring is just around the corner, which means flea season is, too. To protect your pet (and home) from the pests, whip up this nontoxic flea spray: Bring 2 cups of water to a boil, then add a few sprigs of fresh (or 2 tablespoons of dried) rosemary. Simmer for 30 minutes and let cool, then pour into a clean spray bottle. Twice a week, saturate a paper towel with the rosemary water and wipe down your pet. Then give carpets, rugs, and pet beds a good spritz. The herb's scent is pleasant to humans and animals but naturally repels fleas.

Fleaproof your pooch

After finally conquering a flea infestation, you want to ensure the pests stay away for good. What can help: Place a few drops of lemon essential oil on the outside of your dog's collar, in a spot where she can't lick it off. Fleas hate the scent of citrus, so they'll steer clear. Plus, lemon oil contains a chemical called linalool that will kill any fleas that do land near the collar. (The oil can be toxic to cats, so use this tip for dogs only.)

Shop here to save on meds

Prescriptions for your pal can be costly, but there's an easy way to save: Many pet meds (for everything from allergies to high blood pressure) are available at human pharmacies for lower prices than what vets charge. In fact, Walgreens has a list of veterinary meds for $4 per 30-day supply, compared with the $20 or $30 you might pay at your vet.

Fast relief for Kitty's eye irritation

Recently you noticed that one of your cat's eyes looks watery and irritated. The possible culprit: an infection caused by wind, cold weather, dust, or other irritants. To remedy it, some cat owners swear by soaking a cotton ball in a mixture of 1 tablespoon of raw, unfiltered apple cider vinegar and 1 tablespoon of filtered water, then dabbing it on the back of the cat's neck and between her shoulder blades. When she cleans herself, she'll distribute the healing solution to her eyes. (Check with your vet before treating and again if you don't see an improvement after 2 days or if the condition seems to worsen.)

Cure for kitty constipation

Indoor heat can encourage shedding, which leads to Fluffy ingesting more hair—and that can make it tough for her to "go." If your cat's stools look hard and dry, try stirring ½ teaspoon of mayonnaise per 5 pounds of body weight into her food daily. The oil in mayo will help hair glide through her digestive tract, plus cats love the condiment's flavor.

Quickly cool down an overheated cat

On sweltering days, your cat sometimes starts panting on and off—a sure sign that she's too hot. For a fast, easy way to keep her comfortable, wet a clean washcloth or paper towel with cold tap water and use it to gently stroke your kitty in the places where cats get the warmest: the stomach, paw pads, armpits, under the chin, and on the outside of the ears. Dabbing cold water on these spots will help bring down her body temperature immediately.

Keep your pup cool and comfy

To protect your dog from getting overheated on your walks, make him a cooling collar: Fill a clean tube sock with a few crushed ice cubes (use two socks for large dogs) and tie loosely around his neck so you can fit two fingers under it. The frosty collar will lower his body temperature on hot days.

Outsmart a pill-wary pet

You've tried hiding your buddy's pills in his food, but he somehow finds a way to pick around them. Next time, try the secret ingredient many vets recommend: cottage cheese. Simply take a spoonful of cheese and blot any excess liquid with a paper towel. Form the curds into a ball over the pill. Most pets love the taste of cottage cheese, and since it's not high in lactose, it won't upset his tummy. Your pal will happily gobble down the pill while thinking he's getting a treat!

Protect your pal from sunburn

Your cutie loves to lounge in the sunshine, but exposure to UV rays can burn the sensitive skin on the bridge of his nose, the tips of his ears, the belly, and the groin area. To keep his skin safe, apply an all-natural sunscreen formulated for sensitive skin or babies on any spots that aren't covered by fur. Choose a formula that does not contain zinc oxide, which can be harmful to pets if ingested.

Fast relief for itchy bug bites

Pesky mosquito and flea bites cause your furry pal to scratch incessantly, which can lead to infection. Dabbing milk of magnesia on itchy areas can help. Vets say the magnesium salts and potassium in the medicine (which is safe and free of side effects if a small amount is accidentally ingested) stop the itching and help heal the bite so Fido gets relief in no time.

Fend off fly bites

Flies love biting the thin skin on a dog's ears, which can lead to irritation and infection. To keep the pests away from your sweetie, try this natural repellent: Bring 1 cup of water and 1 basil leaf to a boil. Remove from the heat, then add 1 tablespoon of eucalyptus essential oil and 1 cup of apple cider vinegar; let cool. Before your pup goes outside, use a clean cloth to apply the liquid to the tips of his ears. The scent of basil and eucalyptus will ward off flies, while the vinegar helps heal old bites.

Cure for canine stomach woes

When your pup has an upset belly, try giving him Pepto-Bismol. The pink stuff will coat his stomach, providing relief from cramps, diarrhea, and vomiting. The dose some vets advise (but check with yours first): 1 milliliter of regular-strength liquid Pepto per pound of body weight every 6 to 8 hours. (Some dog owners soak bread in Pepto and give that to their pup to eat.) If there's no improvement after 3 hours, call your vet. Note: Don't give Pepto-Bismol to cats.

Soothe spring allergies

If your pal has watery eyes or is scratching more, he may have a pollen allergy. What can help: Wipe down his coat and paws with a wet paper towel after each walk. In addition to getting the irritants off him, this will minimize the amount of pollen that gets tracked through the house.

Rx for sniffles

Achoo! If your pal has come down with a cold, help her kick the bug fast by supplementing her diet with immunity-boosting vitamin C. Some vets suggest adding 250 milligrams of powdered vitamin C per 10 pounds of body weight to your pet's food daily. (Check with your vet for the ideal dose for your cat or dog.) Vitamin C supplements for humans are generally safe for animals, but if you'd like to buy one designed for pets, try Halo VitaGlo Xtra-C.

Preserve your pal's eyesight

If you've noticed your pet has been bumping into things or having trouble finding his way around in dim light, his vision may not be as sharp as it used to be. To improve his eyesight, give him bilberry extract. Plant compounds in bilberries support the growth of a pigment in the retina that enhances night vision. The daily dose vets recommend (but check with yours first): $\frac{1}{4}$ teaspoon for cats and dogs under 10 pounds, $\frac{1}{2}$ teaspoon for pets 11 to 25 pounds, and $\frac{3}{4}$ teaspoon for pets more than 25 pounds. Simply sprinkle the powder on his food daily.

Sweet help for a gassy pup

Max has mastered the "I'm so hungry . . . and so cute" look—and he uses it to convince your dinner guests to sneak him bites under the table. Unfortunately for him (and anyone sitting near him), his indulgences usually lead to stinky gas. The Rx: Feed him 1 teaspoon of honey up to three times a day until his symptoms subside. Honey inhibits the growth of gas-causing bacteria in the digestive tract, relieving his upset tummy.

Rx for bee stings

While exploring your flower bed, your curious four-legged friend got stung! To ease his ouch: If you see the stinger, remove it by scraping the area with a credit card or your fingernail. (If you're doing this on a cat, swaddle him in a towel to keep him from scratching you.) Next, mix 1 tablespoon of baking soda with just enough water to create a paste and apply it to the sting. The alkalinity of the baking soda will neutralize the acidity of the bee's venom to soothe the pain. If you notice swelling, your pal may be having a mild allergic reaction to the sting. Some vets advise administering Benadryl (one 25-milligram capsule to cats or dogs under 30 pounds, 50 milligrams for dogs 31 to 80 pounds, and 75 milligrams for dogs over 80 pounds). Check with your vet for details before dosing.

SOS for Fido's tummy troubles

As you were giving your furry friend a belly rub, you noticed she seemed a little bloated—and she's been a bit gassy lately, too. To help settle her stomach, add plain yogurt with live and active cultures (some vets recommend 1 tablespoon of yogurt for every 10 pounds of body weight) to her food each day. Yogurt's healthy probiotics will help balance the overabundance of gas-forming bacteria in your dog's gut. Plus, the probiotics will give her immune system a boost that will help her stay happy and healthy as you move into the colder months.

Soothe kennel cough

Your pooch loves socializing at the dog park, but the outings can lead to a case of kennel cough—a dry, incessant cough that irritates the windpipe. To speed her recovery: Steep a wild-cherry-bark tea bag (found at health food stores) in 1 cup of boiling water and stir in 2 tablespoons of honey. When cool, pour one-third over her kibble. Cherry bark's antiseptic qualities will treat the infection, while honey eases irritation.

Winterproof your pet's paws

To ensure harsh deicing chemicals on sidewalks don't irritate your pal's paws, apply a thin layer of petroleum jelly to his paw pads before going out for a walk. After your stroll, wipe your pup's paws with a warm washcloth, then another thin layer of petroleum jelly to keep his skin from drying out.

Freshen your pup's breath with this

Your pal loves to lavish you with kisses, but sometimes her breath is too stinky to handle. What can help: Chop up 1 teaspoon of fresh parsley and sprinkle it over her food. She'll happily gobble up the herb, which will instantly mask odors. Better still, parsley's chlorophyll has antibacterial properties that help eliminate the odor-causing bacteria that feast on food deposits in the back of your dog's mouth. Bring on the kisses!

Fend off ear infections

A simple cleaning strategy that will help keep your pal free of ear mites: Every 3 days, dampen a cotton ball with rubbing alcohol and gently wipe it around the outside of the ear and along the inside edge. The alcohol will kill any pesky bugs before they can cause irritation or infection.

Clever Pet Clean-Ups

You've probably seen it all—or stepped in it—when it comes to pet messes. As much as you love your pets, sometimes they create a bit of chaos. Try these hints for cleaning up after your furry friends.

The accessory that nixes doggy odors

You're getting ready for tonight's company when you catch a whiff of Fido—*shoo-whee!* To help him smell fresh in a flash, try this trick: Dissolve ½ cup of baking soda in 2 cups of water, then soak a bandanna or cute holiday scarf in the mixture and spread it out to air-dry. When dry, tie it around your pup's neck. Not only will he look adorable, but the baking soda will absorb odors from his fur. (Tip: Soak a few bandannas at once and store them in a zipper-lock bag, then tie a fresh one on him each day.)

No more muddy paw prints!

To keep the mess of slush and mud off your floors after Spot comes in from a walk, use a "mud mitt." To make: Fold a dish towel in half and stitch two of the open sides shut to form a pocket. After a walk, put one paw at a time into the mitt and rub any muck off. The grime will stay inside the towel pocket instead of falling on the floor. And after using, you can simply shake the mitt over the trash or toss in the washer as needed.

Say good-bye to scattered kibble

Instead of setting bowls on a plastic mat that doesn't do much to minimize a mess, try this: Cut an old, clean yoga mat to the desired size. The mat is slip-proof, so it will be tough for your pet to move his bowls. Plus, the mat's texture will keep food from getting scattered across the floor. And it's easy to wipe clean.

Remove fur from carpets with ease

Fall shedding season is in full swing, and your little buddy is leaving so much fur on the rug that even vacuuming doesn't get up every bit. The tool that works wonders: a squeegee. Simply swipe the window cleaner back and forth across the floor. The rubber end will loosen any embedded hair so you can drag it into piles, then just pick up and toss out the clumps. You'll have a fur-free carpet in no time!

The kitchen fix for litter-box odor

We love those deodorizing powders that keep the litter box smelling fresh, but we're not so fond of the price tag. So we were happy to discover an alternative that costs a fraction of the price: citric acid, which is sold as a food preservative at grocery stores. The citrus-derived crystals are actually an active ingredient in many pricey powders, thanks to their ability to neutralize odor by trapping ammonia from urine. Just sprinkle a light layer of the crystals on the litter—your cat will activate them as he steps in the box.

Keep pet bowls in place

Ugh! Your little buddy keeps pushing his bowl across the room as he drinks, leaving a mess of splashed water for you to mop up. To prevent this in the future, stick removable Velcro mounting squares to the floor and the bottom of the bowl. These squares (which stick to most surfaces, including wood, metal, glass, tile, and plastic) are strong enough to keep the bowl in place as your canine companion drinks. And when it's time to refill his water, you can simply lift the bowl, then set it back down on the Velcro squares when you're done. Problem solved!

Silence jingling tags

It's so sweet when your pal lovingly follows you around the house, but you could do without the incessant clanking of the ID tags on her collar. To make the jingle-jangle stop, cover the edges of the metal tags with rubber key covers (found at hardware stores). You'll get peace and quiet—and you'll add a pop of stylish color to your cutie's favorite accessory.

Neatly contain doggy bags

Instead of digging through the closet or under the sink for a plastic bag to take when you walk Rover, upcycle a coffee can or other drink mix can into a handy doggy-bag dispenser. Simply decorate the outside of a clean, empty coffee can with contact paper or gift wrap, if desired. Then cut a large X in the center of the can's plastic lid and bend the "points" to make the opening more flexible. Stuff plastic bags into the can one by one, then pop on the lid. For easy access, stash the can next to your dog's leash and pull out bags as needed. No more plastic-bag clutter!

Simple Pet-Training Secrets

Yikes! Your pup's been digging in the garden again. Pets can be a little naughty and rambunctious, but a little bit of training can improve your furry friend's behavior in no time!

Put a stop to early morning meowing

Earlier sunrises set off Fluffy's internal clock, sending her meowing at your door an hour before your alarm. To halt this unwanted wake-up call, place a fan just outside your door and turn it on so it's blowing outward. Since cats can't stand the feeling of wind in their faces, your kitty will associate the breeze with your bedroom at sunrise and learn to steer clear until you've woken and turned off the fan.

10 Brilliant Uses
for CANE SUGAR

1 Outsmart kitty-litter clumps
Ugh! When your cat scratches around in her litter, she tears the liner—and that leads to sticky clumps on the bottom of the box. The fix: Sprinkle sugar in the pan before you add a new liner. The granules will absorb any liquid that seeps through the tears, so clumps won't form. (Don't worry about ants—the litter will mask the sugar's scent.)

2 Get the grill fired up—fast!
The burgers and kebabs are ready to be cooked, but you're having trouble getting the coals to burn. For a simple way to jump-start the flames, toss a few spoonfuls of sugar onto the briquettes, then try lighting again. When exposed to high temperatures, sugar rapidly decomposes and forms a chemical that easily ignites. Ready, set, grill!

3 Stop wasps from crashing your barbecue
It's a perfect day for outdoor dining, and you want to make sure stinging pests don't spoil your fun. To make mini traps, mix equal parts sugar and water and bring to a boil; pour into cups, cover with foil, and secure with rubber bands. Poke holes in the foil and place the cups around your yard. The aroma will lure the insects into the cups—but they won't be able to climb back out.

4 Instantly soothe a burned mouth
If you accidentally singe the roof of your mouth on a hot slice of pizza, place a pinch of sugar on your tongue and hold it against the sore spot. As the granules melt, they'll stimulate the release of endorphins—feel-good brain chemicals that help ease the pain.

5 Clear a pimple overnight
A quick fix for summer blemishes: Mix 1 teaspoon of sugar with a few drops of water, then dab on affected skin and let sit while you sleep. The sucrose will inhibit the growth of bacteria, reducing redness and swelling by morning.

6 Whisk away grinder grime
Coffee bean residue stuck in your grinder can give your morning brew an off flavor. The save: Once a month, pour 1/4 cup of sugar into the appliance and run it for 2 minutes, then dump out the remains and wipe the grinder clean. The abrasive sugar granules will scour away buildup and absorb stale odors, ensuring a perfect cup of joe.

7 Gently remove paint from skin

Your freshly touched-up fence looks fantastic, but your hands are a different story—they're covered in paint! Instead of using skin-irritating paint thinners to remove the color, pour 1 teaspoon each of sugar and olive oil onto your palms, then rub your hands together. The oil will break down the paint's bond so the stains slide off your skin, and the mildly abrasive sugar granules will gently scrape off any stubborn, lingering pigment.

8 Tame too-spicy salsa in seconds

Your salsa is always a hit—it has just enough oomph without setting mouths on fire. But if a batch comes out a bit too fiery, you can tone down the heat by adding sugar to the bowl, $\frac{1}{2}$ teaspoon at a time, until the salsa is to your liking. Since sweetness and heat are on opposite sides of the flavor wheel, the sugar will neutralize the salsa's bite.

9 Double the life of fresh flowers

For a bouquet that lasts and lasts, fill your vase with 3 tablespoons of sugar and 2 tablespoons of white vinegar per quart of warm water. The sugar will nourish the flowers, while the vinegar will kill bacteria in the water to keep the blooms fresh and perky.

10 Enhance the natural sweetness of corn

Mmm . . . one of the highlights of your end-of-summer cookouts is enjoying the juicy corn that's now in season. To ensure this farm-stand favorite tastes its best, add a little sugar to the water (about 4 teaspoons per gallon of water) when boiling it. The sucrose doesn't sweeten the corn itself—rather, it prevents the kernels' natural sugars from leaching out during the cooking process. Delicious!

Put an end to off-limits chewing

Being cooped up on cold, rainy days can lead even the most obedient dog to root out "new" chew toys—like your favorite shoes! The strategy trainers use to keep household items safe: Lightly touch the back of your pup's neck to get his attention, then hug the item close to you while retaining eye contact. This communicates that the object belongs to you (the alpha of the pack) and is off-limits. Then offer him one of his toys to gnaw.

Stop Kitty from getting underfoot

Your playful cat loves to snake between your legs and bat your ankles as you walk down the hall. Next time she does this, stop walking and pick her up by the scruff of the neck, then firmly tell her, "No!" and move her out of the way. Experts say holding a cat by the scruff for a few moments will command her full attention but won't hurt her. (This is how mother cats move kittens out of harm's way.) She'll quickly get the message that this isn't a game, and your ankles will be safe from scratches.

Deter Fido from digging

Argh! Your canine pal has taken up the habit of digging holes in your yard. An easy way to curb his behavior: Place a bit of chicken wire in the holes before refilling with dirt. The next time your pup goes rooting around, he'll touch the wire, which will startle him. He'll quickly realize that something unpleasant lies beneath the grass and quit digging for good.

Say good-bye to toilet-paper shredding

The white "confetti" strewn all over the bathroom floor can mean only one thing: Fluffy's been playing with the toilet paper again. To prevent this from happening in the future, place a few drops of orange or lemon essential oil in the cardboard center of the toilet-paper roll. Cats generally dislike the scent of citrus, so your cat will steer clear. And as a bonus for you, each time the roll is spun, a subtle citrus aroma will freshen your bathroom. (Caution: Keep essential-oil bottles out of cats' reach.)

Deter Kitty from eating plants

Your frisky feline seems to think the houseplants are her personal playground. To stop her from chewing on the leaves, combine 1 teaspoon of white vinegar and 2 cups of water in a spray bottle, then mist plants with the solution twice weekly. The scent of vinegar is unbearably pungent to cats' sensitive noses, so your fluffy friend will steer clear. Bonus: Vinegar neutralizes the pH of water, helping plants absorb more vital nutrients.

No more "hello" tinkling from Fido

You love seeing your dog when you come home, but you could do without his excited piddling. To curb his habit, try this trainer-approved strategy: Instead of acknowledging your pup the moment you walk through the door, give him some time to calm down first. After a few minutes, approach him with your body turned sideways and avoid eye contact until you can kneel beside him. Then say hello softly and take him outside to relieve himself.

Prevent playful nipping

Ouch! You know she's only playing, but your pup's bites during a friendly tug-of-war session can hurt! To break her habit, grab one of her back feet whenever she tries to nip. Dogs have a defensive reflex to withdraw when their feet are touched unexpectedly, so doing this will train her to stop nipping—stat.

Make sure cats won't claw furniture

Your frisky feline thinks the legs of the dining room table are the perfect scratching posts. To deter her, try dabbing a small amount of mentholated ointment (like Vicks VapoRub) near where she claws. The petroleum-based balm is virtually invisible and won't harm polished wood, but the powerful menthol scent will be too intense for your kitty's keen sense of smell, so she'll be sure to keep her distance.

Safeguard pets from tree water

He has perfectly good water in his bowl, but your pal keeps sipping out of the Christmas tree stand—not ideal, since trees are often sprayed with pesticides that can leach into the water and trigger a tummy ache. To sidestep, wrap plastic wrap around the lower part of the trunk and the opening of the water basin, then cover with a tree skirt.

Stress Solutions for Pets

Pets can become pretty anxious while in a vet's office or when friends visit your home. Try these stress-soothing ideas to keep your dog or cat in a peaceful state of mind.

Ease vet stress

If your dog or cat requires an overnight stay at the vet or boarding kennel, quell her anxiety with this strategy: Toss her favorite soft toy or blankie into your dirty clothes hamper for a few hours to embed it with your scent. Then bring the item along with your pet to the vet. The familiar scent will make her feel more secure and content in unfamiliar surroundings.

Soothe your pal's winter blues

A pet that's acting anxious or clingy may be experiencing a bout of the winter blahs brought on by gloomy weather and lack of exercise. Lift your furry friend's spirits with this acupressure trick: Starting at his bottom rib, count up to the fifth rib (moving toward your pet's head), then move your fingers along the fifth rib toward the spine. Using small circular motions, gently massage the small indentations on either side of the spine for 5 minutes. Stimulating these acupressure points releases feel-good brain chemicals that will help your pet feel calm and happy.

Know when Fluffy has had enough

Ouch! Your cat usually loves to be stroked, but every once in a while, she suddenly swats or grabs your arm angrily in the middle of a petting or play session. To accurately read her changing moods and avoid painful claw marks in the future, keep this tell-tail sign in mind: If your kitty's tail starts swishing fast (either the whole tail or just a rapidly twitching tip), you should stop petting her immediately. The movement indicates that she's getting aggravated. As soon as you move your hands away, she'll calm down and you'll stay scratch-free.

Calm an anxious pet

With holiday visitors popping by, changes to your home decor, and delivery men constantly knocking at the door, your pet has been acting skittish. To soothe your pet, rub a couple of drops of lavender essential oil onto her collar. Just as it does in humans, the floral aroma instantly fosters feelings of relaxation in both cats and dogs. Plus, every time you cuddle your pal, the scent will help soothe you, too!

Ease a cat's fear around strangers

You love having visitors during the holidays, but strangers make your kitty skittish, and sometimes she hisses to show her displeasure. To help her feel at ease, ask guests to avoid eye contact with her. Cats interpret eye contact from someone they don't know as a challenge or threat—which explains why felines usually take to the one person who ignores them most.

Soothe anxiety with a ditty

When guests come to visit, your pup gets so anxious that he piddles on the floor. To help ease his stress, try this trainer trick: Hum or whistle a special song when he's playing and happy—doing this a few times will help him form a positive association with the tune. Then when your four-legged buddy is exhibiting fearful behavior, hum a few bars of the song. He'll relate the sound to pleasant feelings and instantly relax.

Massage here for instant calm

If your pooch tends to get a tad too hyper after a romp in the park, settle him down with some strategic ear strokes. To do: Hold the base of each ear between your thumb and forefinger, then gently stroke all the way to the tip with even pressure. (Try to get into a rhythm of one stroke per second.) Massaging the many acupressure points on the ears releases the feel-good brain chemical dopamine, which will have him relaxed in no time.

Pet Entertainment Ideas

It's a blast playing with your little buddy! But you can't be there all the time to keep your pet entertained. Here are some brilliant ideas for keeping playtime fun.

Keep Whiskers entertained for hours

Your kitty loves when you bring home a new pack of cat toys, but within days, all the playthings are either destroyed or MIA. To replenish her toy stash without spending more cash, try this: Save your wine corks and thread string or ribbon through the holes made from the corkscrew, then knot to secure each side. You can make the corks even more appealing by misting with catnip spray, or hang the cork from a doorknob so your pal can bat the toy around.

The homemade toy that cleans Kitty's teeth

Trying to brush your cat's teeth can be anxiety provoking for her and you. To avoid the stress, toss her a DIY dental toy. Simply boil a clean, natural

loofah (about $1; look for one made with vegetable dye, which is safe for cats) for 10 minutes. Then use a serrated knife to slice off ¼-inch disks and trim any loose fibers with scissors. While your pal nibbles on the loofah, its fibers will scrub plaque and food particles from her teeth. Note: Your cat won't be harmed if she ingests a tiny piece, but supervise her so she doesn't bite off chunks, which can be a choking hazard.

Kitty "immune" to catnip? Try this!

Hoping to keep Whiskers busy (and curb her destructive behavior), you offered her a few new catnip toys, but she showed zero interest and went right back to batting the curtains. The possible reason: Your kitty could be one of the 50 percent of cats who have no reaction to catnip. Give her a honeysuckle-based toy instead—many cats find the scent more appealing than catnip. Plus, honeysuckle doesn't lose its potency, so you won't need to replace the toys anytime soon.

Effortlessly entertain your playful pets

Your pal loves to romp outside on warm days, but sometimes you're too tired to play. The solution: Fashion a play pole (which will look a bit like a fishing pole) to tucker her out fast. To do: Buy a 4-foot-long piece of ¾-inch PVC pipe and 10 feet of rope at the hardware store. Thread the rope through the pipe and tie a knot at the end to keep it from slipping out. Then tie a toy to the other end of the rope. With a flick of your wrist, you can use the pole to fling the toy around and watch your pet try to catch it. She'll get a workout while you get a rest!

Boost visibility on p.m. strolls

The sun sets so early at certain times of year that it often feels like you're walking your dog in total darkness. Instead of buying a reflective or glow-in-the-dark leash to make your pal more visible to passing cars, simply take a roll of 2-inch reflective fabric tape and cut it to fit on his lead and collar. Your furry friend will be just as flashy for a lot less!

DIY puzzle toy for dogs

You're so go-go-go these days that sometimes you don't have any extra free time to entertain Spot, so he's taken to entertaining himself by . . . chewing on your shoes. To give him a better outlet for his energy, set out this easy-to-make interactive puzzle: Place four or five puppy treats in the wells of a muffin pan and cover several of the wells with balls, then place the pan on the floor. He'll be so wrapped up in finding the tasty bites under the balls that he won't have time to get into mischief.

10 Brilliant Uses
for CAR WAX

1 Prevent dog tags from rusting
The fate of your pup's last set of ID tags: rusted within months. To protect his new ones from the corrosive effects of moisture, use a soft cloth to apply a thin coat of car wax to the metal and let dry before reattaching to his collar. Then simply reapply the wax every 2 months or as needed—you'll keep the tags looking new for years to come.

2 Effortlessly change outdoor lightbulbs
The bulbs on your patio are prone to rust, which "glues" them into their sockets so they're impossible to remove. To prevent this, rub 1 teaspoon of car wax over the bulbs' metal threads before screwing them into place. The clear film will act as a sealant to stop water from seeping in so rust doesn't form. When it comes time to change the bulbs, they'll twist out sans struggle.

3 Easily clean a greasy range hood
Last time you tried to remove the film that forms on your range hood (a combination of grease and dust), you had to seriously scrub. But next time it will be a breeze. Simply wash the hood with soapy water, then rub in 2 tablespoons of wax in a circular motion. The wax's polishing agents will whisk away grime, while its silicone restores shine.

4 Critterproof your bird feeder
Every time you peek out your window to see the colorful birds enjoying their feeder, you notice squirrels seated at the seed buffet. Keep the furry thieves away by greasing the pole with a generous amount of car wax. The backyard bandits won't be able to get a claw hold on the slippery surface, so they'll be forced to take their appetites elsewhere.

5 Stop garden shears from sticking
Ugh! Whenever you trim your hedges, the sap from the branches gums up your clippers. The save: Use a soft cloth to buff car wax into the shears' hinges and blades before you start pruning. Thanks to the slick coating, the tool will remain sap-free.

6 Save a scratched CD or DVD
If a favorite disc starts skipping, buff a dime-size amount of car wax onto the scratched area, using short strokes. Rinse with water and let dry. The wax will fill in any tiny imperfections, and the disc will play without a hitch.

7 Outsmart stubborn toilet stains

A trick that will enable you to go twice as long between toilet-bowl scrub-downs: Turn off the toilet's water supply, then flush until the bowl is empty. Apply a thin layer of wax to the inside of the bowl, let sit for 10 minutes, then turn the water back on. Any stains will slide right off the wax, leaving your toilet spiffy for up to 2 weeks.

8 Keep chrome fixtures sparkling

File under *totally frustrating!* Within an hour of cleaning your bathroom faucets, they're covered with water, soap, and toothpaste splatters. To put an end to the constant mess, use a soft cloth to apply a small amount of car wax to the fixtures after cleaning. The wax will leave an invisible shield that prevents buildup from sticking to the metal—so the shine will last well past the next tooth brushing.

9 Silence squeaky shower rings

The screech of shower curtain rings scraping against the metal rod is the last thing you want to hear early in the morning. End the racket by using a soft cloth to apply 2 tablespoons of car wax to the curtain rod, then buff to remove any excess. The wax will form a slick, invisible coating that will allow the rings to glide silently across the bar.

10 Guarantee a fog-free reflection

On go-go-go mornings, waiting for the bathroom mirror to defog after a shower can be stressful—you have to apply your mascara, and the clock is ticking! To the rescue: car wax. Simply coat the glass with a thin layer, then wipe it off with a lint-free cloth. The wax will leave behind a transparent film that will ward off condensation buildup for up to 30 days.

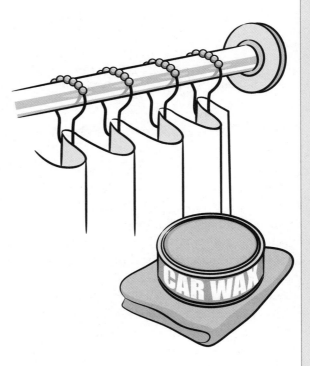

Keep Whiskers busy with a treat puzzle

A curious kitty can get into all sorts of mischief in the kitchen—jumping on counters, toppling the trash can, and tripping you up—especially when you're prepping holiday meals. To keep your pal occupied, make him this fun toy: Cut small holes (just large enough for a paw to fit through) into the sides of a shoe box. Next, roll paper and foil into small balls and place them inside, along with a few treats and a sprinkle of catnip. Finish by sealing the top of the box in place with duct tape. Whiskers will be so focused on his new puzzle that he'll be out from underfoot for hours.

Save on chew toys

Your buddy loves his chew toys so much that he goes through them faster than you can get to the pet store to buy more . . . but if you don't, he'll take to gnawing on your shoes. To keep him happy— and save some cash in the process—make a simple chew toy with items you have around the house: Slip an empty 20-ounce plastic bottle inside an old, clean tube sock and tie a knot at the end to prevent the bottle from sliding out. When chewed, the bottle will make a fun crunching sound that dogs love, but the sock's thick fabric will prevent your pup from chewing through the plastic.

Cozy Corners for Cats and Dogs

Nothing makes a pet feel more at ease than a comfy bed. From creating the ideal napping spot to making a DIY bed, read on for pet-bed pointers that will make your little friend feel happy and secure!

Create a purr-fect sleeping spot for your cat

If Whiskers loves nestling inside your dresser drawer or baskets of folded clothes (covering your shirts and pants with fur!), try making him a comfy sleeping space of his own: Simply tuck one or two throw pillows or small cushions inside a cleaned-out old planter. Kitties instinctively love the feeling of being contained in snug, cozy spaces, so the planter's small size and high sides will make her feel safe and protected. If your cat needs a little convincing to snuggle up in her new bed, spritz a few of her toys with catnip spray and place them inside.

Pick the perfect doggy bed

In the market for a bed for Fido? Make sure he'll love snuggling up in his cozy new spot by inspecting how he likes to sleep: If your pal usually snoozes with his legs sprawled, he'll most likely feel comfortable on a flat bed without side bumpers. But if he prefers sleeping curled up, a bumper bed is the way to go. This quick check will ensure he finds his new bed so appealing that he'll stay out of yours.

Transport Kitty with ease

Whether you're taking your cat on a road trip to visit family or to the vet for a checkup, getting her in and out of her carrier can be a hassle. To avoid scratched-up arms, use a carrier with a removable top instead of a traditional door, which will make her less likely to fight or flee. The easy DIY: Place your kitty in a sturdy plastic laundry basket with a pillow to keep things cozy, then set another basket of the same size on top and use bungee cords to secure the two together, running one cord lengthwise and two crosswise. Your cat won't see the basket as a threat, so she'll be comfy and content as she travels.

Make a pet bed for pennies

Designer pet beds can cost more than $100, but you can create a chic lounger for a fraction of the price by upcycling an old suitcase. To do: Find a case that your pet can lie in comfortably, then cover an old pillow or cushion with a pillowcase and place it in the suitcase. If the suitcase's top doesn't have pockets (which are perfect for storage), tie a wide ribbon across the back to hold toys.

Pet Nutrition Needs

Food and water smarts are essential for keeping your dog or cat healthy and happy. Try these quick food and water fixes that will ensure your pet is well fed and hydrated!

The supplement that slims

If your pal has packed on a few extra pounds over the winter, consider supplementing his diet with L-carnitine, an amino acid that stimulates the liver to burn fat for energy. Some specialty pet foods contain the nutrient, but giving your pal a powdered supplement can save you about $13 per month. One to try: Life Extension Acetyl-L-Carnitine 500 mg. Simply open the capsules and sprinkle the powder over your pet's regular food. The daily dose some vets recommend (but check with yours first): 1,000 milligrams for pets up to 25 pounds; 2,000 milligrams for pets 26 to 50 pounds; and 2,500 milligrams for pets over 50 pounds.

Keep ants out of pet bowls

You like to have a bowl of pet food on the patio for your pal to nibble on when he's spending more time outdoors, but a parade of ants also likes to feast on the kibble. To fend off the pests, try this trick: Place your pet's food bowl in the center of a serving tray or baking sheet, then fill the pan with about $1/2$ inch of water. Since ants can't swim, the water will prevent them from getting into the bowl. To prevent mosquitoes from breeding in the water, just be sure to empty the pan before heading inside for the night.

The doggy snack that's low in calories

If you're trying to help your sweetie lose a few pounds but finding it hard to resist those puppy-dog eyes when he begs for a treat, give him a plain, unsalted rice cake to nibble on. Vets often suggest these crunchy cakes as a substitute for regular dog treats because they're low in calories and sodium and dogs love the taste. Bonus: Since rice cakes are less expensive than biscuits and other pet treats, you'll save money, to boot!

A smart—and stylish!—way to keep Sparky hydrated

With all the exercise your pup gets in the yard, you want to make sure he has access to plenty of water. An easy, attractive idea: Place his bowl in a flower urn (available in various sizes and colors for about $6 at garden-supply stores). Fill the urn with sand or rocks to prevent it from getting blown over by wind or pushed around by your pal, then set the bowl on top. In addition to looking neat on your patio, there's a health benefit: Bending over to drink can strain your dog's back and neck, so the elevated bowl will make him more comfortable during water breaks.

Pique a cat's appetite

When temperatures begin to skyrocket, many cats lose interest in eating. To whet your feline friend's appetite so he stays healthy and energized during the "dog days" of summer, try feeding him a frozen dinner. Just pop open a can of his favorite wet food and cut it into chunks, then set the pieces on a plate and freeze for a few hours before serving it. Your cat will love licking and nibbling the frosty meal, which will keep him cool and well fed.

Easy cleaning for pet bowls

To avoid those dried bits of food clinging to your dog or cat's bowl, give the inside of the bowl a light spritz of cooking spray before filling with pet food. The vegetable oil will prevent the food from adhering to the bowl.

Sure cure for dehydration

Buster went nosing around in the garbage and ate some things he shouldn't have, which led to a bout of diarrhea. If you notice that he's acting lethargic or drooling after having tummy troubles, it could mean he's dehydrated. To help him feel better fast, give him Pedialyte. Just as in humans, the drink will help replenish fluids and electrolytes. Simply pour some of the liquid into a bowl and offer it to your dog or cat, or use an oral syringe to squirt a dose into his mouth. The dose some vets recommend (but check with yours first): 2 to 4 milliliters of Pedialyte per pound of body weight every 2 hours.

Key to keeping Kitty hydrated

To ensure Whiskers drinks enough water during the sweltering "dog" days of summer, crush a pinch of dried catnip between your fingers and sprinkle it into her bowl. Like a magnet, the irresistible treat will draw your feline friend to the water bowl and entice her to drink twice as much, so she'll stay happy and healthy!

Create a homemade elevated feeder

Bending down to eat out of bowls on the floor can strain an older pet's neck and back. To keep feeding time from being a pain for your pal, craft this clever feeder, inspired by the folks at Apartment Therapy.com: Measure your pet from paw to shoulder and divide that number by two—this is roughly how high the feeder should be. Next, hot glue four "legs" to the bottom of an inexpensive serving tray to raise it to the right height. (Try empty thread spools or napkin rings for small animals and cans for big dogs.) Then place bowls on top. Nice!

Upcycle popcorn tins into stylish food containers

Jumbo-size bags of pet food save you a bundle, but they often lead to messes—either because the food spills out when you try to pour it or because your buddy chews through the bag when he wants a snack. Sure, you could buy a special canister to solve the problem, but they can cost more than $50 at pet stores. Instead, make your own container from a holiday popcorn tin. Simply spray-paint the can and lid, then add a label with a cute paw print or your pet's name for extra flair. Easy!

Stop cats from sloshing water

Splish-splash! If your kitty tends to make a major mess every time she takes a drink, the problem could be the size of her bowl. Many cats don't like deep, narrow vessels because their extremely sensitive whiskers rub against the sides. To avoid this, they knock water out of the bowl and drink off the floor. The fix that will cut her stress and keep your floor dry: Trade her water bowl for an old pie pan or other large, wide dish that lets her drink without her whiskers ever touching the sides.

Chapter 9

A HAPPIER, HEALTHIER YOU

Let's Get Physical

Ever wonder how to cure a headache without opening the medicine cabinet? Need the secrets to better sleep? Here, you'll learn tips and tricks that are guaranteed to make you happy, healthy, and unstoppable.

FROM SNEEZES TO SNORING

Quiet a cough that just won't quit

To soothe a nagging cough and sore throat, simply mix 1 tablespoon of lemon juice, 1 teaspoon of honey, and a pinch of cayenne pepper, then swallow. The lemon juice will reduce inflammation and deliver a dose of immunity-boosting vitamin C, the honey will coat irritated throat tissue, and the pepper will rev circulation to speed healing time. Money saved: $6 for a bag of cough lozenges

Fast-acting hiccup cure

If you're out to dinner and suddenly get a case of the hiccups that no amount of water gulping and breath holding can stop, try sucking on a slice of lemon for a few seconds. The sour-tasting fruit will give your system a surprising jolt that will interrupt the diaphragm spasms that cause hiccups, so you'll be breathing easy in no time.

Sure cure for stubborn hiccups

The next time you find yourself suffering from a pesky bout of hiccups, try slowly eating a spoonful of peanut butter. The effort it takes to chew this sticky childhood staple and remove it from the roof of your mouth and your teeth interrupts your breathing pattern, which will put an end to the hiccups.

Sniff this to turn off hunger

You know 3 p.m. has arrived when the urge to visit the vending machine hits you. To resist temptation, pop a piece of minty gum or apply mint-scented lotion to your skin. According to research at Wheeling Jesuit University in West Virginia, the scent of mint is a natural appetite suppressant, and people who sniffed it throughout each day consumed 3,000 fewer calories per week—that's almost a pound of weight loss a week!

Soften the itch from wool sweaters

Years of washing and wearing can leave your favorite wool sweaters stiff and scratchy and you itchy and scratchy, too. The fix: Soak the garment in cold water, gently press the water out, and work a liberal amount of hair conditioner through the fibers. Let sit for 30 minutes, then rinse and press out as much water as possible. Lay flat to dry. Because conditioner is formulated for protein-based fibers—such as human hair and wool—it will make the garment softer and more pliable.

The kitchen staple that ends snoring

The loud noise that woke you from a peaceful sleep? Your own snoring. (We've been there!) To prevent the habit from keeping you up at night, try downing 1 teaspoon of olive oil before heading to bed. The oil will coat and lubricate throat tissue to help air flow more smoothly through the respiratory tract. Bonus: A shot of olive oil soothes a scratchy or ticklish throat.

EASE THE ACHES

Ease weekend warrior aches

When summer is just around the corner, your body is used to the slower pace of winter, and those active outings can leave you aching. The fix: Nibble on candied ginger. Its anti-inflammatory compounds reduce muscle pain by up to 25 percent overnight.

Relieve a leg cramp in seconds

Ouch! Just as you are falling asleep, you're awakened by a painful charley horse in your calf. To get rid of the cramp fast, use your thumb and forefinger to firmly pinch your upper lip (just under your nose) for 20 to 30 seconds. This technique, known as acupinch, is a favorite of sports physicians and has been shown to be 90 percent effective in reducing the pain and duration of muscle cramps.

Eliminate nighttime leg cramps

Thanks to the recent heat wave, your legs feel so swollen and achy every night that you can't sleep. Try a yoga pose called Legs Up the Wall. To do: Lie on your back with your legs flat against a wall, forming an L shape with your body; hold for 1 minute. Calf muscles often become swollen during the day, impeding bloodflow when you lie down and causing cramps. Yoga experts say that elevating the legs eases fluid buildup to reduce this swelling.

Fast relief for tired feet

Those new shoes look fabulous, but after 8 hours of wear, your feet are aching. The fix: Rub medicated lip balm on sore spots, like overworked heels or arches. The balm's menthol will offer instant cooling relief, while its anti-inflammatory camphor will heal irritated skin. Money saved: $9 for a container of foot balm

TREAT MINI MEDICAL MISHAPS

Cure athlete's foot for less

You had fun splashing around in the community pool . . . but it's led to a case of athlete's foot. The Rx: vinegar. Its acetic acid kills fungus and soothes itching. Just soak feet in equal parts warm water and vinegar for 15 minutes twice a day, then dry thoroughly (you could use a blow-dryer on "cool"). The itching should ease right away, but repeat daily for 3 weeks for total relief. Money saved: $7 for antifungal spray

Painlessly remove a stubborn splinter

While cleaning off the deck for winter, you got a splinter in your finger that even tweezers can't remove. Squirt a bit of liquid glue on the spot and smear it all over the problem area. Once it dries, peel it off. The glue will securely grasp even the tiniest splinter so it comes right out.

Soothe a wasp sting in seconds

A painful little fact: Wasps become more aggressive in the fall, when their natural food supply starts to dwindle. But the pain and itchiness of a sting can be eased by smoothing on a small amount of Vicks VapoRub. The menthol in the ointment will act as a local anesthetic to reduce pain, plus stimulate temperature-sensitive nerves to produce a cooling sensation that will relieve itchiness.

Grab toothpaste for an itchy bug bite

Having a picnic is always loads of fun—until the mosquitoes arrive. For quick relief, rub a dollop of mint-flavored toothpaste onto the irritated area. When a mosquito bites you, it injects a bit of saliva into your skin. This leads to a mild allergic reaction that stimulates the body to release histamines, inflammatory compounds that can cause itching and swelling. The fluoride in the toothpaste will work as an antihistamine to counteract this effect, while its menthol will help calm temperature-sensitive nerves and produce a cooling sensation that relieves itching.

Quick relief for a mosquito bite

Watching the sunset from your deck seemed like a great idea, but now you're left with a mosquito bite. For quick relief, rub a drop or two of lemon juice or vinegar on the bite as soon as possible. Since insect venom tends to be alkaline, applying something acidic to the area can help counteract the poison, preventing it from spreading and becoming itchy and irritated.

Soothe sunburned skin in a pinch

While helping to set up your church's ice cream social, you lost track of time and forgot to apply more sunscreen. Now that you're home, your shoulders are tingling painfully, but a quick search of your medicine cabinet reveals you're all out of aloe vera gel. For fast relief, reach for your shaving cream and smooth a dollop over the burned areas. Shaving cream contains skin-soothing ingredients like lanolin and emollients—some even contain aloe vera—that will soothe the burn immediately. Plus, the light foam won't trap heat against your skin.

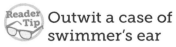 Outwit a case of swimmer's ear

"I spent the first day of my beach vacation splashing around in the ocean with my kids—and ended up with a painful ear infection. When I called my mom for advice, she suggested I mix 1 teaspoon of white vinegar and ¼ cup of boiled water in a small bottle, then put 2 drops in both ears after each swim. The vinegar kills infection-causing bacteria, so the next day I was pain-free and ready for another dip in the ocean!"

—Ashley Lorrell, Carmel, CA

The throwaway that soothes a hurt

Keep a stash of leftover condiment packets from takeout in the freezer to use as small ice packs when you have a bruise or burn yourself in the kitchen. It's a lot easier than breaking out a big bag of peas and less messy than holding an ice cube.

No more scalp sunburns!

"I'm usually good about protecting my skin if I'm going to be outside, but recently I forgot to bring a hat to the pool, and my scalp got fried. It hurt so bad that I could barely brush my hair! I was complaining about it to a friend, and she shared this tip: Run a stick of lip balm with SPF along your part and hairline. You get protection right where you need it, and you don't have to worry about making your hair oily with sunscreen or dealing with hat hair."

—Angela Brady, Atlanta, GA

Soothe a bee sting in seconds

If you get stung and don't have a first-aid kit on hand, try this in-a-pinch Rx: Remove the stinger if necessary, then mix a bit of dirt and clean water (or saliva) and smear it onto the affected area. As the mud dries, it will draw out the pain-inducing venom. Note: If you're allergic to bees (signs include swelling, trouble breathing, and dizziness), skip the mud poultice and seek immediate medical care.

Fast sunburn relief

"One recent afternoon I was having so much fun lounging outside with my friends that I forgot to reapply my sunscreen and got a nasty burn. Luckily, one friend suggested soaking a few paper towels in white vinegar and gently pressing them onto my skin. She said vinegar's acetic acid works to ease the pain and puffiness, so I'd feel soothed in no time. She was right!"

—Carol Barnes, Baytown, TX

Coax out a stubborn splinter

Ouch! While dragging your Christmas tree out to the curb for pickup, you got a nasty sliver of wood stuck in your finger, and you just can't grasp it with your tweezers. To the rescue: baking soda! Simply mix 1 tablespoon of the pantry staple with enough water to create a gooey paste, then apply it to the punctured area and cover with a bandage. Leave on for 15 minutes, or until the paste is dry, then gently remove the bandage. As the paste hardens, your skin will swell slightly, drawing the splinter to the surface so you can easily remove it.

Tuck this under your collar to repel gnats

Weeding the garden would be a lot more enjoyable if it weren't for the cloud of gnats that forms around your head. Instead of wasting time swatting them away, tuck a few fabric softener sheets under your collar or bra strap. According to a study in the journal *HortScience*, the dryer sheets contain linalool, a colorless alcohol known to be toxic to insects, and beta-citronellol, a natural insect-repelling compound.

Tasty way to nix heartburn

A fresh-off-the-grill cheeseburger and an icy cola hit the spot at a Memorial Day gathering . . . until that painful burning sensation sets in. For fast relief, snack on a handful of almonds. Their fatty acids have been shown to neutralize stomach acid within 15 minutes, while the nuts' fiber speeds digestion so the body can produce less acid. Also smart: enjoying almonds before a meal to ward off a bout of acid reflux.

BANISH HEADACHES

Ease a headache in 60 seconds

After arguing with the gate agent about your bumped flight, you're left with a nasty headache. Just locate the protruding bones behind your ears, then move your fingers down and toward one another to find two small depressions. Press for 1 minute. Acupressurists believe that tension headaches are caused by an energy imbalance in the Gallbladder Meridian. Stimulating this spot, called GB20, will boost blood circulation to melt away the pain.

Roll away a headache

Oh, no! In the middle of a fun family outing, you feel an ache starting to build up behind your eyes. To keep the pain from intensifying, grab a golf ball and roll it under your foot (from big toe to heel) 10 times. This makeshift massage will put pressure on reflexology points that boost bloodflow throughout the body and stimulate the production of mood-boosting neurochemicals, helping to ease a headache.

Natural help for a throbbing headache

"Not now!" you think to yourself as you feel a familiar pain around your temples. To relieve your headache before it gets worse, drizzle some extra-virgin olive oil onto your lunchtime salad or use the oil as a dip for bread. According to research in the journal *Nature,* the antioxidant oleocanthal in the oil may inhibit enzymes that cause pain and inflammation as effectively as ibuprofen. The study-proven dose: 2 teaspoons whenever head pain strikes.

Sure cure for a tension headache

To find relief when your head starts to throb, hold a pencil between your teeth (without biting down on it) for a few minutes. Stress and anxiety lead to unconscious jaw clenching, which strains the muscle that connects the jaw to the temples and triggers tension headaches. But this action will unclench your jaw to relax facial muscles and ease the pain.

10 Brilliant Uses
for BLACK
TEA BAGS

1 Ward off an unsightly bruise
Ouch! You banged your knee on the coffee table, and you just know it'll result in a nasty bruise. To minimize the mark, soak a black tea bag in water and hold it against the area for 5 minutes. Tea's tannins constrict blood vessels, which reduces swelling and inflammation. If you do end up with a bruise, it will be smaller and will heal faster.

2 Soothe a minor sunburn for pennies
The sun was more intense than you realized, and now you have splotches of pink skin. What can help: Dip black tea bags in cold water and place on burned spots. Tea's polyphenols and tannic acid will relieve the burn and speed healing. (For widespread sunburn, place 10 tea bags under the faucet while filling the tub, then slip in for a soothing soak.)

3 Enrich a sluggish compost pile
During the heat of midsummer, it's easy to assure decomposition in a compost pile. But as temperatures start to dip in September, the bacteria that create compost become less active. As a result, your pile may need a helping hand. To do: Toss a few used black tea bags into the heap. Tea is rich in nitrogen, which supplies bacteria with the energy they need to dial up decomposition.

4 Get pans sparkling—without scrubbing!
Your gang flipped for your casserole . . . but now you have to get the stuck-on food bits off the pan. Rather than spending precious time scrubbing, fill the pan with hot water, toss in two black tea bags, and let sit overnight. The hot water works with the tea's tannic acid to soften and lift stubborn food particles. The next morning, a quick rinse will be all it takes to get your pan gleaming.

5 Heal dry, chapped lips
Keep your pucker kissably soft by pressing a moistened black tea bag to your lips for 30 seconds. Tea's antioxidant polyphenols will help repair damaged skin cells and speed cell renewal. Repeat three to five times a week, or as needed.

6 Rustproof a cast-iron skillet

Guarantee your trusty skillet stays rust-free by wiping it with a damp, used black tea bag after every cooking session. The tea's tannins will coat the pan with an invisible protective layer that prevents rust-causing oxidation.

7 Fast fix for mirror spots

For a chemical-free way to rid your bathroom mirror of toothpaste splatters and the like, simply save the damp black tea bag from your morning brew and rub it over the spots, then dry with a soft cloth. The tea's tannic acids will gently break down the grime, ensuring that your glass is crystal clear.

8 Freshen up an area rug in no time

You decided to get ahead on spring cleaning, starting with your area rugs. But even after being beaten outdoors and vacuumed, they still smell a little funky. To freshen up the rugs: Grab a dry, used black tea bag; split it open; and sprinkle the leaves over the rugs. Let sit for 10 minutes before vacuuming the tea away. The leaves will absorb smells and odor-causing moisture, so when you vacuum them up, the rugs will look and smell refreshed.

9 Relieve bleeding gums instantly

If you've ever had damage to your gums, especially after having a tooth extracted, you can relieve the tender area by placing a dampened black tea bag over the area and gently biting down. The tea's healing tannins have astringent qualities that will dull the ache and stop any bleeding fast. The tea will also form a protective layer over the exposed tissue, which will help keep infections out.

10 Soothe your pup's salt-cracked paws

Poor Sparky! Salt sprinkled on the sidewalk after a snowstorm irritated his paws, and now he's chewing on the red spots in an effort to get relief. What can help: Press a damp black tea bag against his footpads for 1 minute twice a day. Tea's plant polyphenols ease irritation and speed cell renewal, so he'll be feeling better within a week.

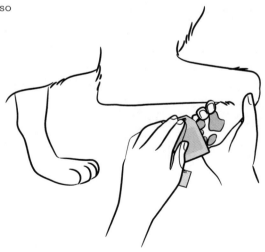

CONGESTION CURE-ALLS

The snack that dials down fall allergies

The sure signs that the seasons are changing? Your runny nose and itchy, watery eyes. To stop the sniffles, enjoy two 6-ounce containers of Greek yogurt on days when your allergies flare up. *Lactobacillus casei,* a strain of probiotic bacteria commonly found in this creamy treat, has been shown to lower the body's levels of immunoglobulin E, an antibody that triggers the release of the inflammatory histamines responsible for allergy symptoms.

Relieve sinus pain in minutes

Forget sniffling, sneezing, and wheezing—the sure sign of fall allergies is the throbbing pain we feel in our sinuses. Our new go-to fix: the peppermint tea in our pantry. German researchers discovered that inhaling the tea's vapor is supereffective at soothing sinus pain—and the results kick in fast. The credit goes to peppermint's natural anti-inflammatory compounds and pain relievers (like menthol), which relax constricted sinuses.

Hum away spring sinus pain

You know your allergies have kicked in when you start to feel that throbbing pressure in your sinuses. A surprising remedy: Hum your favorite song. According to research in the *American Journal of Respiratory and Critical Care Medicine,* humming optimizes the flow of air between the sinus and nasal cavities, which helps keep them properly ventilated to ease the pain.

SOS for sinus pressure

An easy acupressure trick can offer relief for allergy-induced congestion and sinus discomfort. Simply use the thumb and index finger of one hand to firmly pinch the webbed area between the thumb and index finger of your opposite hand. Hold for 1 minute. Experts explain that this area, called LI-4, corresponds to the sinuses. Applying pressure to the spot will restore energy flow to the nasal passages, reducing stuffiness.

The body trick that eases congestion

For a surprisingly simple way to unblock a stuffy nose, try this: Alternate between gently pushing your tongue against the roof of your mouth and using your index finger to press the spot between your eyebrows. This rhythmic back-and-forth action will cause the vomer bone (which runs through the nasal passages to the mouth) to rock back and forth, loosening congestion. After 20 seconds, you should feel your sinuses start to drain. Continue until your sinuses are clear, and repeat as often as needed.

Soothe a sore throat—deliciously!

Forget foul-tasting syrup—you can ease an aching throat with a childhood treat: Jell-O! Prepare your favorite flavor according to package directions, but instead of letting it chill, heat it in the microwave for 30 seconds, then add 1 teaspoon of honey. The warm gelatin will coat and soothe your throat, while honey's antimicrobial properties will help kill infection-causing bacteria.

HOW TO REMEMBER ANYTHING!

Use these simple tricks to help you remember PINs, combinations, and household hiding spots.

Your ATM PIN

ATM codes are easy to forget, especially since banks suggest avoiding familiar (but easy-to-hack) numbers like your birthday. To safely keep your PIN on hand, create a fake contact in your cell phone whose initials spell out PIN, like Pete Ingels. Input a bogus phone number for the contact, making the last four digits your PIN. If you draw a blank at the ATM, remembering is as simple as checking your cell. And if your phone is lost or stolen, the code will be disguised from thieves.

A lock combination

This trick makes recalling any lock combination as easy as remembering your birthday. If your combination is 22/41/17 and your birthday is 8/15/70, add each of the separate numbers together (22 + 8 / 41 + 15 / 17 + 70), then write the sum (30/56/87) in permanent marker on the back of the lock. Even if someone sees the code, they won't be able to use it to open your lock, but since you know the trick, you'll never forget the combination again!

Items you need at a store

When you're about to make a quick stop at the store sans list, try the "memory palace" technique. To do: Before you leave, mentally tour your home, picturing a needed item in each room—eggs on your bed, milk on the stairs, etc. Just imagining these items helps ensure you won't forget any essentials. At the store, just walk through the route again—you'll be able to "see" every item.

Household storage spots

Whether it's tax documents, holiday decorations, or out-of-season clothes, take a picture of the storage space so it's easy to recall later. Upload the photos to your computer and label them with the name of the stored item ("tax documents"), then put the pictures in a folder on your desktop labeled "storage." Too late? Try looking up and to the left. Brain scans have shown that moving your eyes this way stimulates the visual memory portion of your brain, helping you picture the location.

MOUTH PAIN GONE!

Cure a cold sore quickly

You came home from a day at the beach with a healthy glow, sand in your shoes . . . and the start of a cold sore. For fast relief, dab a little honey on the blister. Repeat two or three times a day until the spot heals. Researchers in Dubai discovered that applying antioxidant-rich honey at the first sign of a cold sore reduces the breakout's duration by two-thirds, so it heals 43 percent faster than when treated with prescription antivirals. Money saved: $10 per tube of cold sore cream

Heal a cold sore—stat!

To banish a fever blister, mix 1 teaspoon of baking soda with a drop of water, then use a cotton swab to apply the paste to the sore. Let it harden for 10 minutes before rinsing. Repeat daily for a week. The sodium bicarbonate in the soda will reduce bacteria around the sore, speeding healing time. Money saved: $13 per tube of OTC cold sore treatment

The kitchen fix for tooth pain

If you start to feel a bit of an ache in your tooth but can't get to the dentist right away, soak a cotton swab with vanilla extract and dab it on the sore spot. The extract's alcohol will quickly numb the pain, while its aroma helps promote feelings of calm that can relieve physical discomfort. Money saved: $8 for a tube of numbing gel

Boost Your Brain

Sharpen your mental focus with these simple tricks. Whether you are experiencing brain fog, need a quick pick-me-up, or want a better night's sleep, you can incorporate these ideas to help you feel smarter, more creative, and a whole lot more relaxed in minutes.

IMPROVE FOCUS INSTANTLY

Clear brain fog in seconds

Popping a stick of gum into your mouth when your focus starts to fade can save you from an unproductive zone-out. That's because the act of chewing causes more oxygen to be delivered to the brain, which improves alertness by up to 35 percent. Bonus: Pick a brand that contains xylitol, like Spry, to help fight off oral bacteria.

Crunch away brain fog

To get back on your A-game when a slump threatens your productivity, snack on some salt-and-vinegar chips. UCLA scientists say the combination of crunch, salt, and vinegar will heighten your senses to boost alertness fast.

The swish that improves focus

To overcome the productivity slump that seems to strike at 3 p.m. every day, add a pinch of sugar to a glass of water, then swish the liquid around in your mouth for a few seconds before spitting it out. Simply tasting something sweet has been shown to stimulate the brain regions that govern focus, allowing you to power through your to-dos.

Back-to-work blahs? Gone!

Getting into the groove after the holidays can be tough. To regain your focus, try placing a few twigs from your Christmas tree in a bowl on your desk. The natural compound that gives pine its scent has been shown to activate the brain's energy and alertness center. After a few deep breaths, you'll be raring to go!

Switch this to be even smarter

An easy way to banish brain fog: Move your mouse to the opposite side of your computer and use your nondominant hand to click for 2 minutes. This will stimulate neural connections between brain hemispheres to sharpen thinking. And when done daily, it will increase the number of nerve fibers in the brain for a lasting mental boost.

Make yourself mistakeproof

The next time you need to type an important e-mail, enjoy some coffee or another caffeinated beverage before you get started. Consuming 200 milligrams of caffeine (the amount in 2 cups of java) has been shown to improve performance in the brain region that controls language-related functions. Researchers say this makes it easier to catch and fix grammatical errors.

Boost motivation with a glance

Every day we vow to start that freelance project at home . . . and every night we get distracted by chores and other to-dos. If you've ever been in that boat, try this trick we learned to stimulate productivity: Place a happy photo (like that great family vacation shot!) in a red frame and display it on your desk. Studies show that just looking at the color red prompts action by releasing adrenaline. Plus, the activity in the photo is subconsciously seen as a reward, providing inspiration that can be channeled into the task.

Increase your motivation fast

You vowed to jog around your neighborhood four times a week. But after just one lap around the block, you're ready to throw in the towel. The fix: Rather than think about how far you have to go, admire how your legs move or concentrate on driving your elbows forward and backward. This distraction strategy, called chunking, shifts your attention to just one part of your body, so the rest of you doesn't feel as tired.

Watch this to boost your resolve

Tuning in to see if your favorite dancer nails her solo on *So You Think You Can Dance* or who makes it to the finals on *America's Got Talent* can enhance your resolve and improve your decision-making powers, psychologists report. The reason: The can-do attitudes featured on such shows are "contagious," infusing viewers with inner strength. But since temptation is also easy to "catch," experts advise bypassing programs that showcase bad habits.

SECRETS FOR IMPROVING SLEEP

The snack that helps you sleep

When a warm bath and dimmed lights fail to get you in shut-eye mode, try a slice of watermelon. Here's why: In an Australian study, people who ate a snack high on the glycemic index (like watermelon) before bedtime fell asleep twice as fast as those who consumed slower-digesting treats. Plus, the juicy fruit increases the production of tryptophan, an amino acid that boosts levels of the sleep-inducing hormone serotonin. Sweet dreams! Money saved: $7 per box of over-the-counter sleep-aid supplements

No more tossing and turning

If you find yourself wide-eyed when you want to be sleeping, enjoy a late-night almond snack, like almond butter on crackers. These nuts are a rich source of magnesium, a natural tranquilizer that relaxes muscles, plus tryptophan, an amino acid that boosts the production of sleep-inducing brain chemicals.

The postparty trick for sound sleep

You had a great time at the holiday bash, but now your feet are aching and you're too wired to sleep. To soothe your mind and body, pour marbles into a basin, fill it with warm water, and add ½ cup of Epsom salts. Then dip your feet in and roll your soles over the marbles for a few minutes. The salts will increase circulation to relieve sore feet, while the marbles will activate acupressure points that relax the entire body and encourage deep sleep.

Press here to fall asleep faster

When a nagging worry has you tossing and turning, use your thumb to rub tiny circles on the outer edge of your inner wrist (under your pinkie) for 2 minutes. Acupressure experts say stimulating this spot will slow heart rate, helping you drift off easily.

Sing your way to deeper sleep

To put a stop to snoring (and next-day fatigue), try singing along to some of your favorite tunes for 20 minutes a day. Regularly singing helps tone muscles in the throat's upper airways, which enables you to increase your oxygen intake as you sleep. The result: You'll be snoring less within 3 months and jumping out of bed feeling totally refreshed!

CONFIDENCE CLUES

Instantly boost self-confidence

If the holidays thrust you into the spotlight, try tilting your head back, angling your chin slightly upward. This small movement will change your thought process by sending feel-good signals to your brain, which results in the production of more confidence-boosting hormones. Plus, a slightly raised chin shows others that you're self-assured—always a good thing.

Stop self-doubt with a nod

You're about to present a new budget strategy to your boss when your nerves kick into high gear. Before you start doubting yourself, subtly nod your head up and down a few times. According to researchers at Ohio State University in Columbus, nodding is a form of self-validation that instantly boosts confidence and assurance in one's own thoughts.

Banish nagging self-doubt

If, after you fall short of a goal, that voice inside your head starts putting you down and making you question yourself, try this study-proven trick: Close your eyes and make your inner critic sound like a cartoon character with a funny voice that makes you smile, such as Donald Duck or Betty Boop. Researchers say that the pleasant memories associated with these silly characters will create an alternative perspective that instantly wipes out the bad feelings created by even the harshest inner critic.

NIX FORGETFULNESS NOW!

Never forget a password

Your bank is requesting that you update your online password—again—and you're having a hard time coming up with one that's obscure enough to keep people out yet easy enough to remember. Here's a clever method you can try: Create a password using the first letter of each word in the first few lines of a well-known or much-loved song. For example, a password referencing the first two lines of "Happy Birthday" would be "HbtyHbty." If the Web site requires that you include numbers, simply count the letters in the string you just created (in this case, 8) and tack that onto the end of your password—like "HbtyHbty8."

Be even smarter

Is it just us, or are names and dates becoming harder and harder to recall? Brain maps show that the nerve endings on fingertips connect with more areas of the brain than those anywhere else on the body. That's why women who play the piano, do needlework, and otherwise challenge their digits stay sharper. In fact, new research confirms that finger exercises help increase brain mass and boost brain circulation. Hello, knitting needles!

Rev recall with this little trick

You're scheduled to present a proposal at tomorrow's town meeting. To help commit the words to memory, try typing the speech in a small, hard-to-read font (like 12-point Bodoni) instead of a large, clear font (like 16-point Arial). In a study at Princeton University, participants remembered 14 percent more of what they read when challenging fonts were used. The reason: These fonts force you to slow down and concentrate, sending information deeper into the brain's memory-processing areas.

Remember numbers effortlessly

You recently switched phone companies and had to change your home number. To commit your new digits to memory, write them out by hand. Handwriting activates the brain's working memory, the ability to mentally store and manipulate information. Plus, it leaves a motor memory in the sensorimotor part of the brain, which helps us recognize characters.

CLEVERLY CREATIVE

Have your next aha moment right now!

Need to come up with a smart solution to a pesky problem? Simply visualize an empty pitcher. Cognitive therapists explain that picturing emptiness creates space for new ideas in the cerebral cortex, the brain's problem-solving center. So you'll be hit with a flash of genius in a matter of minutes.

Be even smarter—in minutes!

Need to come up with a brilliant solution to a pesky problem? Spend a few minutes reading a "nonsense" book like *The Cat in the Hat* or *Where the Sidewalk Ends*. Studies show that people who read silly literature have a heightened ability to recognize hidden patterns and think outside the box. That's because the mind tries to find meaning in whatever it encounters—and the less sense something makes, the harder the brain works to find a solution.

Boost creativity with this hue

You were thrilled when the local library asked you to help organize their annual book sale. To come up with new, fun ideas, toss on a violet shirt or dress. According to color-therapy experts, the electromagnetic frequency of this hue increases levels of oxytocin, a hormone that aids in creativity. Plus, purple is 50 percent red, which stimulates the logical left side of the brain, and 50 percent blue, which sparks the intuitive right side for a perfect balance.

Brighten Your Mood!

STOP STRESS—STAT!

Bracing for a busy day? Do this

You haven't even changed out of your pj's and already you're feeling overwhelmed as you ponder your to-do list and wonder how you'll manage it all. The trick that can help you breeze through your day: While brushing your teeth, stand on one leg and think about just one of the items you need to tackle. This balancing act increases bloodflow to the brain region that governs the ability to plan, so you'll be better able to map out your schedule and focus on what needs to be done.

The scent that nixes stress

Feeling frazzled by your mile-long to-do list? Try rubbing on a coconut-scented body lotion or lighting a coconut candle. This tropical scent is study proven to reduce levels of the stress hormone cortisol by up to 24 percent. The reason: It stimulates the limbic system, the area in the brain responsible

for mood. Plus, since the aroma is associated with carefree beach vacations, your mood will immediately improve.

Instantly release stress

A trick that will help you stay calm in any situation: Rub your hands together when you start to feel tense. Experts explain that when anxiety hits, the nervous system directs bloodflow away from the hands to the body's larger muscles—which causes hands to get chilly. By warming them up, you send the body a signal that it's okay to calm down.

The salty fix for nervousness

To ease entertaining jitters, take a moment to enjoy a salty snack, like a small handful of pretzels or peanuts. A hit of sodium will slow the production of a key anxiety-triggering hormone while prompting the brain to produce the calming hormone oxytocin. The result: a sense of relaxation that sets in within 15 minutes.

The staring contest that ends stress

It's been that kind of day: Traffic made you late for work, you stepped in a puddle (without rain boots), and your son's teacher called you for a conference. Feel better fast by having a staring contest with your pet. In a study in the journal *Hormones and Behavior*, when dog owners maintained eye contact with their pets for about 2½ minutes, they experienced a 20 percent spike in oxytocin, a feel-good hormone that banishes negative feelings and encourages calm and relaxation.

The spice that helps you relax

For some reason you woke up on the wrong side of the bed this morning and are feeling sad and tense. To stop the blues from taking over your day, add a few dashes of nutmeg to your breakfast. According to researchers at Texas A&M University in College Station, the myristicin in this sweet spice induces relaxation by increasing brain levels of the calming hormone serotonin.

PERFECT YOUR PEOPLE SKILLS

Try this to get closer to anyone

A surprising way to strengthen your relationship with a loved one: Whisper something caring into his or her left ear. Emotional words have a greater impact when heard in the left ear than when heard in the right, according to psychologists. That's because the left ear is controlled by the more emotional right side of the brain, ensuring your loving messages will be heard loud and clear.

The trick that makes you appear friendlier

While waiting in line at the supermarket, you strike up a conversation with the woman in front of you. Turns out she just moved in across the street! To start off on the right foot with her, shift your gaze between her right and left eye while you chat. This movement will signal that you're interested in what she's saying by maintaining eye contact but without appearing too intense.

Do this to be more persuasive

While explaining a new budget strategy to your team at work, you're getting more blank stares than enthusiastic nods. To make sure you are understood, repeat your points using several related hand gestures. (For instance, draw a slope in the air to indicate increasing profits.) You may feel silly at first, but according to the Association for Psychological Science, people catch on to new concepts up to nine times faster when the speaker illustrates key points with hand movements.

How to make people listen

The next time you need to get your point across, ensure that you're taken seriously by making yourself appear larger. Simply stand with your feet about 6 inches apart and place one hand on your hip or gesture with both hands as you speak. According to body language experts, this pose projects an air of confidence and power.

10 Brilliant Uses
for COCONUT OIL

1 Remove makeup the gentle way
Instead of using harsh (and pricey) store-bought products, put a dab of coconut oil on a cotton pad and sweep it over your lids. In addition to removing every trace of makeup, this supermoisturizing oil will make the delicate under-eye skin look younger—in one study, it was shown to reduce fine lines and wrinkles by 42 percent in 8 weeks.

2 Effortlessly speed slimming
Using coconut oil to sauté foods is an easy way to trim inches and boost energy. Just replace the butter or vegetable oil you'd normally use with an equal amount of coconut oil, letting it melt in the pan before adding veggies or meat. This simple switch will provide a dose of medium-chain fatty acids, which rev metabolism by 50 percent.

3 Ease "down there" dryness
To improve sexual comfort, apply ¼ teaspoon of coconut oil instead of storebought lubricant. The oil will minimize friction for instant relief. Plus, if used daily, its caprylic and myristic acids improve elasticity and moisture retention in vaginal skin for lasting benefits. (The oil damages latex, so don't use with condoms or diaphragms.)

4 Eliminate stubborn acne
The sweaty season is here, but you can quickly erase any blemishes that crop up on your face, chest, and back by rubbing a dab of coconut oil into affected skin until it's absorbed. Coconut's lauric acid is 15 times more effective than benzoyl peroxide at killing breakout-causing bacteria—and it won't clog pores. Hello, clear skin!

5 Whip up healthier baked goods
The next time you make cupcakes, swap out the butter in your recipe for coconut oil. Because the oil is a saturated fat like butter, your treats will be just as fluffy. But they'll also be a whole lot healthier, thanks to unique fats in coconut that reduce heart disease risk.

6 Polish wood sans chemicals
A natural way to get your coffee table gleaming: In a small bowl, combine 1 part lemon juice and 2 parts coconut oil, then dip a soft cloth into the mixture and rub all over the surface of your furniture until it's absorbed. The lemon will dissolve dirt and grime, while the oil will seep into the wood's pores, locking in moisture and restoring the fixture's vibrant, glossy finish.

7 Soothe an itchy bug bite

You made sure to apply and reapply insect repellent, but mosquitoes *still* feasted on your arms and legs. Ease the itch by rubbing a dab of coconut oil into the bites. The oil's anti-inflammatory properties will quickly stop the itching sensation, while its immunity-boosting natural acids will help speed the healing process.

8 Heal a dog's hot spots—fast

Summer's heat and humidity can cause canine hot spots to flare up. To calm your pup's painful sores, gently rub a dollop of coconut oil onto the problem areas daily. Coconut's lauric acid will kill irritation-causing bacteria, plus protect skin from further infection. Also consider stirring the oil (½ teaspoon for every 20 pounds of body weight, once a day) into your dog's food to nourish his coat from the inside out.

9 Silence squeaky cabinet hinges

Your kitchen cupboard screeches when you open it, but you don't want to use WD-40 on a white cabinet. The save: Using a dropper, coat the hinges with coconut oil. (If the oil is solid, warm a very small amount in the microwave to melt it.) The colorless oil will lubricate the metal, ensuring smooth, quiet movement.

10 Repair damaged hair while you sleep

A day at the pool or beach is a much-deserved break for you—but sun, salt water, and chlorine can dry out your tresses and lead to split ends. To the rescue: coconut oil. Before bed, warm 1 tablespoon in your hands, massage into damp hair, and distribute with a wide-tooth comb. Then pop on a shower cap and go to sleep. Shampoo as usual in the a.m. Coconut oil's fatty acid molecules will penetrate the hair cuticle down to the cortex for deep, nourishing hydration.

INSTANT PICK-ME-UPS

Snack on this to feel happier

For a tasty way to boost mood in minutes, nibble on a handful of popcorn. This complex carb has been shown to increase levels of tryptophan, the amino acid used to produce the feel-good neurotransmitter serotonin, by 42 percent.

Sniff this to feel sunnier

Inhaling the sweet-tart aroma of a green apple (or slathering on some apple-scented lotion) is an easy way to bring on smiles. According to aromatherapy experts, the scent will stimulate pleasure receptors in the brain and spur the production of feel-good serotonin.

60 seconds to happy!

Need a quick hit of positive energy? Noshing on something spicy—like chips and ¼ cup of salsa or a couple of hot cherry peppers—can brighten your mood in as little as 1 minute. The credit goes to capsaicin, a plant compound that stimulates a rush of endorphins to the brain.

Feel more love every day

"When it comes time to put away my holiday decorations, I always feel bad tossing the family photo cards I've received throughout the season. So this year I used my cell phone to snap a picture of each card, then I updated my contacts with the holiday photos. Now when I get a call from friends and family members, I'm greeted with a gorgeous photo of them."

—*Tara Westin, Hays, KS*

Life—A Little Bit Simpler

Having trouble zipping up the back of your dress? Need a fast fix for cracked eye shadow? Wondering how to untangle earbuds? These little issues can make for hassles and headaches. But don't worry—the great ideas here are unique hints guaranteed to fix these problems and make your life easier.

FAST FIXES

Unstick a stubborn zipper in seconds

"I scored a gorgeous woven handbag on sale a few months ago and have been using it nonstop ever since—so I was upset to find the zipper stubbornly stuck last week. Luckily, my friend knew of a remedy: Just lightly rub an unlit candle along the teeth on both sides of the zipper. The wax will lubricate the metal just enough to get the zipper moving again without damaging the bag's fabric."

—*Lily Walsh, Bristol, VA*

SPEED THROUGH ANY ERRAND

We hate going out to run a "quick" errand only to encounter unexpected crowds or traffic. That's why we asked the experts for the best days to tackle all our to-dos.

SUNDAY: Book a hotel room

Revenue managers who manage rates for rooms don't typically work on Sunday, which means you'll have better luck getting a room for less. Since front desk workers are more concerned with filling rooms than securing the highest rate, you'll get the best deal in the least amount of time.

MONDAY: Return unwanted items

Because most shoppers wear themselves out over the weekend, Mondays are quiet days at the mall. While you don't want to do your actual shopping on Monday (since you'll miss out on sales that will be advertised later in the week), it's wise to use this time to return unwanted items—you'll zip through the returns line and benefit from more attentive staff.

TUESDAY: Visit the post office

In 2009, when asking Congress to consider cutting postal service from 6 days a week to 5, then-Postmaster General John E. Potter suggested eliminating mail delivery every Tuesday, citing it as the second-slowest day of the week. (Saturday is the slowest day for mail delivery but one of the busiest in-house.) The exception: Tuesdays after federal banking holidays, which tend to be superbusy.

WEDNESDAY: Shop for groceries

According to a 2008 study by the Time Use Institute, the busiest supermarket days are at the end of the week, with Sunday a close second. But on Wednesday there's a lull in supermarket traffic, so your trip will average just 36 minutes (versus 46 minutes on Saturday). Bonus: Many supermarkets get shipments on Monday and Tuesday, so by Wednesday the freshest foods will be on the shelves.

THURSDAY: Get your car serviced

Most people head to the body shop or service station on Friday or at the beginning of the week (right before or after taking weekend trips). That makes Thursday the least crowded day of the week to get your car serviced.

FRIDAY: Catch up on e-mails

In 2005, the e-mail marketing service Exact Target studied 2.7 billion e-mail messages from more than 4,000 organizations. Their finding: People open more e-mails on Friday than any other day of the week. Plus, another study found that the fewest e-mails overall are sent on Friday. The reduced volume in people's in-boxes will increase the visibility of your e-mail, so your messages will be read ASAP.

SATURDAY: Have fun!

Everyone deserves a day off! In a study in the magazine *Harvard Business Review*, people who were guaranteed 1 night off a week from their usual duties were not only happier but also more productive overall—so you'll still get all your to-dos done.

Unravel a tangled necklace with ease

"After sharing how I spent 20 minutes trying to get the knot out of my gold necklace one morning, a coworker revealed this detangling tip: Place the jewelry on a hard surface to avoid staining, then apply a few drops of baby oil to the knot to lubricate the metal. Next, use a safety pin to gently pull apart the tangle. Just wipe off the necklace afterward."

—*Kathy Nader, Deltona, FL*

 ## Easily untangle kinked earbuds

"I accidentally put my earbuds through the washer and dryer, and although they still worked, the cords were all kinked up. Luckily, my techie son had a solution: Wrap the earphones around a coffee cup, taping the wires down so they lie flat, and fill the cup with boiling water. Let sit for 15 minutes, or until the water cools. When I took the earbuds off the cup, they were kink-free and ready for me to use."

—*Karen Gadskill, Savoy, IL*

 ## Quick fix for an earring emergency

"Sometimes when I'm rushing in the morning, I drop the back of an earring—and retrieving it is next to impossible. But recently my friend told me how she copes with a lost earring back: Cut a small square from a rubber band and secure it to the metal post. Now I keep a few cut-up rubber bands in my jewelry box just in case."

—*Ann Carter, Winslow, AZ*

Rethread a drawstring

"The other day the drawstring came out of my yoga pants, and I had the hardest time rethreading it. I mentioned what a hassle it was to a friend, and she offered this advice: Thread the drawstring through a plastic straw and staple one end to secure, then push it back through the waistband. The straw's length and flexibility make rethreading a cinch."

—*Madison Grayson, Boone, NC*

Runproof tights

To ensure your tights make it through the last few weeks of winter without a run, soak them in a solution of $\frac{1}{4}$ cup of salt and 4 cups of water for 30 minutes. Rinse with cool water and let air-dry before wearing. The salt will penetrate the nylon fibers, making them stronger and resistant to snags. Money saved: $9 for a pair of tights

 ## Quick save for cracked shadow

"I clumsily dropped the compact while applying my favorite eye shadow one morning, causing it to break into pieces. Luckily, my sister offered this tip: Add a few drops of rubbing alcohol to the crushed powder, then push it back into shape with the back of a spoon. As the alcohol evaporates, the product will meld together."

—*Daisy Carter, Durham, NC*

Cool off a too-hot laptop

Frustrated by slow or skipping videos on your laptop? Try placing it on a wire cooling rack. Streaming videos often cause laptops to overheat, which interferes with viewing quality—but this trick will keep air circulating and lower the computer's temperature by up to 10°F. Money saved: $20 for a laptop tray

Shoe odor—eliminated!

If the sneakers you've been sporting all summer start to smell a little off, try this: Set a few pieces of orange or lemon peel, colorful side up, inside the shoes and let sit overnight. The spongelike white pith will absorb moisture and odor, while the peel's citrusy scent will freshen up the shoe. Money saved: $6 to $10 for shoe deodorizer

Reader Tip: De-crumb a bag in a flash

"After a beach trip with my friend, I was trying to shake the sand out of my bag when she suggested that I run a lint roller along the inside. It worked like a charm—the sticky pad picked up every speck. Now I do this for my handbag once a week to remove any crumbs and lint."

—*Sarah Graham, Corpus Christi, TX*

GET MORE FROM EACH PURCHASE

Genius way to use expired sunscreen

While stowing away your bottles of sunscreen for next summer, you see a few are about to expire. Instead of tossing them, use the lotion as shaving cream. The thick formula will provide a barrier that prevents razor burn. Plus, most sunscreens have soothing, moisturizing properties. Money saved: $4 for a can of shaving cream

Keep energy bars intact on the go

On busy mornings, you often toss a snack bar into your bag before rushing out the door. But when you pull it out later, it's deformed—or worse, in little crumbly bits. To keep the bar in one piece for easy snacking, try stashing it in an old eyeglass or plastic pencil case. The case is the perfect size to hold the bar, and its hard outer shell will prevent it from getting smashed in your bag.

Perfume—good to the last drop

You can see there's still enough of your signature scent left in the bottle to last you a few more days, but you can't get it to spray. The fix: Remove the lid and nozzle (depending on the bottle, this may require the use of pliers), then add a few drops of the perfume to a dollop of unscented lotion. Bonus: The cream's oils lock in the fragrant notes, so your scent won't fade as fast as it does when you simply spritz.

Extend the life of a wireless mouse

Ugh! The batteries in your wireless mouse are constantly going dead—and they usually need to be replaced right when you're in the middle of an important project. To prolong the life of your batteries, consider switching to a light-colored mouse pad. According to computer experts, using the mouse on dark, dull, or rough surfaces forces the tracking sensor to work harder, depleting the device's battery power. But navigating on a reflective, lighter-hued surface helps conserve energy—and money!

10 Brilliant Uses
for WITCH HAZEL

1 ***Revive limp, greasy summer hair***
August really takes a toll on your tresses. That's because high temperatures prompt scalp glands to churn out more oil, resulting in a "dirty" look. The fast fix: Once or twice a week, dab a solution of 1 part witch hazel to 10 parts water along your hairline and part after you shower. The witch hazel will dissolve grease on contact and reduce the amount of oil your scalp secretes, so your hair will look bouncy and fresh all day long.

2 ***Diminish under-eye puffiness***
You made sure to go to sleep early so you would look refreshed for your sister's wedding photo—but instead, you woke up with puffy bags under your eyes. To perk up your peepers, beat 1 egg white and 1 teaspoon of witch hazel until foamy. Dab the mixture under your eyes and let sit for 15 minutes, then rinse off. The albumin in egg whites will temporarily tighten skin, while the anti-inflammatory witch hazel will help reduce puffiness.

3 ***Lift set-in bloodstains with ease***
Your honey must have nicked his neck shaving yesterday, but you didn't notice the bloodstain on his collar until after the shirt went through the wash. To remove the stain, tie an elastic band around the discolored area to isolate it, then immerse the stain in witch hazel for about 30 minutes. Remove and rinse with cool water, then launder as usual. The alcohol and other solvents in witch hazel will break down and evaporate the proteins in blood, easily erasing the stain.

4 ***Shrink stubborn varicose veins***
If varicose veins have been making you feel achy and self-conscious, try this: Steep a couple washcloths in witch hazel, then wrap them around your problem areas after showering and let sit for 5 minutes. Witch hazel has astringent and vasoconstrictive properties that will temporarily lighten the appearance of varicose veins and reduce painful inflammation.

5 ***Effortlessly remove sticker adhesive***
Yikes! You found a clothing sticker stuck to your dresser, and it's leaving behind a sticky residue. To get rid of the grime, saturate a cotton ball with witch hazel and apply it to the affected areas. Hold it firmly in place for 2 minutes (this will give the witch hazel time to dissolve the adhesive), then scrape gently with a spatula or another flat kitchen tool. The astringent properties in witch hazel will break down the stickers' bonding agents for easy removal.

6 Rid photographs of fingerprints

To erase smudges from your favorite vacation snapshots, pour a little witch hazel onto a cotton ball or soft cloth and gently wipe them away. The alcohol in the witch hazel will quickly lift and evaporate any oily residue from fingerprints. (Be sure to test a small corner first to ensure the finish stays intact.)

7 Make razor-burn bumps disappear

No matter how gentle you are with the blade, you always develop razor burn around your bikini line. Witch hazel to the rescue! Dip a soft cloth into the liquid and apply it generously to the unsightly blemishes. The soothing antibacterial solution will reduce inflammation and redness so you can don a swimsuit with confidence.

8 Relieve poison ivy itch in seconds

After walking in the woods, you sprouted a nasty-looking rash. For fast relief, soak a paper towel in witch hazel and dab the irritated areas as often as needed. The witch hazel's astringent properties will draw out the allergy-causing urushiol oil from the poison ivy and help dry out the rash. Plus, its eugenol will act as a natural anesthetic to help soothe the itch.

9 Ensure Fido's ear are squeaky clean

During the hot and humid months, your furry pal often suffers from itchy, smelly ear infections. To keep his ears clean and fresh, moisten a cotton ball or soft cloth with witch hazel and gently wipe the inside of his ears every other week. The liquid will loosen any waxy buildup so it comes off with ease.

10 Protect yourself from mosquitoes

You love eating outdoors with your family this time of year . . . that is, until the sun goes down and the mosquitoes decide to come out and feast on you. Keep them away from your next outing by combining witch hazel and a few drops of peppermint oil in a spray bottle. Spray this homemade mosquito repellent all over your arms and legs. The combination of scents will naturally repel bugs while masking other aromas that attract the critters, so you'll be able to enjoy a bite-free night.

More life from a dying cell phone

Halfway through the workday, you notice your cell phone is on its last bar. Problem is, you feel uncomfortable driving alone after dark without a working phone. To do: Take out the battery, place it in a sealed plastic bag, and stash it in the office freezer until you're ready to leave. Let the battery come to room temperature before reattaching it to the phone. Cell phone batteries degrade more rapidly in warm temperatures, so a stint in the freezer will help you get a few more minutes of talk time.

DAILY DOABLES

Reader Tip — Swallow large pills with ease

"I recently came down with an infection and was prescribed antibiotics to clear it up. But the pills were enormous and hard to swallow. When I called my pharmacist for advice, she told me to tilt my chin down while swallowing rather than lifting it up. This helps open the esophagus and close the windpipe so the pill slides down easily."

—Lisa Minkel, Saratoga Springs, NY

Here's a supersafe way to pack a razor.

30-Second Storage

Reader Tip — Fasten a bracelet without help

"One of the biggest annoyances I have with living alone is that it's next to impossible to fasten my jewelry. Silly, but true! My friend suggested this trick: Unfold a paper clip, then slip the "hook" into the circle end of the bracelet. You can use the paper clip to hold the bracelet in place with one hand and fasten it with the other hand."

—Abbie Burns, Merced, CA

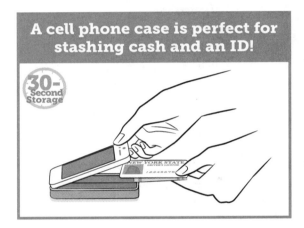

A cell phone case is perfect for stashing cash and an ID!

30-Second Storage

Butter up a pill for easy swallowing

Getting a large pill to go down can be a struggle, especially when you have a sore throat. To make capsules easier to swallow, lightly coat each one in butter before swallowing with water. The butter will act as a lubricant to help the pill glide down your throat.

Finger-friendly way to open a key ring

To avoid breaking a nail when adding a key to your chain, slide the edge of a butter knife or staple remover between the rings and lift. Spreading that stubborn opening apart will be a cinch.

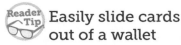 ### Easily slide cards out of a wallet

"I recently replaced my worn-out old billfold with a pretty new one—but the leather is so tight that it's tough to access my ID and credit cards when I need them. My save: I used clear tape to create small tabs at the top of each card. Now I just pull the tab and the card comes right out."

—Sue Ostanger, Fort Sill, OK

Make earbuds stay put

Listening to your favorite tunes makes everything from strolling around the block to sweeping the kitchen floor a bit more enjoyable. But those little earbuds have a way of slipping out when you're moving and grooving, which disrupts your flow. To keep them in place: Run the cords behind and over your ears before inserting the buds. This will provide a more secure fit, ensuring you won't miss a beat.

The easiest way to keep track of water intake is with a Sharpie.

30-Second Storage

An empty lip balm tube is perfect for hiding cash at the pool.

30-Second Storage

Lip Balm skin protection

 ### Spillproof your to-go coffee cup

"When I run out of time to make coffee in the morning, I grab a cup at the local coffee shop. But while I'm driving to work, the brew often spills out of the cup's opening and gets all over my car. One day the barista showed me this clever trick: Fold a plastic straw in half and tuck it into the hole. Presto—no more spills!"

—Candice Logan, Perry, FL

 ### The silly way to stay glass-smart

"During the last girls' night at a friend's house, my pals and I kept mixing up our wineglasses—until our hostess grabbed some of her daughter's old Silly Bandz bracelets to use as wine charms. The different colors and shapes eliminated any glass confusion. They're so cute that I bought a 24-pack at the drugstore—for $3!—to use when I host."

—Penny Evans, Morristown, NJ

Pull tabs made of tape make it easy to slide credit cards out of your wallet.

 30-Second Storage

Charge a cell phone in no time

It can seem like a fact of modern life: Whenever you need to power up your cell phone, you don't have time to plug it in for more than a few minutes. To get the most possible charge in the least time, go into your phone's "settings" menu and turn on "airplane mode." (Most smartphones and traditional cell phones have this setting.) This switches off the applications that drain the battery and cause the phone to charge at a slower pace, so your battery will power up quickly and you'll be able to get on with your busy day.

De-germ for pennies!

To sanitize your toothbrush in seconds, simply soak the bristles in 2 tablespoons of 3 percent hydrogen peroxide for 5 minutes, then rinse with warm water. Repeat once a week. Also smart: stashing your brush in an upright holder, which ensures that the bristles dry properly to prevent bacteria growth. Money saved: $10 for a toothbrush sanitizer

Reader Tip — Make zipping up a back-zip dress easy

"The other day I was putting on my favorite dress and no one was around to help zip me up. After a few minutes of unsuccessful twisting and turning, I knotted a piece of string to the end of a safety pin and attached it to the zipper. Then I was able to grab the string and pull the zipper up—no painful contortionism required!"

—*Jill Sorenson, Bellevue, WA*

Keep soda cans safe from bees.

NEVER WAIT AGAIN!

Instead of getting impatient waiting for your turn, get smart about it with these time-savers!

If you're . . . looking for a parking spot

The fastest way to find a spot in a crowded lot? Make a beeline for the back and weave your way closer. In a study published in the journal *Transportation Science*, drivers who headed toward the "fringe" spots at the back and edges of the lot found spaces 14 percent faster than those who went straight to the lanes closest to the entrance. Also, take the first spot you see. Researchers at Christopher Newport University in Newport News, Virginia, found that people who search for "good" spots end up no closer to the store than those who parked in the first spot they saw.

If you're . . . calling a customer service line

Is there anything more frustrating than being stuck in an automated voice-message chain when trying to reach a customer service representative? The quick trick that will get you through to an operator in no time: mumbling. If you confuse the system, it will realize that it has to connect you to a person. Other ways to confound the system and get to a live representative faster: pressing zero or the pound key.

If you're . . . checking out at a busy supermarket

When faced with chaos at the checkout counters, aim for a lane with fewer people, even if they have more items in their carts. On average, it takes cashiers 2.8 seconds to scan one item, but greeting a new customer and completing payment takes 48 seconds—so it would be faster to add 17 items to a line than adding just one extra person.

If you're . . . going through airport security

The secret to bypassing long airport security lines: Head left. A survey at Arizona State University in Tempe showed that Americans are most likely to turn right when entering a building or confronting a forked path, so lines to the left tend to be shorter and move faster.

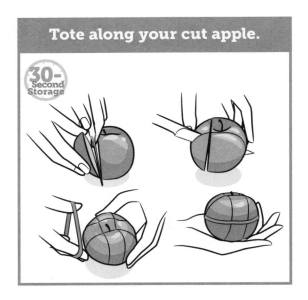

Tote along your cut apple.

30-Second Storage

Add traction to slippery shoe soles

You were thrilled with the new heels you bought—until you tested them out around the house and started slipping and sliding all over the place. To wear the shoes without worry, gently rub the soles with medium-grit sandpaper. The rough texture will make the soles slightly uneven, allowing them to firmly grip the floor.

Safely keep SSNs on hand

Reader Tip

"I've saved my family members' Social Security numbers as contacts in my cell phone (adding an extra zero), using each person's middle name as an alias. If I lose my phone, I don't have to worry, because the digits look like a phone number."

—*Amber Cahill, Rensselaer, NY*

Quick fix for tough-to-open nail polish

Ever struggled to open a stuck bottle of nail polish? Us, too! So we were happy to learn this easy fix: When you're done with the polish, dab petroleum jelly on the bottle's ridges (where the cap screws on). The jelly will create a lubricating barrier that will keep polish from gathering on the ridges and hardening.

Thread a needle with ease

Reader Tip

"Last weekend I decided to get started on my holiday crafts. As usual, it took me several tries to get the needle threaded. When I mentioned it to a friend, she clued me in on this great solution: Spritz a bit of hair spray on the tip of the thread to stiffen it so it will easily pass through the needle's eye. It worked like a charm, and now I always thread my needle on the first try!"

—*Cindy Schroeder, Chicago, IL*

Sort scarves with shower rings.

30-Second Storage

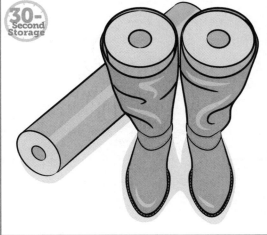

Keep boots upright with pool toys.

30-Second Storage

Use this to store bobby pins

"I used to get so frustrated: I knew I had dozens of bobby pins lying around but could never find one when I needed it. Thankfully, my sister offered this trick: Store the pins in an empty Tic Tac container. The rectangular box is perfect for holding the tiny pins and fits easily into the medicine cabinet, so I'll never have to waste time searching again."

—*Karen Payton, Amarillo, TX*

An eyeglass case can work beautifully as a travel nail kit!

30-Second Storage

Reader Tip **Genius use for old pill bottles**

"Instead of tossing old prescription bottles, I turn them into mini nail polish removers. I simply cut off a piece of sponge, pop it into a cleaned bottle, and saturate it with nail polish remover. Then, to take off a manicure, I dip my fingers in the bottle and swipe them against the sponge—no more scrubbing with cotton! I add remover to the vials as needed, and they last for months."

—*Cassidy Grisser, Chico, CA*

Reader Tip **Never lose another earring**

"My mother's cat loves to swat my jewelry off the nightstand when I stay over in the guest room. After losing one too many earrings, I now thread the studs through the holes of my wristwatch strap, then attach their backs. Even if the cat swats the watch off the table, I can easily find it on the floor, along with my earrings."

—*Ann Mattei, Colby, KS*

Reader Tip **Messproof mineral makeup**

"I love mineral makeup, but traveling with it can be a hassle—the loose powder always seeps through the sifter holes, so when I open the container, the makeup spills out. When I mentioned this to my sister, she suggested placing a cotton round over the holes, then screwing on the container's lid. I tried it on a recent trip and arrived without any spills. Now I swear by this!"

—*Allison Hiller, Salina, KS*

Save space with a mini makeup kit

"I can never cram my lip gloss, foundation, and blush into my party clutch—but I want those essentials on hand in case I need a quick touch-up. Then I had the idea to take an old contact-lens case and add a few squirts of foundation to one side and cream blush or lip gloss to the other. The case easily fits inside my clutch, and it's a cinch to wash out and refill for the next party!"

—*Melissa Lemmon, Boston, MA*

A shower curtain ring is perfect for organizing hair ties.

30-Second Storage

Index

Arts and crafts projects, 205
Aspirin tablets, 24, 50, 278
Asters, 147
Astringents, 26
Athlete's foot, 309
ATM pin, remembering, 315
Attic door air leaks, 158
Avocado, 91
Awning, 127

B

Baby oil, 11, 62, 326
Baby powder, 54, 270, 276–77
Baby wipes, 62, 194
Back, cooling, 271
Bacon, 75
Bacon bits, 75
Bad breath, pet, 291
Bag caddies, 17
Baked potatoes, 87, 93
Baking, 18, 107–8, 218, 322. *See also specific baked good*
Baking cups, 133
Baking soda
  as ant repellent, 23
  for bee sting relief, 291
  for carpet-stain removal, 57
  for cleaning, 1, 3, 9, 12, 63, 66, 68
  for cold sore relief, 316
  cooking with, 69, 77, 97, 102
  as deicer, 68–69
  for drain declogging, 53
  in dry skin, 69
  for eye puffiness, 279
  as fabric softener, 46, 68
  for food stain removal, 69
  for heat mark removal, 63
  for itchy skin, 69

for pesticide removal from fruits, 68
for pet odor removal, 69, 292
for refrigerator odor removal, 258
for sensitive skin treatment, 246
for shiny hair, 233
for splinter removal, 310
for tooth stain removal, 69, 256
for yellowed toenails, 266
Balancing exercise, 320
Balloons, 136, 141
Ballpoint pen, 15
Banana peels, 184–85
Bananas, 91, 278, 281
Bandanas, 126–27, 292
Bangs, trimming, 233
Barbecue entertaining, 141–43, 224–25, 294
Basement, musty, 57
Basil leaves, 99, 113, 249, 290
Bat garland, 148, **148**
Bath pillows, 197
Bathroom
  cleaning, 10–13
  decal removal, 34
  fern in, 131
  odor removal, 13
  storage, 22
Baths, 249, 268–69
Batteries, 27, 29, 137, 330, 332
Bay leaf, 23
Beans, 83
BeautyFix.com, 194
Beauty Insider Club, 193
Beauty recipes, natural, 275, 278–80. *See also* Hair; Makeup; Skin

Bedding
  cleaning, 8
  deals on, 195
  pet, 302–3
  storing, 22
Beef, 75–77
Beef bouillon, 79
Beer, 20–21, 37, 40, 216, 221. *See also* Alcohol
Bees, 40, **332**
Bee stings, 40, 290–91, 310
Be Koool Soft Gel Sheets, 270
Bell peppers, 87
Belts, 265
Benadryl, 291
Berry stain removal, 48, 54, 108
Beverages, 6, 99–101, 141, 143. *See also* Alcohol
Big-box store shopping, 191
Bilberry extract, 290
BimboBakeries.com, 221
Binder clips, 4, 14–15, 30, 56, 263
Biotin, 272
Birds, wild
  droppings, 129
  feeders, critterproofing, 300
  food, 81
Biscuits, 102
Blackboard eraser, 43
Blackheads, 250
Black tea bags, 250, 312–13
Blanching basil, 113
Blankets, 22, 140, 142
Bleach, 25, 57
Bleach gel, 12
Blemishes, skin, 249–50, 266, 278, 294, 322
Blenders, 2, 10, 111–12, 226
Blisters, 9, 250, 259
Bloodstain removal, 8, 49, 328

Rust removal/prevention
   apple cider vinegar, 52–53
   beer, 21
   black tea bags, 313
   car wax, 300
   lip balm, 244
   nail polish, 13
   rice, 169

S

Safety pin, 332
St. Paddy's Day entertaining, 133
Salad dressing, 6, 89, 96–97, 286
Salad dressing stain removal, 48
Salads, 96–97, 286
Salad spinners, 45
Saline solution, 255
Salons, 194
Salsa, 113, 295
Salt
   as air freshener, 63
   for cleaning, 11, 49
   cooking with, 15, 76–77, 79, 83–85, 92
   for drain declogging, 12
   dusting and, 152–53
   Kosher, 249, 256
   as meat tenderizer, 75
   for odor removal, 50, 63
   for oily skin treatment, 246
   sea, 194
   for skin care, 194
   for stain removal, 49
   for stress management, 320
   for tights, runproofing, 326
   as weed killer, 33
Salt stain removal, 56
Salt-water solutions, 38
Sand, 28, 267, 276

Sanding tips, 58, 136
Sandpaper, 58, 70, 334
Sandwich bags, plastic, 14
Sangria, 272–73
Sauces, 113–14
Sausages, 74, 145
Scallops, 79
Scissors, 70, 99, 233
Scones, 102
Scratches
   car, 44
   CD/DVD, 184, 244, 300
   dishes, 4
   flooring, 57, 58
   LCD screen, 173
   sunglass, 265
Screens, computer, 27
Screwdrivers, 67, 70
Screw holes, stripped, 67
Screws, rusty, 128
Scuff marks, 4, 55, 136–37, 173, 185, 264
Seafood, 78–79, 95
SearsOutlet.com, 201
Sea salt, 194
Seashells, 146, **146**
Seaside party entertaining, 143, 146
Seaweed, powdered, 268
Secondhand items, buying, 181. *See also* Yard sales
Seed planting, 172
Seed storage, 33
Self-confidence, boosting, 318–19
Self-doubt, eliminating, 319
Self-talk, 319
Self-tanning lotion, 251, 266
Seltzer, 90, 116
Sensitive skin, 246
Serveware, 221. *See also* Dishes

Serving platters, 218
Servings calculator, 217
Sewing, 51, 55, 58, 222
Shades, window, 164
Shadow boxes, 51, **125**, 125
Shampoo, dry, 232
Sharpening tools/utensils, 2, 70, 233
Sharpie pen, **331**
Shave lotion, 266
Shaving, 250–51
Shaving cream, 12, 54, 309
Shaving cream substitute, 327
Shedding pets, 283–84, 292
Sheets, 22
Shelf liner, 142
Shelves, 17, 124, **124**, **125**, 125, 126–27
Shipping packages, 219–20
Shirt boxes, 103
Shirts, 150
Shoe boxes, 18, **29**
Shoelaces, 245
Shoe organizer, 17, 33
Shoes
   blisterproofing new, 259
   displaying, 126
   leather, 55, 185
   odor removal, 327
   online specialty stores, 192
   polishing, 55, 185
   reshaping squishy, 197
   shopping for, 192
   slippery soles on, 334
   stretching too-tight, 264
ShopAtHome.com, 201
Shopping cost savings
   appliances, 200–201, 202, 203
   bulk shopping, 193
   clothing, 189–92

First

for women

Your worries...
solved

Little tips that end big stress

BEAUTY ❖ STYLE ❖ HEALTH
NUTRITION ❖ MIND ❖ FOOD
HOME ❖ PETS ❖ MONEY

WHY MISS AN ISSUE?
SUBSCRIBE AND SAVE 52%*!